THE TYRANNICIDE BRIEF

Geoffrey Robertson QC is a leading human rights lawyer and a UN war-crimes judge. He has been counsel in many notable Old Bailey trials, has defended hundreds of men facing death sentences in the Caribbean, and has won landmark rulings on civil liberty from the highest courts in Britain, Europe and the Commonwealth. He was involved with cases against General Pinochet and Hastings Banda, and in the training of judges who will try Saddam Hussein. His book *Crimes Against Humanity* has been an inspiration for the global justice movement, and he is the author of an acclaimed memoir, *The Justice Game*, and the textbook *Media Law*. He is married to Kathy Lette: they live with their two children in London. Geoffrey Robertson is Head of Doughty Street Chambers, a Master of the Middle Temple, a Recorder and visiting professor at Queen Mary College, University of London.

ALSO BY GEOFFREY ROBERTSON

Reluctant Judas
Obscenity
People Against the Press
Geoffrey Robertson's Hypotheticals (Vols. I & II)
Media Law
Does Dracula Have Aids?
Freedom, the Individual and the Law
The Justice Game
Crimes Against Humanity

GEOFFREY ROBERTSON

The Tyrannicide Brief

The Story of the Man who sent
Charles I to the Scaffold

VINTAGE BOOKS
London

Published by Vintage 2006

8 10 9 7

First published in Great Britain in 2005 by
Chatto & Windus

Vintage
Random House, 20 Vauxhall Bridge Road,
London SW1V 2SA

www.vintage-books.co.uk

Addresses for companies within The Random House Group Limited
can be found at: www.randomhouse.co.uk/offices.htm

The Random House Group Limited Reg. No. 954009

A CIP catalogue record for this book
is available from the British Library

ISBN 9780099459194

The Random House Group Limited supports The Forest Stewardship
Council (FSC®), the leading international forest certification organisation.
Our books carrying the FSC label are printed on FSC® certified paper.
FSC is the only forest certification scheme endorsed by the leading
environmental organisations, including Greenpeace. Our
paper procurement policy can be found at
www.randomhouse.co.uk/environment

Printed and bound in Great Britain by Clays Ltd, St Ives PLC

For Kathy

Contents

List of Illustrations

Plate Section I

We are not traitors or murderers or fanatics but true Christians and good commonwealthsmen, fixed and constant in the principles of sanctity, truth, justice and mercy, which the Parliament and army declared and engaged for, and to that noble principle of preferring the universality before particularity. We fought for the public good and would have enfranchised the people and secured the welfare of the whole groaning creation, if the nation had not more delighted in servitude than freedom.

John Cooke, letter from prison, September 1660

That afternoon, going through London – I saw the limbs of some of our new traitors set upon Aldersgate, which was a sad sight to see; and a bloody week this and the last have been, there being ten hanged, drawn and quartered . . . After dinner to my Lords, and from there to the Abbey . . . and so to the Crowne in the Palace-yard – I and George Vines by the way calling at their house, where he carried me up to the top of his turret, where there is Cooke's head set up for traitor, and Harrison's on the other side of Westminster Hall. Here I could see them plainly, as also a very fair prospect about London.

Diary of Samuel Pepys, 20/21 October 1660

Silver Medal, struck in John Cooke's honour by Thomas
Simon, 1649 (British Museum, misdated 1660)

Preface

This is the story of an obscure lawyer once called upon to make history. The severed head that spoiled Pepys's pleasant view over London had previously been attached to body parts inspected by John Evelyn, another diarist whose wit has proved congenial to modern times. He gloated 'Oh, the miraculous providence of God!', at the sight of a basket just brought from the gallows to feed the stray dogs at Aldersgate. It contained hearts, testicles and penises, 'mangled, and cut, and reeking', of men hanged, drawn and quartered at Charing Cross. One was John Cooke, for the past decade a judge acclaimed for law reform and for championing the poor, the first to propose a host of institutions we now take for granted, including a national health service and legal aid. Cooke had been executed for demanding the kind of justice that, 350 years later, the world at last would want: the ending of impunity for rulers responsible for making war on their own people.

That such a man should have been torn quite literally to pieces after a rigged trial at the Old Bailey, remains one of English history's most shameful episodes, white-washed by lawyers and ignored by historians. Today, John Cooke is only mentioned as a passing wraith in books which dismiss him as an embittered Puritan fanatic or as a dodgy lawyer prepared to do the dirty work for the rising Cromwell. These caricatures are so at odds with the actual records – his published writings, the transcripts of his speeches and what can be gleaned of his personal life – that fairness requires a belated defence for this bravest of all barristers, who died for the highest principle of advocacy.

The bad press received by 'the regicides' has been attributed to the fact that history is written by winners, and John Cooke's actions have certainly been interpreted by historians with their own agenda – in the words of W. S. Gilbert's sentient sentry, 'either a little liberal, or else a little conservative'.

1

For Tory writers, the trial and execution of Charles I were straightforward crimes of treason and murder. The Whig historians who refurbished Cromwell's reputation were inclined to accept the unlawfulness of the proceedings, passing over them quickly with the excuse (attributed to Cromwell as he inspected the King's corpse) of 'cruel necessity'. Neither school has bothered about the regicide trial, other than to praise Charles II for confining his vengeance to those who had prosecuted his father. Left-wing authors have preferred to celebrate the Levellers – the journalist-agitators who first suggested that the King should be prosecuted but who went to water (or to the country) when the hard decisions about that trial had to be made, and later forged shady alliances with royalists. It is doubtful whether any English author, even today, can approach the King's trial without some antagonistic sentiment – it seems so wrong to have cut off the head of the only English monarch who cared about culture.

On the groaning shelves of literature on the English revolution, John Cooke rates only a few mentions – usually as the barrister who acted as the King's prosecutor. In this role he has been ill-served by twentieth-century accounts which distort an event precisely recorded by skilled law reporters. Editorship of *The Trial of Charles I* in the 'Notable British Trials' series (1928) was entrusted to a ranting royalist, J.G. Muddiman. His worst mistakes were exposed in 1964 by Dame Veronica Wedgwood in *The Trial of Charles I* (1964) but this book also has factual errors and a different interpretative bias: Dame Veronica thought the trial a disaster for 'the good old cause' and blamed its 'overzealous' prosecutor. More recent studies have pointed out that the trial was not the foregone conclusion alleged by its detractors, but have not effaced Wedgwood's impression. There has been no study of Cooke's own trial in 1660: curiously, this bloody assize has never been the subject of serious analysis, either by historians or by lawyers. Although most barristers supported Parliament against the King, their Inns of Court have since striven to cover up their republican past by genuflections to the royal family – especially Gray's Inn, which today makes no mention at all of Cooke and Bradshawe, its members who did most to change the course of history. Its largest portraits are of Charles I, Charles II and the future Charles III.

My own interest in Cooke began by chance, when I was invited to Gray's Inn to dispute a paper delivered by Justice Michael Kirby on the 350th anniversary of the trial of Charles I. I accepted only because of a long-standing friendship with Michael, whose paper concluded that the trial was 'by legal standards a discreditable affair'. This seemed indisputable, until I dug out a very old edition of the *State Trials*, purchased in my youth as an investment (foolishly: most of these reports may now be read for free, and without dust, on the internet). I blew away cobwebs and settled down to absorb *The Tryal of King Charles the Firſt, accuſed of treaſon and ſubverting juſtice*. I did know something of the history of criminal law and procedure, and to my surprise I found this trial to be far from discreditable – on the contrary, it appeared for its time as an oasis of justice and fairness, the *most* creditable proceedings that had yet taken place in an age where those accused of treason were usually convicted within a few hours. Defendants were tortured if they refused to plead, and any who offended the judges of the King's own Star Chamber had their ears cut off and their noses slit. My sense that Kirby and Wedgwood might have got it wrong deepened when I found in my volume a transcript of the trial of the regicides, held eleven years later. The contrast could not have been more marked: if ever a trial was a 'discreditable affair', this was it. The defendants had been locked up for months in plague-infected prisons, and were brought to the Old Bailey in shackles and leg-irons to be viciously mocked and abused by the partisan judges of Charles II, who instructed vetted jurors to convict without bothering to leave the jury-box.

John Cooke struck me as a pivotal figure: he was at the centre of both the trial of Charles I in 1649 and the trial of the regicides in 1660: the prosecutor of the King now prosecuted by the King's son, courageously arguing that it had not been treason, but professional duty, to accept the tyrannicide brief. The events in which he participated are, of course, the stuff of countless histories of the English civil war, interregnum and Restoration. My reason for offering a new reading of them is that John Cooke's arguments resonate today in ways that historians have not appreciated. For example, the King's trial may now be seen as the earliest precedent for trials of modern heads of state – political and military leaders like Pinochet and Milosevic, who attempt (just like Charles I) to plead sovereign immunity when arraigned for killing their own people. Cooke's case against the King was the first modern legal argument against tyranny – based (as Bush and Blair might more credibly have based their case against Saddam Hussein) on a universal right to punish a tyrant who denies democracy and civil and religious liberty to his people. In contrast, the trial of the regicides deserves to be stigmatised as 'victors' justice', a barbaric act of royalist revenge to satisfy the blood-hatred of Charles

II who (according to Evelyn) personally attended Cooke's disembowelling.

This was a transitional time, when post-Renaissance minds could be moved by the poetry of Shakespeare yet approve the most savage torture in the interests of public order. It was a time when the rooted English obsession with social rank was briefly challenged by men from Cromwell's favourite constituency, 'the middling sort' of tradespeople and lesser gentry. Cooke, a poor farmer's son, was able to rise above the social caste first noted, at the time of his entry to Oxford University, as 'plebeian'. Although the occupations and preoccupations of mid-seventeenth-century society are long gone, it is the lawyers (and the prostitutes) who have changed least. Barristers were as numerous, comparatively, in London in 1640 as they are today, located in the same places – the Inns, the courts and Parliament – where they still study, think and argue by the same plodding mix of precedent and principle. Their ethics, their practices and their attitudes are more highly developed, but their peculiar and indulged professional vices remain: a genteel interest in money, patronage through old boy networks and political preferment, a social exclusivity and a calculated deference to the wealthy and the well-connected. It is possible, even in today's Inns of Court, for ghosts to walk into reasonable focus. I write this in my flat overlooking the Middle Temple, where the famous equestrian portrait of Charles I, attributed to van Dyck, now hangs. Charles II came to a feast in the Temple in 1661 to honour his own Solicitor General for prosecuting his father's judges. Legend has it that on some such occasion the King became so drunk that he could not stand for the loyal toast, and said to the Masters of the Bench, 'remain you also seated, both tonight and hereafter.' Today, we still obey him.

No life of Cooke has been attempted before. There are no surviving records of the man amongst his family and friends, other than in the much-edited memoirs of Edmund Ludlow, the Puritan MP who fled to Switzerland in 1660 to escape royalist revenge. Even the prolific genealogical websites are bereft of any reference to his wife, Frances, or to his assumed second marriage or to the death of his young son or to Freelove, the daughter who made life anew in the colonies. But his conduct of the King's trial and courageous self-defence at his own trial have been fully transcribed, and amongst the Thomason tracts – an exhaustive collection of the pamphlet literature of the period – are some half-dozen lengthy booklets which Cooke wrote between 1646 and 1652. There is an account of the speech he made on the gallows, and the affecting last letters written to his wife ('let us not part in a shower . . . God hath wiped away all tears'), and to his baby daughter, Freelove – moving enough for Charles II's government, which did not question their authenticity, to prosecute all who dared print them. There are, alas, few contemporary documents to provide details of his judicial work in Ireland where the public records of the period were destroyed in a fire in 1922. No one has sought to draw together the strands of the remarkable, indeed sensational, life and death of Britain's most radical lawyer.

In doing so, I am conscious of having tiptoed across historical minefields. But my reading of events that turn so much on trials and their procedures and beliefs about constitutional rights has been informed by a long professional life as a trial lawyer. My sense of what was really happening at the Old Bailey, the Inns of Court and Westminster Hall sometimes differs from that of historians. It is astonishing, for example, that almost all of them, Wedgwood included, relate with embroidered detail how Cooke opened the King's trial by reading the charge, when this was in fact done at great length by the court clerk. Such a simple mistake, misreporting the opening of the most significant trial in English history, suggests they may have made more deep-seated errors of analysis and appreciation. This is a further reason for offering a new account of events whose actors, however driven by long-past religious passion, first expressed our modern belief in civil liberties and democracy. In order to get their message across the years, I have made minor changes in their language, updating spelling and calligraphy (and occasionally grammar) and modernising some sentence constructions and forms of address ('you' replaces 'thou', for example). It has been necessary to edit trial transcript extracts, I trust without unfairness to the original speakers. Seventeenth century surnames were erratically spelled. I have preferred 'Cooke' because that is how John signed himself, although his name often appears without the 'e'. At that time the calendar year began on March 25th, so contemporary records confusingly record, for example, the King's trial in January 1649 as having taken place in January 1648. I have followed the usual updating practice.

British history is too often told – to children and on television – through the indulged lives of kings and queens, and never through the lives of lawyers. Yet men from the Inns of Court dominated that action-packed age, 1641–60, the crucible years in which they forged many of the ideals the world today most cherishes: the sovereignty of parliament; the independence of judges; freedom from arbitrary arrest and detention; the right to silence; comparative religious toleration – in short, freedom from tyranny. Any rational people would take pride in the events of 1649, the critical year for this ideological progress. But it has been the British way to ignore the Republic, to deplore the prosecution of the King and to pretend that liberty dates from what is dubbed 'the Glorious Revolution' of 1689 – a milksop affair neither glorious nor revolutionary, which merely retrieved from the fall of the Stuart kings some of the gains made in 1649. This mental blockage about giving credit or celebrity to the 'Commonwealthsmen' is exemplified by the school syllabus: at age 13 schoolchildren are falsely taught that what appeared on the currency as 'the first year of freedom by God's blessing restored' was really no more than a time of bloody turmoil and revenge. There is national amnesia about the persecution of republicans in 1660, at an Old Bailey show trial of Stalinesque proportions. Although I forbear from urging the Criminal Cases Review Authority to refer John Cooke's treason conviction back to the Court of Appeal for posthumous quashing, and a royal pardon somehow seems inappropriate, this book may serve to commemorate the integrity and vision of a man who in these qualities at least was beyond his time. He was a tyrannicide in the noble Roman sense, rather than a king-killer. Cromwell's chaplain, Hugh Peters, was right to congratulate him in Westminster Hall on a 'glorious beginning of this great work' of ending the impunity of despots.

That work continues today, in far-flung tribunals where the proceedings in Westminster Hall echo ironically. Saddam Hussein after his capture addressed the court with the same challenge that Charles I threw at his judges: 'By what legal authority do you try me?' Slobodan Milosevic at The Hague at first played the King's gambit, refusing to enter a plea. General Pinochet notoriously asserted the law's immunity for heads of state – the same sovereign impunity that John Cooke devised a means to circumvent. He did so by formulating the crime of tyranny to punish a leader who destroys law and liberty, or who bears command responsibility for the killing of his own people, or who orders the plunder of innocent civilians and the torture of prisoners of war. Cooke's charge, and the evidence to support it, was produced in less than ten days, with (in fact, despite) the help of a Cambridge academic and a committee of MPs: an achievement, for which his own life was the hazard. Cooke realised that the King's determination to live or die as a divinely ordained, absolute and hereditary monarch made compromise impossible: as Solicitor-General, he must push England to where logic ('right reason') led, where law (Magna Carta) pointed and where God (the first

Book of Samuel) approved, but where no other nation at the time or for another century would reach: a proto-democratic republic with constitutional guarantees for civil and religious liberties.

Roundheads of John Cooke's stamp are in short supply in modern Britain, where 'radical barristers' are contradictions in terms and former political firebrands kiss the monarch's hand on taking their oath of cabinet office or self-importantly stroke their ermine in the House of Peers. Monarchy still exerts its vainglorious magic, from Eurostarry princesses to feudal Saudi royals to the virgin-deflowering King of Swaziland. Australians, normally a sensible people, voted in 1999 to keep a-hold of the Queen of England rather than have an Australian as their head of state: the republican campaign made no mention of 'the good old cause' or the historic part it played in securing liberty throughout the British commonwealth. At the Old Bailey in 1660, the prosecution alleged that the King's execution was the culmination of a terrorist plot devised by Puritans in Massachusetts, who despatched Peters and young Henry Vane to implement it in conspiracy with Cromwell and Cooke. Today in the United States the regicides are remembered in street names, but John Cooke's life demonstrates that their true legacy is the use of criminal law to end the impunity of tyrants. That was the instruction written on his brief and it was the cause for which he sacrificed his life. That cause has now taken shape in an International Criminal Court, and it is (so to speak) a crowning irony that the Bush administration, for all its proclaimed Puritan religiousity, has sought to destroy one institution that can deliver on Cooke's proposition that rulers who oppress their people must be brought to justice.

This book has benefited from research by George Southcombe and Ian Williams and from the nurturing editorship of Jenny Uglow. My thanks additionally to Wilfrid Prest, Tim Lello and Seamus O'Keefe for convivial discussion, to Gill Rushton at the Hampshire Record Office, Lesley Whitelaw, Middle Temple Archivist, Gray's Inn librarian Theresa Thom, to Chris Pigott and Wayne Gunthorpe, distant descendants who helped to trace Freelove Cooke's happy ending – and to Michael Green who located for me at Vevey the graves of Ludlow and others who escaped the King's vengeance. I have been assisted (in so far as its restricted opening hours could permit), by staff at the British Library. Tabitha Peebles worked prodigiously on manuscript drafts, which David Williamson has already turned into a moving play. All errors, I am happy to say, are mine alone – the difference in writing a history book rather than a legal text is that you actually look forward to having them pointed out.

Prologue: There But For Fortune . . .

The law can be a matter of luck – as much for lawyers as for their clients. It is known, well enough, how litigants may draw hostile judges or prejudiced jurors, or lose good cases on a sudden technicality. It is less appreciated, but no less true, that the career of a lawyer may also be governed by chance: the elevation to senior rank, or to a judgeship bestowed by a political patron or through the timely influence of a friend or relative. In the life of an advocate in Britain, fortune most often smiles (or grimaces) in the guise of the delivery of a 'brief' – a set of papers, traditionally tied in pink tape, directing an appearance in court on behalf of a particular client. Some briefs can make you or break you at the bar of public opinion – because people will, naturally enough, identify pleaders with the cause for which they plead. As an elementary protection for those who act for unpopular causes or villainous clients, barristers today adopt the professional conceit that they have no choice: just as a cab driver may not turn away an unprepossessing but paying passenger, so an advocate must, once an appropriate fee is proffered, accept any case that is capable of argument. This principle – now called the 'cab-rank rule' – is the kerbstone of the barrister's right to practise, and the guarantee that any party, however unpleasant or unpopular, may have the benefit of a counsel learned in the law. For those who hold fast to this principle it still brings certain dangers, usually in the post – excrement if you defend paedophiles, the prospect of a letter-bomb for prosecuting terrorists. In some places – Belfast and Bogota and Baghdad provide recent examples – vengeance can come to lawyers in the form of an assassin's bullet. This great – if perilous – principle was first asserted by John Cooke, barrister of Gray's Inn, into whose hands history's most fateful brief was delivered by parliamentary messenger on Wednesday 10 January 1649.

The day itself was ferociously cold. The Thames had frozen, with the consequence of a modern tube-strike, since it immobilised the boats that carried passengers from the pier at Westminster, where the civil courts and Parliament sat, to the Temple and then to the Tower where traitors awaited trial, the easternmost end of this compact and crowded city of half a million citizens. It was not until the dusk had thickened that Parliament's messenger arrived on horseback at Gray's, the northernmost of the Inns of Court which sprawled up from the Temple to provide lodgings and offices for the fast-growing ranks of lawyers, in chambers which spiralled around compact squares and gardens. A few pinpoints of light from candles and fireplaces punctured the gloom, as the clerk dismounted and asked for directions to the chambers of a barrister of the Inn. The arrival of this brief was not unexpected, and it was indeed the very reason why the Inns on this early evening were eerily quiet: semi-deserted, despite the imminent start of the legal term.

Most lawyers had fled to the country 'purposely to avoid this business' as Bulstrode Whitelocke put it. He was one of the first to flee – and he was Lord Chancellor. He was followed by the Chief Justice – one of Cromwell's closest friends – and many others. Those who remained, like John Cooke, argued agonisingly at dinners in their Halls and later in the taverns, over both the wisdom and the legality of 'this business', a professional engagement which might spell death and, what was much worse, eternal damnation. Cooke turned down offers of a carriage ride to his family home near Leicester. 'I must wait upon God,' he replied, a reference to the unshakeable belief, which would remain throughout his life, that nothing happened to him but by the will of his Maker. He was waiting, puffing at a long pipe in his smoky chambers, when Parliament's messenger arrived at his door to deliver a parchment. It was a brief, and it had his name on it, 'to prepare and prosecute the charge against the King'.

John Cooke would have felt the thrill that excites every advocate on receiving a portentous retainer. It is a rush of egotistic pleasure that others think you the best (or only) person for this particular job, cooled by a nervousness that your performance might affect your career, for good or ill. But this brief was unlike any other, before or since. It was a set of instructions to formulate a criminal charge against a king widely regarded as ruler by divine right, in a credulous age when people believed their skin diseases could be cured by a touch from a monarch who was God's representative on English – and Irish and Scottish – earth. Even to contemplate laying a hand on the

Lord's anointed was treason, punished by death if and when the royalists returned to power. More immediately, it would make Cooke an instant target for assassination, in a city infiltrated by de-plumed but re-pistolled cavaliers.

Apart from this physical danger, there was a looming professional problem: there was simply no basis that legal minds at the time could conceive for prosecuting the King, the source of law, who by definition could do no wrong. That was what the kings and queens of England, and their governments, had always believed, and lawyers had always presumed. Since *Rex* was *lex*, a case of *Rex v Rex* was a contradiction in terms. Besides, since Magna Carta guaranteed every defendant a jury of his peers, how could the King, who obviously had no peer, be put on trial? These riddles were insoluble, said all the judges and most of the lawyers whose opinions were delivered by their feet as they scurried away from this lethal paradox, and from the Inns of Court.

Cooke could have chosen to leave town at any time in the past few days, as whispers that he might be appointed to prosecute began to reach the Inn. He felt a crippling sense of his own unworthiness: he was not one of the 'great lawyers', either in rank or birth or the size of his practice. He was consumed not with fear but by self-doubt, that one of the lowliest barristers would be chosen for such an awesome task. But this appointment, like every-thing else that happened to him, was a manifestation of divine will: his very obscurity, he reasoned, would in some way serve God's purpose.

John Cooke was forty. He was highly respected by younger lawyers for his legal knowledge, his wisdom and the extent of his independence from the familiar circles of patronage and power. He was lacking in social stature and family wealth, being the son of a poor-to-do Leicester tenant farmer who had risked bankruptcy to support his education at Oxford and the Inns of Court. The youthful barrister, unable at first to afford chambers in London, had taken employment in Ireland with Thomas Wentworth's administration, earning enough to take a continental tour and a spiritual semester with the Calvinists of Geneva, before setting up practice at Gray's Inn. He soon displayed a quality rare in this period – integrity. He had taken up causes that were morally right but politically incorrect, and had damaged his career.

What made Cooke unique – a man beyond his time – were the social and legal reform ideas that he had begun to express, in booklets that were sold from the stalls in St Paul's churchyard and around the law courts of

Westminster Hall. These tracts were visionary to a degree his contemporaries could scarcely envision: he argued for the abolition of the death sentence other than for murder and treason; the end of imprisonment for debt; the abolition of Latin in the courts and many other reforms that did not come about for centuries. He was the first to claim that poverty was a major cause of crime (so offenders who acted from hunger and desperation should be put on probation) and the first to suggest that the state should provide a national health service and a system of legal aid for the poor. He urged barristers to work *pro bono* (free of charge) in 10 per cent of their cases. These ideas were not calculated to endear Cooke to the leaders of his profession, much less to the many pettifogging lawyers described by popular pamphleteers, accurately enough, as 'vipers and caterpillars of the Commonwealth'. They were outraged when Cooke urged Parliament to set limits to their fees, by passing a statute upon which self-interested MPs – namely lawyers – must not be allowed to vote. This was the ultimate insult: for his mercenary colleagues, Cooke was a cuckoo in their nests, threatening their nest-eggs.

In short, John Cooke was respected but not trusted. He tended to do and say what he believed was right, rather than what was popular or politic or likely to ingratiate him with the prevailing power, be it the King or Parliament or a bench of judges. He would do nothing merely to please, unless it were to please God. So he was a risky choice to be entrusted to stage-manage an event as momentous and unprecedented as the trial of the King. He had not previously spoken out in favour of a trial, and indeed at a dinner the previous week he had loudly and succinctly expressed a view on 'Pride's Purge' and the political and military factions that were jockeying for power: 'I think they are all mad.' His appointment as 'Solicitor-General of the Commonwealth' – a job that came with his acceptance of the brief – was a measure of Parliament's desperation, as more senior and more reliable barristers ran for cover.

There was one safeguard. As Solicitor-General, Cooke would be responsible for collecting the evidence and writing the legal arguments, but would not have a leading, or even speaking, part in the trial itself. The Attorney-General, William Steele, would sign the all-important charge against the King, and would be the prosecutor in the public eye, harrying Charles Stuart to conviction and perhaps to a sentence of death. Steele also had chambers in Gray's Inn, where the messenger called first to deliver the leading brief.

It must have seemed, to the parliamentary committee which made it, a sensible arrangement – Cooke would be a learned and zealous junior, complementing the forensic skill of Steele, who had proved a 'safe pair of hands' in the courtroom. That was before Steele sent a message to the court, claiming that he was seriously ill.

By this stroke of providence, John Cooke came to lead the prosecution. It was by now but a week before the trial. Its success would have to depend on Cooke, who would have the task of persuading the court – and, more importantly, the world – that neither divine right nor sovereign immunity permitted a head of state to enjoy impunity after oppressing his own people. The word 'impunity' in its modern sense, which describes the freedom that tyrants should never have to live happily ever after their tyranny, enters history in Cooke's brief. The parchment, scored in the elegant sloped hand of a parliamentary clerk, instructed the counsel to appear before this new High Court of Justice, established

> To the end that no chief officer or magistrate may hereafter presume traitorously or maliciously to imagine or contrive the enslaving or destroying of the English nation, and expect impunity for so doing . . .

In this final flourish is found the principle that justified the trial of Charles I in the eyes of weary soldiers and their supporters in Parliament and the city. It was a means of deterring future tyrants from maltreating their own people. It was designed to end the impunity which Machiavelli had argued in *The Prince* should always protect rulers from the consequences of their crimes. When General Pinochet was denied impunity, 350 years later, this prosecution theory appeared very new and very radical: in 1649 it was so far before its time that later historians have failed to comprehend Cooke's purpose. They treat the trial as Cromwell's elaborate exercise in *realpolitik* – a 'cruel necessity'. But the King could have been removed much more conveniently and quietly, by poison or court-martial or by having him shot while trying to escape. The first wonder of this trial was that it took place at all, and the second was how John Cooke, in a frantic fortnight, managed to locate the Achilles heel of sovereign impunity.

The first civil war had begun in August 1642 when King Charles I raised his standard at Nottingham to attack the forces of Parliament. It ended almost four years later, when the King was ignominiously sold to Parliament by its Scottish allies. Thereafter, whilst a prisoner in his own palaces, he contrived to direct a second civil war which took the form of a series of revolts, riots and incendiary flare-ups throughout the spring and summer of 1648. These were painfully extinguished by General Fairfax and his deputy, Oliver Cromwell, but scarcely had the killing stopped than Charles began plotting a third war, in which Parliament's New Model Army would be opposed by Scots (to whom he made secret promises) and by Irish loyalists, assisted by old cavaliers and fresh forces from Catholic allies in Europe. Yet so fundamental was monarchy to contemporary conceptions of government that the majority of the House of Commons – mainly Presbyterian MPs – naively proposed a power-sharing treaty with their untrustworthy King. For the army and its MP supporters, this was a certain recipe for a third civil war: so in early December, with Fairfax's approval, Colonel Pride marched to Westminster and 'purged' the House of Commons of its appeasers, by refusing them entry. In Westminster over Christmas (a holiday uncelebrated by Puritans), the army and the 'Rump' of MPs left in Parliament began to plan an action never before imagined, in England or elsewhere: of putting the King on trial.

The enormity of this exercise, in its place and time, cannot be overstated. It would, for a start, amount to treason, under a statute of 1351 (still in force today) which had remained in regular use. The offence was of wide definition: 'compassing or imagining' the death of the monarch was punishable by public execution. For treacherous nobles, aristocrats and persons of breeding, death would come instantly and surgically, as the executioner's axe severed the cervical vertebrae: the legs and abdomen would twitch reflexively as the assistant displayed the aristocratic head to the crowd, with the awesome cry *'Behold – the head of a traitor'*. For those of common birth, however, there was a torture as barbaric as the times could devise, known as 'hanging, drawing and quartering'. The miscreant would be drawn on a hurdle, facing backwards, to the place of execution: he would be forced up a ladder, hung for a few moments to the jeers of the crowd, then cut down whilst still conscious. His penis and testicles would first be cut off, and dangled in his face. The executioner's knife would deftly extract a few feet of bowel, which would be set alight by a torch, before his boggling eyes. Oblivion, in the stench and excruciating pain, was delayed as long as possible, and would be followed by cutting pieces off the carcass ('quartering') before it was dragged away behind the sledge: the severed head, arms, legs and torso would be boiled and preserved for exhibition on pikes at various public places in the city, *pour encourager les autres*. This obscene ritual was laid down in the law books: it was intended as the ultimate deterrent to any commoner who might think of deposing a king. It was the main reason why, on that afternoon of 10 January, the Inns of Court were so empty.

When that brief arrived, did John Cooke have any precognition of his own torture by rope and knife? Did his father Isaac, a frail presence in the corner of his chamber, picture the horrible death of the son of whom he was so proud? His wife, Frances, knelt and prayed for his safety. Across the Gray's Inn courtyard the Attorney-General was hiding under his bedcovers. At another chambers in the same Inn, the wife of John Bradshawe, the only English judge prepared to sit at the trial, was begging him to have nothing to do with it. To mollify her he had his hat lined with lead: it could deflect an assassin's bullet, if not time's arrow.

Despite the danger and the entreaties from his friends, John Cooke showed no hesitation and took no precautions. Over the following days, as he prepared the evidence against the King, he became a marked man: death threats, hand-written, were slid under the door of his chamber and attached to stones thrown at his windows at night. He experienced, for the first time, the sting of British gutter journalism: the royalist news-sheets (called *Mercuries*) had been banned in the capital, but that served like all censorship only to encourage their circulation and the new Solicitor-General soon became a target for character assassination. There were plenty of real assassins in London as well: the long nights in this freezing January brought fogs that could camouflage any act of murder. Cooke came under siege from young barristers he had befriended or tutored, who besought him to have no part in the business. One of them, James Nutley, wept openly as he begged his mentor not to hazard his life and his professional standing. Cooke answered by reference to what his profession would later call the cab-rank rule: 'I cannot avoid it. You see, they put it on me.'

The trial of Charles I was a momentous event, and not only for Britain. After thirty years of continental war, the kingdoms of Europe had, by the Treaty of Westphalia in October 1648, given some guarantee of the rights of religious and ethnic minorities within their domains, but as sovereign states that would police themselves. It was fundamental to this treaty, the foundation of international law, that a prince could not be overthrown for violating the liberties of his own subjects. But the most important thing about the Treaty of Westphalia was that England was not party to it. Just a few months later, John Cooke devised a way of ending the impunity it guaranteed to sovereigns, crafting out of the common law and the law of nations and the Bible, a theory which could bring hereditary dictatorship to an end. This message, filtered through the philosophy of Locke and Montesquieu, provided inspiration for the French Revolution and the War of American Independence: we can see it now as the precursor of a much more recent development which began at Nuremberg, namely the use of criminal law to punish heads of state and political and military leaders for war crimes and crimes against humanity.

Cooke's charge began with a fundamental proposition: the King of England was not a person, but an office whose every occupant was entrusted with a limited power to govern 'by and according to the laws of the land and not otherwise'. It had been with the criminal object of securing unlimited and tyrannical power that Charles I had levied war against Parliament and had set out to destroy the very people whose life and liberty he was obliged to preserve. To bring home his guilt for the crippling loss of English life on both sides in the war he had started in 1642, Cooke invoked the doctrine which is called, in modern war-crimes courts, 'command responsibility':

> By which it appears that he, the said Charles Stuart, has been and is the occasioner, author and continuer of the said unnatural, cruel and bloody wars and therefore guilty of all the treasons, murders, rapines, burnings, spoils, desolations, damages and mischiefs to the nation acted and committed in the said wars, or occasioned thereby.

The charges against Milosevic at The Hague conveyed the same idea – the responsibility of the commander for all the natural and probable consequences of his commands. Cooke alleged not only high treason, but 'other High Crimes', which he spelled out in the final paragraph: Charles Stuart he impeached as 'a tyrant, traitor, murderer and public and implacable enemy to the Commonwealth of England'. In a nutshell, what the Solicitor-General had created was a new offence, one that could condemn most of the crowned heads of Europe at the time, and many of the dictators and undemocratic rulers who would come to power in the nations of the world in the following centuries. He had made tyranny a crime.

On Saturday 20 January – only 10 days after accepting the brief – Cooke signed the charge, the document that was to seal the King's fate and his own. That afternoon, a procession of sixty-eight judges in black cloaks or gowns solemnly entered the Great Hall at Westminster, for the public opening of the trial. Accompanied by 120 soldiers with long pikes, they presented a powerful tableau to thousands of citizens who crammed into the public galleries. Preceded by a clerk carrying the sword of state, Judge Bradshawe made his way to centre-stage where his crimson velvet chair had been placed, behind a desk on which a crimson cushion bore the parliamentary mace. The judges sat behind him, on benches hung with scarlet: the chair in which Charles would sit was directly in front of them. The prosecutor – John Cooke – stood immediately to the right of the King's chair. The proceedings began with the deep-voiced ushers shouting the traditional 'Oyez' still heard at the opening of every English criminal court:

> Oyez, oyez, oyez. All manner of persons who have any business in this Court, draw near and give your attendance.

The assembly waited to see a sight that had no parallel: the bringing of a king to a place of public justice. There were some – the soldiers in particular – whose thoughts were of retribution against the man they held responsible for the blood of fallen comrades, but most of the crowd would have had in mind the set of traditional beliefs about the monarch's 'divine majesty'. When Charles did enter, it was with a certain dignity. The sergeant-at-arms, mace held aloft, escorted him towards his centre-stage seat. He was not in chains, nor under obvious restraint: the halberdiers who followed him might have been his own retinue. This was no ordinary prisoner, as his behaviour imme-diately showed: resting upon his familiar silver-tipped cane, he looked with unblinking sternness at the judges, displaying his contempt for the court by refusing to remove his hat. He was, for these few moments, still a king in command.

'Charles Stuart, King of England . . .' Judge Bradshawe's words were respectful, his tone measured and polite: 'the Commons of England have constituted this High Court of Justice before which you are now brought, and you are to hear your charge, after which the Court will proceed.'

This was John Cooke's cue. He brandished the parchment upon which the charge had been written – the charge that he had signed as Solicitor-General for the Commonwealth. 'My Lord President,' he began – at which point he felt a sharp tap on his shoulder. The King had hit the prosecutor with his cane, a walking staff with an ornate silver tip. 'Hold,' Charles commanded, and rose to speak, poking the low-bred lawyer again with his cane to emphasise his command to give way.

If Cooke had yielded, the entire enterprise would have faltered. But the barrister ignored the King, and continued to address the court: 'My Lord President,' he went on, 'according to an order of this High Court directed to me for that purpose . . .' At this point, he suffered a third blow from the cane, a palpable hit, hard enough to dislodge its silver tip, which rolled down the counsel's gown and clattered on to the floor between the two men. Their eyes met, and the King nodded for Cooke to bend and pick it up. But the barrister did not blink, much less stoop. Ignoring the little man beside him at the bar rail he continued, coldly and precisely:

'I do, in the name and on the behalf of the people of England, exhibit and bring into this Court a charge of high treason and other high crimes whereof I do accuse Charles Stuart, King of England, here present.'

Under Cooke's wounding words, the King seemed to shrink, into a small cranky prisoner with dirty hair. In that character, slowly and painfully, under the astonished gaze of his people, the King stooped to pick up the silver tip from the floor at Cooke's feet. There were gasps: Cooke paused for the significance of the moment to sink in before handing the indictment to the court clerk, Andrew Broughton, for its formal reading.

The symbolism of this incident was plain to all. The King, the divine majesty, had bowed, powerless before the majesty of human law. In an age when everyone was on the look-out for signs and portents, this was taken as the direst of signals. The King told his friends that he believed it a bad omen, and the news-sheets reported how Charles had been forced to stoop to retrieve the silver tip: 'This it is conceived will be very ominous.' Few had really thought this unprecedented public spectacle would be taken seriously, but Cooke's resolve at its outset transformed expectations. It now had the appearance of a real trial in which the monarch would have no special favours. *'Be ye ever so high, the law is above you'* had been an empty aphorism for those who had tried to bring the Stuart kings to the bar or the battlefield: this defining historical moment gave it meaning. It was the moment for which John Cooke would never be forgiven.

Part I

Revolution

1

A Man of the Middling Sort

The first recorded existence of John Cooke is in the register of All Saints church in the village of Husbands Bosworth, just south of Leicester. Here he was baptised on 18 September 1608, an indication that his birth had taken place a few days before. He came from poor but healthy farming stock: his father, Isaac Cooke, was twenty-five, and would live until the age of seventy-four. Isaac was one of twelve children of Abraham Cooke, who would die in 1620 at a similar age. If John could come through his early years, in this period when a third of all infants died before reaching five, he could be expected to live through all the seven ages of man predicted by Shakespeare, at this time writing his final plays for the London theatre. His family were God-fearing farmers, with allotments that dotted the countryside for twenty miles to the town of Burbage. Husbands Bosworth was named for all its husbandmen – tenant farmers whose smallholdings sustained their families but little else – and that would have been his parents' expectation for baby John. What mattered most to Isaac and Elizabeth was that he would live an abstemious and pious life, his ability to do so being regarded as an outward sign that he was one of the 'elect' predestined for paradise when the Son of God returned to claim the earth.

This mattered so much to these Puritan parents that for the baptism of their first-born they had travelled from their own farm, just outside Burbage, where the rector was a well-connected Anglican who obeyed the bishop, to Elizabeth's austere family church.[1] Its minister was willing to dispense with 'impure' rituals, like motioning the sign of the cross over the head of the baptised infant. That such a tiny gesture could become a major bone of contention between the bishops of the Church of England, who were sticklers for rituals and symbols, and those Puritan worshippers who wished to 'purify' the Church of all such distractions, was typical of the internecine squabbling that had rent the Anglican religion. Puritans like the Cookes were thick on the ground in the Midlands and the eastern counties and many local ministers were sympathetic to their preference for deritualised worship, which was anathema to King James and his bishops.

James I had been invited from Scotland (where he ruled as James VI) to take the English throne on Elizabeth I's death in 1603. The optimism among Puritans in England that a man from the austere Calvinist Kirk would look sympathetically on their similar form of worship had soon been dashed: James was obsessed with his God-given right to rule as an absolute prince, through a hierarchy supported by archbishops and bishops, alongside his councillors and favourite courtiers. From the outset of his reign he urged the Anglican authorities to discipline ministers who refused to follow approved rituals or who spoke on politics from the pulpit. James I was very far from being 'the wisest fool in Christendom': he was highly educated and very canny, and he knew exactly where the Puritans' hostility to hierarchy in their church would lead: 'no Bishop, no King'.

James warned his son to 'hate no man more than a proud Puritan'.[2] He did not persecute them, but encouraged the Church to discriminate against them and to sack their ministers. The King's edicts, on matters of Sunday observance in particular, were often at variance with the strict moral code of these godly communities, and the profligacy and debauchery of his court further outraged them. As John Cooke grew up, there was much prurient gossip amongst the faithful about a monarch who claimed divine authority yet who maintained a luxurious and licentious court, financed by selling titles and monopolies, and who boasted that his favourite pastimes were 'hunting witches, prophets, Puritans, dead cats and hares'. After all, James had a grotesque parentage: his mother was Mary, Queen of Scots. He was in her swollen belly when it was clutched at by her lover, David Riccio, as he was being dragged to his death at Holyrood House by a team of assassins led by James's father, Henry Stuart. Mary had later arranged for Henry to be strangled and had eventually been executed for plotting to kill her cousin and sister-queen Elizabeth I. If there *was* anything in the theory of hereditary right by which James acceded to the throne, it did not bode well for the Stuarts.

The farming community where the Cookes lived was small – there were only seventy families at Burbage (then named Burbach) and a handful in their hamlet of Sketchley. The town's name – a construct from 'burr' (a kind of thistle) and 'bach' (a rivulet) – indicates the kind of countryside in which he played as a boy, although play was not encouraged by Puritans: they had been outraged when James issued a 'Book of Sports', permitting certain recreations after church on Sundays. As a young man, Cooke was well aware that the brand of religion on which he was raised was not in government favour. At school, where he excelled, he belonged to a group of Puritan children ostracised in the playground just as their parents were often excluded from worship in the church. There was one faith that suffered worse discrimination: the stateliest house in the area, Bosworth Hall, was owned by a Catholic family related to Sir Thomas More, and their secret celebration of Mass was the cause of occasional raids authorised by the local Justices of the Peace. Especially after the Gunpowder Plot of 1605, Catholics were regarded as potential terrorists, but the strength of their faith intrigued the boy, and would later tempt him to explore it before settling on his own. He spent long hours learning the Bible (the King James edition was printed in 1611, and widely distributed) and was brought up to believe that powerful men who had failed God's election were abandoned to sin – a belief readily corroborated by reports of corrupt behaviour at court.

James, more homoerotically fixated as he became older, elevated his young male favourites (first Robert Carr, then George Villiers) to titles and positions of power entirely beyond their abilities. Scandalous rumours were rife throughout Cooke's youth, confirmed by trials in 1616 which gripped the nation. The Countess of Essex, married to Robert Carr whom the King had made Earl of Somerset, arranged for Sir Thomas Overbury to be murdered, by having arsenic put in his food and then, when that failed, by administration of an enema filled with poison. Various of the poisoners were convicted and hanged, but not the earl or the courtiers who had procured the murder, who were pardoned because of their status. Puritans got the message: although their birth might be low on the social scale, in death God would raise them far above kings and courtiers. Another message – that there was no justice to be had in the King's courts, at least in cases concerning the King and his favourites – would soon concern a new generation of lawyers for whom the common law of England, rooted in Magna Carta, brooked no such exceptions.

Another telling event of Cooke's youth was the execution in 1618 of Sir Walter Ralegh, that great Renaissance Englishman – historian, explorer, poet, philosopher, intellectual and adventurer. He had been convicted in 1603 on trumped-up charges of plotting with Spanish interests to overthrow the newly crowned King James. His treason trial had been notable for the invective of the prosecutor, the ambitious Attorney-General Edward Coke:

COKE: You are the most vile and execrable traitor that ever lived.

RALEGH: You speak indiscreetly, uncivilly and barbarously.

COKE: I want words sufficient to express your viperous treasons.

RALEGH: I think you want words indeed, for you have spoken one thing half a dozen times.

COKE: You are an odious fellow; your name is hateful to all the realm of England . . . I will make it appear to the world that there never lived a viler viper on the face of the earth than you.

This abuse of the defendant was what passed for cross-examination in treason trials, after which jurors who had been hand-picked by the King's officials were expected to convict. This time, unusually, Coke's venom backfired: Ralegh's dignity earned him such popular support that James, cautious at the outset of his reign, felt it politic to suspend his death sentence. Sir Walter lived in modest comfort in the Tower of London, in rooms that can still be viewed, and was released in 1616 to mount an expedition in search of Spanish gold. It was unsuccessful, but it rekindled Spain's hatred of the man who had sunk so many of its galleons and had razed Cadiz. His execution was demanded as a condition of fulfilling James's pet project of marriage between his own heir (Charles) and the Spanish princess. James could hardly put Ralegh on public trial for attacking England's traditional enemy: instead, he ordered his Chancellor, the brilliant but bent Francis Bacon, to arrange to have the 1603 death sentence put into effect. Ralegh went to his long-delayed execution with memorable dignity, after a scaffold speech which persuaded everyone of his innocence and which convinced two of the onlookers – the MPs John Eliot and John Pym – that the Stuarts could not be trusted to govern the country. James was depraved, unpopular and idle: now he had killed an English hero at the request of Spain. There remained a general belief that he had been appointed by God, but by the end of his reign it had occurred to many MPs to examine more closely the terms of that divine appointment.

James had only one male heir, the small (5 feet 4 inches) stammering and petulant Charles, born in 1600. He was made Prince of Wales in 1616, after the death of Henry, his more popular elder brother. While John Cooke spent his boyhood in the bosom of a loving family circle, Charles had to endure long periods of separation from his mother, at the insistence of an unloving father who had him indoctrinated with the divine right of the Stuarts to rule and to be obeyed. James had set down these precepts in a small volume, *Basilikon Doron*, a handbook for the divine right monarch. From it, Charles was made to believe that his God-given authority over his people was like that of a father over his children. James preached the benefits of what would now be described as a benign political and spiritual dictatorship, in which the King governed through an elite, chosen and discarded at his own discretion, comprising his ministers, his bishops and judges, who must *never* question the royal prerogative, for 'that is to take away the mystical reverence that belongs to those that sit in the throne of God'.[3] In this Stuart utopia, Parliament was irritating and irrelevant and alternative religions were positively dangerous. James had written another book to refute the claim – by Geneva Calvinists – that monarchy entailed a contract with the people, who might resist and remove a king if he breached it. On the contrary, the monarch is 'the absolute master of the lives and possessions of his subjects; his acts are not open to inquiry or dispute, and no misdeeds can ever justify resistance'.[4] It was an argument that Shakespeare, in context ironically, put thus in *Pericles*:

> Kings are earth's gods; in vice their law's their will,
> And if Jove stray, who dares say, Jove doth ill?

One Englishman who dared to quarrel with the King over whether God gave him power to override the common law was Sir Edward Coke. He had been appointed Chief Justice after his Crown-pleasing (if not crowd-pleasing) prosecution of Ralegh. His legendary confrontation with James at a Privy Council meeting in 1608 arose when the King claimed that since he was divinely ordained and thus the supreme judge on earth, he could override the decisions of any of the other judges, all of whom he had appointed and could dismiss at will. Judges might (as Bacon had said) be 'lions under the throne', but they were *under* it, and tethered. The Chief Justice disagreed: God's prodigy the King might be, but he was bound to obey the common law: 'The law is the golden metewand and measure to try the causes of your majesty's subjects, and it is by that law that your majesty is protected in safety and peace.' At this, James flew into a rage, screaming that it was treason to say that he was under the law. The King lurched forward to punch Coke, but the Chief Justice prostrated himself and begged for mercy. It had been a courageous moment and Coke's short-lived defiance reverberates today,[5] but at the time had little support. James I's subjects believed that the King's authority was bestowed by God, a belief endorsed by all his other judges. Monarchical government was ordained by God and resistance to the King's power was both mortal sin and treason.[6]

James's assertion that the King could do no wrong would never be tested during his reign. Judges were not minded to assert any power over him, even if (as Coke contended) they had it, because they lacked tenure of their office and could always be sacked if they displeased him. Coke himself was dismissed from the Chief Justiceship for that very reason in 1616: he had infuriated James once again, this time by refusing to concede that the King was entitled to summon the judges for a private 'consultation' about a case to which the King was a party. But Coke, despite his intellectual courage, was as corrupt as all other gifted commoners when it came to advancing his career or his wealth. He sought to worm his way back into royal favour by forcing his fourteen-year-old daughter to marry the Duke of Buckingham's idiot brother, tying her to a bedpost and whipping her until she gave a sobbing consent, and battling, on the streets and in court, with his wife who opposed the match. Challenging the absolutist claim of royal power would require a different breed of men, with a faith firm enough to transcend trivial temptations of earthly wealth or privilege. Disappointed, Coke became a baleful anti-Stuart presence in Parliament, and wrote his justly famous *Institutes*, a textbook which taught John Cooke's generation of law students to revere Magna Carta as the source of English liberty and that kings, for all their 'natural reason', could not be accepted as interpreters of the common law, since they lacked training in 'the artificial reason and judgment' by which the laws of the realm of England were to be understood and applied. Coke's point – that 'law is an art which requires long study and experience, before a man can attain to the cognizance of it'[7] – was not just a denial of the theory of the monarch-judge, but a claim to a professional monopoly. The prospect was congenial to students slaving over tedious texts and precedents for the seven long years of study at the Inns of Court.

At the royal court, however, divine right doctrine was drummed into Charles the young Prince of Wales: he lived it in the lavishness of the surroundings and the sycophancy of the courtiers. The only 'outsiders' that he could be bothered to meet at a social level were artists like the tame playwright Ben Jonson and Inigo Jones the architect, happy to create private masques in which the royal family could join in the singing of their own praises. Significantly, these expensive and exclusive self-celebrations were Charles's greatest delight: both as youth and man he played out idealised stage roles as sincerely as if he were living the fantasy of a prince adored alike by angels and subjects. He grew up in a narcissistic cocoon, unconcerned about the feelings and aspirations of other classes and citizens – merchants and land-owning squires and ambitious lawyers – who believed that their new-found prosperity, which had grown during the peace which was the greatest achievement of James's reign, should give them some stake in national policy. Many of these hard-working, ambitious men were Puritans, a religious caste towards whom Charles had inherited his father's uncomprehending distaste. Among them was Oliver Cromwell, born in 1599, the only son of wealthy and well-connected Puritan gentry in Huntingdon. He was a man whose massive talents any sensible regime would seek to harness. But in the 1630s Cromwell was so disillusioned about his prospects under Stuart rule that he seriously considered emigrating to America – a course which over 20,000 Puritans actually took, in the decade after Charles prorogued Parliament in 1629.

John Cooke was a generation behind Cromwell and from a different class entirely: a class of husbandmen who always had to worry about money. A census in 1619, when John was eleven, shows two younger brothers (James and William) and two baby sisters.[8] Isaac, at thirty-five, had yet to acquire the land or the income of £40 per year that would entitle him to the status of 'gent',[9] and he could not afford to provide his precocious eldest son with a university education at nearby Cambridge. In Oxford, however, a college had recently been founded 'for poor and needy scholars' by the will of a wealthy West Country Protestant, Nicholas Wadham. Cooke met its conditions for entry, having been born in wedlock to a family which could not provide him with an income of more than £8 per year. He was impressive enough for Wadham to accept him at fourteen, the youngest age possible. His class was recorded as 'plebeian', and he came as a 'battellar' who would reduce cost to the college by looking after himself as much as possible. College records show that he lived for his first year in a chamber underneath the chaplain's lodgings, and his good behaviour may be inferred from the fact that his 'caution money', deposited in case of misconduct, was returned in full when he left Wadham in 1624. He had to attend the twice-daily chapel services, at 5 a.m. and 8 p.m., and eschew such pleasurable pursuits as might have been available (few were: to remove temptation, all servants had to be male except for the laundress, who was required to be elderly and of unblemished repute).[10] Rhetoric, logic and moral philosophy were taught, along with Greek and Latin, but theology suffused all teaching. It was designed to prepare the students for a good life – by which was meant a life godly enough to continue after death.

At Wadham, Cooke's contemporaries included Robert Blake, who grew up to become Cromwell's mighty admiral, vanquisher of the Dutch and Spanish and French fleets, and Nicholas Love, later a lawyer MP who would serve as one of the judges at the King's trial. Carew Ralegh, Sir Walter's son, was there as well – he had been thrown out of the royal court for frightening the King, who took him for the ghost of his father. A friendship between Carew and Cooke led the latter to read Sir Walter's banned *History of the World*, which emphasised the deceit and oppression of kings who 'pulled the vengeance of God upon themselves'.[11] Cooke would later salute the work as an example of the 'application of those twin lode-stars, nature and right reason'.[12] It must have staggered these boys as they came to realise how cruelly the life of the greatest living Englishman had been sacrificed, by order of a king who wanted to curry favour with a hostile power whose Armada had, within the memory of many of their tutors, been scattered by Ralegh's ships and fellow captains.

Students at Wadham in the 1620s would have surveyed a Stuart court that was financially and morally bankrupt. James paid for his pleasures by selling knighthoods and preferments and by privatising royal monopolies like the collection of taxes and customs dues. The court continued its licentious ways. George Villiers, dashing but dim-witted, had been elevated to become the King's leading minister and created Duke of Buckingham: James privately called this catamite courtier 'my sweet child and wife'. Gossip at the colleges and the Inns of Court was more of Lot's wife and the horrible punishment for sodomy 'as we had probable cause to fear, a sin in the prince as well as the people', recorded Simonds D'Ewes, a student at the Middle Temple, in his diary for 1622. He confided, in code, his concern about the King's 'base and cowardly nature' and the sexual preference for which he was 'laughed at by the vulgar.'[13]

Zealous young Puritans like D'Ewes and Cooke could level an even graver charge against James: he had betrayed the Protestant cause. He had refused to help the troops of the Protestant elector Frederick, under attack by Catholic forces of the Holy Roman Empire, despite the fact that Frederick was married to James's own daughter Elizabeth. His foreign policy was set upon forging an alliance by marrying Charles to the King of Spain's daughter, so he gave permission for a hare-brained scheme conceived by Buckingham and Charles, which made them the laughing stock of Europe. It involved their travelling incognito to Madrid, for Charles to woo the princess in person. Philip III took advice from the Pope, then kept them waiting while adding conditions to the match which would require toleration for Catholics – a policy anathema to most of the English and blasphemy to the Scots. The unsuccessful suitors returned home to public joy, more over their failure than over their return. Indeed, the insouciance with which James and Charles and the despised Buckingham could contemplate a Catholic alliance caused deep disquiet. When an alternative foreign alliance was forged, through Charles's marriage to Princess Henrietta Maria, it was with France, the lesser of the two Catholic evils. But the priests who attended on her, and the open Catholicism of her 'court within a court', would remain a grumbling provocation throughout her husband's reign.

James died on 27 March 1625 after contracting a malaria-like fever. Buckingham had forcibly kept the royal doctors from his bedside and arranged for his own servants and his mother to treat the King with mysterious potions and poultices. Rumours swept the nation that Buckingham and Charles, fast friends after the Madrid escapade, had poisoned the old man. The following year one of the King's doctors went public with this charge against Buckingham, and it was inconclusively investigated by a parliamentary committee. No allegation could be made against Charles, who was now King and hence above the law. But the evidence against him, of complicity in an unnatural plot to inherit the throne by hastening the death of his own father, was avidly discussed at the Inns of Court in Cooke's first year. In that questioning but protected forum, it was possible to argue that the Lord's commandment 'Thou shalt not kill' applied to kings, as well as to commoners.

Cooke was a student at Gray's Inn from the outset of Charles's reign. It was a long apprenticeship to become a barrister: seven years of study at an inn, followed by satisfactory performance of practical exercises under the direction of a senior barrister for three years after call to the bar. Cooke was 'called' (allowed to begin supervised practice) in 1631, at the age of twenty-three. Although James had ordered that no one should be admitted who was not a 'gentleman by descent', this was widely flouted, and Cooke took his place with other sons of plebeians – farmers and tradesmen who had scrimped and saved to clothe their sons in the velvet breeches and silken doublet of a law student. The Inns had provided a special education to the sons of English gentry for several hundred years. Most students did not in fact go on to practise law but the education gave them sufficient knowledge to operate as administrators of provincial government or of the large family estates that, if first-born sons, they would soon inherit. By 1625, however, the Inns had become more accessible to men from the lower middle classes, who saw the practice of law as a means of obtaining a measure of wealth and position.

After completing his seven years of legal study, Cooke did what is now termed 'pupillage' with a bencher of the Inn, Thomas Brickenden, who had to supervise his work for three years. Brickenden was a cautious and respected practitioner, of noted Puritan piety, who took over as dean of the chapel after the death of Richard Sibbes. That he was prepared to take Cooke as his apprentice was an indication of the youth's religious intensity and capacity for grinding legal research. Brickenden advised him to study a tedious book by Justice Littleton on land tenure. It was 'like a lump of beef after a grand dinner', Cooke recalled, 'Littleton being undoubtedly the most crabbed author to begin with any science in the world'.[14] He read the more practical *Doctor and Student* with greater aptitude, because it dealt with actual cases, rather than 'moot points and speculative conceits'. The seven-year bar course had been heavily loaded with theology, and Cooke was irritated by attempts to make legal science turn on biblical examples. Law was a man-made discipline: the first three years of the course should be spent on the study of divinity followed by four years on the unadulterated principles of the common law.[15]

The role of 'divinity' in law was to give it super-human strength. The

Bible was a book of precedents, integrated into the common law with the help of preachers as well as professors, and the most influential in Gray's Inn was Richard Sibbes – 'heavenly Doctor Sibbes' as Cooke described him – who would tell the young lawyer again and again to 'study the law, but practise divinity' because it was empty vanity for a barrister to advise a client unless he had himself been 'a client at the throne of Grace'.[16] Cooke was imbued with the teaching that God was no respecter of persons: 'of all the men in hell, the torment of great men is most, because they had most comfort in this world. Mighty men shall be mightily tormented, that is all the privilege they shall have in hell.'[17] There was only one Divine Right – and that was God's right to rule kings: 'Kings reign by Him . . . it is a treason against God to betray the Kingdoms that He has given them into the hands of his enemies.'[18] The message from the Gray's Inn pulpit was that kings might be held to account for leading their people astray and it was superstition, not true religion, that immunised them from punishment for breaching the law. Over such challenges to sovereign immunity, hostility between the new King and his Parliament would quickly develop.

Charles's first mistake was to cling to his father's favourite, the unpopular Duke of Buckingham. The two became inseparable: Charles, it was said, preferred Buckingham's company to that of Henrietta Maria, his new wife. The young King appointed the inexperienced duke to lead a series of military excursions which ended disastrously. The first, to the fury of English Puritans, unintentionally helped the French attack fellow Protestants at La Rochelle. Then the English fleet, under Buckingham the Lord Admiral, failed ignominiously to take a small French garrison protecting the Ile de Rhé. Successive Parliaments attempted to impeach the duke, for offences ranging from misfeasance in office to the murder of James. But Charles always dissolved the House before it could lay hands on him, warning MPs 'that Parliaments are altogether in my power for their calling, sitting and dissolution'. The King's fatal loathing for the institution began in 1628, when Buckingham was murdered by a disaffected sailor named Felton, who claimed that his crime had been instigated by the accusations made against the duke in the House of Commons. Charles, distraught at the death of his best friend, was all too ready to believe him and to blame MPs, led by Sir John Eliot, for inciting the assassination. Buckingham's death was celebrated throughout the land by bonfires and bell-ringings and ballads in Felton's honour: these were mortal insults the grieving King would never forgive.

Although Charles was in certain respects an improvement on his father – he was sober and serious, and much more attentive to the duties of government – he had not inherited James's street-wisdom and was hopelessly lacking in any ability to compromise with or to care about the aspirations of any section of his people. He had no empathy with the gentry. The landowning class was represented in the House of Lords (many because of the titles they had bought from James) and were now being elected to the Commons in large numbers, often defeating candidates who had the King's support. After Buckingham's death, Charles vowed that he would suffer Parliament to meet only for the purpose of voting him money; it would not be allowed to criticise his foreign policy or to speak up for the liberty of his subjects, either by objecting to his power to imprison them or by dissenting from the arrangements he chose to make for their Anglican worship. In this frame of mind, Charles denounced, deceived and dissolved successive Parliaments between 1625 and 1629 which refused (other than upon conditions he could not accept) to vote the loans and taxes he required. By so doing, he provoked the enmity of a class of powerful men who were ultimately to bring him down, with the help of doctrines forged by the generation of lawyers currently in training at the Inns. The MPs Cooke supported as a student – 'Puritan squires' like Eliot and Pym and Hampden – were sustained in their opposition to the King by Coke's vision of the common law as the guarantor of liberty and by a more self-interested disinclination to suffer taxation without consent. But most crucially, the obstinacy they were to display in these first years of resistance to the King was a response to his challenge to their religious faith.

James had not carried out his threat to 'harry Puritans out of the land', but his son soon chose to promote, as bishops and court favourites, those Anglican divines who were keen to harry their ministers out of the Church. They were led by William Laud, an archbishop committed to hierarchical rule and to rituals (like the wearing of a surplice and signing the cross at baptism) and symbols (altar rails and stained glass) that most Puritans abominated. Laud and many of his supporters were 'Arminians' who doubted the Calvinist doctrine of predestination, believing (like Catholics) in the prospective salvation of sinners. They argued vehemently that it was mortal sin to disobey the sovereign's command, and in consequence they preached obedience to one command that Parliament could never accept as lawful – the 'forced loan' that Charles decreed in order to raise money without its consent.

Charles had instructed his Privy Council in 1626 to order various taxes, like customs duties ('tonnage and poundage') without parliamentary approval. Some MPs who refused to pay were imprisoned, and five of them took out writs of habeas corpus requiring the King to justify their detention. Habeas corpus, 'the great writ', requires the state to show lawful cause for the applicant's imprisonment. The MPs took their stand on that bedrock principle of English liberty, Clause 29 of Magna Carta, the Great Charter:

No free man shall be taken or imprisoned, or be deprived of his freehold, or liberties, or free customs, or be detained, or exiled, or any otherwise destroyed; nor will we pass upon him, or condemn him, but by the lawful judgement of his peers, or by the law of the land. To no man will we sell, to no man will we deny or delay, justice or right.

It was a crucial issue, the first in a succession of legal challenges by the parliamentary leaders to the royal prerogative. The King sacked the Chief Justice (Sir Randall Crewe) for expressing doubts about the legality of the forced loan, and his Privy Council directed the warden of the prison to answer the habeas corpus writ merely by stating that the orders to commit the MPs to prison without trial 'were and are by His Majesty's special command'. This was not a lawful answer, the barrister MP John Selden argued in *The Five Knights' Case* which followed in 1627,[19] because Magna Carta required that no person can lose his liberty except by due process of law: 'His Majesty's special command' was not a law, let alone lawful reason for indefinite detention. On the contrary, replied the Attorney-General, the King's command was the law: 'the very essence of justice under God upon us is in him'. The order for indefinite imprisonment of the loan-refusers was an 'act of state', an exercise of the royal prerogative into which the courts could not enquire. The pliable new Chief Justice, Nicholas Hyde, agreed: he declined the MPs' request to rule on the legality of non-parliamentary taxation, and ordered that they should stay in prison.

This decision generated a great controversy, which escalated when Selden discovered that the Attorney-General, under pressure from the King, had secretly entered in the official court roll a final order which had not been approved by the judges, who claimed (when questioned in the House of Lords) that they intended only to make a provisional ruling.[20] It appeared, to infuriated MPs, that the King and his legal acolytes were stealthily asserting a royal right to imprison subjects indefinitely without trial, for refusing to pay an unlawful tax. Selden's argument was endorsed by the elderly legal colossus, Sir Edward Coke ('it weakens Magna Carta . . . Magna Carta is such a fellow he will have no sovereign'[21]) and fervently supported by John Cooke and his fellow students at Gray's Inn, where seditious notes were passed around in drinking pots and an anonymous libel was printed urging 'all English freeholders' to refuse to pay the forced loan.[22] But the judges of the King's Bench were beholden to the King, who could sack them if displeased with their judgment or (as in Chief Justice Crewe's case) even by an indication that they might give it against the King. That is why they ducked any decision on the legality of the exaction, and refused bail. Many more gentry – including John Hampden, Sir John Eliot and Sir Thomas Wentworth (then a leader of the opposition to the King, and much admired by Cooke) – were imprisoned until they forked out for the 'loan' – on any view, a form of taxation that had not been approved by Parliament.

The MPs, blocked in the courts, tried another tactic: they offered to consent to a number of new taxes if the King would approve a Bill of Rights, to be entrenched in legislation drafted by Sir Edward Coke. It would have reversed the decision in *The Five Knights' Case* by giving overriding statutory force to Magna Carta and by removing the King's arbitrary power to imprison. Charles refused, but an apparent compromise was briefly reached by his acceptance of 'the Petition of Right' – not a statute, but a 'declaration' by both Houses of Parliament of how existing laws should be interpreted. There was to be no taxation without parliamentary consent: no forced billeting of hungry and rapacious soldiers on civilian households; no use by the King of martial law in peacetime; and most importantly, no imprisonment (as in the *Five Knights' Case*) of any man 'without being charged with anything to which they might make answer according to the law'. The King's agreement to the petition produced bonfires and bell-ringing, but Charles had no intention of honouring it: when he heard that Parliament was preparing to remonstrate against his imposition of 'tonnage and poundage' he dissolved the House of Commons, expostulating that by approving the Petition of Right he had granted no new liberties nor had he agreed to limit his prerogative in any way. So the decision in the *Five Knights' Case* still stood: the King could tax and imprison as he pleased, irrespective of Magna Carta and the common law.

In 1629 matters came to a showdown when the King, desperate for more funds, recalled Parliament and invited it to approve further financial exactions. Instead, the House of Commons proceeded to debate three resolutions pointedly aimed at the King's counsellors and advisers (it would have been treason to direct them at the King). These resolutions condemned as 'capital enemies to the commonwealth' any ministers who should advocate the levy of any tax not approved by Parliament, or who should – like Laud – attempt to impose innovation in religion (i.e. 'Popery or Arminianism'). When Parliament met on 2 March the Speaker, Sir John Finch, refused to permit the debate. The King, he announced, had ordered the House to adjourn and he could not allow the motions to be put ('I will not say I will not put it to the question, but I must say I dare not'). There was uproar: Finch tried to adjourn by leaving the Speaker's chair, but was held down by Denzil Holles and other MPs. The doors were locked while Eliot passionately advocated the resolutions, which were passed with acclamation while the King's soldiers hammered loudly on the outer doors.

It was in any view an extraordinary moment in English history – Parliament's most dramatic defiance yet of the sovereign's will and of the sovereign's armed officials. Simon Schama overstates it as 'the birth of English public opinion', although it was reported in the news-sheets and debated at taverns and meeting-places throughout the land.[23] But the uniqueness of this occasion really lies in the wording of the resolutions: it was the first assertion by Parliament that a capital offence could be committed against 'the commonwealth', in circumstances where the principal offender, albeit immune from justice, would be the sovereign himself.

Charles dissolved this turbulent assembly a few days later. Although incandescent with rage, he condescended to the new power of the press by publishing his decision in the news-sheets, in a lengthy diatribe against his enemies, in particular the lawyer MPs. After a typically arrogant beginning ('Howsoever princes are not bound to give account of their actions but to God alone . . .') his declaration accused MPs of trying to extend their privileges in ways 'incompatible with monarchy' – namely by setting up parliamentary committees which dared to summon his officials, and by criticising his government and his Star Chamber: 'Young lawyers sitting there take upon them to decry the opinions of the judges,' he exclaimed. This kind of behaviour 'under pretence of privilege and freedom of speech' was 'to force us to yield to conditions incompatible with monarchy' – by which he meant, incompatible with absolute monarchical power.[24]

Charles had nine MPs arrested for disorderly behaviour in the House: they claimed parliamentary privilege, and their habeas corpus petitions were initially granted by judges who did not realise just how determined to destroy Parliament the King had become. Charles ignored the court order, and directed that the MPs should be transferred to the Tower of London, where they would be at his mercy. The price of their release, he decided, would be an abject apology and provision of sureties for good behaviour – an admission of guilt. Eliot and four others refused to grovel, and remained in prison for over a year. After deliberate delays engineered by Charles, their prosecution for assaulting the Speaker and creating disorder in the House came before the Court of King's Bench.

The judges knew that words spoken or actions taken in Parliament could not be punished in the courts – this privilege of free speech within the House dated back to the first Parliament of Queen Elizabeth. The MPs argued that only Parliament, as the highest court, could discipline its members and claimed their privilege in the appropriate way, by refusing to enter a plea. In consequence, the duty of the judges was to investigate their claim and indeed to uphold it (nobody doubted its validity). But instead they decided to treat the refusal to plead not as a claim of privilege but as a refusal to acknowledge the court.[25] A refusal to recognise the court meant that the defendant's silence when called upon to answer the charge must be taken *pro confesso*, i.e. as a confession of guilt. By this device, and after one judge had been suspended by the King because he wanted to uphold parliamentary privilege,[26] the cowered bench contrived to uphold the King's behaviour and to find the MPs guilty. They were heavily fined (Eliot a massive £2,000) and imprisoned at the King's pleasure. Charles was not pleased to release any of them without an unqualified apology and was particularly pleased when Eliot, whom he principally blamed for inciting Buckingham's murder, died in the Tower from consumption in 1632. His death, Eliot's supporters would always remember, was hastened by the King's refusal to allow a fire in his cell. Another petty act of royal spite was the refusal to allow his body to be buried in the family vault. Sir John Eliot was Parliament's first martyr, a man who disdained to save his own life by the expedient of an insincere apology.

John Cooke would not forget Eliot, or the 'five knights'. The law student had closely followed the twists and turns of these cases and observed some of the hearings in King's Bench, one of the higher courts of justice which sat in a partitioned section of Westminster Hall. Twenty years later, in framing the charge of tyranny against King Charles, Cooke recalled Sir John Eliot's attack on the forced loan: 'Upon this dispute not alone our lands and goods are engaged, but all that we call ours. These privileges, which made our fathers free men, are in question. If they be not the more carefully preserved, they will I fear render us to posterity less free, less worthy than our fathers.'[27] Cooke was not, of course, of the same rank and station as these valiant lawyer MPs who first defied Charles I. They were men of great estates, Puritans for the most part, backed financially and politically by barons whose ancestors had forced King John to seal Magna Carta. Their faith and their fortune gave them the courage to disobey a monarch who was abusing the law, but none of them would have dreamed of demanding a republic. They could not conceive of England ruled by other than a king: their insistence was that he should govern with the wisdom of Parliament, and under the restrictions of common law. They stood for Parliament's place *alongside* the King: for its right to consent to any taxes on the class its members composed, to influence his foreign policy in a Europe beset by popery, and to ensure that he kept the faith – the Protestant faith, preferably purged of rituals and observances.

Charles could not abide their pretensions. He dissolved Parliament and entered upon eleven years of personal rule. From 1629 to 1640 he reigned free of all irritations and provocations from Sir John Eliot's colleagues – men of the stamp of John Pym, John Hampden, Denzil Holles and Oliver St John. A few defected, attracted by the prospect of exercising power: Thomas Wentworth joined the King's Privy Council and later became the Earl of Strafford, while Edward Hyde, a constitutional monarchist, went over to Charles I and in due course would shepherd his son back to the throne. He had no doubt, writing later as Lord Clarendon, that the true cause of the civil war lay in 1629:

No man can shew me a source from whence these waters of bitterness we now taste have more probably flowed, than from this unseasonable, unskillful, and precipitate dissolution of Parliament . . .[28]

2

Strafford, Ship Money and a Search for Self

The crucial events of the 1630s – the decade of King Charles's personal rule, when he refused to call Parliament – can only be understood in the context of a society where everyone, from the highest to the most lowly born, was obsessed with attaining salvation. The ever-present physical pain – from rotting teeth or untreatable injuries or countless poxes – had no analgesic other than prayerful contemplation of a graceful transition to a heaven which was self-evidently too small to hold everyone. The Church of England was not seen as the result of Henry VIII's frustrations over divorce; rather it was the true Church, arising from the ashes of the heroic divines whom Queen Mary (Henry's Catholic daughter by his first marriage to Katherine of Aragon) had burnt at the stake for condemning the Pope as the anti-Christ. Their torments and their courage in facing death – unrepentantly and with famous last words – were required reading in a magisterial tome, *Foxe's Book of Martyrs*. This was the most influential textbook, available in every school and every church, with illustrations of the true Protestant saints departing this life in the fires of Smithfield. Catholics, those dangerous devotees of the anti-Christ, must be suppressed – other than in Ireland, where they coexisted as a despised lumpen proletariat, kept down by rigorous rule and a policy of transmigration under which great estates were progressively bestowed on Protestant settlers.

For English Puritans, Geneva was the 'city on a hill' both spiritually as the custodian of Calvin's legacy (he had lived and taught there) and liter-

38

ally: its high towers had resisted all attacks by land armies of the Catholic kings of Savoy, most famously in *l'Escalade* of 1602. A substantial English community had settled there in Calvin's time, refugees from Mary's persecution. When Elizabeth I re-established the Church of England, it was as 'a Protestant creed decently dressed in the time-honoured vestments of Catholicism'[1] – and it was precisely such vestments that the Puritan movement sought to strip bare. Catholicism was superstition, dangerous because directed by a foreign power, and as Calvin's successor Theodore Beza had famously said, tolerating other religions was a diabolical idea 'because it means that everyone should be left to go to hell in his own way'. The Puritans wanted to 'purify' the Church by removing not only papist remnants, but all aspects of worship for which they could find no biblical support – and in the bible there is no reference to bishops.

The bishops, led by Laud, wanted Puritans out of the Church of England, and from Charles I they had every support. In 1629 England was in the grip of economic misery unrelieved, for the God-fearing middle classes, by any prospect of political power: removing from them as well the power to worship in their church made Charles's realm unendurable. John Winthrop, a lawyer friend of Sir John Eliot, planned a 'bible commonwealth' beyond the seas in New England, where 'we shall be as a city upon a hill, the eyes of all people are upon us . . . we shall be made a story and a byword throughout the world'.[2] So he wrote, mid-Atlantic, on board the *Arbella*, leaving a country upon which God had turned His back for a settlement where proper worship by 'the elect' would attract His blessing. Over the next decade, more than twenty thousand religious refugees followed, as Laud's inquisition excommunicated congregationalist ministers in England. God did seem to favour their sails – of 198 ships which made the crossing carrying Puritan settlers between 1630 and 1640, only one was lost.[3] Hugh Peters, who would be indissolubly linked with Cooke later in life and death, crossed the seas for Massachusetts, to become a minister at Salem (half a century before the witch trials which demonised the town). He travelled with young Henry Vane, who became the State's first governor (at the age of twenty-three) and the daughters of an Essex puritan, Edmund Reade, who married into the Winthrop family (two of their descendants – George W. Bush and John Kerry – were to contest the U.S. Presidency, 370 years later). Peters played an important role in the early days of the settlement, standing up for rationality and learning against those who urged guidance by 'inner light' and he was the most active of the founders of Harvard College. His pious precept, 'an hour's idleness is a sin, as well as an hour's drunkenness' became a motto for Harvard freshmen. Its Board of Overseas would send him to Europe in 1641 on what was probably the first college fund-raising drive, and he promoted settlement in Massachusetts by issuing a prospectus with Harvard education as the main selling point. But Hugh Peters did not return: by then, the battle with the King drew him into the parliamentary army and in due course he became Cromwell's personal chaplain.

The achievements of these Puritans in Massachusetts provide the clearest example of the political and social consequences of their philosophy. They quickly abolished primogeniture, the feudal law which ensured that vast estates (including the Crown) were passed down to the eldest male. They refused to acknowledge aristocratic titles, although they maintained a social order which distinguished the gentle folk from the labourers and servants. Government was by the wise, or 'selected', who organised town meetings with the object of obtaining general agreement after discussion and debate. Churches were the barest of meeting-rooms, with a pulpit and no decoration other than a severe Magritte-like eye painted on the wall behind it, staring down on the congregation as a reminder of the all-seeing deity watching their every move. The sermons were long lectures which took the form of a literal exegesis of a biblical text, followed by a discussion of its true meaning. Pagan feasts and holy days that had been adopted by Christians were abolished – including Christmas and Easter. One province, New Haven, took note that the Lord slew Onan after he 'spilt his seed upon the ground' and so prescribed death by hanging for this sin of emission – in the very year that the King's physician, William Harvey, discovered that hanging, by breaking the cervical vertebrae, caused ejaculation. The work ethic ('improving the time') ensured that the colony did not founder, although work was rigorously suspended on the Sabbath when all tools were downed – married couples were required to refrain from sexual intercourse on Sundays.

The modern perception of the joyless Puritan comes partly from confusing them with really joyless Presbyterians, but also from the protective self-discipline of America's founding fathers, whose faith was 'one of the most harsh and painful creeds that believing Christians have ever inflicted upon themselves'.[4] Cooke, who was later to urge Christians to abandon cruel punishments, had to acknowledge that harsh necessity might justify harsh laws: he contrasted the punishment of death for adultery in 'the new plantations' with its punishment in England, where adulterers merely had to stand for a night in the pillory clad in a cold sheet.[5] Certainly there was less zealotry among the leading Puritan families in England. There, the 'unreproved joys' of the landed gentry included 'hunting, hawking, fencing, bowling, dancing, making music and playing chess' not to mention conversing over strong ale with crude jokes and japes (for all its modern associations with sexual repression, Puritan writing on sex was robust and explicit – so much so that its republication became impossible in Victorian times).[6] In any event there was much joy and 'good neighbourliness' to be had amongst the congregations which gathered around preachers and at meeting-places, a world away from the back-stabbing of the Court and the strict class divides of the country.

There was pessimism in Calvin's theology, of course, because original sin doomed mankind to permanent depravity. This was the first of its five principles settled by the Synod of Dort in 1619. Christ died to atone for the sins of very few (the second principle), the 'elect' already chosen by God, and there was nothing the unelected could do about it (the third principle). But the doctrine of irresistible grace (the fourth principle) brought daily joy, as it entitled members of the congregation to retreat into an internal ecstasy – a 'state of grace'. Indeed, the ability to enter such a state was a hint – no more – of one's election. The fifth principle stressed God's infinite love and mercy and enjoined the saints-in-waiting to love each other selflessly and look after the poor and oppressed – again, the ability to manifest such love provided a premonition that the good Puritan had the nod from God. Since the elect would obviously live according to Christ's precepts, an upright life was a necessary, but not a sufficient, condition of salvation. This was the theological spur for John Cooke's passionate concern for the poor and sick.

The young barrister completed his pupillage with Brickenden in 1634. He lacked the inherited wealth to take, like his contemporaries, a grand tour to the Protestant centres of Europe, and the prospects for law practice in New England were not, at this point, enticing. He had no money and no status: to make his way at the English bar required both. His solution was to move to Ireland and seek employment. Dublin was only a week's travel time from home and religious diversity was tolerated, as it had to be, in a country where most were Catholic. In 1634, he was admitted to the Dublin bar as a member of King's Inn and he was soon offered a job by Thomas Wentworth, the 'Lord Deputy' – the King's regent and the effective ruler of Ireland. The young lawyer seems to have cut a dashing figure – an enemy later recalled him 'strutting in his plush and velvet, cringing for acquaintance and screwing into the favour of the Earl of Strafford, who at length took notice of his fair deportment and saw something in him that might deserve his countenance'.[7]

Thomas Wentworth had arrived to rule as the King's deputy in Ireland in the summer of 1633: his administration continued for six years. 'Black Tom' was a remarkable leader and administrator, if utterly unscrupulous in amassing power and wealth. He had trained at the Inns of Court and became an MP: back in 1628, Cooke had admired his leadership of the Parliamentary clamour for a Bill of Rights. Then, opportunistically, Wentworth had accepted a senior position in the King's government, where he worked with Archbishop Laud to attack the rising Puritan power in the kingdom. He was a man from the lower aristocracy, which partly accounts for his obsession with improving his position according to the way the political wind was blowing. His colleagues called him 'the grand apostate', but his defection gave him the opportunity to exercise his administrative genius as a member of the Privy Council. In 1633, Charles seemed unassailable in every part of his kingdom except Ireland, so it was to that unruly domain that Charles appointed his most talented civil servant.

Ireland was a melting pot with ingredients that refused to melt. It was a separate kingdom, but regarded as an English colony – unlike Scotland, which was a separate kingdom with a Presbyterian Church and an independent Parliament. Most of its two million people were poor, uneducated and Catholic: the 'Old Irish' native people, Celtic in origin and Gaelic in language, were organised on a tribal basis with their own noble chiefs and their ancient 'brechon law' that defied comprehension by English common lawyers. The great estates, however, belonged to 'Old English' (or 'Norman Irish'), the original planter-class families who had unjustly acquired vast swathes of the best land in the country long before the Reformation: they too were predominantly papist. But the post-Reformation colonial expansion, followed by the Puritan exodus from England, brought waves of migrants to form a third class of 'New English' settlers, planted Protestants determined to grab as much land as possible and exploit it for maximum profit whilst despising the primitive 'wild Irish' and their idolatrous religion. When Wentworth arrived, reliable central government was confined to 'the Pale' – an area comprising Dublin and its surrounds, full of Old and New English. It was his genius to extend his administration 'beyond the Pale' and to provide a modicum of law and order throughout the land. But in 1641, two years after his departure, the whole structure broke down in barbarous civil strife. His regime had eventually disaffected all these factions, by milking them in the interests of the King of England – and of the future Earl of Strafford.

Wentworth had an English Puritan's contempt for the Old Irish, but he insisted that 'the meaner sort' be tried fairly. He removed tainted judges who accepted bribes, and punished one judge who wrongfully convicted a defendant in order to obtain his land after his execution.[8] For these tasks he relied on 'can-do' lawyers like John Cooke. He revitalised but controlled the weak Irish Parliament, which at his direction voted taxes to the King – unlike the malcontents at Westminster. He cleaned up the collection of customs and other revenues, to the disadvantage of some powerful lords (whose noses were even more out of joint when they realised that Wentworth had put his in what used to be their trough). He tried, more creditably, to reform the land tenure system, although his impatience led him to take discreditable steps – in Galway, for example, he punished a jury that refused to find for the King in a land claim against an 'Old English' lord. In this instance, the King's claim had been justified and the jury had been perverse – it had been stacked by the sheriff with relatives of the nobleman.[9] But Wentworth's irascible behaviour, in punishing not only the sheriff and the jury, but counsel and even the county, was cited by his enemies as an example of his autocratic style.[10] In his regular correspondence with Archbishop Laud, his friend and fellow Privy Counsellor, Wentworth referred to his policy as 'thorough'. This word he used in the sense of driving through, or riding roughshod over, interests that lay in the path of fiscal religious or administrative unity, however long settled or indigenous those interests might be. English writers, irrespective of their political sympathies, have generally saluted Strafford as a great administrator, whilst Irish historians condemn him as despotic and venal. Both perspectives are correct.

Cooke served in Wentworth's entourage between 1634 and 1636 and the Deputy found the fledgling lawyer worthy of advancement. Cooke was employed to draft the reform legislation that Wentworth was pushing through the pliable local Parliament: these laws he had printed in 1635 'in a small but stately volume bearing cherubs and cornucopia on its title page, followed by the royal arms and the arms of Wentworth'.[11] He was involved in a project to reduce legal fees and to punish lawyers and officials who overcharged, and the idealistic young Puritan may have suggested a scheme whereby all who got themselves drunk in Dublin of an evening had to pay for it the next morning – literally, by a fine of one groat. This he thought would raise many hundreds of pounds, but of course it proved impossible to enforce, although its failure did not deter Cooke, years later, from advocating a similar cure for alcoholism in England.[12] Cooke would later apologise to Strafford for leaving his service after only two years, notwithstanding the career opportunity it provided. The King's Deputy was noted for looking after his employees, and Cooke could have expected a profitable supply of government briefs had he stayed to practise, with further lucrative work from the grand 'New English' plantation owners.

So why did this talented lawyer abandon a budding career in Ireland? Many years later, a royalist mudslinger would falsely allege that he had pocketed the money for printing the statutes and had absconded to Italy until after Strafford's execution in 1641.[13] The truth is very different. As Cooke explained to Strafford, he was at this time 'wanting to myself'[14] – an indication of spiritual crisis. Strutting in plush and velvet had not overborne the Puritan upbringing of this poor farmer's son, but easy association with Catholics had aroused deep unsureties about the true path to salvation. He was twenty-eight, with sufficient earnings now to travel to the alternative centres of religious learning – to Rome and Geneva. So John Cooke left the King's Irish service, to search for the best way to save his soul.

It was usual for the sons of notable Puritan families to go on a 'grand tour' of the continent after their study at the Inns – a kind of gap year in which they might learn something of the civil (i.e. Roman) law practised there, pass with distaste or disputation through Catholic regions and sojourn piously in Calvinist Geneva. Cooke's trip was belated but extensive: he travelled through France and Spain (he was unimpressed by Spanish inn-keepers, who required guests to shop for their own food and wine).[15] In Madrid, where he inspected the city's new prison, he was told the sort of joke that has been current for centuries. A horse refused to leap aboard a ferry across the river, until a passenger whispered in its ear, whereupon it leapt quickly onto the boat. The ferryman asked the passenger how he had made the horse move so rapidly. The man answered: 'I told him to leap into the boat as fast as the soul of a lawyer goes to hell.'[16]

Cooke's tour was not for pleasure or cultural observation. His Protestant faith needed strengthening, by exposure to the alternatives. He was in Basle in 1637, asking a leading Calvinist, 'Where was your Protestant church before Luther?' – only to receive the answer that he was too young to meddle with such a hard question.[17] But meddle he did, by registering to study at the University of Padua, the most liberal institution in Catholic Europe because it came under the relaxed authority of Venice.[18] In this period (1637–8) his presence is recorded on two occasions at the English College in Rome, run by Jesuits as a fly-trap for visiting Protestant gentlemen: all were invited to partake of its hospitality (the wine was fabled) in the hope that conversation with a cardinal might lead to conversion. Cooke dined there, as did the young Milton, in the spring of 1638.[19] Government spies reported back to London, and many years later a royalist libeller would falsely claim that Cooke had joined the Jesuits when in Rome.[20]

It was in Paris that Cooke himself locates his temptation – from Dr Smith, an Englishman who kept the Cardinal's library, 'a subtle man and a great scholar who was very earnest with me to reconcile myself into the bosom of the Roman church'. Smith argued that the English Protestants would soon destroy themselves by persecuting each other – look at the way the bishops were persecuting the Puritans. 'We allow a greater latitude in the Church of Rome, notwithstanding the inquisition.' Cooke was able to resist Dr Smith's blandishments, whilst accepting that there were attractions in disciplined Catholicism, which encouraged good works by inviting everyone to find salvation through them: after all, he mused, 'If good works do not merit, who will do any good works?'[21]

The young lawyer wavered, but did not succumb. His friend Edmund Ludlow later recalled that 'Cooke in his younger days travelled through France and Italy; and being at Rome spoke freely on the behalf of the reformed Religion and so far discovered his zeal and abilities therein that no endeavours were wanting for drawing him to own the Popish interest. But he, as enlightened from above, was not the least shaken by their temptations.'[22] Ludlow protests too much – obviously the young Puritan was wavering in his religious beliefs at this time. However, his faith was not lost: by August 1638 he had left Rome for the Calvinist city on a hill, where Ludlow continues: 'Residing for some months in Geneva, at the house of Mr Diodati, he was observed to live a very strict and pious life, and to be a constant frequenter [observer] of public ordinances.'[23] This does ring true: the poet Milton, who was Cooke's exact contemporary, stayed in Geneva in 1638–9 and records that in a place 'where so much license exists, I lived free and untouched by the slightest sin or reproach, reflecting constantly that although I might hide from the gaze of men, I could not elude the sight of God. In

Geneva I converse daily with John Diodati, the learned professor of theology.'[24]

Diodati was minister of the Italian church in Calvin's city (where licence was not as available as Milton imagined) and he offered a comforting retreat for young English Puritans. Cooke stayed with Diodati long enough to observe what he later described as 'the nature of democracy, where the power resides in the people, as all lawful power originally is . . . Geneva is a pure democracy [because] every inhabitant has a voice in the election of the Grand Council'.[25] This system appealed to Calvinists (much taken with selection of the wise) and to democrats, and worked well in a fortified city: but could it be translated to a nation? It was a topic of discussion amongst the émigré Protestants who had settled in Geneva as refugees from the Thirty Years War and the English descendants of the Marian refugees. They reproached Cooke vehemently about Charles I, who they believed had betrayed La Rochelle and the Protestant cause in France. Cooke spoke out in defence of his monarch: Charles, he explained to Diodati, was wise, and friendly to their church. The theologian smiled: 'Christ commands us to forgive our enemies, but not our friends'. To the embarrassment of his young English guest, Diodati would often say 'the Protestants have Charles I's body, but the papists have his heart'.[26]

Both Cooke and Milton stayed with Diodati at this time and speak of Camillo Cerdogni, an Anglophile Neopolitan nobleman who insisted on recording autographs and messages from visiting Englishmen in his *Album Amicorum*. When adding his own signature in August 1638, Cooke was most struck by a message left by an Englishman who had stayed with Cerdogni back in 1612.[27] It was a quote from Seneca: 'Whoever is too much known to everyone, is unknown to himself.'[28] It had been inscribed by his former patron, the young Thomas Wentworth, who had never suffered fools gladly – and back in England, those he had treated as fools were no longer prepared to suffer him.

Wentworth's former colleagues in the fractious parliamentarian class of '28 had prospered during the years of Charles's personal rule. Most were directors of corporations formed to foster and benefit from Puritan settlement abroad, such as the Massachusetts Bay Company and the Providence Company in the Caribbean (in the latter case, they showed little scruple in benefiting from the exertions of slaves on the sugar plantations). Corporation meetings provided commercial cover for seditious discussions, and what these Puritan grandees refused to tolerate was the King's threefold attack – on their parliament, on their place in the Church and on their well-gotten gains.

In the Church, the influence of William Laud and his episcopalian faction waxed because it had the King's blessing: Laud became the most powerful figure in the Privy Council. His purge of Puritan ministers continued and congregations were forced to accept his preferred rituals and his insistence, against their wishes, on fixing the place of the communion table.[29] Such insults offended many believers, but what made them ripe for rebellion was their outrage at the Court of Star Chamber. This prerogative court comprised all members of the Privy Council (i.e. nominees and favourites of the King – in effect, his cabinet) and two subservient judges. As a court, it had power to arrest, to torture and to sentence to indefinite imprisonment ('at his Majesty's pleasure') for political offences such as seditious libel. Its punishment of Puritan propagandists was ferocious, and took place in public, attended by Laud himself, who took a vicious satisfaction in observing the agonies to which he had sentenced his critics.

In 1633 the barrister William Prynne had his ears cut off for a polemic against the theatre, on the theme *Women Actresses Notorious Whores*, shortly after the Queen had acted in a masque. In prison, he penned an attack on the bishops, so was arraigned again, in June 1637, along with the Puritan divine Dr Henry Burton, who had preached a sermon attacking Laud's innovations as anti-Christian, and Dr John Bastwick, a Presbyterian who had penned a popular satire on the grossness and greed of the bishops. The Star Chamber, with Laud as a judge, condemned these three learned men to sit in the pillory at New Palace Yard and to have their ears (in Prynne's case, the stumps of his ears) cut off, to be branded on the face with a hot iron, fined the massive sum of £5,000 and then thrown into prison for the rest of their lives. A vast crowd gathered around the pillory at New Palace Yard: to them the three preached and with them, prayed, inspiring their audience (and, through the pamphlets which described the scene, the whole country) with their courage in the face of the Star Chamber's cruelty.

This cruelty was attributed not to the King but to his counsellors – particularly to Laud and Wentworth. This was a convenient way of exculpating the monarch, in whose interests and with whose approval the punishment had been imposed. Wentworth's advice from Ireland was that 'to be shut up and kept in the dark all their lives is punishment mild enough for such savages

. . . It is not prelacy they would end with . . . They begin to let forth the very life-blood of monarchy itself.'[30] The result, of course, was to make them martyrs, and one hot-headed youth who had been at the front of the crowd around the pillory was inspired by their example to smuggle their seditious books back into the country. On his arrest, John Lilburne refused to answer his Star Chamber interrogators, claiming that as a freeborn Englishman he was entitled to a right against self-incrimination. The court found him in contempt and ordered him to be whipped, all the way from Fleet Street to New Palace Yard. The sentence was carried out viciously, in the sight of a large crowd that gathered to cheer the youth they dubbed 'Freeborn John'. It was a catch-cry that would be heard again – and again . . .

In the same year, 1637, came another legal challenge, over the very serious issue of ship money. Charles had managed to survive financially in the first years of his personal reign by the sale of patents and monopolies and from the exaction of customs duties, exempt from the historic rule that taxes must be approved by Parliament. But the King's expenses were heavy, even though the country was at peace, and another revenue-raising device was required. The King's legal advisers found it in the ancient duty of every coastal county to provide and pay for a ship for the Royal Navy. By extending this duty to *all* counties, whether they bordered the sea or not, and by collecting the money through individual assessments, the King could raise sufficient funds not only to provision his navy, but (so it was feared) to extend the army and pay for the court. He might never need to recall Parliament – so long as his judges upheld the dubious argument that ship money was not a tax and the even more dubious argument that the King had the power to levy it whenever, in his unchallengeable judgment, there was peril on the sea.

It was to be another mighty test of strength, a decade after the *Five Knights' Case*, between the King and his government on the one hand and the prorogued parliamentarians and the landowning fraternity on the other, played out in courts where kings had no compunction about exploiting their influence over the judiciary. The test case involving John Hampden was heard in November 1637. His ship money levy had been a paltry 20 shillings, but there was a fundamental principle at stake, as his counsel, Oliver St John, explained to the twelve justices. It was the monarch's right to declare war but Parliament alone was empowered – and best qualified – to decide whether and how to raise any tax to fight it. St John's clinching argument was that the country was not at war, nor was any war in prospect: the writ recited only that the King had been told 'that certain thieves, pirates and robbers of the sea, as well as Turks' were abroad on the oceans. This might endanger some merchant shipping, but not the navy – let alone the kingdom. There was, in short, no national emergency of the kind that alone could justify a tax so urgent that its imposition could not wait the forty-day interval between the summoning of a new Parliament and its meeting – especially since it would take seven months to build a ship. This was the factual basis upon which the court should have quashed the writ for ship money.[31] The Attorney-General could only reply that the argument was populist: 'What would be the consequence of it, but the introducing of democratical government?'

Judgment was delayed for several months, until February 1638. It was not 'handed down' but read at length and by each of the twelve judges in turn, the junior ones first, over several days – which gave the ship-money decision something of the tension of a lengthy penalty shoot-out.[32] 'The King may dispense with any laws in case of necessity,' declared Justice Vernon – obsequiously and wrongly. Sir Robert Berkeley accepted that in normal times the King could not take away property rights without Parliament's consent, but it would be 'utter ruin and subversion' if the King could not exercise such a power urgently: 'The law knows no such King-yoking policy. The law is of itself an old and trusty servant of the King's; it is his instrument . . . it is common and most true that *Rex* is *Lex* . . . The King cannot do wrong.' Three more judges then found for the King.

So far, so predictable. The King was ahead five–nil. But the sixth judge was Sir George Croke, a man remembered by his contemporaries at the bar for having 'more piety, religiosity and zeal of justice' than ordinary lawyers, and for leaving the Bible and Foxe's *Book of Martyrs* open in his waiting-room for his clients to peruse.[33] This closet Puritan was the first to declare in favour of the defendant – on the ground, in effect, of no taxation without representation. 'Ship money' was in reality a tax, for which the common law required parliamentary authorisation – no claim by the King of necessity or danger could override this inflexible rule. That night they joked at the Inns that the King would have his ship money 'by hook, but not by Croke' – and the next day Croke's vote was followed by the eighth, ninth and tenth judges. With the score at six to four it fell to Chief Justice Finch to deliver the match to the King. Finch had been that spineless Speaker who in 1628 had to be held down in his chair so Eliot could speak: now he apologised for his dissident brethren and wrote that 'none are more happy than we' to live under a king who 'is of God alone'. The King, he ruled, had unlimited discretion to act for what, in his unchallengeable subjective view, was the public good: his good faith had to be assumed on the question of whether the kingdom was in danger. Finch outraged Parliament and the common lawyers by his ruling that nothing had changed since the *Five Knights' Case*: the King was above the law.

John Cooke had been abroad whilst these momentous events had taken place, but in 1639 he returned from Geneva, having stayed and prayed with a community of English Congregationalist exiles in the Netherlands on his journey back to London.[34] His talent for disputation asserted itself with these fractious separatists, who (unlike mainstream Puritans) wanted no place in the Anglican Church. 'I stood as stiffly as I could for episcopacy', he recalled later, of his support for bishops at this time, but like every good advocate he was conscious of the flaws in his argument.

Back in London, affected by the criticism of Charles he had heard from fellow-Protestants on his travels, he quickly identified the flaw in the ship money ruling: 'if the King may take what he please in cases of necessity, and be judge of that necessity, England must needs be a necessitous people – as Louis II said of France, it was a meadow he might mow or not as he judged it necessary'.[35] The problem was that the judges were 'pusillanimous': their ambition to be 'grandees at Court' had caused them to betray their trust as guardians of the people's liberty by acting as tools of the government and over-extending the royal prerogative.

Cooke set up chambers in Gray's Inn and began to practise at the bar. It was through his association with Congregationalists in London that he acquired a celebrated client – 'Doctor' William Trigg, a herbalist famed for refusing to charge the poor and for staying in London to treat victims of the plague, at times when registered doctors – members of the College of Physicians – fled the city. The college was a royal monopoly that vigorously prosecuted unlicensed rivals, and had secured Trigg's first conviction in 1631 (asked whether, like all approved practitioners, he was a servant of the King, he had defiantly replied 'I am God's').[36] Cooke defended Trigg in 1640, when he was tried before the King's Bench. The college prosecutors called an elderly lady who testified that Trigg had some years before prescribed medicine that made her sick, but Cooke pointed out that 'the woman has been well ever since – she is a lusty, merry old woman who possibly might, but for that medicine, be in her grave'.[37] The young barrister showed skill in avoiding imprisonment for his incorrigible client, who had been sent to prison for the offence before: this time, he was fined £155.[38] Cooke moved to appeal the conviction to the House of Lords, but to his annoyance the King (whose consent was necessary) refused permission. None the less, the case was a harbinger of success at the Bar, so long as his conscience, well-honed through his time in Geneva, could fit the fashion of the times.

Ironically, the very narrowness of the King's victory in the ship money case had sent a contrary message throughout the kingdom that the tax was in truth unlawful: the fact that five judges, the most respected on the bench, had refused to buckle under the King's demands was a signal that the dissenters must be correct. Before the case, most of the gentry had paid ship money without demur. But by 1640, it was estimated that only one third of the exactions had been paid.[39] England was in the grip of widespread civil disobedience – so much so that Finch issued a practice direction from the Star Chamber to all English judges as they departed for Assizes later that year: 'My lords, it is your part to break the insolence of the vulgar before it approaches too nigh the royal throne.'[40] That insolence was already directed at the bishops – significant sections of the middle and upper classes were seriously upset at the way Laud was disciplining their preachers, and the London mob was reading 'Freeborn John' Lilburne, from whose prison cell there flowed a series of bishop-bashing pamphlets. To cap it all, there was soon a genuine emergency – a war, no less, with Scotland.

Exactly what mix of pride, arrogance and belief in his own divine inspiration made Charles interfere with the quiet but heartfelt devotional practices of his one and a half million Scottish subjects is difficult today to comprehend. At the time, when the doctrine that the King could do no wrong meant that all blame had to be borne by ministers, it was put down to the High Church obsessions of William Laud, his Archbishop of Canterbury. But the King as well as Laud found the Presbyterianism of the Scots offensive: it exuded an unreconstructed Calvinism, in spartan churches (kirks) in which local ministers were entrusted with expounding the literal meaning of the Bible. There were riots in the kirks in 1638 when the King and his bishops tried to foist upon them a book for uniform prayers: a national covenant was drawn up by Archibald Johnston, another radical lawyer (a breed that was to become the bane of Stuart monarchy) and rapidly subscribed to by many Scotsmen, high and low. What made this covenant so radical was the pledge to maintain the authority of Parliaments (i.e. the English and Scottish Parliaments) 'without which neither any laws nor lawful judications can be established'. Otherwise, the covenanters protested that they had no intention to 'diminish the King's greatness and authority'. That was not how Charles read it: 'I will rather die than yield to these impertinent and damnable divines.' In anger, he made a rash plan to 'reduce that people to obedience' by force.

For a monarch to invade his own kingdom, to kill subjects loyal to him in all but their method of devotion, was irrational. To do so without a proper army or the money to furnish one was absurd. Ship money was not forthcoming, the nobility was unconvinced of the justice of the King's cause whilst many of the gentry sympathised with the beliefs of the Kirk and were already upset at the King's failure to assist Protestants fighting (and losing) the war with Catholic powers on the Continent. But in April 1639, Charles advanced on Scotland at the head of such forces as he could muster, by which time the Scots had put together a better trained and motivated army under banners which read 'FOR CHRIST'S CROWN AND COVENANT.' The King, recognising that in any pitched battle he would face certain defeat, saved as much face as he could by concluding this 'First Bishops War' – in which not a shot had been fired, despite the fury on both sides – by a deal in which he promised that before imposing uniformity in worship he would consult with the Scottish Parliament and the National Assembly of the Kirk. This was just one of many expedient promises that throughout his life Charles made without any sense of obligation and broke with no sense of shame. He returned to London angry and vengeful, determined to raise a force to destroy the Scots. It was for this purpose that he recalled Thomas Wentworth, who came to his side from Ireland in September 1640.

The advice that Charles sorely needed was to stop lying to the Scots – to withdraw the prayer book and grant them liberty to worship through the Kirk, and then to show a degree of regal humility by visiting the kingdom occasionally, bringing blessings rather than men in arms. But Charles was fixated on punishing the Scots, so Wentworth's advice was suitably bloodthirsty: he should gather a superior army, and reduce the kingdom to the status of a colony – the status effectively of Ireland governed by a Deputy like Wentworth. So far so bad, but Wentworth followed up with advice that was to have momentous consequences. He was, after all, an old Parliamentary hand – a leader of the MPs in 1628 – and he had effortlessly managed to persuade Irish Parliaments to support the King. Since the royal coffers were empty, and ship money was uncollectable, there was nothing for it but to recall Parliament to vote the funds for the new war. Wentworth of course was out of touch (he thought his former MP comrades would vote the funds in gratitude for being recalled) and Charles still lived life as if performing in a masque. He issued the writ for a new Parliament and ennobled Wentworth. It was as Earl of Strafford that this hard man awaited what he imagined would be parliamentary spaniels, unaware that they would come back as hungry lions.

In April 1640 they mainly returned – his old colleagues from the Puritan gentry Parliament of 1628, who remembered him unfondly as the 'grand apostate'. Pym and Hampden, Oliver St John and Denzil Holles, Essex and other wealthy lords of the Providence Company were in no mood to vote money until their grievances were expounded and redressed. Finch, once the cowardly Speaker they had assaulted and then the Chief Justice they despised for his ship-money decision, was now Lord Keeper (of the Great Seal of the State) who presided over the Star Chamber and was blamed for its excesses. He opened the Parliament, praising the King and demanding money to pay for war against the treasonable Scots. The House heard him with mounting contempt, and proceeded over the next three weeks to lambast the evils perpetrated by the government. MPs maintained the traditional fiction of the monarch misled by bad ministers, but this fooled nobody – and Strafford was nobody's fool. He advised the King to dissolve this 'Short Parliament'; that done, the Privy Council imprisoned several MPs, and ordered searches of homes and offices of Puritan leaders.

Charles now called his cabinet together for a council of war – with Scotland. Strafford was the war's leading proponent, urging a forced loan from the City of London to fund it. His remarks were noted by old Sir Henry Vane whose son, young Henry, had returned from Massachusetts to sit as an MP and disclosed the notes to Pym. They were to the effect that having been let down by Parliament, this was a case of necessity and necessity knew no law – the King was 'loose and absolved from all rules of government'. Strafford said he had an army in Ireland that 'you may employ here to reduce this kingdom'. Did he mean Scotland, or by 'this kingdom' did he mean England – arguably a treasonable proposition, even though made to the King? It was an ambiguity that would soon cost Strafford his life.

War with the Scots was unpopular in London, where it meant forcible pressing of young men to be soldiers, as well as an enforced loan. This 'Second Bishops' War' began, none the less, in August but ended the same month – ignominiously for the King, when the Scots invaded England and routed his forces. Charles made peace, on terms which once more he had no intention of keeping, although he realised that to get away with breaking this agreement he would need the support of the great Puritan peers, who were angrily petitioning for a new Parliament so that 'the authors and counsellors of great grievances may be there brought to such legal trial and condign punishment as the nature of the several offences shall require'.[41] Charles called another Parliament because defeat left him no alternative way of raising money to fight the Scots, but the threatening language of the peers' petition should have given him due warning.

The 'Long Parliament' – it was to last for the next thirteen tumultuous years – first met in November 1640. Its initial act was to impeach the Earl of Strafford for high treason: the second most powerful man in the country was arrested and taken to the Tower. A few weeks later he was joined by the Archbishop of Canterbury, also accused of treason. The trifecta was narrowly missed: Finch was impeached after several of the ship-money judges confessed that he had improperly pressured them to give judgment for the King, but he escaped to exile in France. This was a heady time for the MPs and their supporters – the excitable 'trained bands' of London apprentices, the sober congregations of Puritan tradespeople, and the lawyers at the Inns of Court. Parliament kept flexing its muscles: it declared ship money unlawful and it ordered the release of the Puritan martyrs – Prynne, Burton and Bastwick – whose return to London from their provincial prisons was triumphal: they were accompanied by a hundred coaches and two thousand horsemen, and welcomed by a massive crowd. It was not long before a voice in Parliament demanded the release of John Lilburne.

That voice, 'sharp and untunable', came from an unknown MP. His plain cloth suit 'seemed to have been made by an ill country tailor'. He had a 'swollen and reddish countenance' and there were specks of blood on his collar suggesting that he had cut himself while shaving.[42] Thus did Oliver Cromwell strike one somewhat sniffy courtier at the time. That Cromwell should be the first to champion Lilburne would later become one of the minor ironies of the time. But it was a popular cause, which played well to the crowd – and from the very start of this Parliament there was a sense, certainly in the Commons, of the advantages in playing to the mob. In the streets of London there was a feeling that most of their grievances against the government were the fault of 'Black Tom Tyrant' – so the leaders of the House turned to devise ways and means of sacrificing Strafford.

Most of the leading MPs were lawyers, well aware that high treason, then as now, was conclusively defined by the Treason Act of 1351, as 'compassing or imagining' the death of the King, or levying war against the King or adhering to the King's enemies. So their accusation against Strafford was that he had led the King astray. Other charges concerned his actions as Deputy Lieutenant in Ireland, such as organising miscarriages of justice (e.g. punishing the Galway jury) and tolerating Catholic 'mass-houses' in Dublin. More serious were accusations that he had advised the King to wage war on the Scots and to bring the Irish army to the mainland 'to reduce this Kingdom'.

The impeachment process was settled by long tradition. The House of Commons would vote to bring particular charges, then present them to the Lords for judgment at a trial in Westminster Hall. MPs would prosecute and would call witnesses against the defendant, who would be permitted to call defence witnesses and retain counsel to argue points of law. It would, in the case of the newly ennobled Strafford, literally be a judgment by his peers, or such of them as turned up to vote. He had the reassurance, at the end of the day, of the King's power to pardon. But it was a trial of strength, and the House of Commons lawyers – led by Pym – spared no effort in preparing for the prosecution in the early months of 1641. There was plentiful evidence provided by Strafford's enemies in Ireland, and the London crowd was kept at boiling point by pamphlets exaggerating his tyrannies. Strafford meanwhile was kept in close confinement in the Tower: his visitors and his correspondence were closely monitored and agents provocateurs were sent in vain efforts to entrap him. In this atmosphere, only a brave man would step forward to help the most hated prisoner in the realm.

John Cooke stepped forward. In a letter he must have known would be intercepted, he wrote to Strafford offering to testify for his defence. The Lord Deputy had never exceeded his powers in the two years that the barrister served in his administration. 'I have known many that have felt the reviving heat of your Lordship's speedy justice', Cooke recalled, but this was not in subversion of the laws but rather in support of them: justice delayed was justice denied and his reforms had enabled poor suitors to contend equally with great ones. 'Whilst I was in Ireland', he wrote, 'the poor cried there had never been so good a Lord Deputy before.' When Strafford dispensed with jury trial it was only to avoid miscarriages of justice – 'For I have known juries to go strangely against the evidence.' Cooke volunteered to testify to Strafford's reputation for religious orthodoxy. 'That your Lordship should be over-indulgent to the Catholics more than what reason of state did require, I do not believe, for I knew your Lordship zealous to suppress mass-houses in Dublin.'[43] What is remarkable, even at this remove, is that the young lawyer, who had nothing to gain, could take the risk of hitching his career to such a falling star.[44]

His help extended to offering arguments on the law. This very junior barrister presented his 'humble mite' of legal knowledge on high treason 'which is but as the pissing of a wren into the sea of your learned counsel's experience'. Treason was a subject on which he would in due course become over-familiar. 'We young lawyers', he wrote, doubtless echoing the views of many at the Inns, conceived that the most serious article of Strafford's impeachment was the accusation of subverting law by making it subservient to the power of the King rather than Parliament. In all treason there must either be some hostility to the King or some intention to destroy the state, so a Lord Deputy cannot be guilty for mistaking the law or governing over-strictly or even recklessly – 'Who knows what bridle is best for any horse 'till he knows its condition?' Cooke argued, abandoning legal Latin for a homely metaphor.

Strafford's trial was a sorry affair for both sides. It was conducted fairly at first, with due pomp in Westminster Hall. The King was present, his sympathies signalled by his direction that the ceremonial axe – traditionally on display in treason cases to symbolise the inevitable sentence – should remain locked up in the Tower. The 'managers' of the trial – MPs led by Pym, Oliver St John and young Sir Harry Vane – presented the charges to the peers of the realm. Strafford was permitted counsel – the best constitutional lawyer in the Kingdom, Matthew Hale, defended him – and his answers, both written and oral, sounded convincing. One witness, who had claimed to overhear him say (from twelve yards' distance) 'the King's little finger should be heavier than the loins of the law', was quickly proved to be stone deaf. The witnesses from Ireland, reeking with malice, were sarcastically dispatched.

But as the weeks went by, the cumulative effect of the evidence left no doubt that Strafford had enriched himself greatly both in land and in finances from his deputyship and that many of his decisions striking at local worthies, particularly at the money-grubbing 'new English' grandees with friends among the MPs, had been made arbitrarily and without due process, however much they may have been justified. Strafford soon found it politic to promise to retire from public service if the verdict went in his favour. His basic argument – and it was undoubtedly correct – was that which had been sketched out by Cooke: the charges, even if proved, could not amount to high treason because his abuses of power did not constitute an attack on the monarch on whose behalf they were committed. As for his comments about the worthlessness of parliamentarians, there was obvious point in his response that 'if all choleric expressions of that nature should be accounted treasonable, there would be more suits of that kind flying up and down Westminster Hall than common law'.[45]

After three weeks the outcome of the trial hung in the balance. The evidence had damaged Strafford, but not terminally. The 'smoking gun' that was produced by the prosecution, Vane senior's note of the advice Strafford had given to the King about bringing over the Irish army, was ambiguous. Prejudice aside – although prejudice could not be put aside by the Puritan nobles who sat in judgment on a man whose death many of them thought would be in the interests of the state – there was insufficient evidence to convict. The longer the trial continued, the more the murmuring public who had been led to expect a death sentence felt they were being cheated of their prey. At this point a new MP, Arthur Haselrig, made the first of his many controversial contributions to public life: he introduced into Parliament a bill for the attainder of the Earl of Strafford. This device, when passed by both Houses, became a statute which decreed conviction and sentence of death.

Parliament was the highest court and could ordain death by statute, without a trial and subject only to the King's approval – an unlikely prospect, of course, given his support for the earl. The Bill passed the Commons without difficulty, and it was then presented to the Lords by the newly appointed Solicitor-General, Oliver St John. He adopted the same inflated rhetoric which had characterised Coke's prosecution of Ralegh, describing Strafford as a 'beast of prey', whose extermination was of no more moment than the killing of a fox or wolf. 'He that would not have had others to have a law, why should he have any himself?' Strafford could only raise his eyes and hands towards heaven – a reply, the court reporter notes, that was all 'dumb eloquence'.[46] But jurisprudentially, Parliament was widening the legal definition of treason, hitherto a crime involving denial of allegiance to the King, to include political attacks on his realm – e.g. by subverting the laws or abusing delegated powers. This extended definition would leave open the possibility – unforeseen at this time – that treason might be committed by a king who attacked another sovereign institution – i.e. parliament.[47] The Lords eventually voted 26–19 to pass the Act, but it required the King's ratification, and Charles had written to Strafford a few days before its passage with the solemn promise 'that, upon the word of a king, you shall not suffer in life, honour or fortune'. Two weeks later, Charles ratified the Act. On hearing the news, Strafford famously spluttered, 'Put not your trust in princes.'

The earl's beheading was a great public event: 100,000 people attended, their eyes raised to the high scaffold on Tower Hill. Wenceslas Hollar drew the scene with almost photographic accuracy: the audience was sober and well dressed with many gentlewomen present. Puritan England attended in force to celebrate the demise of 'Black Tom Tyrant'. Many travelled from outlying counties as if to witness a political epiphany. Strafford stood for the bishops whose greed for power was suffocating their Church, and there was a fitting moment of pathos when old William Laud, the arch-heretic, stood at his prison window in the Tower to bless Strafford as he was taken to his execution. There was a roar of approval as the executioner held aloft the severed head with the cry 'Behold, the head of a traitor.' There were bonfires and bells and by nightfall the appearance of a new symbol of hope: a lit candle glowing in every Puritan window.

Strafford's fate had been sealed by the behaviour of the King who could not comprehend the determined demand for change in government policy. The Puritans who flocked to the execution craved a sign that he would support the way of life they had developed over almost a century since the end of Mary's bloody reign. His failure to empathise would lead them to the perception that only Parliament could safeguard their liberty – a Parliament which was regular rather than occasional and which would have a much broader function than merely voting taxes. The mistake made by the Stuarts was to perceive the Puritans as bent on destruction of monarchy and therefore as a movement to be suppressed. There is no evidence, as late as 1641, that any Puritan leader envisaged anything like a republic. They wanted Strafford dead and buried to symbolise change and in order that his undoubted genius would never again be available to counsel the King: as Essex, the leader of the pro-Parliament faction in the Lords, put it on the eve of the fatal vote, 'Stone dead hath no fellow.'

It is therefore remarkable that John Cooke stood up to be counted as a Straffordian just as his career was getting under way. But he knew first-hand that some of the charges were false, and he genuinely admired those aspects of Strafford's policy which provided more equal and speedy justice for the poor in Ireland. The 'young lawyer' in him was sufficiently honest to acknowledge that Strafford was not guilty of high treason as charged. That did not mean that arbitrary and tyrannical government, or the levying of war against the people of England, could never constitute treason as the law then stood. It meant that the King's Deputy, acting with royal approval, could not be convicted of a crime of disloyalty to the King, *either* because the King could do no wrong (the discredited ship money ruling) or else because the wrong in such circumstances should be attributed directly to the King. The youthful barrister, fresh from his disputations in the capitals of Europe, must have noted the momentous but logical consequence of that alternative.

Cooke's courage in helping Strafford was all the more remarkable because he had no political truck with his cause: the others who aligned themselves with the earl were out-and-out royalists, staking their future on the King's fortunes, or grand lawyer/MPs like Edward Hyde (who became Lord Chancellor Clarendon) and Orlando Bridgeman, later the Lord Chief Justice who presided over the regicide trials. But Cooke, humbly born and Puritan, could expect no favour from the King, and his identification in 1641 as a Straffordian explains why his practice dried up for a time and he fell into debt – he had to eke out a living tutoring law students.[48] He missed out on parliamentary briefs during the Civil War – although he was frequently recommended for employment in parliamentary matters, his support for Strafford cast doubt over his loyalty to the cause.[49] There was danger too, in Cooke's stand: Pym's faction had begun to experiment with street propaganda, inciting crowds to appear in New Palace Yard chanting 'Justice' whenever Strafford or his judges passed through the hall. After the Commons vote, wall posters appeared pointing the finger at named Straffordians and describing them as 'enemies to their country'. One was 'Mr Cooke'. It was a common enough name (there were several barristers and an MP who bore it) but it should have alerted the young lawyer to the danger of letting his conscience dictate his support for public enemy number one.

3

A King in Check

The execution of the Earl of Strafford was a turning point – or no-turning-back point – in the struggle for parliamentary power. That the King could be forced to bend his absolute will to a political demand backed by demonstrations on the streets of London convinced Pym and his supporters, now in the majority, that now was the time to pursue the agenda they had devised after their ship-money defeat. Judicial independence must be secured. Never again should judges bow to pressure from the King: their duty was to invoke Magna Carta and the common law to protect the liberty of the subject *against* the King. Parliament would have to sit in regular sessions to protect Protestant worship from popish innovations and bishops, and against the threat (much exaggerated) from Catholic courtiers surrounding the Queen. These parliamentary presumptions were anathema to Charles: he would never forgive himself for consenting to Strafford's death and would never forgive Parliament for demanding that consent. From this point onwards, he devoted himself to stratagems to turn the clock back to the time of his personal rule. King and Parliament thus set themselves on a collision course, and over the next five years there would be lethal collisions in the muddy fields of middle England – from Edgehill to Marston Moor to Naseby – which took the lives of one in every ten adult males in the kingdom. Several hundred thousand died in 'collateral damage' from siege warfare and disease and starvation: for years to come, the streets of London would be lined by maimed and bandaged beggars, the veterans of these wars.[1]

Parliament had pressed on in the wake of Strafford's execution, clipping the King's prerogative by abolishing his Court of Star Chamber, because its judges 'have undertaken to punish where no law doth warrant'. Henceforth, the King must come to the ordinary courts of justice, staffed with judges whom he could not sack other than for gross misconduct. This historic Act, premised on Magna Carta, separated the powers of executive government and the judiciary: no longer could the royal prerogative be exercised to try or imprison the King's subjects. It also marked the abolition of torture, which had long been condemned by common lawyers as 'something practiced by the French' but which had been a regular Star Chamber punishment, inflicted upon political and religious dissidents. The Star Chamber was the last tribunal in England to accept evidence obtained by torture. (In 2005, the Act which in 1641 abolished the Star Chamber was invoked to stop the UK government using such evidence in its anti-terrorist courts). Ship money, too, was in the same year declared illegal.[2] All this and more the King suffered in comparative silence (he spent much of his time networking in Scotland, sounding out the possibility of armed support against Parliament) but on his return in December 1641 he was asked to cross one bridge too far. He was presented with the 'Grand Remonstrance', a long indictment by Parliament of all the evils of his reign thus far – intimidation of judges, toleration of bishops and their Laudian innovations, selling offices and monopolies, and so forth. It was prefaced by the usual disingenuous protestations of loyalty and by the pretence that all grievances were caused by bad advice from courtiers who were papists or traitors – hence its insistence that bishops must be excluded from the House of Lords and that the King's councillors should in future be approved by Parliament. The Grand Remonstrance passed after a bitter and prolonged debate between Pym's faction and the moderates led by Edward Hyde. What gave the narrow victory to Pym was panic rather than principle – the vote followed a few weeks after dramatic news reached London of a Catholic uprising in Ireland.

The domain formerly ruled by Strafford's iron will had come apart at the seams. The native Irish had combined with 'Old English' Catholics to wreak revenge upon the newly settled Protestants from England and Scotland with a genocidal ferocity. The impact of atrocity pictures – woodcuts of 'wild Irish' skewering pregnant women on their pikes and barbequing babies – was heightened by rumours that the King was seeking support from Strafford's Catholic army, which was implicated in the massacres. The newsbooks reported that over 100,000 English Protestants had been slaughtered. The number was closer to 5,000, but the atrocities perpetrated by pro-royalist Catholic leader Phelim O'Neil, who pretended his revolt was authorised by Charles, were not invented.[3] The impact of the news in London was dramatic: it swung many moderates – John Cooke included – against the King.

This steeled Pym's supporters in Parliament: not only did they pass the Remonstrance, but they had it printed and distributed to the people. Charles hit back by ordering his Attorney-General to indict Pym and four other MPs – the ship-money heroes John Hampden and William Strode, the new radical Arthur Haselrig and the old Presbyterian intemperate Denzil Holles. They were accused of high treason, in that 'they have traitorously endeavoured to subvert the fundamental laws and government of the Kingdom of England' – a tit-for-tat charge echoing their indictment of Strafford, but a dangerous precedent for Charles himself. The next day, 3 January 1642, he arrived at the Commons at the head of 400 armed loyalists, to arrest the MPs personally.

It was a *grand guignol* moment when the King entered the House, whose members all knew that the five MPs had left. They had been tipped off by a sympathetic lady of the court, in time to slip away and take a boat from Westminster to their friends in the City. Charles, oblivious to their escape, commandeered the Speaker's chair, standing upon it to cast his eyes over the faces of the MPs, who had all doffed their hats in ritual reverence. Like a bad-tempered schoolmaster he shouted for Pym and he called for Holles, but answer came there none. The King then turned to the Speaker, William Lenthall, and asked whether the five MPs were in the House. Lenthall was not a brave man, but the fate of his lickspittle predecessor Finch helped to fashion an immediate and immortal reply. He fell at the King's feet:

May it please your Majesty. I have neither eyes to see nor tongue to speak in this place but as the House is pleased to direct me, whose servant I am here, and humbly beg your Majesty's pardon that I cannot give any answer than this . . .[4]

The King could no longer contain his anger. 'Well, since I see all the birds are flown, I expect you will send them unto me, as soon as they return hither.' Charles stormed out, while MPs emboldened by their Speaker's defiance pursued him with cries of 'Privilege! Privilege!' It was a cry taken up by the London mob the next day, when the King in a last desperate gambit rode into the City to demand that its aldermen hand over the famous five. But the City was fiercely protestant: its walls were still plastered with posters bearing the Commons' 'protestation' of the previous year, and its 'trained bands' – a part-time army of apprentices – were commanded by a Pym-supporting MP. By 10 January, Charles could bear the animosity of his unruly capital no longer: he left it, never to return in freedom.

And so to arms the country's men were called – as 'cavaliers' (probably an abusive corruption of *caballero* – a Spanish trooper given to torturing Protestants) and 'roundheads' (from the crop-headed city apprentices who supported Parliament, although the name might have stuck from a slighting reference by the Queen to John Pym's round and balding head). The King sent Henrietta Maria to Holland with the crown jewels, to purchase arms and foreign mercenaries. Loyalty to him was firm in Wales and the south-west and north of England, whilst in Ireland the rebellion had forged a powerful Catholic 'confederacy' which volunteered its services to the King – at the time, a great embarrassment to Charles (since it was responsible for the massacres of English protestants) but a potential source of reinforcements. The King retained the loyalty of most of the Lords, and of MPs who shared the moderate views of his new chief counsellor, Edward Hyde. The parliamentary forces drew most support from London and the home counties and the near north-east, although it would be a mistake to think of a clear geographical division – counties, towns and families were split in their allegiance.

There was a degree of social divide, certainly in the armies: cavalier officers were men of 'quality' and birth. Cromwell's famous preference ('I had rather have a plain russet-coated captain that knows what he fights for, and loves what he knows, than that which you call a gentleman and is nothing else') was soon reflected in the middle ranks of the parliamentary forces. There was a tendency for established gentry with large estates to side with the King, whilst the 'new men' from the professions and the tradesmen and artisans in the cities rallied to a House of Commons whose members shared their aspirations. The clearest division was religious: Puritans and Presbyterians alike mainly took up arms for Parliament. Catholics supported the King, fearing the anti-papal virulence of parliamentary supporters. So of course did the bishops and most of their clergy, and many of the Anglican worshippers who craved order and traditional ceremony. Nobody owned up to being an atheist in mid-seventeenth-century England: Henry Marten, an agnostic Buckinghamshire MP, fought for Parliament.

What is certain is that nobody went to war for a republic, and when Henry Marten first suggested one, he was immediately clapped in the Tower.[5] Instead, Parliament drew up, in June 1642, the terms upon which it required the King to govern in future. After ritual expressions of love and humility, and ritual blaming of the 'evil counsels of disaffected men' who had brought the kingdom to the brink of disaster, these '19 Propositions' proposed a constitutional monarchy in which power would be shared between King, Commons and Lords. Parliament would have the right to approve all ministers of the government, officers of the army and senior judges. Charles must consent to parliamentary control of the army and supervision of the Church. Judges would take an oath to uphold Magna Carta and the Petition of Right and would no longer be capable of removal at the King's pleasure. But Charles would have none of this: he replied that the House of Commons 'was never intended for any share in government, or the choosing of them that govern'. He condemned the '19 Propositions' because they encouraged the common people to think they might be equal with men of estate, thereby destroying distinctions based on family or merit – in short, they were a prescription for 'democracy' – a word with contemporary undertones of anarchy. Clearly, there was in the summer of 1642 no common ground: there remained only the battleground. On 22 August, in a field outside Nottingham Castle, the King declared war against those of his own people who chose to follow Parliament.

This momentous declaration was, by eye-witness accounts, an unimpressive occasion. The standard – a flag with streamers, crudely depicting a hand pointing to the crown, with the motto 'Give Caesar his due' – was carried out of the castle by a troop of horse and set up in a nearby field: a small crowd heard the herald stumble over the proclamation which Charles at the last minute had decided to alter in his own illegible handwriting. Eventually the herald cried 'God save the King!' and called for all loving subjects to help suppress the rebellion. A gusty wind that night blew the standard down – an ill omen that was widely reported. Charles made Oxford his new capital and held court at Christchurch College: the city remained the royalist headquarters throughout the war. The first pitched battle was at Edgehill, where his nephew Prince Rupert of the Rhine, the 'laughing cavalier', showed his flair and his experience from the continental wars by breaking through the sluggish ranks of the Earl of Essex's parliamentary army. The day would have been won for the royalists had not their cavalry continued its charge in order to plunder the enemy's baggage train, allowing the parliamentarian forces to re-group and attack the now unprotected royalist infantry. Edgehill ended as a clumsily fought draw – but three thousand Englishmen were left dead on the field.

This appalling consequence brought neither side to its senses. By the end of the first year of fighting there had been a string of royalist gains throughout the country and John Hampden lay dead from wounds at Chalgrove Field. Pym himself was wracked with terminal cancer, but this wise old Elizabethan had one last trick up his sleeve. In September 1643, a few months before his death, he brought off an alliance with the Scots. Both parties had an obsession with protecting their Calvinist-based religion and had suffered lengthy frustrations at Charles's duplicity and unreliability. The Scots demanded a heavy price: it was a measure of Pym's desperation that he agreed that Parliament would sign up to 'the Solemn League and Covenant', promising (or so it seemed to the Scots) that it would accept Presbyterianism as the basis for what would become, after their victory, 'the Kirk of England'. This was a devious deal and unacceptable to Pym's more radical Puritan supporters, but they had to swallow their pride for the time being, until God changed sides. The first sign of this providential development came at the battle of Winceby, where Prince Rupert's cavalry, hitherto unbeaten in the field, was unexpectedly routed by the parliamentary horse, commanded by two officers who had never before fought together. Oliver Cromwell and Sir Thomas Fairfax had begun their sensational partnership.

The civil war swung in Parliament's favour. It now had the support of the Scottish covenanters, in the form of a 20,000–strong army under a seasoned General Leslie, and it had a cavalry under the outstanding leadership of Fairfax and Cromwell. At the battle of Nantwich, royalist gains in Cheshire were reversed by Fairfax, who captured one of the most proficient of the King's commanders, George Monck. After a spell in the Tower, Monck offered to fight for Parliament (one of history's great hypotheticals is how it might have changed if his offer had been refused). Heavy damage was inflicted on the royalists at the battle of Marston Moor, outside York, in mid-1644. 'Give glory, all the glory, to God,' said Cromwell, who had deserved much of it. The King's army lost 4,500 dead, with 1,500 taken prisoner. 'God made them as stubble to our swords.'[6]

But it was a measure of the ineffectiveness of Parliament's chief commanders – the aristocratic generals Essex and Manchester – that they failed to press home the advantage. The King partly recovered, with victories in the south and the midlands, and a brilliant campaign in Scotland by his ally, the Duke of Montrose, against the covenanters. Most dangerous of all for the parliamentarians was the possibility that the King might call upon the Catholic forces who had rebelled in his name in Ireland. Charles had not scrupled to hock the crown jewels to pay for foreign mercenaries (French soldiers, mainly, who were blamed for the high instance of royalist rape). He would stop at nothing to win the war, and the parliamentary high command was showing distinct signs of discomfort at the prospect of continuing it. In November 1644 the Earl of Manchester confronted the paradoxical position of a Parliament which fought a king it wanted to reinstall as its own commander-in-chief:

The King need not care how oft he fights, but it concerns us to be wary, for in fighting we venture all to nothing. If we fight a hundred times and beat him ninety nine times, he will be King still. But if he beat us once, or the last time, we shall be hanged, we shall lose our estates, and our posterities will be undone.

Manchester's dilemma admitted of only one resolution: to hang the King. But since this was unthinkable, Cromwell's reply was to beg the question: 'My Lord, if this be so, why did we take up arms at first?' Since they refused to contemplate a republic, parliamentarians had the choice either of surrendering to a king who would never accept parliamentary sovereignty, or fighting on, defeating the King and somehow reaching a new settlement that might guarantee stability. It was this idea of 'peace through continuing the war' that Cromwell made his theme, taken up by the 'war party' of MPs convinced they must push on to defeat the King outright and as soon as possible. They suspected Manchester and other Presbyterian leaders of the 'peace party' of spinning out the war inconclusively – to maintain their power and to lobby for post-war positions in the settlement they sought with the King.[7] So the Independents persuaded Parliament to bring into effect a 'Self-Denying Ordinance' in April 1645, which discharged all members of either House from any military command or service. The army was to be remodelled as a professional fighting force:

a 'new model' army. It was to have a war aim that was clear and brooked no debate or appeasement: to advance Christ's kingdom. Its mission was to scourge the land of papists, bishops and superstitious clergy and to 'bring to justice the enemies of our church and state'.

Thus the army was reinvented as an independent institution – a new power in the land. No longer would it be led by barely competent earls with little stomach for the fight or by one-upping MPs with rival agendas. This professional army would be under the control of one general, Sir Thomas Fairfax. He was heroic and religious, upstanding and able, inarticulate and unambitious: in all, an uncanny man. He would, of course, need to choose a deputy. He chose the best person for the job, an MP whose military brilliance, although self-taught, was undeniable. Oliver Cromwell must, Fairfax told Parliament, be excepted from the self-denying ordinance.

The New Model Army soon engaged the King and Prince Rupert: the date was 14 June 1645 and the field was Naseby, south of Leicester. Battle began with Rupert's familiar cavalry charge, scattering the force of a newly promoted general, Cromwell's son-in-law Henry Ireton. But the years had not taught discipline to Rupert's horsemen: they galloped on in search of the baggage train, whilst Cromwell and Fairfax advanced on the unprotected royalist infantry. It was Roundhead day, and this time it was decisive – 5,000 cavaliers were taken prisoner after more than 1,000 were slaughtered, while the New Model Army suffered only 200 casualties. Most importantly, the royalist baggage train was captured, with the King's correspondence – proving him guilty of all that Parliament had suspected. He had been writing to the leaders of the rebel Irish, hoping to bring their troops to his aid in England. He had been plotting with the Queen to obtain funds and forces from France – in return, he promised what was (regrettably) anathema to most Englishmen, namely toleration of Catholics. He had, in short, been conspiring with the enemies of England, to levy war with foreign troops against his own people.

This was treason in anyone else – and if in anyone else, why not in the King? It was a question that nobody dared ask, at least out loud, but the contents of 'the King's cabinet' were soon published and diminished his support. His remaining forces were painstakingly mopped up by the New Model Army in siege after victorious siege of loyalist towns. By April 1646, Fairfax had surrounded Oxford, the King's last redoubt.[8] Charles finally recognised the inevitable. Disguising himself as a servant, he made a last humiliating exit from his high-spired headquarters and headed towards London.

He reached Harrow-on-the-Hill, and looked down on his former capital. That was when second thoughts assailed him, namely that a better reception might be waiting in his northern kingdom. He struck north, and on 5 May surrendered himself to the Scottish army at Newark. The civil war was over – apparently.

Charles I had fought it with more credit as commander than he is usually given. Throughout the four years of fighting he had headed his troops with ostentatious courage, never hesitating to rally them in the main battles, often within range of enemy musket-shot. This 'hands-on' generalship, in councils and court-martials and in the field, had another consequence: it indubitably fixed him with what is now called 'command responsibility', namely liability in law for the criminal conduct of troops which he controlled, or could have controlled had he wished. The laws of war in this period were well known. Only combatants could be killed but not after their offer of 'quarter' had been accepted. Women and children must be left unmolested and prisoners treated with civility: torture was prohibited and captives could be executed only after conviction by a court-martial for some recognised war crime. Prince Rupert was not a scrupulous adherent to these rules: he punished parliamentary strongholds by plundering and then burning them down. Both he and fellow royalist General George Goring were regularly accused of using poisoned bullets and allowing their troops to rape women and kill harmless citizens of towns they had besieged. In Scotland, Montrose was equally brutal. Royalist campaigns invariably left evidence of the torture and maltreatment of prisoners.

The parliamentary forces were much better disciplined: its godly generals scrupulously punished any soldiers guilty of pillage or rape.[9] But post-Naseby, an unsettling blood-thirstiness overcame Cromwell's battle-weary troops at the Catholic stronghold of Basing House: incensed (quite literally) at its papist icons, they exulted in killing its defenders who had unwisely sought no quarter. There was an investigation, but the report was made to Parliament by Cromwell's personal chaplain, who was more interested in celebrating the destruction of a 'nest of idolatry'. This canon of Christianity was Hugh Peters, returned from Massachusetts, whose ability to preach the parliamentary cause and to fundraise for it, together with his position as personal chaplain to Cromwell, had made him a power in the land. Cooke met him when Peters came to preach at St Bride's, a church off Fleet Street which the barrister would attend during the London legal term. His sermonising was a call to arms: if the enemy prevailed over Parliament, Peters warned, then very few would be spared execution. Cooke found himself in agreement: Peters, he concluded, was 'a man of pure evangelical spirit, who goes about doing good and may be a looking glass for others'.[10]

Hugh Peters was no intellectual, but he was a powerful and entertaining speaker, hiding manic depression behind manic public activity. Cromwell and Cooke were imbued with his 'bible republicanism'. Harvard, the college he helped to found, held its first graduation in 1642: most graduates came over to England to join the parliamentary cause, together with many other young colonists. They were recruited in particular by a kinsman of Cromwell, the Reverend William Hookes, who urged them to give up ploughshares and take up swords across the sea (*New England's Tears for Old England's Fears*). In 1660, it would be alleged by the prosecution at the Old Bailey that 'American fundamentalists' like Peters and Vane had been sent as terrorists by the Massachusetts preachers, to persuade Cromwell to kill the King. Another emissary from the colony was Edward Winslow, who was to play a notable part in Cromwell's administration, and George Downing, the second man to graduate from Harvad, who left his name on Britain's most famous street. (He was to become Cromwell's Kissinger, the arch-diplomat of the Republic who later turned into its arch-traitor, rounding up old round-head comrades after the Restoration). The colonials, especially the Harvard graduates, were to promote 'the new England way' in English churches and in due course in the government of the English republic.[11]

More through luck than management, the war had not spilt into London: there the city continued its business more frenetically than ever, between the twin hubs of Westminster, home to the courts, the Parliament and the army, and St Paul's – citadel of the aldermen and merchants, surrounded by preaching-houses and the shops of Puritan tradesmen. In between, as if holding politicians and common people in equilibrium, were the Inns of Court: an intellectual market-place where any argument could be had for a price. To this haven John Cooke, chastened by the experience of supporting Strafford, had retreated to teach and to practise law according to Sir Edward Coke's *Institutes* and the Christian principles expounded by Richard Sibbes. As victory followed victory in the wake of Naseby, Puritans did indeed give all the glory to God: they hoped, Cooke as firmly as Peters and Cromwell, that He had predetermined their triumph in order to prepare the way for the establishment of His government on earth. This was the period described in the Book of Revelation as 'the Rule of the Saints', a wholesome human interregnum crowned by the second coming of Christ.

Cooke had spent these war years in the capital, 'adhering cordially and constantly to the Parliament on scripture grounds and reasons of state'[12] but also because of his weak frame and intellectual frame of mind ('I was no swordsman').[13] His support for Strafford having disentitled him to Parliamentary briefs, instead he scrabbled a general practice in conveyancing property. 'Master Cooke the lawyer' drew up the deeds of sale for Winchester House in Southampton which John Lilburne later bought – after checking the title with Cooke first.[14] He also defended debtors, obtaining their release from prison after their arrest. He dabbled in what passed for family law, including suits for breach of promise of marriage, an area of law in which some practitioners were little better than blackmailers.

Cooke believed that a legal profession with integrity would serve the public benefit, but the system he experienced encouraged misconduct. One typical example was of a client arrested on his wedding day for an alleged debt of £1,500: he could not raise enough bail money, so the wedding had to be cancelled. The allegation had been made out of spite, to stop the match, and Cooke had the suit dismissed, but recovered only 7 shillings and 2 pence in costs – less than his own fee. His client lost his money, his liberty and his wife – an heiress, for 'it was the occasion of his utter undoing'. Cooke reported this case in 1646, as an example of the need for reform – both of costs of fighting malicious actions, and the 'inhumane practice of arrest for debt'.[15] So unjust was the justice system of his time that after seven years of practice, John Cooke decided to expose it publicly.

4

The Breath of an Unfee'd Lawyer

Reform of the law, Cooke maintained, was the 'one great thing that my honoured friends in the army told me they fought for'.[1] The 'soldier's catechism' issued in 1645 by the New Model Army included as a war aim 'the regulating of our Courts of Justice, which have been made the seats of iniquity and unrighteousness'. Oliver Cromwell certainly agreed: 'The law as it is now constituted', he complained to Colonel Ludlow, 'serves only to maintain the lawyers and to encourage the rich to oppress the poor.'[2] Opposition to the King had been fomented almost entirely by lawyer MPs, yet ironically the consequence of their victory was to unleash an unprecedentedly vitriolic attack upon their profession, whose privilege and status 'encountered the most searching critique they have yet sustained in the long course of English history'.[3] Abolition of the Star Chamber had ended censorship and Parliament never managed to put the genie of free speech back in the bottle – as Milton predicted, the attempt of the Presbyterian MPs in 1644 to reintroduce censorship was rather like the exploit of the gallant farmer who sought to keep the crows out of his field by shutting the gate. The result was a flood of print – George Thomason collected 12,548 pamphlets from 1642 to 1649 – and, after Naseby, much of the vitriol was about the law and the lawyers.[4]

Parliament had begun the great work of making the justice system more just in 1642, when it removed the King's power to dismiss judges and abolished Star Chamber, his cruel prerogative court. But the exigencies of fighting the civil war had occupied the Long Parliament's legislative time until the glorious summer of 1646, when after the King surrendered to the Scots it seemed at last that peace was at hand. That was when the demands began in earnest to rid the commonwealth of its 'caterpillars' and its 'pettifoggers' and clean out its augean stables – invariably identified as the courts in Westminster Hall. There have been lawyer jokes from time immemorial, generally about the profession's greed or smugness or tendency to 'strain after a gnat and swallow a camel'. Now, these post-war pamphlets reminded readers of St Luke's gospel, where Jesus Christ embraced lepers and tax collectors, but drew the line at lawyers: 'Woe unto you also, ye lawyers! for ye lade men with burdens grievous to be borne, and ye yourselves touch not the burdens with one of your fingers . . . ye have taken away the key of knowledge.'[5]

In England in the 1640s, there was – as Cooke was first to admit – ample cause for public antipathy. The number of lawyers had increased dramatically: in 1560 there was one attorney for every 20,000 citizens, but in 1640 there was one for every 2,500 – roughly the proportion today.[6] This proliferation had not been permitted to bring about competition so as to reduce fees: the Inns of Court had jealously guarded their monopoly. Many judges, and almost all court officials, were on the take (the latter were badly paid, and their acceptance of bribes saved public funds). The elite barrister rank of sergeant (similar to modern Queen's Counsel) was open to purchase.[7] A handful of barristers who were judicial favourites monopolised the practice in particular courts. Severe delays were endemic in all civil actions. Many of the judgments were incomprehensible – most of the statutes and the law reports had, since the Conquest, been written in an archaic Norman French, which meant that law had become the preserve of those who could read it. This was not merely a means of entrenching a professional monopoly: as a measure of class stability, the Privy Council had been concerned to keep the public in ignorance of the law, lest they be tempted to take it into their own hands. Judges assisted by delivering decisions in pig-Latin, often to cloak their pig-ignorance. The 'common law' – so called because it was common throughout the realm – included Magna Carta, statutory principles and judicial decisions. It was a crazy jumble of thousands of badly reported precedents, reduced to some order in textbooks by Littleton and Coke. Lawyers needed to train for seven years at the Inns in order to understand them.

The criminal law was not so much severe as savage: in an age without a police force, crime could, it was thought, only be deterred by punishing grotesquely the few who were caught, by devices like disembowelling (for treason), burning (for heresy or witchcraft), branding with hot irons and ear slitting (for sedition); all who stole more than one shilling were hanged by the neck until dead. But those who were educated were allowed their first crime without penalty, through a device called 'benefit of clergy'.[8] Beneficiaries were branded on the thumb: prisoners were always called upon to hold up their hand for inspection before their trial could begin, to determine whether they were any longer eligible for 'clergy'. There were occasional witch-hunting crazes, most notably after Sir Harbottle Grimstone, the Presbyterian magistrate and MP, authorised Matthew Hopkins to frighten confessions out of lonely or unbalanced old women. The procedure, laid down in a treatise of James I, was to search for 'teats' on which devilish 'familiars' (spirits in animal form) were believed to suck. In certain cases a prosecuting lawyer – always a married man – would examine the genitalia of the female suspect, and testify to finding (or not) a 'devil's hood'. The prisoner's possession of a wart, haemorrhoid or prominent clitoris was thus regarded as scientific proof of daemonic possession, although in unenlightened villages the people preferred the old method of 'swimming' a suspected witch, who would be guilty if she floated (because water would reject those who denied their Christian baptism.) Only drowning was proof of innocence.

The enforcement of debts began in most cases with the arrest of the debtor at the instance of his creditor – a procedure ripe for abuse, since debtors then became prisoners with insecure rights to bail. Prisoners who could afford to pay jailers might live well, but most were kept in filthy and insanitary courtyards where 'gaol fever' was so rife that they often spread the infection from the dock: judges plunged their noses into flower and herb bouquets (nosegays) in an effort to deflect the germs. Treason trials might be preceded by torture to extract confessions[9] and defendants were not allowed to have counsel (on the pretext that the judge could be relied upon to look after their interests) other than to argue points of law. Defendants, invariably shackled in irons throughout trials that lasted no more than a few hours, were not permitted to cross-examine prosecution witnesses, although they might put questions in the form of comments on the evidence as it was given against them. There was no appeal, unless the trial judge decided to refer a point of law to a higher court.

Before the civil war, judicial positions and administrative posts in the courts (which could be very lucrative) were sold to the highest bidder: bribery was common and Bacon, when Lord Chancellor, was alone in being caught out and forced to resign, although he suffered no other punishment.[10] Corruption's twin pillars, nepotism and favouritism, were much in evidence. Appointments were made only rarely upon merit – judges like Coke and Croke were exceptions. Most promotions were secured either by connections or by cash – as one historian puts it, identifying the characteristics of Stuart administration, 'by patrimony, patronage or purchase'.[11] The most authoritative study concludes that 'judicial corruption was a fact of life in pre-Civil War England and barristers played an integral role as go-betweens in the corrupt relationships of judges with litigants'.[12] In short, the rich had nothing to fear from the law: they had benefit of clergy and could buy the best advocates (or best-placed favourites) and bribe their way to victory over, or at least frustration of, a poorer plaintiff who was in the right.

Cooke had none of these levers to pull: his parentage was humble and as an old Straffordian he lacked political patrons. As the royalists later said of him, in their superior way, he was a man 'of inconsiderable birth and of small and mean fortune'. The class from which he came – the artisans and yeomen who made up much of the New Model Army – had thus far gained nothing from the law, and in any post-war settlement they wanted access to the courts for speedy and effective justice. John Cooke decided to give their aspirations an empathetic and expert voice: no other barrister was prepared to do an 'inside job' on his own profession.

By 1645 Cooke had spent seven years in study, three in apprenticeship, two in Strafford's service and six in practice. His ability was respected, to the extent that he gained at least one important client, General Fairfax,[13] whom he had advised concerning the Fairfax family estate at Nun Appleton. But he was not wealthy: he gave most of his fees away to the poor, since the giving of alms was the only way for lawyers to avoid the woe that was threatened them in the gospel according to St Luke. But the most ethical of lawyers have palms that itch by habit: as Cooke himself admitted: 'Such is the corruption of my nature, that when I have had a client in my study I have made my dear father stay in the [bed]chamber till I have gotten my ten pounds.'[14]

Like most barristers Cooke lived in term-time at his Inn, in 'chambers' that consisted of an all-purpose sitting room/study with fireplace and chimney, and an adjoining bedchamber. There were four law terms when the London courts were crammed with business but these lasted for less than four months in total, leaving the rest of the time – 'the vacation' – for paperwork and riding out of London on circuits to pick up work at assizes. He would have had a clerk – probably a young relation – to carry books, arrange conferences with clients and accompany him on the downstream boat to Westminster Hall. This was another expense – the boy would have to be clothed and fed (clerks had a special table in hall) and accommodated – although he probably slept in a truckle bed in the sitting room. Cooke was imbued with the Puritan work ethic, which called for morning prayer at Gray's Inn chapel at 6 a.m., followed by a quick breakfast and a water taxi to Westminster where the courts sat from 8 until the early afternoon, although the criminal court at Old Bailey might sit until midnight to complete a trial within the day. Paperwork and conferences were in the evening, as was evensong at St Bride's; the courts sat on Saturdays and no good Puritan could work on the Sabbath. (The royalist judge, David Jenkins, taunted Cooke that by applying himself every Sunday, he worked one year more in every seven.)[15] It was a tough profession for most jobbing barristers, requiring good health and hard work and much interruption of conjugality – it was said that 'a common lawyer's terms are his wife's vacations'. The wife of one distinguished bencher of Gray's Inn was heard to complain 'that all women would take heed of her for marrying with a lawyer, and would say she had been better to have married to a thresher, for such when he had had his hire would come home at night and be merry with her'.[16]

Cooke himself and his family had suffered through the law's delays and booby-traps. He had been in debt in 1641. His father was unjustly sued for £300 and harried from law to equity, where his defence finally succeeded – but at the irrecoverable cost of £700 in court and legal fees. Jacob Cooke, his brother, had taken over the tenancy of a bankrupt's estate, but the bankrupt later paid off his debts and sued Jacob for £1,500, threatening to have him clapped into prison in London. Jacob 'for peace sake' gave him £700 to drop what Cooke described as a blackmail action ('As any full-pursed malicious man may ruin a man with whom he is displeased'). Arrest for debt was a common terror among the middling classes: bail was not easy to obtain in the City of London.

His brother-in-law, named Clapham, had an even worse experience in the notoriously corrupt Court of Wards. He took a yearly tenancy in 1642 of some lands in Leicestershire which he relinquished because the civil war was raging in the area, but his sheep and cattle were seized to guarantee the rent.

Cooke went as his counsel to the Court of Wards to obtain an order to hand them back, and reached an agreement with one of the court officials that his brother-in-law would not be arrested for any rent that the other party claimed he owed. The official invited them to his home to ratify the agreement – and demanded a bribe for having arranged it. Cooke refused to pay, whereupon Clapham was arrested on the charge that he owed rent of over £1,000. Cooke was furious: it was expected of barristers at the time that they would act for their family and friends, but instead of protecting Clapham he had been outwitted by a perfidious court official. To make matters worse his sister, on hearing of the arrest, immediately went into labour. The official jeered that the city court would accept nobody of less rank than an alderman as surety for bail, but Cooke found a judge who was prepared to take his father and a friend, as well as himself, as sureties. Then Cooke had the case removed from the Court of Wards to the Court of King's Bench where he was better known, and obtained a court order for £40 against his brother-in-law's persecutor. Clapham, he noted sadly, would rather have paid £100 to avoid the temporary disgrace.

Clapham's legal problems were not over: after the Court of Wards was abolished by Parliament in 1645 – its corruption had become notorious – he tried to get his sheep and cattle back by suing another official who had taken them into his own custody, but in 1650 that official was held to have immunity from suit. Then the original landlord sued Clapham in the Chancery division where the suit was delayed for five years and Clapham almost ruined by the continuing legal expenses and the loss of his livestock. Such experiences were not uncommon and they left a mark. 'I do bear a personal animosity towards the practice of the law, my friends having suffered so much by it', Cooke later admitted.[17]

It was not so much a personal animosity as a love-hate relationship, and Cooke had suffered it for some years. His views were widely known in the Inns: he inveighed openly against bribery and favouritism, and his nickname at the bar, 'White Cooke', may have referred to his incorruptibility rather than his pasty complexion. For powerful lawyers and judges he was not 'one of us', and his European learning and radical leanings made him the chief suspect as the anonymous author of the first devastating critique of the legal profession, which hit the streets soon after Naseby.[18] A *Looking Glass for all Proud, Ambitious, Covetous and Corrupt Lawyers* counselled its readers against electing to Parliament 'men whom fools admire for their wit, namely lawyers'.

This was a topical question, since well over 300 members of the Long Parliament had attended at the Inns of Court and seventy-five of these were practising barristers. The argument was simple: the great jurisconsuls of Rome had acted for the poor without fee: the English scions of the Inns, by demanding large fees, had become 'hackney pettifoggers and hucksters of the law'. The anonymous author recalled a time within old men's memories when competition thrived: lawyers would stand at the corner of Chancery Lane and at Temple Bar and by a pillar outside St Paul's and 'cap in hand, courteously salute their countrymen, enquiring what business brought them to town, not unlike watermen plying for a fare'. But this halcyon image of cheap legal services was long gone – now it was impossible to obtain an audience with a great lawyer without a large fee paid up front, while pleadings cost a pound for every line written in incomprehensible law French. To succeed in a particular court, it was necessary to retain the judge's 'favourites' who had special access: 'Oh misery! Poor men cannot afford the price of justice and rich men are oft undone by buying it.' The proliferation of lawyers (especially the new breed of solicitors) was oppressing the country – they were like locusts swarming over the land, devouring and impoverishing it. Lawyers were a bold and talkative ilk: elect them, and they would be nominated to chair parliamentary committees where their habit of taking fees for talking would encourage corruption. 'It is to be feared that the commonwealth, though founded by the laws, will be confounded by the lawyers.'

It was a powerful, witty and well-informed indictment of the profession, all the more so by being written from a Puritan perspective: its thesis that a Parliament full of lawyers would never countenance effective law reform 'because they got more by the corruption and delays of the law than by the law itself' was insightful and proved in time (and to Cooke's despair) all too true. The pamphlet's message was immediately taken up by John Lilburne, in a blast entitled *England's Birthright Justified*, and then by his fellow Leveller William Walwyn, in *England's Lamentable Slavery*, and in the following years by booklets with titles that speak for themselves: *Hell, Rome and the Inns of Court; The Corrupt Lawyer Untrussed, Lashed and Quashed; Everyman's Case, or Lawyers Routed; The Lawyer's Bane; The Chief Judge of Hell; St Hilary's Tears Shed Upon All Professions from the Judge to the Pettifogger; A Rod for Lawyers, Who Are Hereby Declared Robbers and Deceivers of the Nation.*

What was emerging from these powerful propagandists, who had receptive audiences in the ranks of city tradesmen and in the middle echelons of the New Model Army, was a dangerous streak of hostility to common law and even to Magna Carta, which Walwyn claimed was an irrelevance because it was a charter for barons and not for common people. This was the voice of Jack Cade (in fact, the shout of his comrade, Dick the Butcher): 'The first thing we do, let's kill all the lawyers.'[19] It was a worrying prospect that a post-Naseby world would renounce the very basis upon which the revolution had been fought, namely for common law and Magna Carta against the prerogatives of the King. John Cooke was known to be in sympathy with ideas in the original pamphlet and was widely accused of writing it. That accusation must have been given greater force when he accepted a brief to act for 'Freeborn John' Lilburne. It was time to make his real position clear – which he did in a book-length pamphlet published in February 1646.

This remarkable publication *The Vindication of the Professors and Profession of the Law*, began with an astute dedication to the 'noble senators' of the Lords and Commons, 'from whom the King's majesty can no more be divided in his political capacity than the head from a living body' (an ironic reminder of how this concept of shared sovereignty, accepted at the end of the Civil War, would become outdated just three years later, when the King's head *was* severed from his living body). Cooke urged Parliament to progress towards realisation of Magna Carta's promise of speedy justice. He looked forward to the day when civil actions might be commenced and completed in one law term – i.e. in months rather than years – and made very clear that he was not blaming the judges (before whom he had to appear) for deciding hard cases: that was the result of the bad laws they were obliged to uphold. Reform of those laws was a matter for Parliament, not for the courts and certainly not for the King. This was, indeed, the great strength of the common law, which distinguished England from less happy lands which lacked parliaments: 'I may most truly say that the laws of England are either actively, or potentially, the best in the world, because if anything be amiss, the Parliament may reform it.'[20]

Cooke made his message to the Commons clear from the outset:

Politicians observe, as the greatest misery in war is to see a man's wife ravished before his face, so certainly one of the saddest spectacles in peace is to see might overcome right – a poor man's righteous cause lost for want of money to follow it . . . Look with eagle eyes into the poor man's sorrows and oppressions, and see that justice be done them for such fees as they are able to pay.[21]

Cooke warned that there could be no peace without justice, and that meant restocking the bench with godly and learned judges who preferred 'right reason to precedent'. This was the most important post-war task. He proudly eschewed in his own writing the 'untunable jarring' of Latin phrases and strongly advocated the abandonment of law French and the discontinuance of legal documents couched in Latin: 'I am ashamed that a sub-poena should be served on a countryman in Latin when peradventure scarcely anyone within five miles understands it.'[22]

Cooke commenced his critique confidently, by reprinting in its entirety the pamphlet to which he was responding so that his readers could, in fairness, appreciate the other side. He began with a heartfelt attack on anonymous authors: 'Why should he who thinks he writes truth be ashamed to own to it?' He easily dealt with the silly suggestion that it was dishonourable for a lawyer to accept a fee, although he conceded it had to be moderate and earned by good and faithful service. Cooke was writing, in effect, the first book of legal ethics and he began it with a rule against touting: 'I hold that to seek for clients is as preposterous as for a woman to go a wooing, or a physician to seek for patients.'[23] The barrister who is paid a fee is trustee of the money under a tacit contract: he has a duty to return it if he does not do the work. The fee ensures that the lawyer 'lays it to his heart as if it really was his own case'. But since litigants are like sick men – 'distempered, passionate, willful and extremely in love with their own cause' – the advocate has a duty to advise them emphatically to drop an action that is unlikely to succeed. Cooke always did this with his own clients and noticed 'how disconsolately they have gone away with gouty hands, as if I had been their professed enemy'. Although honey in the mouth produces money in the hand, the advocate's duty is to give advice on what the law is, not what might be achieved through exploiting it by perjury and other tricks. As for the common cavil that lawyers will take any side irrespective of truth, 'the truth lies many times in such a deep well that each lawyer has a bucket to draw'; estate law, for example, was so difficult and complex that 'the judge has one ear for the plaintiff and the other ear for the defendant, but counsel has both ears for his client'.

The *Vindication* continues much in this vein, setting out what now appears ethical orthodoxy, although Cooke was articulating some of these rules for the first time – for example, the rule that no barrister should charge a fee for advising a fellow barrister, a professional courtesy that was in the process of crystallising.[24] His concern that clients should be served by counsel who gave honest advice was directed at the ambulance chasers who led them into court at their peril and not at the lawyers who undertook unpopular causes, as Cooke himself was often to do. He endorsed the ethical rule that a barrister was entitled to appear for any client who had an arguable case, so long as he did not participate in any deception of the court.[25] But in stating these rules of 'vindication', Cooke underpinned them with a commitment to justice and the defence of the poor which was unparalleled in England up to that time. It was certainly unheard of for a lawyer to advocate, as did Cooke, a 'cap' on professional earnings, beyond which all work should be done free of charge for the poor.

Drawing upon the lessons preached at Gray's Inn by 'heavenly Dr Sibbs' and some proto-socialist ideas he had picked up in Italy, Cooke urged that 'no man should get above twenty thousand pounds by his profession or occupation, which being acquired he should either desist or give away to others'[26] (in modern value, lawyers should stop earning once they have made their first million). Since the purpose of any occupation is to serve God by serving mankind, earnings vastly in excess of what was needed to maintain home and family should either be waived in respect of services to the poor or else given away for good causes. It was a rule fashioned not only for lawyers, whose well-being was a reflection of the kingdom's prosperity, but for the clergy who grasped for tithes and physicians whose high charges for visiting the sick were gains ill-gotten indeed – more grievous to their patients than the illness itself. Cooke's demand was that the rich should practise philanthropy, on the payback principle that those who profit from a community have a moral duty to dispense charity.

Cooke contended that a surfeit of lawyers was a sign of a flourishing country, but he deplored the way the profession and the law itself had been permitted to develop under the Stuarts. Reason must be the basis for all law, although he was careful to point out, with a clear echo of Coke's advice to King James, 'that which we call the reason of the law is not every natural man's reason but a practical and studied experience acquired by much industry and long observation'.[27] (There had to be some benefit in seven years of study followed by three more years of apprenticeship.) But he identified cruelty in many of the accepted notions of the time: the rule that all a suicide's property should go to the King, for example, was unfair to the grieving children left to beg on the streets. He condemned the rule that defendants could not call witnesses on oath, that they were not permitted counsel when their life was at stake, that oversights in the highly technical rules for pleading indictments enabled many murderers to escape justice. The rules were even more technical in civil cases, which could be won or lost by minor errors in arcane pleadings, handwritten (at £1 a line) in the incomprehensible argot of Latin-laced Norman French. There were *declarations*, *pleas in bar*, *replications*, *rejoinders*, *rebutters*, *surrebutters*, and so on. Many good causes were lost by defective pleading: 'the loss in such case ought at least to be borne by the counsel or attorney who had been at fault'[28] (this suggestion – that barristers should be liable for their mistakes like other professionals, through a law of professional negligence – did not endear Cooke to his colleagues, and did not come to pass for more than 300 years). Cooke condemned 'benefit of clergy' as both an encouragement to crime and an insult to reason: 'It is a greater offence for a scholar, who knows his duty and the danger of breaking the law, to offend than an illiterate man who knows nothing in comparison.'[29]

The issue that concerns Cooke time and again is the endemic delay in the justice system of the period. He saw no reason why cases in London should not be decided within a month; if a plaintiff failed to bring his case on within three months, it should be dismissed with costs. Although critics blamed lawyers for spinning out cases so they could obtain more fees, Cooke explained that in fact both barristers and solicitors would benefit financially from speedy justice: they would get through more cases and potential clients would be keener to go to law. Unlike most barristers, then as now, he had a good word to say for that new professional underclass, the solicitor:

If they be honest men – as all of them are for anything I know to the contrary – I know nothing in right reason that can be said against their profession. I believe they are very useful to the client and of great assistance to counsel, who many times in a long business sees much through their spectacles, not having time to peruse depositions.[30]

Cooke defended equity, too, from the critics who condemned it as an extension of the power of the King. Equity was dispensed in the court of Chancery, which had the power to do what was right when statute law was silent or produced an unconscionable result. It gave remedies, for example, against bargains produced by deceit or undue influence, e.g. where children or the feeble-minded were lured into making contracts which might be good in law but were bad in conscience. For Chancery to work effectively, Cooke insisted that it should reject trivial suits and impose sanctions against false actions: the plaintiff should put his claim on oath (so he could be prosecuted for perjury if it turned out false) and barristers and solicitors should take an oath to say nothing to the court that they doubted to be true. 'For my part, when anyone comes for advice about commencing a suit, I tremble and bid him first examine his own conscience seriously: has he been wronged, and in a considerable matter? For I would not have Christians go to court for trifles . . . Law is like a labyrinth, the entry very easy but the exit very difficult.'[31]

The *Vindication* was not only concerned with the law as a set of rules: it was the first informed criticism of the law as it was practised, in the courts that did their business in the Guildhall and behind partitions in the crowded thoroughfare of Westminster Hall. They did not do business often enough: 'No vacations in the Courts of Justice' was Cooke's slogan. The most heart-felt section of his book was that dealing with judicial favouritism – a very practical problem which took courage for a barrister to expose. Scandalously, every court had its 'favourites' whose cases would be called first and who would have private access to the judges. Naturally, they obtained the lion's share of work. Their ease of access gave rise to the perception that they passed on bribes to their judicial patrons, and it certainly distorted the priorities of the court always to hear the favourites first, even when their cases were neither urgent nor important. Cooke argued that matters touching life and liberty should always be heard first, irrespective of the identity of the counsel who proposed the motion. The system of 'favourites' discriminated against other competent lawyers and certainly against their clients. It would destroy the profession, since good men would not study the law once they realised what a lottery success at the bar had become.

Cooke was exposing a raw nerve. As Bulstrode Whitelocke conceded when it was safe to do so (i.e. in his memoirs), favourites were retained by clients because 'they hoped thereby to have more favours than otherwise they ought to have, a kind of bribery' (Whitelocke had been a 'favourite' of King's Bench when his father was a judge, but his annual earnings dropped from £300 to £50 when Judge Whitelocke died).[32] The greatest 'favourites' of all were the sergeants, members of the 'Order of the Coif' who were appointed by royal writ (after a substantial payment – hence the joke 'argent makes sergeant') and who had lucrative rights of audience in the Court of Common Pleas.

On the other hand, ordinary barristers were not as busy as they seemed, as they pranced up and down Westminster Hall:

> I cannot but smile many times, to see what a company of hypocrites we are, striding up and down in our gowns, making men believe that we are full of employment; and so we are indeed in a perpetual motion measuring the length of the Hall but not making motions, perhaps, from the first day of term to the last.[33]

Cooke accepted that justice was a moral rather than a religious virtue ('No doubt there are many good justices amongst the infidels') but he urged that all judges be selected for their learning, prudence and integrity. Courage was required in standing up to the King and if needs be to Parliament, but disaffected royalists could not be suffered on the bench. Charles I had been wary of Puritan judges, but they were least likely to take bribes or draw out proceedings in the hope that a bribe would sooner or later be offered. The only way to obtain good judges was to ensure that the bar from which they were recruited was stocked with good men. The greatest defect in the profession, and hence in the judiciary, was, he thought, the failure of the Inns to teach English history: they produced crick-necked practitioners who could not look back to understand the reason why various legal doctrines had developed.[34]

Cooke did not shrink from tackling the complexities of reforming land law, which remained feudal in origin and perplexing in practice. He condemned primogeniture, the established system under which the oldest son took all, leaving daughters (even if older) to be married off and younger sons to find careers in the army or Church or else to starve. It may be that this obvious unfairness made him think more carefully about hereditary monarchy, which operated on the same feudal principle. But Cooke recognised the virtue of maintaining large estates and was more concerned that poor farmers – like his own relatives – should be able to leave modest portions of their estate to daughters and younger sons.[35] Where he was truly innovatory was in being the first to propose a national land registry, containing records of all contracts, conveyances, leases and charges which might be inspected on payment of a small fee by those who needed to check whether an estate was encumbered. He proposed that no dealing in land should be valid unless and until registered. This system would, when established in

1862, become basic to transfers and mortgaging of land: the advocate for the poor had hit upon a necessary service for the transfer of wealth. Cooke's purpose in suggesting the reform was not only to avoid fraudulent land sales, but to provide a measure of freedom of information: once the truth about estates was discoverable, charlatans could not 'dress in a garb of five hundred pounds a year' and incur debts they could never repay, nor could misers pretend that they were poor.[36]

The *Vindication* was a remarkable mix of what lawyers would call confession and avoidance: a realistic account of the grave practical defects of the law, the courts and the profession, yet at the same time a passionate defence of their proper role. That role included a place in Parliament for lawyers (although not for judges) and Cooke paid fulsome tribute to Hampden, Pym and other notable MPs who had trained at the Inns. He did, however, make one important concession to the anonymous pamphleteer he was refuting: MPs who practised as barristers should be disqualified from voting on regulation of legal fees, redress of court delays or other legal reforms, because no man should be judge in his own cause, and no 'gown man' (as barristers were termed) should be in a position to press his private advantage. Cooke was prescient in fearing the self-interest of his colleagues: in due course his reforms, even when supported by Cromwell, would be frustrated by lawyer-MPs. These obstructionists were not royalists ('malignant lawyers', as Cooke described them, of the 'Oxford party') – on the contrary, they were independent grandees like Oliver St John and Bulstrode Whitelocke, who were not prepared to surrender their professional privileges.

The *Vindication* salutes the courage of the soldiers, especially Fairfax – a member of Gray's Inn – and Cromwell, 'who fears nothing but to offend God'. It reflected a common expectation of a post-war constitutional monarchy: 'The Parliament desires not to diminish his Majesty's just grandeur but to defend themselves and the Kingdom from violence and oppression . . . Oh that his Majesty would yet forsake all his destructive ways, and engage himself with his noble Lords and Commons against all anti-Christian sin and profaneness.'[37] Oh but what if his Majesty did not forsake his destructive ways? In the hope-filled days of 1646, this prospect did not dawn on any of Parliament's supporters, even upon the political thinking of the visionary John Cooke: his thoughts about the monarchy were to run very far and very fast over the next three years.

The *Vindication* was published by the bookseller Matthew Walbank and was sold from his shop at Gray's Inn Gate and from stalls in St Paul's Church-yard and from the booksellers stationed around the courts in Westminster Hall. Publications of this kind – pamphlets the length of a small book – would have a print run of about 1,500 copies with an estimate of ten readers per copy,[38] mainly in London where a very high proportion of the citizenry – 80 per cent of men, at one estimate – could read.[39] The significance of the *Vindication* as a reference point for law reform literature may have secured it a wider circulation: the work was reprinted by Walbank in 1652, when Cooke was Chief Justice of Munster and his law reform agenda appeared likely to be implemented.

February 1646 was so cold that printing errors in the *Vindication* were caused by the frostbitten fingers of its compositors. It was an important month for Cooke: six days after publication, he made his most celebrated court appearance to date: as counsel assigned by the House of Lords to argue that an old Star Chamber conviction was wrong in law and should be overturned. Cooke was to be led by John Bradshawe, a more experienced counsel and also a friend of Milton. The man whose conviction they would seek to over-turn was an idol of the mob whose fame, then and later, came from speaking for himself. 'Freeborn John' Lilburne had persuaded Parliament, now that the war was almost over, to examine the lawfulness of the sentence passed on him in 1638 by the Star Chamber.

Lilburne had lived eventfully since Cromwell had secured his release from prison. He had enlisted as an officer in Essex's army and survived Edgehill, only to be captured by Prince Rupert's men in a subsequent skirmish and carried off as a prisoner to Oxford, where he was put on trial for high treason. He confounded the King's court by demanding that it adjourn to the nearest field for a medieval trial by battle, in which 'Freeborn John' wished to face Prince Rupert in single combat. Edward Hyde, present at the trial, thought that 'he behaved with so much impudence that it was manifest he ambi-tioned martyrdom for his cause'.[40] A few days before the court was due to sentence him to death, he managed to smuggle a letter out of Oxford to the Speaker of the House of Commons. Parliament had been unaware of this outrageous royalist initiative to put its soldiers on trial for treason – a pretext for executing prisoners whom the King was bound, by the laws of war, to prosecute only for war crimes or escapes. The House immediately invoked the *lex talionis* ('an eye for an eye . . .') and declared that if the Oxford trials went ahead, it would treat royalist prisoners in the same way. But could this declaration reach Oxford in time to save Lilburne? There was no telephone, fax or available pigeon between Westminster and Oxford, and no open line of communication between the two forces. Lilburne's heavily pregnant wife, Elizabeth, persuaded the Speaker to give her a letter authenticating the declaration, and set off on horseback for Oxford, reaching the royalist capital in the nick of time. The King caved in to Parliament's threat and ordered the abandonment of unlawful trials of prisoners of war. Lilburne was reprieved, and later swapped for a royalist prisoner.

Captain Lilburne fought valiantly in Cromwell's troop at Marston Moor, but left the army in 1645 to fight a new enemy – the parliamentary Presbyterians, led by Denzil Holles and his old mentor, William Prynne. These humourless and comparatively conservative MPs had a majority in the Long Parliament (which had lost about 40 per cent of its members through defections to the King) and they were becoming very anxious, as the war turned Parliament's way, to deliver on the Covenant with the Kirk which had been Pym's price for Scottish armed support. The Presbyterians had been the first to reimpose censorship, inspiring Milton's immortal cry for press freedom, the *Areopagitica*. In January 1645 the House of Commons had approved a plan for uniting the kingdoms in Presbyterian worship and Prynne insisted that there must be no toleration either of Anglicans (Laud, old and irrelevant, they cruelly put on trial and then to death) or of Independents, a post-Naseby group of 'war party' MPs called 'Independents' because they wanted a decentralised church broad enough to support separate congregations.

A serious breach in parliamentary unity was slowly opening, and Lilburne, born to stir, determined to widen the gap. He libelled leading Presbyterians and was briefly imprisoned for sedition, choosing John Cooke as counsel to seek his release on bail. Lilburne and his 'Levellers' appeared at this point to be propagandists in the Independent cause rather than extremists, and the House of Lords decision to hear Lilburne's appeal was meant as a concession to this party, which had a significant number of MPs and was widely supported by both officers and men in the army. It would rectify what everyone thought was a miscarriage of justice by the hated Star Chamber, provide the popular Captain Lilburne with some recompense for his wrongful conviction and serve to emphasise the arbitrariness of the King's former rule. The Lords were not prepared to suffer Lilburne in person but they chose the two advocates of whom he could least complain. Bradshawe was a respected and leading barrister with a powerful presentation. If the argument he presented was devised by the radical intellect of John Cooke, Lilburne could be guaranteed a good day in court.

Back in 1638, Lilburne's punishment – pillory, whip and prison – had been ordered by the Star Chamber not because he had been found guilty of the offence it suspected – smuggling seditious books – but because he had refused to take the oath or to answer the judges' questions about his movements and associates. Lilburne had accused the Star Chamber, comprised of the King's ministers and bishops, of 'trying to ensnare me, seeing that the things for which I am imprisoned cannot be proved against me'. Cooke's argument, accepted by the House of Lords, was that it was 'contrary to the laws of nature and the Kingdom for any man to be his own accuser'. Lilburne's sentence was quashed and he was awarded £2,000 in compensation for his wrongful imprisonment (a sum conveniently extracted from the forfeited estates of wealthy royalists). The rule against self-incrimination that Cooke proposed later became known as 'the right to silence': it would live on as one of the foremost civil liberties guaranteed by a common law in over fifty Commonwealth countries and would in due course be entrenched in the fifth amendment to the US Constitution and in the rules of international criminal courts. It contrasts starkly with inquisitorial systems which punish suspects for refusal to answer questions by officials, and it has undoubtedly protected innocent detainees through the ages against making false confessions while frightened or disoriented after arrest or in panicked response to aggressive questioning. Bentham complained that it was the first law that criminals would pass for their own benefit, but even he admitted its value in forcing law enforcement officials to hunt for objective evidence rather than procuring a confession through torture or ill-treatment.

This was a momentous case – Cooke's first '*cause célèbre*'. The coincidence of the hearing with the publication of the *Vindication* made his name – and made him enemies. Some powerful barristers resented his attacks on 'favourites' and their own professional monopolies. But in his late 30s, after six difficult years of graft, he had established himself – sufficiently, at any rate, to take a wife. On 12 September 1646 he married Frances Cutler at St Olave's in Hart Lane, a well-to-do church where Samuel Pepys was later to meet his wife. Post-sermon socialising was a form of speed-dating for the devout, and Cooke had decided it was better to marry than to burn. Besides, he was deeply attracted to Frances, a fellow-congregationalist: their faith, in God and each other, would soon be put to the severest test.

In 1647, Cooke earned the enmity of the medical establishment through the vigour of his defence of the incorrigible 'Doctor' William Trigg, once again charged with administering potions without being a member of the college of physicians. This time, Cooke brought Trigg's patients to court to testify on his behalf and there were still a hundred of them waiting to be called when the judge dismissed the case. Cooke was probably right to attribute more cures to Trigg, using herbal remedies extracted from roots and weeds, than to these College physicians who drew their patients' 'bad blood' by cutting or leeching them. The college then sued Trigg for an unpaid fine, so Cooke drafted a petition on his behalf which attracted more than 3,000 signatures. It claimed Trigg had ministered to 30,000 patients since 1624, and accused members of the college of betraying their trust by fleeing London at times of plague.[41] Cooke published a compelling defence of his client in *The Poor Man's Case*, which appeared in February 1648. But the college could never forgive him for holding its monopoly up to public ridicule: he was described by one of its officials as 'a needy lawyer, an unknown hierophant [expounder of sacred mysteries] and obvious cheat' in an angry letter written to a distinguished legal scholar, Dr Isaac Dorislaus.[42] This doctor of laws was soon to form a rather higher opinion of John Cooke than the outraged doctors of medicine.

These two lawyers – Dorislaus, the unworldly academic who specialised in the republican governance of ancient Rome, and Cooke, the streetwise practitioner with a taste for polemic – would be brought together by Parliament soon enough, to consider the case of the King. But in the summer of 1646, nobody envisaged that Charles would be put on trial. He was a king in temporary quarters with the covenanter army of Scotland: everyone thought it would only be a matter of time before he reached a constitutional settlement with his English Parliament and returned to the throne, his power diluted but not greatly diminished. These expectations faded over the next two years, as the King determined to resist any diminution of his prerogatives, by exploiting the schism in the parliamentary ranks and inciting a second civil war.

5

What the Independents Would Have

The distinctive feature of the English revolution was that it was actually justified by reference to law – Magna Carta, the Petition of Right and the common law, and even by recalling the Saxon legal heritage before the 'Norman yoke' was imposed in 1066.[1] The crown had violated this fundamental law by its 'prerogative courts' like the Star Chamber, by its religious innovations and by spurning Parliament, which shared sovereignty with the King. Henry Parker, a barrister who provided the ideological ballast for resistance, argued that historical precedents demonstrated that Parliament alone had the power to declare law, binding on the King and people alike. His famous conclusion, 'that the sovereign power resides in both Houses of Parliament, the King having no negative voice [i.e. veto]'[2] had been the basis for the constitutional breach in 1642, when the Militia Bill, giving Parliament control over the army and navy, was brought into operation without the monarch's consent. 'The King in Parliament' (i.e. the King in his capacity as executor of Parliament's laws) required utter respect: disobedience was treason. The King outwith Parliament, whether acting by prerogative or on arbitrary whim, might on the other hand be resisted, even by force. Parliament had gone to war on this philosophy: it was the doctrine of constitutional monarchy, not republicanism. Every roundhead read his *Soldiers Catechism*, which began 'I fight to recover the King out of the Popish malignant company'. Any fight to extirpate the King was not seriously suggested – it would have been treason to do so – until 1648.

The dramatic conclusion that 'the common law forged the axe which beheaded Charles I'[3] is simplistic, none the less. A substantial minority of lawyers – including some of the most learned, like Hyde and Bridgeman – stayed with Charles throughout the civil war. It was a common royalist taunt that 'all the great lawyers followed the King', which Cooke answered in his next work (*A Union of Hearts*, published in 1647): 'not so neither, although I am sure the politick lawyer stayed behind [i.e. with the King]: ambition and avarice make many a man argue against their own liberties.'[4] Most barristers were 'trimmers' who cut their cloth (and their hair) to the fashion of government as often as the Vicar of Bray. It was, however, a good measure of the strength of opposition to the King's personal rule that a preponderance of them (about 60 per cent) were supportive of Parliament, even before its victory at Marston Moor: as Cooke pointed out, 'The temptation was very great to be for the King's side in all arguments because Parliaments have been discontinued and shortened'.[5] That most barristers resisted the temptation cannot be attributed entirely to their common law training; it required Protestant passion to move the majority of this conservative profession to take up arms against the status quo. With victory came the question: what *kind* of constitutional settlement should follow?

A compulsory 'Kirk of England' was demanded by the Scottish covenanter allies (in reliance upon Pym's promise) and by the Presbyterians led by Denzil Holles, who in 1646 formed the majority in the Long Parliament. It was resisted by the Congregationalists – their MPs were dubbed 'Independents' – who had widespread support throughout the army, from officers (including Cromwell and Fairfax) and from soldiers. The New Model Army had finished the war as a politicised institution, with promotion on merit rather than on lineage and procedures for presenting the views of lower ranks to the generals, through elected representatives and 'agitators'. In truth, the army was more representative of the general population than was the Parliament, with its gentlemen MPs elected on a very limited franchise by the votes of country squires and other local worthies. At the war's end, the question of what to do about the King (who would spend the first nine months of his captivity in a pleasant enough colloquy with Scots officers) was put on ice. The urgent problem was the growing tension between a Presbyterian Parliament and an increasingly 'Independent' army.

The task of post-war reconstruction was daunting enough: over 100,000 adult males had been killed in the actual fighting, with several hundred thousand non-combatants lost from collateral damage and war-borne disease – in proportion to the population of England and Wales at the time, higher casualties than were suffered in the First or Second World Wars.[6] The New Model Army, which had suffered for Parliament's sake, expected respect for its civil position: instead, Parliament determined to smash it before it became a power base for Independency. Much of the army was to be disbanded, and the remainder sent to Ireland. This was a popular enough policy in London among the merchants and tradesmen: the high taxes to support the soldiers irked the commercial classes. But Parliament's niggardly and unfair treatment of men who had risked their lives to secure its supremacy is only explicable by the growing fear that the army was embracing Independency – a self-fulfilling prophecy as it turned out, because the radicalism of the soldiers, fanned by their Leveller-inspired 'agitators', was fuelled by justified grievances over pay and conditions.

While Parliament shadow-boxed with the army it was in no position to come to a settlement with the King, whose strategy was to exploit the growing split in its ranks: his hope was that 'I shall be able so to draw either the Presbyterians or the Independents to side with me, for extirpating the one or the other, that I shall really be King again'.[7] He was happy to bide his time until he could rally a sufficient force to recommence the war: he had high hopes of anti-covenanter Scots led by his devoted courtier the Duke of Hamilton; the woods of Wales were still thick with royalists (the last Welsh castle did not surrender until the autumn of 1647); and there was always hope of support from the Irish rebels led by his faithful Duke of Ormond, and from the French or even the Vatican. His army commanders were safe on the continent, or had been pardoned in return for pledges that no self-respecting cavalier would keep. So he temporised, happy in the belief that the English political factions needed him more than he needed them. In January 1647, Parliament negotiated a settlement with the Scots covenanter army promising to pay £400,000 for its Civil War services in return for its removing itself from English soil and handing over the King – who considered that he had been bought, and for less than a king's ransom. From his comfortable 'mansion arrest' at Holmby House in Northamptonshire, he smugly rejected Parliament's terms of settlement (the 'Newcastle Propositions') which required that some Royalist officers should be prosecuted for war crimes:

A general act of oblivion is the best bond of peace . . . After intestine trouble, the wisdom of this and other kingdoms has usually and happily, in all ages, granted general pardons, whereby the numerous discontentments of many persons and families otherwise exposed to ruin might not become fuel to new disorders or seed of future troubles.[8]

This demand for a general amnesty came hypocritically from a king who was actively planning to fuel new disorders. But it was a response made from a position of strength: he might be Parliament's prisoner, but the MPs' insistence on having him as their King made *them* his long-term captives. So it came as a considerable shock to Charles, as he was enjoying a springtime game of bowls at the Spencer estate, Althorpe, to hear that he had a visitor. Cornet George Joyce – a very junior officer, although he had consulted with Cromwell before setting out – had come to take him into the custody of the New Model Army. 'Where is your commission?' he asked the polite young soldier who led him away the following morning. 'Here is my commission,' said the corporal. 'Where?' asked the King, expecting to be shown a document signed by Fairfax. 'Behind me,' Joyce answered, indicating the troop of five hundred New Model cavalry waiting to escort them to an army rendezvous at Newmarket. 'It is as fair a commission as I have seen in my life,' Charles acknowledged.

On the chessboard of England at war with itself, Charles had faced Parliament as its King: he now became a pawn in a different game, being played less for civil liberty than for religious toleration. The parliamentary Presbyterians, supported by most of the city fathers and the London mob, wanted to impose upon the whole country the Solemn League and Covenant, with its unity of sombre and sober worship and ordained ministers. The 'Independents' wanted no part of any centralised Church: godly congregations should be entitled to choose their own preachers, whether trained or just divinely inspired. There were other sects too, which spoke in tongues or envisaged the imminent second coming of Christ in ways that variously interpreted the Book of Revelation. Then there were Anglicans – more than anyone realised, as it turned out – who quietly cursed all these Calvinists and wanted to worship at altar rails, with a prayer book supervised by bishops, in the light that played through stained glass. Charles, their champion, was powerless to intervene when, in October, the Independents and Presbyterians briefly made common cause and abolished the Anglican episcopacy, although doubtless he recalled his father's prophecy ('No bishop, no King'). But he was reassured when the two factions fell again to abusing and confusing each other.

It was into this war of angry words that John Cooke stepped in 1647. Realising that the parliamentary cause would be lost without a sensible compromise, he published *What the Independents Would Have*, a tract which sought to define more carefully, and less threateningly, a movement which was already being condemned as 'fanatical'. It was short, at sixteen pages, with large print: it was tighter and more objective than his other writings. He allowed himself only one reminiscence, of the time he was minded to support episcopacy when staying with the separatists in Holland – before being persuaded that bishops, 'the inventions of man', ought not to control an institution committed to Christ. Now, he was writing this pamphlet to answer the question that was being asked all around him: 'What do the Independents really want?' The answer was obvious: they wanted what the Puritans sought vainly from James I, namely liberty of worship,

an entire exemption from the jurisdiction of all prelates and ecclesiastical officers, other than such as themselves shall choose, and to be accountable to the magistrate for what they shall do amiss, submitting to the civil government in all things . . . but otherwise to be free to choose their own company, place and time – with whom, where and when to worship God, as they are in the choice of their wives, for a forced marriage will not hold.[9]

It was a telling simile: a forced marriage was exactly what the English Presbyterians and Scottish covenanters intended, to unify worship in their two kingdoms. Why did the Independents, who were also Calvinists, refuse so stoutly to contract it? Cooke constructs a character – reflective, presumably, of his own – designed to show the Independent as the friend of other Christians (whatever their errors they were fellow believers in Christ) but as an enemy to any form of state-enforced religion: 'to force men to come to church is but to make them hypocrites.'[10] They tolerated not only Presbyterians, but other groups whose errors were not terminal: Anglicans have some 'very comfortable' opinions; sectarians like Anabaptists and Seekers have odd views but may find a way to heaven, as might Fifth monarchists, who thought that Christ was just around the corner, and 'millenarians' (so called because they believed that the thousand-year 'rule of the saints', promised by the Book of Revelation, which would precede the second coming, was at hand). Your Independent 'knows no hurt in a million millenarian-like errors. Who would not be glad to see Jesus Christ?' These cults had crawled from underneath 'the world turned upside down': as a result of the war, families crazed with grief tried to reunite with soldiers they believed to be now in heaven. (The outbreak of spiritualism after the carnage in the trenches of the First World War had a similar effect.) Cooke has been depicted as a millenarian, but the quoted passage demonstrates that he was merely tolerant of their 'million errors'. Given the limited capacity of Heaven, the great mistake of Catholicism was its doctrine that Christ died for all (although he admits it is a clever way of encouraging good works as a means of attaining salvation). But unusually for his time he does allow the possibility of tolerating Catholics, since their praiseworthy aim is to honour and exalt Christ.

Cooke's urgent message was that 'the sword has no capacity to settle religion'. The appalling prospect of war between Parliament and its own army was becoming very real and his Independent 'thinks it strange that those who can least justify them – Christians – should have most wars', a paradox put down to 'this one depraved principle, to suffer no opinion but your own. How can truth appear, but through argumentation?' It was a barrister's point of view, perhaps, but it echoes Milton and predates the 'free marketplace of ideas' of John Stuart Mill. Look at the settlements in New England, Cooke expostulates: there, Independency has worked to the public benefit. He urges Presbyterians to be moderate, not rigid: it was the rigidity of the bishops, after all, that proved their downfall.

'The Independent has always been a faithful well-wisher of King and Parliament,' said Cooke in 1647, the last year in which this statement could be made with a straight face. Independents were still a minority in the Commons, although MPs of the stamp of young Henry Vane, Oliver St John and Arthur Haselrig had led the 'war party' which ran political rings around Holles and Prynne and their cohorts. The 'recruiter' elections towards the end of the war strengthened the Independents – they brought to Parliament Cromwell's son-in-law, Henry Ireton (another lawyer), Charles Fleetwood, Robert Blake (Cooke's Wadham contemporary), Thomas Harrison, Edmund Ludlow, Thomas Rainborough (soon to earn fame at the Putney debates) and Fairfax himself. Henry Marten was readmitted to their ranks after his suspension for urging a republic. By the summer of 1647 he was still, in this respect, in a minority of one.

That attitudes towards a republic changed so radically over the next eighteen months was primarily due to the conduct of the King, who had been relocated with full retinue, in his old palace at Hampton Court, under relaxed surveillance after giving a solemn promise not to escape. Throughout the civil war and obsessively after it, Charles determined to restore his divinely bestowed privileges by force of arms. He cared little about the killing of his countrymen: their deaths were the tribute paid by his subjects towards the restoration of his former powers. He had no compunction about begging armed assistance from Ireland and France or committing the ultimate crime (in the eyes of his English subjects) of soliciting the Pope's support by promising to repeal anti-Catholic laws. (The Vatican in expectation did send a papal nuncio to Ireland, who stirred up plenty of trouble in the royalist interest and made secret treaties for 'home rule' under a Catholic lord lieutenant.) His tactic was to play for time and to play the factions off against each other until his supporters were ready to start a second war that would return him to power. The problem for Charles was that none of this secret scheming remained secret for long. His letters were often intercepted on the high seas or found in captured baggage trains or besieged castles.

The most crucial development in 1647 was the politicisation of the New Model Army, as a result of shabby treatment by the Parliament and the consequent receptiveness by its ranks to Leveller ideas. Denzil Holles led the rigid Presbyterian majority in the House of Commons: they showed no gratitude to the veterans, proposing to cut the pay they were owed before they disbanded. In March, Fairfax forwarded a petition from officers and soldiers asking only for fair treatment in terms of pay and conditions: the MPs' response, at a late night sitting, was to deplore their temerity and warn the war heroes that if they persisted they would be treated as 'enemies of the state and disturbers of the public peace'. This 'Declaration of Dislike' was a graceless and provocative act, as John Cooke was among the first to point out:

> That such gallant men, who have kept some of the chief contrivers' heads on their shoulders, for a humble petition presented to their noble General (which all soldiers by the law of armies may do) should be voted enemies and disturbers for that which since has been acknowledged to be but just, was the most monstrous ingratitude that ever was

heard of under the sun since the first moment of its creation . . . But whom God will destroy for their great provocations, he first makes demented . . .[11]

Cooke had read his Shakespeare – Holles was mad as Lear. Cooke dubbed him the 'chief incendiary' because he had persuaded the Commons, against Cromwell's opposition, to order the public hangman to burn copies of a Leveller petition. Cooke reported that 'many honest people are much troubled at the burning of this petition which was lately presented to the honourable House; what greater mischief can befall a people in time of Parliament, than that those who have ventured their lives for the Petition of Right, should be denied the liberty of petition?' Although much latitude must be allowed to governments acting for the public good, Cooke warned that some commonwealth men were becoming 'private wealthsmen' and 'turning the edge of the axe of power against the people who put it into their hands'. It must have been in this period that Cooke was briefed to advise the army as an advocate-general at courts martial: his writing begins to show a familiarity with its operations.

Fairfax held a council with his senior officers at Saffron Walden in May, which decided to summon a 'general rendezvous' of the whole army, in defiance of Parliament. Cooke's description of their meeting explains what drove these Christian soldiers onwards: they fasted, then led by Fairfax

lay grovelling upon their knees and pouring forth fervent prayers . . . when they rose to eat, their countenance was no longer sad. The Lord had, by the powerful influence of his good spirit, given a sweet return for their prayers. The horse and foot met with such general rejoicing and such a unanimous resolution to live and die together, for the just rights of King and people, that it is most admirable to consider that money, which is the lode-stone that draws the iron hearts of most soldiers, is no more reckoned by them than dirt in comparison to just liberties. I am confident that they which kick their heels against this army will in the end break their necks.[12]

The massed ranks of the New Model Army cheered Fairfax and made a solemn engagement that they would not suffer themselves to be disbanded until their just grievances were met. As if to live up to Cooke's expectations, they issued a declaration by which they vowed:

> that we were not a mere mercenary army, hired to serve any arbitrary power of state, but called forth and conjured by the several declarations of Parliament to the defence of our own and the people's just rights and liberties.

Out of this assembly came the blueprint for a General Council comprising the most senior officers and an elected representative of each regiment: this General Council would determine the political direction of the army, and in due course of the state. Its first business was to settle the 'Heads of Proposals' that Ireton personally put to the King: the very fact that they were more emollient than Parliament's 'Newcastle Propositions' was misinterpreted by Charles as a sign of weakness. He temporised, as usual, duchessing the army leaders whilst waiting for his two great enemies to fall out. This they proceeded to do – the army wanted to impeach Holles and ten other 'incendiary' Presbyterian MPs who had been instrumental in the 'Declaration of Dislike'; they in turn rallied the London mob which staged a violent peace demonstration against the 'war party' of independent MPs, who thereupon left the city (taking the mace with them) to seek the protection of Fairfax. The army marched apprehensively into London in August, but all seemed well: there was a fine show of trumpeting and drumming and the public turned out proudly for the parade. Their huzzahs augured well for John Cooke's latest work, published that month: *A Union of Hearts between the King's most Excellent Majesty, the Right Honourable Lords and Commons in Parliament, His Excellency Sir Thomas Fairfax and the army under his command; the assembly and every honest man that desires a sound and durable peace, accompanied with speedy justice and piety*. King and Parliament, army and people: four estates that needed reminding, in what little space was left on the cover, that '*The falling out of lovers is the renewing of love*'. The problem was that the King had never been in love with his Parliament or its army or with his people and the consequence was not yet apparent to Cooke (or to anyone else). His new work attempted to find a basis for rapprochement with the King, but his argument came very close to justifying a republic, where rulers could be put on trial for murder or for maladministration.

'I know very few who have gained anything by publishing, besides their own contentment', Cooke began, with reference to 'hard censures' earned from fellow lawyers for the *Vindication*. None the less, he volunteered some basic propositions:

1. that all men are born free;
2. that nature gives talents unequally – some are gifted to command and others to obey, since 'wise men should govern the ignorant';
3. that all just authority comes from God, who filters it through the people by making their consent necessary for monarchical (or any other) government. God dislikes 'tyrants' – viz, kings with unlimited power. People should free themselves from tyranny if and when they can;
4. that no government is approved by God unless it is just and rational. It cannot be rational to obey one man in all things 'for wise men are but men';
5. that tyrants may act oppressively by maladministration as well as by conquest. The English people, long before the Norman Conquest, *voluntarily* submitted to monarchy, by consenting to a contract which bound the monarch to call parliaments to make new laws. To these laws the King was not obliged to consent, but if his continued refusal would endanger the people, Parliament was entitled to bring the law into operation notwithstanding.

Cooke accepted that there were opinions by judges to the contrary, but

By whom were they made judges? By the King. How came they by their places? The echo [rumour] is: they bought them . . . all judicial places were bought and sold, as horses in Smithfield; one thousand pounds for a chief justice's place – and for how long to continue? During the King's pleasure. Was it safe for such judges to argue for the liberty of the subject against the King's prerogative . . . ?[13]

Why, Cooke asks, should any more value be put on opinions by these corrupt judges than on decisions by the bishops – were they not both the King's creatures? Take the legal maxim that the King can do no wrong: 'Therefore if he kill or rape it is neither murder nor felony. I say it is against reason and therefore against law: for if the King may kill one man he may kill a hundred and what courtier dare give any faithful advice, when the

98

King may without control kill him or strangle him and not be guilty of blood?'[14] Sovereign immunity offended 'right reason' – the internal logic of the law which the King's judges wilfully ignored in the ship-money case and the *Five Knights'* case: 'how many gallant worthies have they suffered to die in prison when they might have been set at liberty by habeas corpus?'[15]

For all his talk of a renewal of love and a union of hearts, what really emerges is Cooke's bitterness towards the 'rigid Presbyterians', representatives of the war profiteers, who wanted to impose their own narrow religious orthodoxy. His about-face, from the effusive comradeship he offered just six months before, demonstrated how the 'Declaration of Dislike' had soured relationships: to Puritans, the army appeared the last safeguard of religious liberty. Cooke, imagining himself speech-writer to Jesus, prepared an urgent address to the army:

Your work is not yet done. You must stand up for the liberties of your brethren. You must stand upon the gap for me, who alone trod the wine press of my father's wrath for you. Why have I empowered you, but to purchase liberty for my people?

The army commanders continued their negotiations with the King, because he was the only card that could trump the demand of Presbyterian MPs for a compulsory Covenant. But they reckoned without the hostility from their ranks at their dealing at all with the man against whom they had fought for four long and bloody years. Leveller propagandists persuaded the common soldiers that their leaders were bent on appeasing this 'man of blood'. Cooke was Lilburne's counsel, and the Levellers respected his radical intellect, although his writing was often dense and legalistic, relieved by bad puns. The Leveller leaders, by contrast, were outstanding polemicists and neat phrasemakers: *The Agreement of the People*, which they presented to the General Council of the army in October, was a simple and moving document, calling for a new and representative Parliament, elected biannually, for religious toleration and an end to discrimination on grounds of 'tenure, estate, charter, degree, birth or place'. It bemoaned the 'woeful experience' of being 'made to depend for the settlement for our peace and freedom upon him that intended our bondage and brought a cruel war upon us'.[16]

Cromwell and Ireton joined in public debate with their Leveller-inspired critics at a church in Putney over the first week in November 1647. Here, with prayers and passion, the case for liberty and for its limits was memorably stated. The key exchanges were between the cautious Henry Ireton, who feared that universal suffrage would lead to the destruction of private property, and Colonel Thomas Rainborough, who famously extemporised the case for democracy:

> I think that the poorest he that is in England hath a life to live, as the greatest he; the poorest man in England is not at all bound in a strict sense to that government that he hath not had a voice to put himself under . . . Every man born in England cannot, ought not, neither by the law of God nor the law of nature, to be exempted from the choice of those who are to make laws for him to live under, and for aught I know to lose his life under.

When Ireton insisted that universal suffrage would give the vote to persons with no stake at all in the kingdom, Rainborough responded with the question that Cooke had asked in *Union of Hearts*:

> I would fain know what the soldier hath fought for all this while? Hath he fought to enslave himself, to give power to men of riches, men of estates, to make him a perpetual slave?

The upshot of these debates was agreement that the vote should be accorded to all except beggars, servants and women (the poorest she in England would not be enfranchised). The King became the subject of discussion so heated that official note-taking was stopped. Harrison called him a 'man of blood' who should be prosecuted, and Cromwell agreed that he was a danger to national security, but he reminded them of how David could not punish Joab for murder because his brothers were powers in the land and the 'sons of Zeruih were too hard for him'.[17] This was Cromwell's favourite biblical precedent for temporising, but the patience of the army – officers and soldiers alike – was running out. Why, if God had meant us to negotiate with the King, was he proving so stubborn? It was a good question and became even better after 11 November, when Charles broke his solemn undertaking not to escape from Hampton Court. He sneaked out through a secret passage and headed south, to the coast.

The King's escape was an act of calculating confidence. Since his surrender he had never ceased to be 'the King'. His enemies might have won the war but they still, and desperately, needed his agreement to the terms upon which he should be reinstated. They wanted him to turn into some kind of constitutional monarch, deprived of control of the army, forced to share policy with Parliament, and to make a religious settlement which would entrench Calvinism but (if the Independents had their way) with a degree of toleration. At Hampton Court, Charles had held court to factional leaders, receiving in turn Cromwell and Ireton, then Holles and other leaders of the Presbyterian majority, and then the Scottish commissioners with whom he really did want to deal. Their countrymen could not forgive the English for failing to deliver on Pym's promise to accept the Solemn League and Covenant, and were furious at the blasphemous sects which were fermenting in London under the protection of the Independents. Before his flight, Charles had secured in principle their promise to invade England on his behalf: that he headed south rather than north to the border evinced his wish to avoid being in their custody again as well as in their debt. He wanted to place himself where he could rally his foreign and English supporters for a second civil war.

That was not what Charles told the good folk of Newport when, through the bungling of his courtiers, he ended up detained by Cromwell's cousin in Carisbrooke Castle, instead of reaching Jersey or a fall-back base in France. He had come to the Isle of Wight, he announced, through fear of 'a people called "levellers" . . . desiring to be somewhat secure till some happy accommodation may be made between me and my Parliament, I have put myself in this place, for I desire not a drop more of Christian blood should be spilt'.[18] This was colossally hypocritical, even for Charles, who was about to spill another ocean of Christian blood to avoid any accommodation with his Parliament. Leveller voices in the army council had not demanded his execution, and Cromwell was famously insisting that the army must cling to constitutional authority: 'If it be but a hare swimming over the Thames, I will take hold of it rather than let it go.'[19]

For this purpose, reckless radicals had to be jettisoned. At a dramatic army 'rendezvous' at Cork-Bush field, Fairfax eloquently rallied the troops while Cromwell tore up copies of the Leveller 'Agreement of the People' that some wore in their hats. Cork-Bush field effectively ended Leveller prospects of a solid power base in the New Model Army, although their ideas were to remain influential and Lilburne, their leader, was yet to have his finest hour.

Charles's dishonourable escape had finally convinced the army leaders that he could never be trusted, especially after they intercepted his letters explaining to Henrietta Maria that he would not keep any agreements he might make with the army or with Parliament once 'he had power enough to break them'.[20] Charles implacably opposed the abolition of bishops and would insist upon his right to control the army and upon a blanket amnesty – an Act of Oblivion for all his cavaliers accused of war crimes. These were all sticking points: the Houses of Parliament prepared four bills that retrospectively authorised all acts of the Parliament during the civil war, deprived the King of his prerogative to create peerages, placed the army under parliamentary control for twenty years and refused amnesty to the main cavalier commanders, subject to an undertaking to execute no more than seven of them.[21] On 28 December the King sent back from Carisbrooke a robust refusal to sign the four bills, although he still claimed to be committed to a peace treaty which would put his subjects out of their miseries. This response was another marvel of hypocrisy: two days before, Charles had pledged to increase their miseries, by a commitment not to peace, but to a new war. In utmost secrecy, he had reached an 'engagement' with the Scots commissioners that their army would invade England, destroy Fairfax and Cromwell and restore him to power. Once the Scots had mobilised a force under the Duke of Hamilton, and when the King gave the signal, the second civil war would begin.

6

The Poor Man's Case

While the King was plotting to restore his absolute rule over his English subjects at the point of Scottish swords, John Cooke was working out how Parliament might win public support by a new programme of social legislation. The problem that he feared would undo any constitutional settlement with the King was the sudden and alarming increase in the numbers of the poor, in the aftermath of war and a succession of bad harvests. The price of corn in 1648 reached a new high, and wheat averaged 85 shillings per quarter: since a labourer's wage was but 8p a day, hunger gripped the working classes.[1] For all Cooke's increasing legal engagements, he could not remain silent. He had gone back to Leicestershire at Christmas to question the husbandmen and farm labourers he had known in his youth: they told him it was impossible to supply barley and hops in sufficient quantities for the bread and small beer necessary for the townships. He found out about profiteers, who had driven up the price of bread in this 'dear year' by hoarding grain. The war had loosened the paternalistic hold over local communities of country squire and Justice of the Peace: one result had been an explosion in the number of unlicensed alehouses. Drunkards were prone to gamble away the rest of their money, leaving wives and children famished in turn. Cooke realised the danger that the poor might follow the beat of the King's drum and drunkards might cry down the new establishment. In February 1648, he published a passionate plea for social justice, as a means of staving off a new civil war.

The Poor Man's Case begged Parliament to pass an 'angelical ordinance' to lower the price of corn, provide for the proper licensing of taverns, reform drunkards and punish food profiteers. This book, written in an urgent, breathless prose, is a fascinating mix of sociological research, political diatribe and ideas for legal reform, introduced by a philosophical (or at least biblical) commitment to serve the down-trodden. It is difficult to categorise the work – think of some seventeenth-century Michael Moore, citing Deuteronomy. Cooke believed that poverty was an evil allowed by God in order that the rich might have occasion to do good. It followed that doctors should treat poor people free of charge, under a form of national health service, and lawyers should donate one tenth of their time to work *pro bono*: the first time anyone had suggested a system of legal aid. The money for poor relief should come from forfeitures of the ill-gotten gains or goods of criminals, and from a tax on money won at cards (unlike other Puritans, Cooke did not want gambling prohibited – he saw the value in putting its proceeds to better use, as in a national lottery). Royalties from mines and minerals, and all lost property, should go to the poor and not to the King. Drunkards would be forgiven twice, and helped on each occasion towards sobriety, but treated harshly if they were to prove incorrigible. Hoarders and profiteers would be severely punished. In order to set an example of stringency in a time of crisis, Cooke urged his readers to give up drinking toasts – even to the success of the army – and to forbear from purchasing expensive mourning clothes for attendance at funerals.

Suffusing *The Poor Man's Case* is a new concept of the good neighbour – the 'good Commonwealthsman', not merely charitable to the poor but also considerate in business, acknowledging a duty to avoid consequences harmful to consumers or to society, notwithstanding that the business was lawful and profitable. Brewing strong beer was a topical example: it was 'like putting a sword in the hands of a madman'. (Cooke reflected, sadly, that 'Protestants are generally greater drunkards than papists, who are far more libidinous and unchaste'.) It was no sin, in Cooke's book, to make a reasonable profit: his condemnation was reserved for the hoarder and profiteer, 'caterpillars of the Commonwealth'. He argued, importantly, that in sale of goods the Roman law of '*caveat emptor*' (buyer beware) was unsatisfactory: contracts should be avoidable if there was a hidden defect in the product. (Such unfair contracts could be set aside in courts of equity, but not in courts of law, hence Cooke's obsessive crusade to fuse, or combine, law and equity in one court). The alehouses, where strong beer was sold and youth corrupted, should be closed down, and replaced by licensed taverns where landlords might be made responsible for the loss caused by any customer who became tipsy: moral responsibility entailed legal liability. Cooke was for moderation in all things rather than prohibition: a little wine might be healthy, and ale washed down bread, but strong beer conduced to drunkenness; even "that witch, tobacco" might be used "moderately and unlustfully". Cooke was arguing for the opportunity to lead a well-ordered, well-governed life in a well-ordered, well-governed commonwealth, in which law would set the limits to men's earnings so that they would not obsess about money: any wealth which exceeded a reasonable limit would go to the poor.[2]

In Cooke's writings, we get the first sense that petty crime might be the product of social conditions – poverty, drink and famine. He was certainly the first to invoke international standards to condemn penal justice in England, even to require its reform. The conditions of London's prisons shamed the government and the city 'who must answer for the blood of every man that is famished in prison for want of bread, be his offence what it will, for by the law of nations no offender may be poisoned or famished to death, it being abhorred by the law of nature'.[3] England had the most barbaric prisons in the world: the Turks might beat their galley slaves but 'we cast men into a dungeon and suffer them to rot and famish – the most cruel and painful of all deaths'.[4] In an age when theft above a shilling was punished on the gallows, Cooke's lone voice argued for a defence of necessity to acquit a starving man of the charge of stealing bread from a baker or for stealing sheep from a rich man who owns a flock.[5]

Undeserved poverty moved Cooke more than any other contemporary evil: the cries of beggars for bread; the prisoners cast down the hole because they could not pay twopence for their lodging; the starving wife of a man made bankrupt by a vicious creditor; debtors given no time to pay but arrested and kept in prison without bail. These were common spectacles at the time and aroused no public concern: to Cooke they were cruelty and a denial of Christ's example. He referred constantly to Matthew 18 (the parable of the compassionate lord who gave his servant time to pay a debt, only to despair when the servant then cast his own debtor into prison). He urged reform of prisons: improvement in nutrition; a minister in every gaol; weekend release so prisoners could attend Sunday sermons as well as see their families. There was a crying need to provide more poor relief to make begging unnecessary in London: the money 'spent in pageant-like vanities on a Lord Mayor's day would have fed all the mendicant poor about the city'.[6]

Although it would be anachronistic to label Cooke a criminologist, there is real awareness in his writings of the social consequences of deprivation and of the connection between poverty and lawlessness. His analysis preceded by several years that of Gerald Winstanley, founder of the communal 'Diggers' movement, who argued that the temptation of private property was the cause of theft. Cooke concentrated on the effects of the 1647 famine on the behaviour of heads of poor households, who turned to crime in desperation to provide for starving children. He had ridden into the country to investigate their plight and was a familiar visitor to poor tenements and the plague-ridden narrow lanes of London. He was the first to argue that motivation for crime should be taken into account in sentencing and that poverty as a cause of crime should be a powerful mitigation. Judges should refrain from sentencing to death those who rustled sheep or cattle from wealthy estates 'and enquire whether the prisoner was not necessitated to do it, to buy bread for his family or milk and clothes for his poor wife and children'. The judicial enquiry should be whether the prisoner stole 'for want or for wantonness'; if the former, he should be given a second chance and only proceeded against if further thieving demonstrated incorrigibility. At a time when desperate men saw the logic in hanging for a sheep rather than a lamb, Cooke was almost alone in demanding the introduction of mercy into penal law.

The Poor Man's Case maintained Cooke's rage against the profession of medicine, by reference to the case of William Trigg, whom he had been called upon to defend yet again in 1647. Never before had a barrister written for publication about a cause in which he was still acting for a client: Cooke pointed out that he was not taking any fee and 'I know no hurt in it, but so far as it concerns the poor this hard year, I would not gladly omit anything for their advantage: extraordinary diseases must have extraordinary cures'. Bar associations throughout the world still try to stop members writing about their cases, but at a time when barristers were making their professional rules as they went along, this was a reasonable position: Trigg's case was not before a jury so Cooke's writings could not prejudice a trial, and they provided an informative counter-blast to a powerful professional monopoly, which was prosecuting apothecaries and herbalists for using traditional cures which worked much more often than the bloodletting and purging prescribed for 'humours' of the body by physicians who followed the ancient and erroneous Galenic system.

Besides, he was able to generalise from what he had learnt in defending Trigg: that the medical profession was just as covetous and selfish and lacking in courage as the legal profession, albeit by no means as numerous – especially at times of plague, when they were really needed. In order to afford their country estates, city doctors charged heavily for visits ('People in London would rather die than see an apothecary's bill,' said Cooke sarcastically) and they refused to visit the poor. Cooke's proposed reforms were breathtaking in their prescience: he called for something akin to a National Health Service, in which doctors would be assigned free of charge to poor patients. Monopoly licensing by the college should be ended, so as to increase the supply of doctors amongst the City poor. Use of Latin to label apothecaries' bottles must stop: the purchaser must know what he buys and a public health campaign should inform the public about the most tried and trusted herbal medicines and how to make them without having to go to a doctor for a prescription.[7]

In urging such reforms, Cooke was turning his sardonic, rationalising eye on a profession not far removed from quackery. Medical science was hit or miss, but legal science was well developed – already the common law had too many precedents, and publication of Coke's *Institutes* provided more fodder for expensive argument. In *The Poor Man's Case*, Cooke returned once again to the theme of the *Vindication*: high-profile practice now gave him the confidence to advance a more radical prescription for his own covetous colleagues and especially for 'the great practitioners' – the sergeants and barrister 'favourites'. They should donate 10 per cent of their earnings to the poor or else should act *pro bono* in that percentage of their cases. In a passionate appeal to 'all ye who live by the law, whom I may without presumption call brothers' he observed how all the jeremiads rolling off the presses made use of that 'scriptuary weapon' from St Luke, 'Woe unto you, lawyers', and he warned:

All this smoke is not without some fire. He that knows anything about politics may easily foresee there is a great storm gathering in the Kingdom against us lawyers. The only way to prevent it is to keep hold of the principles of right reason and to dispatch poor men's causes free of charge this hard year. In doubtful matters let us dissuade our clients from going to law, and tell them the danger of it, advise them to do as they would be done unto. Let us contend earnestly for the truth rather than for victory. As soon as we discover the cause is unjust let us drop it and advise our clients to make their peace. Let us never utter in court a word we believe untrue. If clients tell us they have no money, let us act for them for their thanks. Then, I warrant you, we will be Parliament-proof and Kingdom-proof: the people will quickly recognise our usefulness, and an honest lawyer will be a necessary member of the Kingdom and the wisdom of the common law will be admired and honoured. But if we make disquiet and trouble for the poor, then believe me the Kingdom will be as weary of us as they ever were of bishops or arbitrary courts.[8]

John Cooke's 'dear father', Isaac, had come to stay with him at Gray's Inn, following John around the courts and criticising the delays and injustices that he witnessed.[9] His dear father was not the only critic – his 'dear friend' Hugh Peters, by now a power in the land as Cromwell's favourite preacher, had turned his righteous rhetoric against the lawyers, and the two friends would meet and dispute long into the night, with Isaac often taking the clergyman's side. Litigants should plead for themselves, argued Peters: in Holland, where lawyers were few, 'You may get justice as often and as naturally as their cows give milk'.[10] Cooke tried to disabuse him of the jejune notion that justice could ever flow so naturally. Peters was all for denuding barristers of their gowns – attachment to which was a mark of the public's enslavement to their monopoly. Cooke replied: 'Were I convinced that my wearing of a gown at Westminster tended to countenance in the least measure the slavery of this nation, I would hang it up in Long Lane and burn all my books but the Bible.'

These differences did not affect their relationship. Cooke admired Peters for his public service and was happy to brief this influential reformer in an effort to make his criticisms more informed, believing, quite correctly, that lawyers would not reform themselves until forced to do so by public clamour or by Parliament. Cooke insisted that he was for 'reformation, not extirpation' and he practised what he preached, announcing publicly that 'for my own part, if any man wants any assistance, I shall freely give him my best advice as cordially without a fee as with it'. He became a one-man legal aid clinic, the first in Britain. But the criticisms from his colleagues weighed him down: 'I must either quit the profession or answer every objection that is made against it' was his response. Since 'justice is as necessary as the sun in the firmament' and there can be no laws without lawyers to explain their clients' rights, then the profession was necessary to the peace of what he still described without irony as 'the Kingdom'. But this was 1648 and Cooke detected trouble ahead: 'All the malignant blood is not as yet drawn out of the Kingdom, there are those that are negotiating to engage us in a second and more bloody and destructive war.' There were indeed, and the chief of these negotiators was the King himself, the 'Man of Blood' obsessed with spilling more of it to regain his own bloodline's supremacy over Parliament.

7

Malignant Blood

The secret 'engagement' between Charles and the Scots commissioners had been wrapped in lead and buried in the yard of Carisbrooke Castle. By the terms of their treaty, the Scots agreed 'to hazard our lives and fortunes' by invading England to restore Charles 'to his government, to the just rights of the Crown and his full revenues' in return for his undertaking to confirm the solemn League and Covenant (subject to an accommodation with the Church of England and its bishops) and to suppress 'the opinions and practices of Anti-Trinitarians, Anabaptists, Antinomians, Arminians, Familists, Brownists, Separatists, Independents, Libertines and Seekers' and, generally, 'all blasphemies, heresy, schism and all such scandalous doctrines and practices as are contrary to the light of nature or to the known principles of Christianity'. In other words, the Scots 'engaged' to fight for the King, to restore his prerogative rights to control the army, select ministers, appoint bishops, bestow honours and to maintain a 'negative voice' (the royal veto over any parliamentary legislation), in return merely for Charles's promise to advance the Covenant and to suppress some minor sects whose behaviour outraged their Calvinist sensibilities. All they asked in addition was to recoup the sum of £200,000 which Parliament still owed them for handing over the King after the first civil war – and Charles cheerfully assented to back-payment of his own ransom.

So the King had once again declared war, silently but irrevocably, on 'his' people and 'his' Parliament. On the day that he rejected the four bills he arranged to leave the Isle of Wight on a ship that might have taken him to Scotland or to France – had an ill wind not blown for several days, by which time orders had arrived from Parliament to keep him under closer guard. Its debates in the early days of 1648 showed how the wind had changed in Westminster as well: for the first time, MPs discussed the possibility of impeaching the King, although as a means of deposing rather than decapitating him. In January, even before the 'Engagement' became public knowledge, the House of Commons debated again the 'Vote of No Addresses', which had been so soundly defeated the previous year: this time it passed, with Cromwell as its main protagonist.

The 'Vote of No Addresses', by which it was determined to break off negotiations with the King, was intended as a rebuke for his high-handed dismissal of the four bills. This occasion marks the emergence of a small group of Independents who can be considered as embryonic republicans – 'commonwealthsmen' – although they had as yet no intention of bringing the King to trial. None the less, to the 'Vote of No Addresses' they attached a Declaration which had the makings of an arraignment, in its call for a requital of 'the sighs and groans, the tears and crying blood (an heavy cry!) the blood of fathers, brothers and children at once, the blood of many hundred thousand free-born subjects in three great kingdoms'.[1] It recited seven attempts to have Charles agree propositions and his seven rebuttals, together with evidence of double-dealing from his intercepted correspondence.

Having established his intractability and insincerity, the Declaration republished Parliament's charge against the Duke of Buckingham in 1626 over his alleged responsibility for King James's death, and alleged that Charles had deliberately frustrated their inquiry. Then followed, in tumbling succession, an indictment of his entire reign: the loss of La Rochelle and the betrayal of the Protestant cause in France; the ship-money oppression and the scandalous sale of monopolies; the prorogation of Parliament and arbitrary personal rule; the whippings and nose-slittings, the brandings and de-earings of the godly ministers; the aggressive war against the Scots; the Queen's cultivation of popery; the King's support for a plot with loyalist officers to free Strafford and bring in the Irish Catholic army (confirmed by the letters captured at Naseby); his attempt to arrest Pym and the other MPs in Parliament; the various attempts (proved by correspondence seized from Lord Digby) to raise troops from Sweden, Denmark and Holland; the pawning of the crown jewels to purchase arms and ammunition; and then, of course, the raising of his standard against Parliament and his attempts to enlist foreign troops to fight his subjects in the civil war.

It was a monumental charge sheet, seasoned with sensational suspicions and weighted with references to documentary evidence from captured correspondence. The Declaration dropped the pretence that the King's misconduct had been caused by 'evil counsellors'. For the first time, evil was imputed not to counsellors but to the King himself. On 15 February 1648, Parliament ordered publication of the Declaration as 'some of the many reasons why we cannot repose any more trust in him'. It was not so much a case for no confidence as a case for the prosecution; soon, news of 'the Engagement' with the Scots would provide proof beyond reasonable doubt that this King was the enemy of his own people. Charles I's crime had been writ large in the Declaration: all that it lacked, since 'treason' was still considered by most lawyers as an offence committed against and not by the King, was a name. In less than a year, John Cooke would supply that name – he was to draw heavily upon the Declaration for his indictment of the King for the crime of tyranny.

The Poor Man's Case appeared at this time, envisioning a utopia in which laws were obeyed out of respect for a Parliament of commonwealthsmen. But that was not the Parliament of 1648. The bigoted Presbyterian majority had produced no popular leader: Denzil Holles and the ambitious lawyer Harbottle Grimstone were prominent but many of their followers wanted to make their fortune before negotiating an agreement with the King which would allow them to keep it. Most legislation derived from the fanatical mind of William Prynne, obsessed with a blasphemy ordinance that would put sectarians to death and with removing from the land all occasions for joy or high spirits. The theatres which had by 1643 become plague pits and for that reason been temporarily closed were now permanently shut by the Presbyterians, because they might spread pleasure. Maypoles were cut down, festival holidays were cancelled, even Christmas was abolished. It is little wonder that the opening shots of the second civil war in 1648 were fired not by royalists but by 'Christmas rioters' in Kent, protesting against the killjoy abolition of the festive season. They went on to form a battalion several thousand strong and to join with cavaliers who were regrouping in Essex.

The country was spotty with disaffection. Parliament was blamed for maintaining high taxes and the army was cursed as the cause and resented for the free board and accommodation required for its soldiers whenever they came to town. London was volatile and unpredictable: the city fathers and merchants would favour any settlement which would let them do their business uninterrupted, and they had thrived under the King's personal rule. The fruits of victory were turning sour: the prevalence on the streets of 'banned' royalist news-sheets, with their scandalous attacks on MPs and army officers, was symptomatic of the failure of Parliament to command loyalty or respect. A substantial part of the country had supported the King and would welcome him back, as would many of the older generation who yearned for Anglican worship and the guidance of prayer book and bishop. In March 1648 the anniversary of the King's coronation was widely celebrated: bonfires were lit on all roads into London and the King's health was jovially drunk in taverns throughout the land. Cooke's gloomy forebodings in the *Poor Man's Case* were coming true, just a month after its publication.

The view from Carisbrooke was roseate enough in March for Charles to decide it was time to escape. But under the wary eye of the castle governor, his attempts failed – on one occasion farcically, as he became stuck between the bars of his bedroom window. None the less, his long-term prospects of reinstatement were good: the Scots were mustering for invasion in the north, royalist diehards had come out fighting in Wales and a cavalier fleet led by his eighteen-year-old son Charles, the Prince of Wales, hovered off the east coast. MPs were on tenterhooks, and attempted to reassure the nation of their fealty: on 28 April they passed a motion promising that the House would 'not alter the fundamental government of the kingdom, by King, Lords and Commons'. The motion calculatingly omitted any reference to the only power in the land capable of governing – the New Model Army, led by Fairfax and dominated by Cromwell, although increasingly reflecting the political ideas of Henry Ireton.

The day after the MPs made this nervous promise, army officers gathered for a prolonged prayer meeting at Windsor Castle. They led a fighting machine that was leaner as a result of parliamentary parsimony and became meaner after the officers searched their souls before girding their loins. As they prayed and wept and begged the guidance of a God who was sending them back into battle, the realisation dawned that they had been guilty of Hamlet's sin of equivocation: the path laid open by the Lord after Naseby had not been taken. So they issued an ominous declaration that 'it was our duty, if ever the Lord brought us back again in peace, to call Charles Stuart, that man of blood, to an account for the blood he has shed and mischief he has done to his utmost, against the Lord's cause and people in these poor nations'.[2]

That was the mind-frame in which the men of the New Model Army set out to fight the second civil war. Fairfax took the eastern campaign, maintaining a controlling presence in London whilst fire-fighting in Kent and Essex and eventually corralling the King's troops at the siege of Colchester. Cromwell put down the insurrection in Wales and then marched north to face a vastly greater Scots army, swelled by cavalier veterans, which he met in battle at Preston. His 8,000 'ironsides' vanquished a force of 24,000 Scots and cavaliers under the inept command of the Duke of Hamilton. 'Surely Sir', Cromwell wrote to the Speaker of the House, William Lenthall, 'this is nothing but the hand of God.' It was not for him to tell Parliament what use to make of his victory, but of course he did: exalt God and 'not hate His people who are as the apple of His eye'. Be kind to Puritans, in other words, was Cromwell's victory message from the battlefield. But he added this warning to the parliamentary appeasers: 'That they that will not leave troubling the land may speedily be destroyed out of the land.' Since the main personage who would not leave troubling the land was Charles Stuart, it was obvious that Cromwell's patience had run out.[3]

A similar iron had entered into the allegedly gentle soul of General Fairfax: at Colchester, which fell to his siege in August, he had two leading cavaliers – Lucas and Lisle – court-martialled and shot. This was in accordance with the laws of war, since they had taken to arms in breach of the condition of the pardon they had received for fighting in the first civil war, but it became a symbol of a more momentous question – of whether the King, who had set them on and in whose name they had fought, should suffer a similar fate. Fairfax made at this point a significant decision: the superior lords captured at Colchester – Goring, Capel and Holland – were not summarily court-martialled, like the two officers under their command, but were detained for a potential treason prosecution. Their fate, bound up with that of the King, would be decided by Parliament. They were soon joined in prison by the Duke of Hamilton, captured in September by Cromwell.

But what, then, did Parliament do? Its officer MPs were still in the field, their lives for the last few months having been put at risk in battles fomented by the King from his 'captivity' in Carisbrooke. To their fury, the Presbyterian majority repealed the 'Vote of No Addresses' and appointed fifteen MPs as commissioners to negotiate a treaty with the King. It feared that the army, returning victorious with its MPs, would make common cause with the 'commonwealthsmen' – the Independents who formed a sizeable minority in the Commons and had the support of the Puritan peers. This coalition would insist on jettisoning the Solemn League and Covenant, which had been Pym's price for Scottish support back in 1644, and require toleration for all manner of blaspheming sects. A settlement with the King was the only power-play which could forestall this, although as army Independents like Ludlow immediately pointed out, Charles was incapable of agreeing to any alliance which did not restore his prerogatives and his bishops, so negotiation was futile. It was a measure of Presbyterian fear – and desperation – that they could even think that the King would accept their terms. But for the next two months, the commissioners talked with Charles in the town hall at Newport, whilst the temper of the army reached boiling-point.

Holles and Grimstone, the senior commissioners, began by prostrating themselves before Charles at a private audience and begged him to yield quickly to Parliament's demands that he become a constitutional monarch, before the army imposed a dictatorship upon them all.[4] The King was pleased to be told how much he was needed: as usual he temporised, and wrote secret letters telling supporters to disregard news of any concessions: he would make them as a means of buying time and would not be bound by them. His hopes of foreign support were buoyed, in mid-October, by the Treaty of Westphalia, the formal end of the Thirty Years War between the continental powers. Now, Henrietta Maria assured him, France would surely intervene on his side. Most heartening was the resurgence of royalist support in Ireland, where the Duke of Ormond had stitched together Catholics and Scots and some Presbyterian forces in a confederate army and was preparing to invade England to restore the King. Charles secretly encouraged Ormond and told him to ignore any treaty that might emerge from the Newport negotiations. But to the commissioners who reported back to Parliament on 1 December 1648, the King appeared to have conceded most of their demands: the sticking points remained, as ever, his refusal to countenance the abolition of bishops or prosecutions of his officers for war crimes.

Meanwhile, the army was taking some final decisions. Henry Ireton, whose regiment had been the first to demand justice on the King for the second war,[5] held discussions with Levellers and Independents at the Nag's Head tavern in central London. He drew up *The Remonstrance of the Army*, for discussion by its officers and men in the course of November. News from the north that the popular and valiant Colonel Rainborough, so prominent in the Putney debates, had been slain by marauding royalists, jolted them into a realisation that the time had finally come to admit the logical conclusion of the second civil war. The interests of justice and the interests of peace in the nation conjoined to demand that Charles Stuart be brought to trial.

The *Remonstrance* argued that it would be wrong to punish the Duke of Hamilton and the other royalist leaders, when 'the capital and grand author of our troubles' was accorded impunity.[6] The King was, demonstrably, incapable of keeping any bargains he made with Parliament: he would always be scheming to recover his lost prerogatives. Any settlement which accorded some power to the King would necessitate that the army be maintained at full strength to stop him seeking more power: the consequent tax burden would make the army and Parliament so unpopular that the public would welcome a return to personal rule. Putting the King on trial was the only course that was just, and it would also provide some measure of deterrence to future tyrants by showing that kings were not above the law. His older sons who had fought with him against Parliament, i.e. Charles, Prince of Wales, and James, Duke of York, should be sent into permanent exile.

The *Remonstrance* reads in places like John Cooke's pamphlets, and it is possible that the barrister had a hand in it, along with his friend Hugh Peters who was identified by royalist newsbooks as one of the authors. Its publication marked a new stage in the debate over the King – the emergence of the argument that justice, and not expediency, required his trial, both as retribution for the blood he was responsible for shedding and as a deterrent to future 'grand delinquents'. Where the *Remonstrance* was notably silent, however, was about the appropriate sentence. Should it be execution (as for traitors) or pardon followed by exile? More importantly, who (if anyone) should take his place as monarch? The document spoke of future kings, with powers strictly limited by a constitution which provided for 'sovereignty of the people': its framers were not prepared to argue the case for a republic, even as late as November 1648. One bright idea – of an *elected* monarchy – had emerged in the course of discussions at the Nag's Head tavern. No future king should reign 'but on the election of and as upon trust from the people'.

Another straw in the wind was the behaviour of Parliament's great lawyers – Whitelocke and Widdrington (the keepers of the great seal – in effect job-sharing Lord Chancellors), John Bradshawe (now Chief Justice of Wales), and its judges, Keble and Thorpe. They were elevated to the rank of sergeants at law on 20 November and appeared in ceremonial procession with 'quoits on their heads and woollen tippets around their bosoms . . . the people broke their hearts with laughing at the good old counsellors'. But it did not escape attention that the traditional climax of this ceremony, when each new Sergeant would dedicate a ring to his Majesty the King, was pointedly omitted.[7] The Levellers were perceptive and sarcastic journalists: they reported the real reason why barristers wanted to become Sergeants (and now, QCs): 'What was this, I pray you, but that they might have their fees doubled by any client?'[8] And they figured that Ireton spoke with Cromwell's voice. On hearing of the King's attempts to escape to join Ormonde, their *Monthly Mercury* for November advised him to try again:

> Oh Charles, Old Noll (thy terror) now draws nigh.
> If thou wilt save thy neck, make haste to fly.[9]

Cromwell all this time had been in the north, far from the army council encamped at St Albans or the smoke-filled rooms of the Nag's Head tavern. But he had been mulling over his philosophy: 'I desire from my heart – I have prayed for it – I have waited for the day to see union and right under-standing between the godly people – Scots, English, Jews, Gentiles, Presbyterians, Independents, Baptists and all.' He had been wrestling with his conscience by his usual convoluted method of 'waiting upon the Lord' (i.e. detecting the ways of God from hindsight). He wrote to Fairfax on 20 November that the men wanted impartial justice done upon offenders 'and I verily think and am persuaded they are things which God puts into our hearts'. The second war he thought a 'more prodigious treason' than the first because it both was a breach of faith and involved an invasion of England by 'foreigners' – i.e. the Scots (conveniently forgetting how Pym had been the first to invite them to invade). By the end of the month he signalled his support for the *Remonstrance*, and was referring to the King as 'this man against whom the Lord has witnessed'.[10]

In mid-November, news reached the Army Council from Holland that Prince Rupert had taken command of the royalist fleet – a signal that he would be back in action, probably in conjunction with Ormonde. The council adopted the *Remonstrance* and Fairfax, always instinctively loyal to consensus, forwarded it to Parliament. On 30 November he prepared for a march on London with an army which announced itself 'full of sad apprehension concerning the danger and evil of the treaty with the King, or any accommodation with the King'. Intercepted messages indicated that Charles was preparing to escape and join with Rupert, so Fairfax on 1 December ordered the removal of the King from Carisbrooke to Hurst Castle, one of Henry VIII's coastal forts, on a windswept mainland promontory from which escape was impossible. On 4 December the Presbyterian majority in Parliament decided upon a showdown with the army: it rejected the *Remonstrance*, declared the King's removal to Hurst had been 'without the advice or consent of the House', and ordered Fairfax to keep his regiments outside London. Fairfax ignored the direction and marched into the city, setting up his headquarters at Whitehall. The climax seemed only to await the arrival of Cromwell, dawdling his way down from the north.[11]

Late into the evening of 5 December the Commons debated the King's responses from Newport, and resolved by 129 to 83 that 'his majesty's concessions are sufficient grounds to proceed upon for the settlement of the peace of the kingdom'.[12] This decision in principle that the King's position could form the basis for a treaty was the last straw for the Independents and the army who believed (with good reason) that further dealings with the King would mean a third civil war. Ireton wanted simply to dissolve this pigheaded Presbyterian Parliament, but the Independent MPs were concerned that fresh elections could backfire by returning the King's supporters. Moreover, unless the King were tried quickly he might not be tried at all. So the next morning, 6 December, Colonel Pride marched a troop detachment to Westminster Hall and stationed them around the entrance to the House of Commons. He stood at the door, consulting a list of names of the MPs who had voted to support negotiations with the King. An independent MP – Lord Grey of Groby – was at Pride's elbow, putting the names to faces of these MPs, who were refused entry.

It was a very English coup – some forty of the excluded MPs were first taken to a cellar full of court records, a hot and musty hole known as 'Hell' and then put under 'tavern arrest' at two hostelries in the Strand. But what must have looked like a *coup d'théâtre* had the momentous consequence of a *coup d'état*. That afternoon, Oliver Cromwell rode into London evincing (or affecting) surprise, saying later that 'since it was done he was glad of it, and would endeavour to maintain it'.[13]

There is no doubt that the purge was approved by Fairfax, the army commander, whose headquarters were, quite literally, across the street. He was always practical and decisive. He had given the order to move the King to Hurst Castle and now he acted again with a simple determination to protect the national interest by sending Colonel Pride to exclude MPs who had not learnt the lesson of dealing with Charles, namely that no deal would stick. On 6 December the secluded MPs were told by Fairfax's messenger, Colonel Axtell, that they were being kept in custody 'by special order from the General and council of the Army'.[14]

'Pride's Purge' cleared the parliamentary deck for disposing of the King without further negotiation. Ireton and army MPs like Ludlow were convinced that a trial was the only way forward. But as every Royalist news-sheet was saying, a trial would only take place once the necessity for it had taken hold in the quirky and fatalistic mind of Ireton's father-in-law, who arrived so fortuitously in London just a few hours after Colonel Pride had secured an Independent majority for a Parliament quickly dubbed, and always remembered, as 'the Rump'.

Part II

Republic

8

To Clutch the Swimming Hare

There was no available blueprint for the trial of Charles I. There were many precedents for treason trials, of course, ever since the Treason Act of 1351: they had this in common, that they always ended quickly, usually with 'guilty' verdicts, followed by sentences of death by beheading for aristocrats, or by disembowelling for common traitors.[1] Trials of commoners were held in public before hand-picked juries, while those of royal status, like Mary Queen of Scots and Anne Boleyn, could be convicted in private by the monarch's own privy council. But the trial of the monarch was a constitutional conundrum. In the first place, there was no court that could try a king: the Star Chamber had been abolished, and there were no privy councillors. The 'Bill of Attainder' procedure used against Strafford and Laud depended crucially on members of the House of Lords sitting as judges – and the dozen or so nobles left in the House were opposed to any trial of the monarch. Then came the legal problems, of how to turn on its head the common law proposition that *Rex* is *lex* and justify a criminal proceeding, *Rex v. Rex*. The King was above the law, and besides, Magna Carta vouchsafed him the right to trial by his peers, but – Catch 22 – a king could not, by definition, have any peers. Credible solutions to these paradoxes had to be found and quickly, if the King was to be put on trial at all.

There had been no serious thought to call the King to account until November 1648. The first demands for his trial, made by Colonel Harrison at the Putney debates and by isolated voices thereafter, had been based on the Old Testament *lex talionis*: retribution for the blood he had shed, by the shedding of his blood. At Putney, Harrison had been answered by Cromwell, another self-made biblical scholar, by reference to 'the sons of Zeruiah' and the analogy was not lost on these bibliophile soldiers: the time was not yet ripe to bring Charles to justice. Over the ensuing twelve months, Cromwell's belief in providence gradually persuaded him that the time was ripening – God-given victories in the second civil war revealed His will that the King, that 'obstinate man whose heart God had hardened', must have his sins requited on earth, as well as in the hereafter. Puritans fervently believed that victory proved that God was on their side – as Cooke wrote in awe, of the defeats suffered by the battle-hardened cavaliers,

> how many veteran commanders, famous in feats of chivalry, have been foiled, broken in pieces, and beaten at their own weapons by a few gentlemen and juvenile mechanics and honest tradesmen, whose hearts the Lord hath drawn forth and engaged to fight his battles; we must needs acknowledge that their valour, prowess and dexterity has either been infused by God, or improved by Him to miraculous proficiency.[2]

In the discussions over the fate of the King, there may be discerned several ideological supports for the 'rightness' of a trial. The most straightforward was retribution for the two civil wars – the latter being the more blame-worthy, since it had been instigated under the deceptive cover of peace nego-tiations and had involved invasion by the Scots. The soldiers' cry for justice on the 'man of blood' had a respectable pedigree not only in biblical blood-guilt, but in the common law of incitement to murder: Charles had given the orders and had been present at many of the battles, egging his men on to kill and to pillage. By alliances with the Scots and the Irish, and with continental supporters rallied by his Queen, he had conspired to achieve the restoration of all his prerogatives, foreseeing widespread death and destruc-tion of parliamentary forces and his own troops. English criminal law was based on the notion of individual responsibility and Charles Stuart was the individual who was most responsible.

Why then should he be exempted from a trial for killing tens of thou-sands in a war of his own making? The doctrine that the King was above the law had been unacceptable when applied by the judges to uphold the ship-money tax, and the decision had been reversed by Parliament. By the same token, kings should not be above the criminal law – even the law of treason, if they so betrayed their trust as to invade their own kingdom.

There was a further reason for a trial – to deter future monarchs from seeking to introduce 'arbitrary and tyrannical government' by ruling without Parliament and by taking up arms against the people. The trial of Charles Stuart would be a warning to his successors: after conviction, he could be humbled and pardoned, and either allowed to continue as a broken man and a limited monarch, or else forced to abdicate – his heirs would rule under a constitutional settlement of the army's making. None of these rationales implied the extinction of hereditary monarchy – quite the contrary.

Logic is rarely permitted to determine history. As late as December 1648, the idea of an English republic had no intellectual progenitor and no contemporary political advocate.[3] The Levellers, for all their democratic ideals and early rhetoric in favour of putting the King on trial, fell strangely silent at this climactic moment. ('Freeborn John' was seized with a sudden desire for wealth: he left London to claim forfeited royalist estates in the north.) Some independent MPs, like Henry Marten and Arthur Haselrig, saw nothing but disaster in hereditary monarchy if the Stuarts were the heirs. But constitutional theorists, such as they were, favoured a monarchy limited by removing the King's 'negative voice' and not the King himself. In practice, this would mean post-conviction elimination of Charles followed by banishment of his eldest belligerent son, the Prince of Wales. The Crown would then descend to his second son, James, Duke of York, or preferably to the untainted and malleable youngest son, eight-year-old Henry Stuart, Duke of Gloucester, a boy king who would be put under the guardianship of a 'Lord Protector' (e.g. Oliver Cromwell). Ireton was more imaginative, and favoured the idea of an elected monarch – but he would be a monarch none the less, a President, in modern parlance, elected (probably by Parliament) to rule for life. It was amidst this intellectual confusion, in a tense and nervous city, its factions all threatened by armed intervention from abroad, that the King's fate came to be determined by the one standard that required compliance: the revealed will of God.

The intellectual architects of the English republic were not inspired by the pagan example of Rome (as the 'neo-classical' Cambridge scholars have recently but ridiculously suggested). They were Puritans like John Cooke, Hugh Peters and John Milton, who came at this time to a revelatory and revolutionary reading of the Old Testament: kings were anathema to God. Kingship was an affliction craved by frail and fallible men who failed to understand that it would only increase their own sufferings. This theory, that human monarchy was a transitory and sinful state of affairs disfavoured by God, was promulgated from the pulpit throughout December by Hugh Peters and is reflected in Cooke's written speech for the prosecution at the King's trial and in Milton's subsequent justification of the proceedings. It was given its most detailed exposition in a tract written by Cooke two years later, with a title that summed it up: MONARCHY *no creature of God's making; wherein is proved by scripture and reason, that monarchical government is against the mind of God.* The frontispiece carried quotations from the book of Hosea which adopted the prophet's adjuration to Israel as a warning to England that monarchs were a divine infuriant:

> *They have set up kings, but not by me: they have made princes, and I knew it not.*

> *O Israel [O England], thou hast destroyed thyself: but in me is thine help, I will be thy king . . .*
> *I gave thee a king in mine anger, and took him away in my wrath.*[4]

Cooke's reasoning was that 'a free people may not make themselves subject to any mortal man'. He was not a modern democrat: he believed that the natural form of government was 'elective aristocracy', because it was 'a principle in nature for wise men to govern the ignorant, as parents their little children that cannot order themselves', it being 'most unnatural for fools to govern wise men'. However, 'the government of one over many' was anathema to God. Monarchs like Charles I 'that assume an absolute supremacy to do what they like, are not creatures of God's ordination . . . God permits such to be, as he suffers sin to be in the world'. Cooke revolted at the notion that God would ordain hereditary kingship, suffering 'millions of people to be subject to the lusts of one man, and that to go in succession to a minor or an idiot . . . reason abhors it, and God approves it not, though he permits it to be'. That permission, however, was contingent on good behaviour, and so far as Charles was concerned, 'Kings that style themselves *defenders of the faith,* if they prove themselves *offenders of the faithful,* God will take away their kingdoms in a way of justice'.[5] The 'way of justice' was a criminal trial.

God's thinking was revealed by Gideon, who delivered the Israelites but disdained their fond demand that he be their king: 'I will not rule over you, neither shall my son rule over you: the Lord shall rule over you.'[6] In the first book of Samuel, Cooke found 'the statute law concerning kings' where it clearly appeared that they were not ordained by God's command but 'from the people's pride and ardent importunity, they were mad for a king to be like unto the heathens'.[7] The story of Nebuchadnezzar, driven out to live with beasts, provided a further proof, as did the fate of his son Belshazzar, for whose feast the writing (*Mene, Mene, Tekel, Upharsin*) was on the wall. How could sensible people contend for monarchy 'when the spirit of God speaks so plainly, that whether kings be good men or bad, I will punish the people says the Lord, so long as they have any kings; it is not a government of my ordination; kings are people's idols, creatures of their own making'.[8] The fatal mistake of the Jews had been their inability to recognise Christ as their expected King because He 'did not exult himself as a monarch, His kingdom being not of this world'.[9] The people of England must now follow the psalmist's injunction – and this became the text for Hugh Peters' sermons in December and January – to take up the two-edged sword 'to bind their kings with chains, and their nobles with fetters of iron'.

The key players in the end game were Bible republicans, not cynical regicides. The Puritan conviction that the institution of monarchy was antipathetic to God provided the moral force which united with the dictates of human reason to turn the King's trial into the event that established a republic. The first book of Samuel clearly warned the Israelites that to seek an earthly king was to reject God: a king would oppress them and they would 'cry out in that day because of your king which ye shall have chosen you; and the Lord will not hear you in that day' (8: 18). Verses from the first book of Samuel resounded from the pulpits of Puritan preachers to hasten the conviction among their congregations that England, like Israel, would be better off without a king.

It became John Cooke's conviction. He admitted that 'many times during the late troubles' he had wished for 'the continuance of a kingly government in England, to have had the pre-eminence and the power in one good, gracious, just, merciful, valiant, faithful and patient man, as a Moses or a Job, who would die for the people'.[10] But in the course of 1648, his Old Testament analysis had hardened into a certainty that kingship, no matter how gracious the incumbent King, was not of God's making and he interpreted the extraordinarily wet summer ('it was mid-winter at mid-summer') as a sign of the Lord's displeasure at those 'wise men who speak of making peace with the King and tying him up so close to law that he should not be able to hurt the people'. Charles would never accept constitutional constraints, and to install a 'King of clouts' with no real power would be an act of national hypocrisy. Symbolic or no, kingship itself had to go.

Cromwell, ever the pragmatist, still had to be convinced that the 'sons of Zeruiah' – the lords and the Presbyterians and the city fathers – would not rise up against any prosecution of the King. The Levellers had run for cover, but cavaliers were creeping back into London in worrying numbers – Fairfax took urgent measures to have them turned away from the city gates but as Cooke later recounted, these 'malignants' came out in the evening with 'swords in their lips' and their 'nocturnal whisperings in taverns against the state and such as are godly in the land'.[11] The Presbyterian MPs, excluded from the Commons by Colonel Pride, were certainly a corrupt and self-seeking group, some of whom merited Milton's jibe that they clung to the King through the Newport treaty negotiations in order to achieve a settlement in which they would feature as the new nobility. But their preachers were not open to this reproach and the army sought in vain, at meetings in mid-December, to win their support for a trial. The Presbyterians appear pathetic in this crucial period and certainly their basic argument against the trial – that Charles had been misled by evil councillors[12] – must have been infuriating to New Model commanders who knew that Charles was plotting to have Ormonde's Irish army join up with Rupert's fleet to launch a third civil war.

The Presbyterians were on stronger ground when citing scripture – the first book of Samuel also carried David's rhetorical question: 'Who can stretch forth his hand against the Lord's anointed, and be guiltless?' (The Puritans denied that Charles was the Lord's anointed, but it was a tricky passage to explain away.) They attacked as unsafe Cromwell's reliance on providence, and argued that the role of the truly godly was to pray for Charles to repent. But turning the other cheek had little popular appeal to men whose cheeks had been bruised twice already. It was a time of national emergency, and some 'purged' MPs began to see things the army's way: they were allowed back to the Commons. By the year's end, Cromwell was satisfied that the Presbyterians in the city would not forcefully or even actively oppose the King's trial.

The only surviving communication by Cromwell in this crucial month is a seemingly insignificant note, dated 18 December, to secure a room in

Doctors Commons – the chambers of civil lawyers – for Dr Isaac Dorislaus. This scholar had once been driven out of his Cambridge professorship as a 'threat to monarchical government' for lecturing on the virtues of the Roman republic,[13] but served as judge-advocate in the New Model Army and had just been sent by Parliament on a diplomatic mission to The Hague. He returned with the dispiriting news that the Dutch were entering a commercial alliance with Ormonde's confederacy in Ireland. On this particular day, Cromwell consulted Bulstrode Whitelocke and Thomas Widdrington, the leading parliamentary lawyers, about the trial of the King, and they expressed serious reservations about its legality.[14] It seems a reasonable inference that Cromwell at this point decided to find other lawyers, like Dorislaus, who could support the prosecution. John Cooke would come into the frame: he was close to Hugh Peters, Cromwell's chaplain; had advised Fairfax; and was a close friend of Colonel Ludlow and other senior officers anxious to put the King on trial.[15]

The King too had been spending time with his lawyers. The description of him as a 'prisoner' since Cornet Joyce took him into army custody is misleading: until his escape attempt at Carisbrooke, he had been permitted to hold court served by a hundred flunkeys and to receive whomever he liked. Afterwards, his retinue was reduced to thirty servants but access to him was readily granted. Parliament had generously approved his request for no less than forty-two expert advisers at Newport, and amongst the array of royalist legal talent was Sir Orlando Bridgeman, Archbishop Laud's defence counsel who would later preside at the regicides' trial and barristers Geoffrey Palmer (later Attorney-General) and John Vaughan, a notable chief justice some thirty years on.[16] The news from London in November was full of speculation about army plans to put Charles on trial, and his legal defence strategy was first planned with these distinguished counsellors. In late November, when a copy of the army's *Remonstrance* reached the King, he noted Bridgeman's preliminary advice on the flyleaf:

> . . . by the letter of the law, all persons charged to offend against the law ought to be tried by their peers or equals. What is the law if the person questioned is without peer?[17]

This point was legalistic, and to a fault. The King was to make it at his trial, and Cooke was easily to dispose of it, then and later, on the basis that no man – not even the King – was above the law. Magna Carta – the 'law' to whose letter Bridgeman referred – was King John's guarantee to the barons that they would be tried by peers (i.e. by barons) and not by kings: if a king were charged with crime, then it would not breach the spirit of the Great Charter to try him before as distinguished and representative a group of judges as Parliament could put together.

Charles had three weeks to prepare, but he spent these December days walking the marshy moonscape around Hurst, gazing at the dark, fast-flowing Solent as if awaiting rescue by Rupert's fleet. But the only ships on the horizon were from Parliament's patrolling squadron. His quarters in the fort were makeshift, and his captors hoped that the discomfort would concentrate his mind: instead, it expanded his fantasies. When Cromwell's cavalry clattered into the keep of the fortress on 19 December to take him to London, he welcomed the chance to rally his loyal subjects. They turned out along the route, to gawp and cheer 'God preserve your Majesty!' Thomas Harrison was in charge of the escort: the King had been told weeks before that Harrison was to be his assassin and was thunderstruck when told the identity of the handsome, gentle and finely attired colonel. The two men almost had an epiphany during pre-dinner drinks that evening at a stately home near Farnham. According to Sir Thomas Herbert's eye-witness account:

> A little before supper, his Majesty discovered Major Harrison at the far end of the room talking with another officer; the King beckoned to him with his hand to come nearer him; which he did with due reverence. The King then taking him by his arm, drew him aside towards the window, where for half an hour or more they discoursed together; the Major in his vindication assured his Majesty, that what was so reported of him was not true; what he had said, he might repeat, that the law was equally obliging to great and small, and that justice had no respect to persons; or words to that purpose; which his Majesty finding affectedly spoken, and to no good end, he left off further communication with him, and went to supper.[18]

It was typical of Charles that he took offence at Harrison's proposition that justice was no respecter of persons. The King's belief that he had no equal was an article of faith, and now a ground of his defence. At Windsor Castle, the King was tearfully greeted by another prisoner awaiting trial, the

Duke of Hamilton. The duke had been visited by Cromwell the previous week, a visit which has proved as puzzling to historians as the flight of Rudolf Hess to another Duke of Hamilton three centuries later. The French ambassador conjectured that it was a last-ditch attempt to enlist the duke to persuade Charles to abdicate the throne in favour of Henry, his youngest son, whilst others have speculated that it may have been to offer the duke a plea-bargain if he gave evidence against the King. In fact, Cromwell went to Windsor at the Duke's request,[19] probably hoping he would divulge the names of Presbyterian MPs who had secretly supported the Engagement. For Charles, abdication was out of the question, and Hamilton's evidence was hardly necessary for a conviction: the King's approval of the Engagement with the Scots, and the letters seized from his cabinet after Naseby, provided ample evidence of aggression against his own people.

If such overtures did take place they were part of a process of testing all options before settling upon a trial. Cromwell's elusive mind would have made itself up by 16 December – the day that Fairfax dispatched the troops to collect the King from Hurst Castle following a meeting of the Army council.[20] Two days later Cromwell was asking the legal grandees for advice about the lawfulness of putting the King on trial, and Isaac Dorislaus returned to report that his mission to The Hague had been a failure. The Dutch government (the States General) had determined to go ahead with a commercial treaty with the Catholic rebel government in Ireland (the confederacy) which was willing to join Ormonde in support of the King. At this time there were worrying reports of Ormonde's waxing strength as loyal Protestants flocked to enlist, and reports from Ireland, always exaggerated, had a propensity to cause panic in the stoutest London hearts. Moreover, Parliament was told of intelligence that Rupert was about to sail his fleet to Ireland to join Ormonde and invade Wales.[21] This was the week when the spectacle of a third civil war loomed with frightening clarity: it would be fought by Ormonde's royalist army, joined with the Catholic confederates and the Prince of Wales's fleet which lay only two days' sail from England, perhaps in new alliance with the awesome Dutch navy. The danger of an invasion from Ireland had been evident for some weeks: the news from The Hague would have confirmed Cromwell's providential intimation that it was time for what Ireton and the Independents had been urging since the *Remonstrance*: the trial of the 'Great Delinquent'.

The decision to put the King on trial did mean rejection (if it was ever seriously considered) of one obvious and time-honoured means of eliminating an inconvenient monarch. According to Clarendon, who was biased and in no position to know, the army had actually discussed the possibility of using poison 'which would make the least noise' or assassination 'for which there were hands ready enough to be employed'. Tempting though it must have been to arrange an historic accident on the winding staircase of Hurst Castle, or to shoot Charles while he was trying to escape (as he often was), the real point is that the army did not take this easy way out. Its discipline was formidable: one officer suspected of encouraging Charles to flee from Carisbrooke so he could be shot in the attempt was court-martialled for his pains. The army firmly protected the life of the King, until it could be taken by process of law.

The choice was not just of a trial, but of an open and *public* trial by a traditional adversary process and not by court-martial. Clarendon complains that this was just another means of king-killing, albeit one 'which would be most for the honour of the Parliament and teach all kings to know that they were accountable and punishable for the wickedness of their lives'. His mistake is in the assumption that a trial entailed conviction and execution: there were only a handful of officers in the Army Council committed to the death sentence. Cromwell's own fatalistic preference was to let justice have its own momentum, and to see where it might lead. Openness was part of the Anglo-Saxon legal inheritance: the trial process which developed after abolition of medieval trial by ordeal was akin to a rather ill-conducted public meeting, involving members of the local community as witnesses, jurors and spectators. Publicity came to be regarded by common lawyers as a defining characteristic of a trial, and even the Star Chamber sat in open court.[22] The open justice rule had not been applied to treason trials of other alleged royal miscreants, like Anne Boleyn and Mary Queen of Scots, which were for that reason alone legally questionable, so publicity would serve as a legitimating factor.

For non-lawyer MPs like Harrison and Cromwell and Thomas Scot, a city alderman, public justice had an altogether different meaning. It would show, quite literally, that they had nothing to hide. The King's trial 'was not to be done in a corner'. This was God's work, and it would be done in the sight of God. These were men who had fought two wars against Charles and now knew they would have to fight a third against his Irish supporters. Their choice of an open trial procedure was not merely to conform with the common law and to deter future tyrants: it was to allow the world to witness the righteousness of their cause, and to let history judge the strength of their case.

The Army Council had an easy and entirely legitimate alternative to a painstaking and unprecedented public trial: the King was an enemy commander who could be court-martialled and then shot immediately, like the cavalier generals Lisle and Lucas at Colchester. The summary justice of the Provost-Marshall had been a feature of wars in England since Edward I: it had become a traditional means of condemning rebels of rank not just after battles but throughout 'turbulent times'. When prosecuting Essex for his revolt in 1601, Attorney-General Coke had explained to the court that 'It was a great mercy of the Queen's that he was not, according to the martial law, put to the sword'.[23] It was merciful of the army – given that Charles had renewed the war by his treaty with the Scots and that his forces were still active and menacing – to put him on trial before a tribunal in which his innocence might be asserted. Under the laws of war, as understood at the time, kings had no immunity during hostilities: 'In war the rules of honour applied universally, binding princes and men at arms equally'.[24] This was the position in international law, agreed by Grotius and the main European jurists – including Alberico Gentili, the Regius professor of civil law at Oxford, an adviser to James I and otherwise a stout upholder of royal absolutism. Since the purpose of victory was to enjoy peace, a captured enemy commander – especially if untrustworthy or in a position to renew the strife – should be put to death. 'A man who is dead renews no war'[25] was the logic of international law in the mid-seventeenth century. In December 1648, it might have been precisely applied to put Charles I before a firing squad.

The decision instead to put Charles before a tribunal tasked to apply the common law, permitting him to justify his cause in public and requiring the prosecution to prove his guilt, was a step as unnecessary as it was unprecedented. In this sense, it was a daring decision, far in advance of the law as it then stood in England or, following the treaty of Westphalia, in the known world. There was no example to suggest that the trial of a Head of State was feasible: it would be necessary to find lawyers who could make it work.

On 21 December, Cromwell asked Whitelocke and Widdrington to put their legal advice in writing. Two days later they met Parliament's legal clerk, Henry Elsyng, who told them he was pretending to be sick because he was opposed to the projected proceedings. A message came for the two great lawyers to attend the Committee to plan the King's trial. 'Are you thinking what I'm thinking?' Whitelocke asked Widdrington, in as many words. 'I think I am,' replied Widdrington, 'I would go anywhere to avoid it.' 'My coach awaits,' responded Whitelocke. Then the two great lawyers, entrusted with the seal of state, rushed downstairs and drove furiously to Whitelocke's country estate in Buckinghamshire, 'till this busness is ended.'[26] Little wonder that Cromwell was nervous: according to Bishop Burnet, a near contemporary, it was Ireton now who drove it on. He 'had the principles and temper of a Cassius in him, and found out Cooke and Bradshawe, two bold lawyers, as proper instruments for managing it.'[27]

9

The Hare, Clutched: Cooke's Charge

The twelve days of Christmas, a traditional festive binge of over-eating and drunkenness, had always been abjured by Puritans, so Parliament sat on Christmas Day to listen to petitions criticising its remissness in failing to bring to 'due and impartial justice' the King and the other 'notorious incendiaries' behind the Scots' invasion. In a Boxing Day debate in the Commons, Cromwell spoke, elliptically but for the first time in public, on his attitude to the fate of the King:

> If any man whatsoever hath carried on the design of deposing the King, and disinheriting his posterity; or, if any man had yet any such a design, he should be the greatest traitor and rebel in the world; but, since the Providence of God hath cast this upon us, I cannot but submit to Providence, though I am not yet provided to give you advice.[1]

Cromwell was still, at least in public, having it both ways: infuriatingly assuming the mantle of high priest of the oracle of providence, he was acknowledging the truth of what his top lawyers had told him on 18 December (that to depose the King was an act of treason and rebellion) but justifying it, reluctantly, as the dictate of destiny. His course was clear, but he was 'not yet provided to give you advice' because he had not yet found lawyers to give *him* advice as to how it might be achieved. Parliamentary counsel Henry Elsying, who had pretended a sudden illness when asked to serve on the committee to consider the future of the King, set up on 23 December, was replaced by Andrew Broughton, the mayor of Maidstone and a figure of considerable gravitas and experience.[2]

Charles, meanwhile, celebrated Christmas at Windsor, decked out from an expensive wardrobe of suits, gowns and cloaks newly made by London tailors in expectation of his entry into the city as head of state. Spurred by reports of this extravagance, the Commons on 27 December took its first vote against such royal waste of public money: it decided to end court ceremonials at Windsor and to reduce to six the number of servants paid from public funds to attend the King. They should no longer serve the King 'on bended knee', but wait upon him in a more dignified and less uncomfortable fashion.[3]

On the same day, the committee on the future of the King reported to the House that a special court should be established to try him, comprising judges who represented the interests of the nation. Its jurisdiction should last for only one month – a measure of the urgency that now attended the question. The committee was co-chaired by Thomas Scot the Puritan city alderman and Henry Marten, the first republican: as an indication of its importance, Cromwell was co-opted. It reported the following day with the draft of a charge, which was so straightforward that it was evident that the committee lacked expert legal assistance:

That Charles Stuart has acted contrary to his trust, in departing from the Parliament, setting up his Standard, making a war against them, and thereby been the occasion of much bloodshed and misery to the people whom he was set over for good. That he gave commissions to Irish Rebels and since was the occasion of a second war, besides what he has done contrary to the liberties of the subject and tending to the destruction of the fundamental laws and liberties of this Kingdom.[4]

In simple language, this charge encapsulated Parliament's complaint against the King. It was a true bill in the sense that Charles could be proved to have committed those acts to which it referred, but the nature of his offence was unclear: the loose constitutional suggestion was that the King was obliged to exercise his power for the public good and might be arraigned for breach of trust if he exercised it for the public bad. This was the sort of argument that might pass muster in a tavern, but not in a criminal court.

The debates continued – on 30 December the House directed the committee to name some judges and 'to make some special provision in case the King should refuse to plead to the charge against him'. Even at this early stage, the King's gambit was predictable, and the failure to make 'special provision' for it was to prove costly to the parliamentarian cause. There is no doubt that the King had discussed tactics with his team of lawyers at Newport: the best criminal lawyer of the time, Matthew Hale, offered his services if Charles decided to recognise the court by pleading 'not guilty'.[5]

On New Year's Day the Commons began to get its act together – or at least its 'Ordinance', for so laws passed by Parliament and brought into operation without royal assent had been described over the previous six years. It 'declared and adjudged' that 'it is treason for the King of England for the time to come to levy war against the Parliament and Kingdom of England'. This was certainly not a republican measure, since it assumed the existence of future kings. The Ordinance set out the prosecution case with much greater particularity and some literary style and flourish. It was passed in the Commons (according to some reports, by only twenty-six votes to twenty) but then stalled by the House of Lords when the dozen or so peers who attended objected to the retrospective definition of the law of treason. 'If the King did levy war first', complained the Earl of Northumberland, 'we have no law extant that can be produced to make a treason in him to do; and for us, my Lords, to declare treason by an Ordinance, when this matter of fact is not yet proved, nor any law to bring to judge it by, seems to me very unreasonable.'[6] They did not reject the Bill, but adjourned for ten days in an effort to stall the Commons, which called their bluff on 6 January by transforming its Ordinance into an 'Act' which it determined should become law irrespective of whether it was passed by the Upper House. This could not be justified on any pre-existing constitutional theory: to have the House of Commons, and a purged House at that, arrogate to itself the right to legislate without the approval of the Lords, was a step that could only have been taken by men who had decided that God, justice and national security all demanded the trial of the King.

The Commons was in urgent earnest now: it named 150 'commissioners and judges' in its Ordinance, without waiting to obtain their consent. They included the chief justices of the three highest courts in England, who made their excuses hastily enough for their names to be omitted from a revised list which appeared in the 'Act' of 6 January. The defection which cries out for explanation was that of Parliament's long-standing legal hero, Chief Justice Oliver St John. He had argued the case against ship money, had prosecuted Strafford and had led the Independents in Parliament during the civil war: he was Cromwell's friend and relation. If he pulled out from principle, he never articulated it at the time, and was back in favour and in power as soon as 'the great business' was done – by others. The leading Puritan lawyers – St John, Lenthall, Whitelocke and Widdrington – were clever, calculating, formidable men: the silence in which they slunk away from the trial and the noise they made when they returned to adhere to the republic six weeks later suggests their motivation was more cowardice than constitutional conviction.

That Charles was responsible for waging war against his own people was a matter of historical record. The Act formally passed by the Commons on 6 January justified his trial on pragmatic grounds (to prevent his raising new 'commotions, rebellions and invasions') as well as on principle – the need to end the impunity hitherto accorded the monarch. The preamble appropriately expressed the long frustration and righteous indignation of the army and the Independents:

> Whereas it is notorious that Charles Stuart, the now King of England, has had a wicked design totally to subvert the ancient and fundamental laws and liberties of this nation, and in their place to introduce an arbitrary and tyrannical government; he has prosecuted it with fire and sword, levied and maintained a cruel war in the land against the Parliament and Kingdom, whereby the country has been miserably wasted, the public treasure exhausted, trade decayed, thousands of people murdered, and infinite other mischiefs committed: for all which high and treasonable offences, the said Charles Stuart might long since justly have been brought to exemplary and condign Punishment. Whereas also, the Parliament well hoping that the restraint and imprisonment of his person, after it had pleased God to deliver him into their hands, would have quieted the distempers of the Kingdom, did forbear to proceed judicially against him; but found by sad experience, that their remissness served only to encourage him and his accomplices in the continuance of their evil practices, and in raising of new commissions, rebellions and invasions. For prevention therefore of the like or greater inconveniences, and to the end that no Chief Officer

or Magistrate whatsoever may hereafter presume traitorously and maliciously to imagine or contrive the enslaving or destroying of the English
nation, and expect Impunity for so doing . . .[7]

This declaration, which a few days later was to serve as Cooke's brief,
identified a particularly grave abuse of power – directing mass-murder, in
furtherance of a design to achieve absolute power – and a compelling reason
for prosecuting, namely to end impunity for heads of state, both to enable
retribution and to deter future monarchs from seeking thus to destroy the
liberty of the people. The denial of impunity to any future 'Chief Officer
or Magistrate' had a special significance: kings would henceforth preside
over the government of the realm without divine ordainment or sovereign
immunity.

For royalists, the flaw in the Act which erected the High Court of Justice
was simply that it touched the untouchable: every sovereign had absolute
legal immunity from criminal prosecution. There was another objection,
namely that it was the result of a vote of a purged Commons, implemented
without the approval of an adjourned (but not yet abolished) House of Lords.
As young Algernon Sidney claimed he said to Cromwell, 'First, the King
can be tried by no court; secondly, no man can be tried by this court.'
Cromwell's alleged reply – 'I tell you, we will cut off his head with the Crown
upon it' – was a pithy rejection of the discreditable doctrine that a king
could get away with murder, but did not confront Sidney's second point –
that the court had been unlawfully established, since the Act had not passed
the House of Lords, much less had it received the royal assent.

Cromwell might have said (Oliver Wendell Holmes said it, 300 years
later) that the constitution is not a suicide pact. What was in effect happening
– although there was no written constitution to express it in these terms –
was a state of emergency, occasioned by an impending resumption of hostilities. The army, in the name of General Fairfax, had in effect declared martial
law, under which it would govern through the medium of an assembly
containing only those elected representatives whom it trusted to legislate
with England's real interests at heart. The elimination of Holles and the
Presbyterian MPs had been justified on the grounds of their corruption, but
peculation was not the problem: it was the corruption of their reason which
held fast to the notion that there was no alternative but to trust Charles
Stuart, the enemy commander, with the governance of England. It was a

true case of necessity and it is a mistake to think that necessity knows no law. It calls for a different kind of law. The army and its supporters rejected a lawless solution (assassination), and declined the lawful but summary justice available under martial law, which permitted enemy commanders to be put before a firing squad. They also rejected the option of a jury trial at the Old Bailey; not because they feared the outcome but because the common law denied juries (made up of commoners) to those of royal blood and they wanted to be as legalistic as possible in this trial without precedent. They were seeking to clutch at Cromwell's swimming hare – the shred of legality – and on 4 January 1649 they found it in the concept of representative government, which entailed the power of the Commons to make law without assent either of the King or of the Lords:

> The Commons of England assembled in Parliament declare that the people under God are the origin of all just power. They do likewise declare that the Commons of England assembled in Parliament, being chosen by and representing the people, have the supreme authority of this nation. They do likewise declare that whatsoever is enacted and declared law by the Commons of England assembled in Parliament, has the force of law, and all the people of this nation are included thereby, although the consent and concurrence of the King and House of Peers be not had thereunto.[8]

For all the derision that was later heaped upon the pretensions of 'the Rump', this was in fact the first modern enunciation of democratic principle by a legislative body purporting to embody it, even though MPs were elected only by wealthy males and 'democratic' was at this time a word of insult, hurled by royalists at Levellers and Independents alike. Yet the 135 men nominated by the Act of 6 January to sit as judges (although they were termed 'commissioners' and have gone down in history as the King's 'judges') were representative of 'the most respectable and substantial elements in the country' – landed gentry, mayors and recorders from a dozen major towns; MPs, lawyers, London aldermen and senior army officers. Some eighty of these individuals attended during the trial and there can be no doubt, despite post-Restoration backsliding by a few, that they did so voluntarily and from 'a sincere conviction that no other course was open to them as God-fearing Christians and lovers of their country'.[9] A typical answer to the call was that of Colonel John Hutchinson; his wife Lucy explained how he prayed for guidance before accepting and found 'a confirmation in his conscience that it was his duty to act as he did'.[10] These judges were attendants upon providence: they had embarked upon a mission, but where it would take them nobody at this stage – certainly not Fairfax and probably not even Cromwell – knew for certain.

The *Act to Establish the High Court of Justice* provided that the court was to have a quorum of only twenty – a reflection of the fact that a number of its judges were away from London on army service and that in the event of the feared invasion, many more would be absent. Others would have difficulty in attending from homes in the provinces, and some would have conscientious objections to serving. They were endowed with discretion to sit wherever and whenever they chose; to administer oaths and to examine witnesses and to appoint all necessary officers and attendants. They were enjoined to charge the King and to receive his 'personal answer' to the charge 'or in default of such answer, to proceed to final sentence, according to justice and the merit of the cause; and such final sentence to execute, or cause to be executed, speedily and impartially'. The death sentence was not inevitable: the King's answer, or else the 'merit of the cause' would determine the appropriate punishment.

A dignified defence, an apology, a show of remorse for the bloodshed on both sides, an offer to share power according to the Nineteen or the Newcastle propositions, or to stand aside in favour of Charles II or Henry IX: the King had everything to play for, if he chose to play the justice game at all. That was not what he had told a well-wisher who asked on Christmas Day what he planned to do if a charge were brought against him. He was reported to have replied 'I would not give any answer. If they put me on trial I will die patiently, like a martyr.'[11]

The Act requested General Fairfax to provide all necessary assistance to the court. The general was unhappy about the prospect of the King's execution, although he had approved the purge of the Commons and then its provisions for the trial. He attended the first meeting of the court, on Monday 8 January, along with fifty-two of the other appointed judges, although he absented himself from the court thereafter, on the ground that he had to run the country. His initial presence gave the tribunal the imprimatur of the army's high command.

The judges had assembled for this brief inauguration in the Painted

Chamber at Westminster: apart from directing the sergeant-at-arms to proclaim the court's existence, and appointing its clerks and ushers, their discussions were mainly about the selection of prosecuting counsel.[12] Dr Dorislaus would have been nominated by Cromwell, while Fairfax's input may have been to put forward a relative, John Aske, as a junior counsel. There are no records of the discussion, but Cooke would have been approved by his friends Edmund Ludlow and Henry Ireton and by Nicholas Love, his contemporary at Wadham, who were present at this first meeting. The minutes refer only to the 'nomination' of Cooke as an officer of the court: he was not formally appointed as Solicitor-General until the next meeting on Wednesday 10 January, presumably after wider soundings had produced no objections, and no better candidates who might be prepared to accept the brief. The more important speaking role of Attorney-General, i.e. the chief prosecutor, went to William Steele. He was the barrister who had prosecuted Captain Burleigh, a somewhat comic cavalier, who had marched on Carisbrooke to liberate the King at the head of a rag-tag band of curious children, one of them blowing a tin whistle. The army had not been amused, and Steele had managed to persuade the jury that Burleigh was guilty of the crime of compassing and imagining the death of the King – by dint of trying to set the King free. It was advocacy of this class that would be needed, if Charles himself were to be convicted of treason.

The judges who first convened on 8 January met regularly in the Painted Chamber to make preparations for the King's trial, which did not commence until Saturday 20 January. Between fifty and sixty commissioners attended each preparatory session, in the long tapestried room adjacent to the House of Lords and overlooking the gardens of a fine house built by the wealthy scholar Sir Robert Cotton, which stood between the Parliament buildings and the river. They sat at trestle tables, their proceedings illuminated in the winter gloom by candles and the flames thrown from a well-tended fire. The proceedings were minuted by two clerks – John Phelps and Andrew Broughton – while six ushers danced attendance and spectators stood at doorways to observe, other than during private sessions when the room was cleared of 'strangers'. Cromwell and Ireton were present at most of the meetings, their eagerness indicated by the fact that they were usually among the first to sign the roll-call. Other prominent participants were Henry Marten, Edmund Ludlow, Nicholas Love, Thomas Scot, John Lisle and Thomas Harrison. Lucy Hutchinson, the wife of Colonel John Hutchinson, was to attest in her memoirs to the keenness and conscientiousness with which they all went about 'the great business': her husband believed it was his duty to his country and his God, 'although he was not ignorant of the danger he ran, as the condition of things then were'.[13]

They had been catapulted into unknown terrain: some had studied at the Inns, but the group was collectively lacking in forensic experience. Their first step had been sure enough: trumpeting and drumming traditionally proclaimed an assize, and Sergeant Dendy made a great impression as he clattered on horseback into the startled courts at Westminster Hall, waving the Parliament's mace and proclaiming the King's trial. He was accompanied by a troop of horse, as well as ten trumpeters and army drummers. The Commons ordered him to repeat this noisy spectacle around the town, at St Paul's and Cheapside and then the Exchange: it was noted with satisfaction that 'the streets are thronged with spectators, without the least violence, injury or affront publicly done or offered'. For all the purported love the people bore their King, and for all the Presbyterian hostility towards the army and the purged Parliament, there was something about a trial – something almost supernaturally appealing about its promise of 'justice' – that was difficult to reject out of hand. Dendy's ceremonial overture aroused public expectations, and the commissioners had very little time (the Act allowed them no more than a month) to raise the curtain.

The commissioners were at a loss without legal leadership. They could do little until they found a judge prepared to preside and counsel prepared to prosecute. On 10 January, they appointed Sergeant John Bradshawe as their president: he had recently been made chief justice of Chester (i.e. of Wales) and had sat as sheriff in the city, where he had strong support among Independent councillors. Bradshawe's family were unhappy that he should play such a leading part in the proceedings – when he arrived for the next meeting on 12 January he earnestly begged to be excused the office. The commissioners refused – there was no one else of judicial rank – and confirmed him as Lord President, a role that he performed punctiliously from then on. His nervousness was not feigned and his reluctance was not entirely, as Cooke would have it, 'out of a humble spirit':[14] the dangers were real and immediate. To calm his wife's fears, Bradshawe lined his broad-brimmed hat with lead to protect his temples from musket fire: the hat is exhibited today at the Ashmolean Museum in Oxford, a reminder both of the danger of these times and of the smallness of the crania of those who lived through them.

His lodgings at Gray's Inn were deemed too exposed to assassins, and a house was found for him in New Palace Yard (and later, the dean's house at Westminster Abbey) where he was guarded around the clock by twenty officers and supplied with the same provisions as the King, who was to be lodged at the Cotton House.

On 10 January the court approved the nomination of John Cooke as Solicitor-General, to prepare the case for presentation by his leader, the more experienced criminal trial counsel, William Steele. The instructions in the brief comprised the Act to establish the High Court (transcribed on vellum) and a note that his first task would be to advise a small committee of commissioners, chaired by Nicholas Love, on 'How to Carry on and Manage the King's Trial'. Plainly, much trust was reposed in the Solicitor-General to make 'the great business' actually work – but would he accept these instructions, delivered that shivery evening to his chambers at Gray's Inn by Parliament's messenger?

John Cooke did not hesitate: this brief was his destiny. 'I readily harkened to their call to this service, as if it had been immediately from heaven.' In humility, he was struck with the discouraging thought that

> my reason is far less than others of my profession; yet considering that there are but two things desirable to make a dumb man eloquent, namely a good cause and good judges . . . and thinking that happily God might make use of one mean man at the Bar, amongst other learned counsel, that more of his mind might appear in it (for many times the less there is of man, the more God's glory does appear) I went as cheerfully about it as to a wedding.[15]

Much more cheerfully, it may be said, than his fellow barrister Steele, who went about it as if to a funeral, namely his own. The Attorney-General took to his bed where he was found a few days later and certified 'very sick'. Doubly sick, so he claimed, at his inability to lead the prosecution, which 'if it should please God to restore him' he would most assiduously do. It did not please God to restore him until the trial was over: on Cooke's humble but willing shoulders fell the task of devising some lawful, fair and presentable way to prosecute Charles I.

Once Bradshawe was in place and Cooke was in action, the court proceedings began to proceed. The prosecution was given power to requisition relevant documentary evidence – original papers and letters, such as those which had been intercepted from the King or found in his cabinet at Naseby – and to summon and depose witnesses. Cooke began to make urgent enquiries among prisoners and soldiers who had previously served the royalist cause for evidence that could implicate the King in war crimes. The court had one important request to make of Cooke and Dorislaus at the first meeting they attended, on Friday 12 January: it wanted them to draft the charge against the King and it wanted that charge ready by Monday morning.

This was a tall order, since not even God's work could be performed on the Sabbath, but the lawyers completed their draft by 2 p.m. on Monday. Cooke read the charge aloud and at length: inevitably, legal drafting under pressure of time is prolix and some of the soldier MPs on the committee wanted the King's crimes writ large. Thomas Harrison, for example, urged that the charge include his responsibility for the loss of La Rochelle and even an allegation that he had been complicit in his father's death: 'Let us blacken him what we can.' John Rushworth, a legally trained House of Commons clerk present at the court's private sitting, reports that the charge 'was very long' and a new committee – including Ireton and Marten – was appointed to help Cooke abbreviate it and to assist him in collecting witness statements. But they were only given two days: when Cooke returned on Wednesday afternoon, the charge was still considered too long. Oliver Cromwell, doubtless at his own suggestion, was added to the committee assisting Cooke, who later said that he resisted pressure from the MPs to include charges that could not be proved, or which were irrelevant, however prejudicial to Charles.[16]

Other court committees busied themselves with matters of security and choreography. Fairfax had not been able to staunch the cavalier infiltration of London and on 13 January someone remembered Guy Fawkes, so the sergeant-at-arms was sent immediately with a troop of soldiers to search the vaults below the Painted Chamber for any trace of gunpowder. Then came the question of where the trial would be held: safely, in front of a selected and screened audience in the Painted Chamber, or in the vast space of Westminster Hall which could accommodate several thousand? Cromwell wanted to play to the larger gallery, notwithstanding the danger, so that the justice of the proceedings could be more widely appreciated. This meant that all the courts which met in Westminster Hall would have to be adjourned for the duration of the King's trial – their partitions were taken down and the scriveners and legal booksellers cleared off the precincts. The judges were to sit on an elevated platform against the south (i.e. river) side facing the King and prosecuting counsel, who would be placed in the railed-off area (the bar) in front of the audience, which would occupy the back half of the hall and some space at the sides. Several private balconies and open apartment windows overlooked the hall: guards had to be stationed to ensure that these vantage points were not used by snipers. There would be soldiers pacing the aisles of the hall to deter disturbances and to monitor the public entrance – 'the great gate' at the north side of the hall. The private passage which led to 'Hell', the cellar where the excluded MPs had been detained after Pride's Purge, would be blocked up for the duration of the trial.

These were elementary precautions which could not have protected either the judges or their counsel from a determined royalist assault or a suicide-assassin. The risk inherent in such a public event, at a time when the second civil war had scarcely ended and the third was almost underway, would have persuaded any prudent administrator to remove the trial to the safety of the Painted Chamber. But for these men, a public spectacle was a form of witness before God of the righteousness of their cause and course. Other than by making special security arrangements to pacify Bradshawe, they took little care for their own safety – Cooke positively disdained protection, notwith-standing death threats. They took more care for the King – also a possible target – and assigned no fewer than 200 foot soldiers to patrol the grounds of the Cotton House, to guard Charles against both rescuers and assassins. He would be allowed to live in some luxury, but privacy was out of the ques-tion: thirty officers would be stationed in the house, two of them perma-nently ensconced in his bedroom. Three servants were permitted to accompany him to the court, surrounded by his special guard: they would enter through the garden and wend their way, through back passages lined with soldiers, to enter the hall from the side closest to the bar, which faced the judges. There the King would sit, on a velvet cushion (a civility insisted upon by Bradshawe), only a few feet from the Solicitor-General.

One thing must have been clear to the organisers, as it is to all who attend events in Westminster Hall today. The acoustics are appalling: a speech from the south end where the Lord President was positioned would scarcely carry past the bar, and the voices of the King and John Cooke, with their back to the bulk of the audience, would not be heard by many behind them. So the judges were particularly concerned that justice must be seen to be done, because it would not be heard to be done. It would be read, at least: twelve short-hand reporters were permitted to form the first press gallery. In order that 'the trial may be performed in a solemn manner' it was decided that only the court's president and counsel should speak during the open court proceedings. The other judges should direct their questions to witnesses through the president and ask him to adjourn if they wished to object to any aspect of the proceeding. They opted for solemn ceremony: they would process in from the Exchequer Chamber, led by the Lord President with the sword of state and Parliament's mace carried before him. The clerk and the ushers should wear gowns, and the court messengers were provided with special cloaks. To add a dash of terror, the court sent to the Tower of London for two hundred halberds, or 'partizans' – long pikes with axe-like blades which soldiers could flourish in the Hall. It must have been hard for men who had risked their lives to worship as they wished in utter austerity, without so much as a tint of stained glass, to recognise that court choreography requires a touch of plush. None the less, they approved a chair of crimson velvet for the president, and a desk with a crimson velvet cushion: the judges' benches too were hung with crimson, setting off their black or 'sad'-coloured suits and broad-brimmed black hats that were in Puritan fashion. In front of the president was a long table covered with Turkish carpet. Here the clerks, Phelps and Broughton, would sit either side of the sword and mace which would lie there, alongside Cooke's charge, while the court was sitting.

On Friday 19 January the commissioners were told that the charge had been 'perfected' and that the Solicitor-General was now ready to present it. Cooke read it to the commissioners three times before they asked him to have it engrossed on parchment and signed: when the trial opened, he should present it 'in the name and on the behalf of the people of England'. The charge (now called an indictment) was a statement of the crime and a description of its 'particulars', that is, of the facts alleged to amount to the offence which the prosecution undertakes to prove by evidence. This indictment was headed 'A *Charge of High Treason, and Other High Crimes*'.[17] Cooke spelled out its juristic basis at the beginning, by alleging that Charles Stuart had been

Trusted with a limited power to govern by and according to the laws of the land and not otherwise; and by his trust, oath and office being obliged to use the power committed to him for the good and benefit of the people, and for the preservation of their rights and liberties.

This embodied the constitutional position Coke had postulated to James I: the sovereign's power was limited, in that he could not encroach upon traditional liberties or breach the common law. The notion that the monarch's power was held in a trust and could only be exercised for the benefit of the people's liberty was new: monarchs had used their powers throughout history to benefit themselves and their favourites. Whether a policy was for the people's benefit was generally a subjective question – but, as this charge went on to explain, a policy of war that resulted in the deaths of tens of thousands of Englishmen could never qualify. On the charge of tyranny, the King's guilty mind (*mens rea* as lawyers call it) consisted in waging aggressive war against his own people for his personal advancement rather than the public interest, in seizing unlimited power to rule according to his royal will rather than law and in particular in abolishing the most precious of the people's fundamental rights, namely access to frequent Parliaments to remedy grievances. With this wicked intent the defendant had 'traitorously and maliciously levied war against the present Parliament and the people therein represented [the main battles of the first civil war were then mentioned, from 1642 to 1646] whereby the said Charles Stuart has caused and procured many thousands of the free people of this nation to be slain'.

There followed an accusation of his command responsibility for the second civil war in various counties in 1648 'by divisions, parties and insurrections within this land, by invasions from foreign parts endeavored and procured by him, and by many other evil ways and means . . . [Charles Stuart] has renewed or caused to be renewed the said war against the Parliament and the good people of this nation'. His brewing of a third civil war was added to the charge: 'for further prosecution of his said evil designs he does still continue his missions to [Charles, Prince of Wales] and other rebels and revolters both English and foreigners and to the Earl of Ormonde and to the Irish rebels and revolters associated with him, and from whom further invasions upon the land are threatened'.

These allegations were capable of proof, in the sense that Charles had commanded in battle, encouraged the renewed fighting in 1648, and had incited Ormonde while he was pretending to parley peace at Newport. The

King's determination to fight Parliament rather than to concede its demands or subsequently the demands of its army, had the consequence, as the charge went on truthfully and movingly to relate, that

> Much innocent blood of the free people of this nation has been spilt, many families have been undone, the public treasury wasted and exhausted, trade obstructed and miserably decayed, vast expense and damage to the nation incurred, and many parts of this land spoiled, some of them even to desolation.

Stubborn, arrogant and selfish Charles I had been, but could Cooke prove that this conduct was criminal? What statute or common law prohibition had he breached? Cooke's conclusion was that the defendant was guilty as 'tyrant, traitor, murderer and a public and implacable enemy to the Commonwealth of England' by virtue of his command responsibility:

> Charles Stuart has been and is the occasioner, author, and continuer of the said unnatural, cruel and bloody wars, and therein guilty of all the treasons, murders, rapines, burnings, spoils, desolations, damages and mischiefs to this nation, acted and committed in the said wars or occasioned thereby.

In the final, formal paragraph of the charge, the prosecutor sealed the King's fate, and his own:

> And the said John Cooke on behalf of the people of England does for the said treasons and crimes impeach the said Charles Stuart as a tyrant, traitor, murderer and a public and implacable enemy to the Commonwealth of England and prays that the said Charles Stuart, King of England, may be put to answer all and every of the premises and that such proceedings, examinations, trials, sentences and judgements may thereupon be had, as shall be agreeable to justice

> Subscribed, John Cooke.

'Tyrant, traitor, murderer . . .' ? There was some doubt whether treason, notwithstanding its extended definition in Strafford's case, could be committed by a king. Murder most certainly could, if the war had been unlawful – but there was some question, even amongst Parliamentarians, about who had really started it, back in 1642. The King had raised his standard outside Nottingham, but he had declared war on his own people in order to safeguard what he sincerely believed were his lawful prerogatives and some thought Essex had over-hastily engaged the parliamentary forces. What the Solicitor-General had hit upon, in a very short time and under intense pressure, was a crime of tyranny, capable of commission by a head of state who begins a widespread and systematic persecution of his own people with the intention of gathering all power into his own hands. On the early morning of 20 January 1649, the Solicitor-General for the Commonwealth formally began the King's trial by signing the vellum parchment upon which his charge had been transcribed.

Cooke's achievement – aided by Aske and Dorislaus – had been remarkable. He had only six working days to formulate the charge and collect the evidence to prove it, harried all the while by a committee which wanted a long press release rather than a technically correct indictment. His final charge was compelling: it reminded the public (and it was widely published in the following weeks) that irrespective of views as to whether the King could or should be put on trial, there was incontrovertible evidence that he bore primary responsibility for the death and desolation of two civil wars. Unlike the trumped-up cases against Strafford and Ralegh and Laud, Anne Boleyn and Mary Queen of Scots, this indictment was a true bill.

10

The King's Trial

On the morning of Saturday 20 January, a troop of soldiers collected the King from St James's Palace, to which he had been brought from Windsor. He was placed in a curtained sedan chair and carried incognito through St James's Park to the nearest landing on the Thames. There, a funereal black barge awaited: he was placed inside its cabin and again his escorts drew the curtain. Shadowed by army boats crammed with musketeers, the barge crunched through the ice floes that had formed on the river overnight and moored at the steps of the Cotton House. The King's arrival could be observed from the high windows of the Painted Chamber, where his judges were meeting to complete their preparations for the opening session. Cromwell, 'white as the wall', stood by the window, announcing in a state of high excitement, 'My masters, he is come, he is come, and now we shall be doing that great work that the nation will be full of.' He turned to Bradshawe, and asked what answer the court should give to 'the first question he will ask us – by what authority and commission we do try him?' Henry Marten stood up and suggested, to general approval, that the King should be told that he was being tried 'in the name of the Commons in Parliament assembled and all the good people of England'.[1]

Charles I was brought to trial at a time when defendants had no rights other than to be tried quickly (cases had to conclude within the day) and were not permitted to give evidence on oath, to cross-examine witnesses or to have the assistance of counsel (other than by leave of the court, and then

151

only to argue points of law). Those who refused to plead were either returned to prison and 'pressed' to do so – by heavy weights which gradually crushed them to death unless they relented – or else were told that their refusal to plead was taken as a confession of guilt. There was no disclosure of the prosecution case, no adjournments and no appeal. 'Prisoners at the bar' might ask the judge to put questions to prosecution witnesses: they could interject and make a final speech but that was their lot. The slightest disrespect to judges was severely punished as contempt of court. Against this background, the King's judges were to show unprecedented consideration for the defendant.

They had good reason to believe that Charles would deny their jurisdiction to try him – this was the refrain of royalist news-sheets – and it was predictable that he would not even accord them the basic courtesy of the age, namely to doff his hat. They decided that royal rudeness should be tolerated and the prisoner generally handled with kid gloves: the court would not insist that he should remove his hat and would give him time to answer the charge if he so requested.[2] The final business, before the seventy judges adjourned to the Exchequer Chamber, the ante-room for their entrance into the hall, was to hear John Cooke read his charge one last time. It had already been engrossed on parchment by a scrivener, and once the court approved it, Cooke signed. His next task was to 'exhibit' it, i.e. present it in open court in the presence of the defendant. This was the formal act which would commence the trial.

It opened in Westminster Hall, the centre of English justice, temporarily cleared of lesser courts and legal bookstalls to make way for this momentous showdown. The Hall was the largest public space in the realm, 300 feet long with a high beamed roof, constructed by William Rufus in 1097. It had been the venue for the trial of Strafford and of the gunpowder plotters, for Sir Thomas Moore's last stand and for Richard II's abdication to Bolingbroke, when the Bishop of Carlisle asked, in Shakespeare's pointed question, 'What subject can pass sentence on his King?'[3] Seventy subjects in black robes emerged at 2pm from the Painted Chamber, to do just that.

The First Session: Saturday Afternoon, 20 January

There was no trumpeting or drumming. The court opened with a solemn procession, led by halberdiers carrying their ceremonial arms from the Tower of London, followed by bearers of the sword of state and the mace. Bradshawe, clad in a long black gown held up by a train-bearer, was accompanied by two lawyers (John Lisle and William Say) similarly robed, and they were followed by sixty-five commissioners in dark suits and high black hats. Bradshawe took his seat on crimson velvet centre stage, in front of the commissioners who sat on tiered benches hung with scarlet, beneath the south window of the hall. Then came the usher's traditional opening proclamation:

Oyez, oyez, oyez. All manner of persons that have anything to do in this court, come near and give your attendance.

As if in response to this invitation, the great gate at the north of the hall was opened and members of the public streamed in and filled up all the places behind and beside the bar. When they were seated, silence was proclaimed and the Act of the Commons establishing the Court was read aloud and loudly by Phelps, standing in front of the Turkish-carpeted clerks' table. Then came the roll-call: each of the judges stood in turn to answer to his name. Sixty-eight were present – given that some of the 135 original nominees had withdrawn or were with army detachments outside London, this counted as a reasonably good attendance. There was a disturbance in one of the abutting galleries when the name of General Fairfax was called: a masked woman (subsequently reported to be Lady Fairfax, the general's wife) shouted out that the general was not present and it was wrong to name him as a judge. (Clarendon claimed she said 'he has more wit than to be here'.) There was a short diversion in the hall and Sergeant Dendy climbed up to the box to investigate, but the lady had departed and the proceedings were not disrupted.

After the roll-call, Bradshawe gave the solemn order 'Send for the prisoner.' It took fifteen minutes for Colonel Tomlinson to fetch the King from the Cotton House and escort him through the maze of passages to his entry point at the side of the hall. There he was met by the sergeant-at-arms and escorted to the bar, where a chair with its velvet cushion, and writing stool with pen, ink and paper, had been placed for him. Normally, prisoners were required to stand at the bar throughout their trials, but the King was no ordinary prisoner.

It had been seven years since Charles had been seen in London, and the spectators were struck by his careworn face and the dirty brown locks which fell from under his hat, which he kept firmly on his head. He was dressed elegantly in black silk with a sky-blue sash; his only decoration the pale blue ribbon and silver medal of St George, emblem of the Order of the Garter. He leant on his white silver-tipped cane and looked sternly at the judges before taking his seat. He rose again, curiosity getting the better of disdain, and turned to survey the audience, but made a point of avoiding the eyes of Cooke, who was sitting a few feet to his right. The sergeant-at-arms called for silence. Charles was spared the demeaning procedure that required the prisoner to hold up his hand on his name being called: instead, Bradshawe made a carefully rehearsed speech, courteously calling him the King of England but at the same time making the court's purpose very clear.[4]

Charles Stuart, King of England. The Commons of England assembled in Parliament, being sensible of the evils and calamities that have been brought upon this nation and of the innocent blood that has been shed in it, which is fixed upon you as the principal author of it, have resolved to make inquisition for this blood, and according to the debt they owe to God, to justice, the Kingdom and themselves, and have resolved to bring you to trial and judgement and have therefore constituted this High Court of Justice, before which you are now brought. Where you are to hear your charge, upon which the court will proceed according to justice.

This was John Cooke's cue. He stood, unscrolling the parchment upon which the charge had been written – the charge that he had signed as Solicitor-General for the commonwealth. 'My Lord President . . .' he began. This is the point at which he felt the sharp tap on his shoulder from the King's cane. 'Hold!' Charles commanded, poking Cooke again. The lawyer ignored him, and addressed Bradshawe: 'My Lord President, according to an order of this High Court to me directed for that purpose . . .' Now Cooke suffered a third blow from the cane, hard enough to dislodge its silver tip. The King motioned for him to pick it up, but the lawyer refused. Instead, he took a deep breath, looked the King squarely in the eye and threw down the legal gage that commenced the trial:

I do, in the name and on the behalf of the people of England, exhibit and bring into this court a charge of high treason and other high crimes whereof I do accuse Charles Stuart, King of England, here present.[5]

Under the astonished gaze of several thousand of his hushed subjects, the King bent to pick the silver tip from the floor at Cooke's feet. 'He stooping for it, put it presently into his pocket. This is conceived will be very ominous', reported the main news-book.[6] It was the moment for which Cooke could never be forgiven – the moment when the King was forced to bend, almost prostrate at his prosecutor's feet, while the law, which he was no longer above, took its course.

The Lord President motioned for the clerk to read out the charge. Charles tried to stop him, with an order: 'By your favour, hold!' The clerk stopped, automatically, but Bradshawe countermanded the King: 'The court commands the charge shall be read: if you have anything to say, after, the court will hear you.'

Charles had been put in his place and that place was the dock. It was a bad start – he was being treated, and beginning to look, like any other prisoner. Now he had to listen to Cooke's charge – even in its slimmed-down form, it would have taken a good ten minutes for the clerk, Andrew Broughton, to read. There is a limit to body language for indifference but Charles did his best – rolling his eyes at the gallery, outstaring the judges, getting up to look behind him at the guards and the spectators. At the description 'tyrant, traitor, murderer . . .' he laughed loudly, as if trying to laugh the charge out of court.[7] It was not a predictable response and it seemed to rattle Bradshawe: Charles had the better of their next exchanges.[8] The judge began ponderously:

Sir, you have now heard your charge read . . . the court expects your answer.

Charles savoured the moment, delayed, then spoke, without his usual stammering, a carefully crafted, but none the less memorable, opening phrase:

I would know by what power I am called hither.

He might have sat down and awaited the answer, but he spoilt the effect by rattling on:

I was not long ago in the Isle of Wight, how I came there is a longer story than I think is fit at this time for me to speak of; but there I entered into a treaty with both Houses of Parliament, with as much public faith as it is possible to be had of any people in the world . . .

He had done no such thing, and everyone knew it. But suddenly he recovered, and returned to his memorable, if poorly memorised, script:

Now I would know by what authority, I mean lawful; there are many unlawful authorities in the world, thieves and robbers by the highways; but I would know by what authority I was brought from thence, and carried from place to place, and I know not what: and when I know by what lawful authority, I shall answer . . .

These words threw back the gage, and the judges must inwardly have cringed. But Charles again spoiled the effect by not awaiting a reply. Instead, he puffed himself up and began to lecture:

Remember I am your King, your lawful King, and what sins you bring upon your heads, and the judgement of God upon this land; think well upon it, I say, think well upon it, before you go further from one sin to a greater . . . In the meantime, I shall not betray my trust; I have a trust committed to me by God, by old and lawful descent. I will not betray it, to answer to a new unlawful authority: therefore resolve me that, and you shall hear more of me.

The accusation of sinfulness could not be taken seriously by men who believed they were doing God's work. But the pointed refrain – show me your authority – unnerved Bradshawe and the King's reference to his hereditary descent provoked the judge:[9]

BRADSHAWE: If you had been pleased to have observed what was hinted to you by the court, at your first coming hither, you would have known by what Authority: which Authority requires you, in the name of the people of England, of which you are elected King, to answer.

KING: England was never an elective Kingdom, but an hereditary Kingdom for near these thousand years; therefore let me know by what Authority I am called hither: I do stand more for the liberty of my people than any here that come to be my pretended judges; and therefore let me know by what lawful Authority I am seated here, and I will answer it. Otherwise I will not answer it.

Bradshawe's use of 'elected' sounds nonsensical to modern ears, but he meant that kings had to be approved by Parliament – a statement with some historical support: James I, after all, had been invited to rule in preference to other candidates. The lesson for Bradshawe (and for any judge) is: do not debate with defendants. This lesson did not sink in:

BRADSHAWE: Sir, how really you have managed your trust, is known: your way of answering is to interrogate the court, which beseems you not in this condition. You have been given your answer twice or thrice.

KING: I do not come here as submitting to the court: I will stand as much for the privilege for the House of Commons, rightly understood, as any man here whatsoever. I see no House of Lords here, that may constitute a Parliament. And the King too should have been. Is this the bringing back of your King to his Parliament? Is this your bringing an end to the treaty done with all the public faith of the world? Let me see a legal authority warranted by the word of God, the scriptures or warranted by the Constitution of the Kingdom, and I will answer.

Charles was on dangerous ground with claim to stand for the privileges of the Commons 'rightly understood' (rightly understood, in the King's view, they barely existed) but again he managed one telling statement – 'I see no House of Lords here, that may constitute a Parliament'. He might have added that he saw no Presbyterian MPs either, which might fully constitute a House of Commons. But this was a special court, not a Parliament, Bradshawe was quick to insist:[10] 'Seeing you will not answer, the court will consider how to proceed,' he announced. 'In the meantime, those that brought you hither, are to take you back again.' But nothing happened – the Lord President had forgotten to issue the command to the guards to take away the prisoner. But then, he asked, as an afterthought: 'The court desires to know, whether this be all the answer you will give, or no.' Charles took his indecision as a cue to admonish the court:

KING: Sir, I desire that you would give me, and all the world, satisfaction in this: let me tell you, it is not a slight thing you are about therefore you shall do well to satisfy first God, and then the country, by what Authority you do it: if you do it by usurped Authority, it will not last long and there is a God in heaven that will call you and all who gave you power to account. Satisfy me in that and I will answer; otherwise I betray my trust and the liberties of the people: and therefore think of that and then I shall be willing . . . satisfy God and me and all the world in that, and you shall receive my answer. I am not afraid of this business.

His demand, made with dignity and force at the outset, now had the irritation of a groove-stuck record. His best point was lost by repeating it, and he did so thirteen times in the course of exchanges with Bradshawe that could have lasted no more than ten minutes. By the end, Charles was much less impressive, whilst Bradshawe had collected himself and now asserted, against the querulous defendant, some vintage judicial authority:

BRADSHAWE: The court expects you should give them a final answer. Their purpose is to adjourn to Monday next. If you then persist in the same temper you are in now, this is as much as if you had said nothing to us. We are upon God's and the Kingdom's errand, and that peace we stand for will be better kept by the doing of justice – that's our present work.

KING: For answer, let me tell you, you have shown no lawful authority to satisfy any reasonable man.

BRADSHAWE: That is in your apprehension – we think it reasonable, and we are your judges.

This time, Bradshawe remembered the magic words which for centuries in English courts have made the defendant disappear: 'Take down the prisoner,' he commanded the guards. 'The King, you mean,' corrected Charles, offended by the word 'prisoner'. The guards advanced to escort him to the staircase leading down to the Cotton gardens. 'Well Sir!' the King harrumphed, as he rose from his seat. As he was led away he pointed with his untipped cane to the parchment containing Cooke's Bill of Indictment, which was lying on the clerk's desk alongside the sword and the mace. 'I do not fear that Bill,' he said loudly, to no one in particular.[11] There were voices in the Hall which now cried out as he left it 'God save the King!', counter-pointed with others which cried 'Justice!' The shouting was stilled by the usher:

Oyez! Oyez! Oyez! All manner of persons that have anything more to do with this court, you are to depart at this time. And this court doth adjourn itself until Monday morning next, at 9 of the clock in the forenoon, to meet in the Painted Chamber, and from thence hither again.

The judges stood up and filed out as they had come in, a solemn procession behind the bearers of the sword of the state and the mace of the Commons. The hearing could not have taken more than an hour: it had started and ended well, and Cromwell and Ireton must have breathed sighs of relief as they compared notes back in the Exchequer Chamber. Although the King's objections read trenchantly on the transcript, his best points had been overwhelmed by the grandeur of the occasion: the impact on the audience, most of whom could not hear a word, was of the majesty of the law rather than the majesty of the King. Bradshawe had carried off the chairmanship with a degree of authority; the fall of the silver tip of the cane was an ominous portent for a defendant who appeared from a distance to be denying the offer of a fair trial. The City that night was quiet, the public engaged – with curiosity, rather than anger or protest. The six licensed newspapers printed more copies, and three new papers had to be licensed to cater for the public appetite to read about the trial. The royalist news-sheets failed to appear, as if cowered by the enormity of the event. This success was more than Cromwell could have hoped, but probably what he expected from providence – although providence had nothing to do with it. Justice always has its own momentum and one thing that was clear from the proceedings of 20 January was that this trial was a deadly serious exercise: now that it had started, it would go on and on – to an end that no one could confidently predict.

In any court, once the prisoners and the judges depart, there is a hubbub as members of the audience, now free to talk, excitedly compare impressions, whilst the barristers gather up their papers and hand them to clerks to carry back to their chambers. The ubiquitous Hugh Peters was first to rush up to Cooke and congratulate him on his performance – especially his coolness when provoked by the King. Holding up his hands as if in thanksgiving, Peters exclaimed, 'This is a most glorious beginning of the work.'[12] These kind words from Peters, now the most influential of the Puritan preachers, must have gladdened the prosecuter's heart. The two friends leant against the bar railing, proud of their part in ending the impunity of sovereigns. The tribunal, they agreed, had resembled that tribunal of the saints promised in the Bible for the day of judgment.

Peters was a populist; Cooke the legalist knew that Bradshawe had yet to provide the answer to the King's challenge to produce lawful authority for the trial. The Solicitor-General would have to find a convincing answer in his final speech – that is, if he was to have a final speech at all. If the King continued in his refusal to plead to the charge he would, by the rules, be taken to have confessed it. That would mean his automatic conviction: the evidence which Cooke had frantically collected over the last ten days would not be heard, and there would be no closing speech, either for the prosecution or the defence. Cooke wanted to play this case, of all cases, by the book (in fact, by two books – the Bible and the *Institutes* of Edward Coke). Peters on the other hand wanted a show trial, in the sense of a trial which would show the world that kings are not above the law.

That Saturday afternoon they went their separate ways: Cooke to begin preparing his opening speech, and Peters his sermon for the morrow. Charles had work to do as well: he refused to spend the night in the Cotton House and was permitted to return to St James's (again by barge and closed sedan chair) to consult his advisers. What had most unnerved him, he confessed to Dr Juxon (the Bishop of London) was the ominous incident with Cooke and the cane. 'It made a great impression – I just don't know how it could have happened, unless Hugh Peters tampered with the tip.'[13] Juxon told him to forget it and concentrate on the next hearing. Charles reproached himself for the day's missed opportunities: he could have told the judges in no uncertain terms *why* they had no legal authority. So a speech was prepared that evening to this effect, for him to deliver when the court reconvened on the Monday.

As for Judge Bradshawe, he abjured his family home behind Gray's Inn gate, and made use instead of the fine lodging appointed for him in New Palace Yard, safely under the guard of army officers. It was just as well: a cavalier named Burghill, armed with sword and pistol, waited for him all night behind the gate.[14] He would have had better luck in assassinating John Cooke, who went back to Gray's Inn with no thought to his own safety. That evening, Cooke was visited by friends who urged him to take care for his own life and indeed to try to save the King. 'They do not intend to take away the King's life, but only bring him to submit to the Parliament,' Cooke reassured them.[15] It was probably an accurate statement of the intention of most members of the court at the outset of the trial.

Sunday was a day of rest for all parties. The judges decided to stay together in Whitehall for fasting and prayer. They commissioned three sermons – the first from Fairfax's chaplain Joshua Sprigge, who preached on the text that had motivated the army: 'Whoso sheddeth man's blood, by man shall his blood be shed.' Then another army preacher took them to task with humiliating thoughts on the subject 'Judge not, that ye be not judged'. These were rather grim and exceedingly long lectures and there was relief when Hugh Peters climbed to the makeshift pulpit to topicalise the text that it was God's purpose 'to bind their kings with chains'. This psalm – 149 – was a favourite since it spoke of the congregation of the saints, amongst which every Puritan hoped to number himself. They intoned:

> Let the high praises of God be in their mouth, and a two-edged sword in
>   their hand;
> To execute vengeance upon the heathen, and punishments upon the people;
> To bind their kings with chains, and their nobles with fetters of iron;
> To execute upon them the judgment written: this honour have all his saints.
>   Praise ye the Lord.

In the mouth of Peters, a skilled and crowd-pleasing evangelist, this psalm had a topical resonance to the judgment on the King. Charles had refused Peters's earnest invitation that he should preach that day to him at St James's, and this gave Cromwell's chaplain – who seems to have had a real talent for stand-up pulpit comedy – a good opening line from Amos, the prophet who insisted on preaching against all the odds: 'The poor wretch would not hear me, but yet I will preach.' Cromwell was observed to laugh at his next joke: the one about the Major, the Bishop and the Bishop's drunken servant. The Major imprisoned the servant, whereupon the Bishop asked by what authority he did so and the Major replied, 'By act of Parliament and neither the bishop nor his man are excepted out of it.' Peters gave the story a topical twist:

> Here is a great discourse and talk in the world: 'What, will you cut off the King's head, the head of a Protestant prince?' But turn to your bibles: *whosoever sheds man's blood, by man shall his blood be shed.* So I will answer them as the Major answered the Bishop, 'By an Act of God – whosoever sheds man's blood, by man shall his blood be shed – and I see neither King Charles, nor Prince Charles, nor Prince Rupert, nor Prince Maurice, nor any of that rabble excepted out of it.'[16]

The Second Session: Monday 22 January

Many of the judges were MPs, and their attendance was required in the Commons when the court was not in session. They began their public duties there on Monday, listening to conflicting messages. The Scottish Parliament had sent a delegation to plead with the House to abandon the trial, but the Commons had little time for their recent enemies: the Scots petition was referred to a committee. More pleasing was a petition from officers on active service in the north, pledging support for the trial and for the 'seclusion' (so Pride's purge was euphemistically described) of corrupt Presbyterian MPs: the present proceedings were 'the work of God alone'. When the business of the House was concluded, those MPs who were also judges joined their colleagues in the Painted Chamber for a post-mortem on the events of Saturday.

This meeting survives only in the short minutes of the clerk, Phelps, but reading between his laconic lines it is evident that the commissioners were troubled by the King's tactics and by Bradshawe's failure to curb them. They realised the long game that the King was playing by denying their jurisdiction – it was to deny the authority of the House of Commons, whether purged or not, to establish a court or to do anything other than to meet at his command, very occasionally, to vote him taxes. Their immediate problem was whether to give the King the opportunity to challenge their jurisdiction, call on Cooke to answer and then deliver a judgment which would establish their legitimacy, or whether they should decline to hear the argument on the basis that a defendant had no right to make it: the court had been established by Act of Parliament, and that was that. Phelps noted that they took 'advice with their counsel learned in both laws', i.e. English common law (Cooke) and continental civil law (Dorislaus). The common law did not, at this stage of its development, permit challenges to jurisdiction: Acts of Parliament, however questionable, could not be questioned in the court that was bound by them because judges were not entitled to investigate the political sources of their own power. The civil law has always been more flexible, and it is likely that Dorislaus favoured what is now the position in international criminal courts, namely that defendants may challenge the lawfulness of the process by which the court was established. Cooke's common law position prevailed, and the court formally resolved that the prisoner should not be suffered to dispute the Act's validity.

Then there was the delicate problem of Bradshawe's inability to shut the King up. The commissioners thought he should be given some help, and drafted an answer for him to give when next Charles demanded to know their 'lawful authority' –

That the Commons of England assembled in Parliament have constituted this court, whose power may not, nor should be permitted to be disputed by him, and that they were resolved he should answer his charge.[17]

The common law rule that Acts of Parliament could not be questioned or investigated justified this answer, as a matter of law. As a matter of reality, this court had not been created by the Parliament, (1) because the Lords had adjourned rather than pass the ordinance and (2) because the army had forcibly excluded from the Commons those MPs whose votes would have defeated it. It was not the creation of 'the Commons assembled in Parliament' but of the Commons disassembled in Parliament by Colonel Pride. But the Rump was nevertheless a *de facto* authority, governing effectively with the support of the army. The interesting point is that in these circumstances its actions were not necessarily unlawful.

The right of a victorious army to detain enemy leaders and put them on trial by court-martial was, as we have seen, an accepted feature of the law of war. Fairfax, a general of considerable scruple, had satisfied himself that he had the power to detain the King, who had himself consulted with some of the best lawyers in the land and never once applied to any judge for habeas corpus, the remedy always available for unlawful detention. There were some judges, especially Presbyterians, who were more than capable of standing up to the army – as William Prynne had proved on 10 January when his lawyers went to a chancery judge to obtain habeas corpus.[18] For all the complaints made by and on behalf of Charles about the unlawfulness of his treatment, he never once challenged it in courts before judges who were bound to entertain his complaint.[19] Lawyers of the calibre of Hale and Bridgeman had considered the point, and must have recognised that the army had the right to detain Charles as an enemy commander. It may be, of course, that a habeas corpus strategy was ruled out because an application to any court by the King could be interpreted as a concession that he *was* subject to the law.

In effect, the army had delegated this power to the Rump. Ireton and Cromwell, officers turned politicians, preferred the Commons to govern the country rather than to fall back on the army's emergency powers. This was a fateful decision because it turned on the alarmingly republican principle that the House of Commons, representing the people of England, was the ultimate repository of all legislative power – absent King and absent Lords. This new constitutional position was first recognised by the High Court on 22 January 1649, by its ruling that the King could not challenge the legitimacy of a court established by the Commons alone.

In the likely event that the King continued his refusal to plead, Cooke reminded the commissioners that the common law had an invariable response: his silence would amount to a confession, and the charge would be 'taken *pro confesso*', i.e. as an admission of every allegation made in it. Charles had three choices: to plead 'guilty'; to plead 'not guilty' and have his day in court; or to maintain his refusal to plead, in which case the charge would be taken *pro confesso*.

Charles was eager to begin. He had brought his speech, finely honed over the weekend – a mixture of legal and political arguments against the authority of the court, written on a paper he held in his hand. He was escorted to his seat after the commissioners, seventy of them, had answered to their names. The court usher hollered for silence and Judge Bradshawe, with a wary eye on the gallery, directed the captain of the guard to arrest anyone who created a disturbance. He nodded in Cooke's direction as a signal for the Solicitor-General to begin, but Cooke was whispering to Dorislaus – both lawyers had their heads down behind the bar, oblivious to the fact that the court was waiting. Charles, impatient to proceed, grasped the opportunity to get his own back: he took his cane (the silver tip firmly glued back) and poked Cooke violently on the shoulder. The barrister turned purple with indignation,[20] but Bradshawe asked loudly, 'Mr Solicitor, do you have anything to demand of the court?' Cooke did indeed, and he quickly recovered:[21]

> May it please your Lordships, at the last court the charge was read over to the prisoner at the Bar, and his answer required. My Lord, instead of answering, he did dispute the authority of this High Court. My humble motion is, that the prisoner may be directed to make a positive answer, either by way of confession or negation. If he shall refuse, then the matter of charge may be taken *pro confesso* and the court may proceed according to justice.

Bradshawe had been primed. He reminded the King of his objections at the previous hearing, and went on:

> Sir, the court now requires you to give a positive and particular answer to this charge that is exhibited against you: they expect you should either confess or deny it. If you deny, the Solicitor-General offers on behalf of the Commonwealth to make it good against you. Sir, the court expects you to apply yourself to the charge, so as not to lose any more time, and to give a positive answer.

Bradshawe had forgotten to explain that if the King should refuse to plead then the charge would be taken *pro confesso*. Charles was unfazed: he consulted his notes and managed to get some way through his prepared speech before Bradshawe interrupted:[22]

> KING: A King cannot be tried by any superior jurisdiction on earth . . . If power without law may make laws, may alter the fundamental laws of the Kingdom, I do not know what subject in England can be sure of his life, or anything that he calls his own. But since I cannot persuade you, I shall tell you my reason as shortly as I can . . . I cannot answer this till I be satisfied of the legality of it. All proceedings against any man whatsoever . . .

BRADSHAWE: Sir, I must interrupt you. I do this unwillingly, but what you do is not agreeable to the proceedings of any court of justice, as all of us who are acquainted with justice know. It seems you are about to enter into argument and dispute concerning the authority of this court, before whom you appear as a prisoner and are charged as a high delinquent. You may not do it.

KING: Sir, I do not know the forms of law, but I do know law and reason. I know as much law as any gentleman in England. I do plead for the liberties of the people more than any of you do.

BRADSHAWE: I must again interrupt you. You must not go on in this course . . .

But he did, arguing with Bradshawe until the judge's patience ran out and he called on the clerk of the court to put the charge:[23]

CLERK: Charles Stuart, King of England, you have been accused on behalf of the people of England of high treason and other high crimes. The court has determined that you ought to give positive answer, whether you confess or deny the charges.

KING: I will, as soon as I know by what authority you sit.

BRADSHAWE: If this be all that you will say, then gentlemen, [addressing Colonel Hacker and his guards] you that brought the prisoner hither, conduct him back again.

KING: I do desire to give my reasons for not answering: I require you give me time for that.

BRADSHAWE: Sir, it is not for prisoners to require.

KING: Prisoners! Sir, I am not an ordinary prisoner.

That was the understatement of the century. At last, Bradshawe was asserting his authority:

BRADSHAWE: The court has considered and already affirmed their jurisdiction. If you will not answer, we will give an order to record your default.

KING: You never heard my reasons yet.

BRADSHAWE: Sir, your reasons are not to be heard against the highest jurisdiction.

KING: Show me wherever the House of Commons was a court of judicature of that kind.

BRADSHAWE: Sergeant, take away the prisoner.

This should have been the end of the day's play. But Charles, as he stood up, turned to the audience and fired a loud parting shot at the court.

KING: Remember that the King is not suffered to give his reasons for the liberty and freedom of all his subjects.

This elicited cries of 'God save the King' although they were ragged (as one observer said of the audience, 'there was an awe upon them'[24]). But the shouts enraged Bradshawe, and he pounced:

BRADSHAWE: Sir, you are not to have liberty to use this language. How great a friend you have been to the laws and liberties of the people, let all England and the world judge.

The King was stung at this and made the mistake of beginning to contest the charges:

KING: Sir, under favour. It was for liberty, freedom and laws of the subject that ever I took . . .

He was about to say 'took to arms', a confession to starting the war. He stopped and checked himself, in obvious embarrassment, and attempted to recover:

KING: I took . . . defended myself with arms. I never took up arms against the people, but for the laws.

The King seemed on the brink of pleading self-defence, but Bradshawe was anxious to adjourn and missed the chance of inveigling the defendant into entering a plea.

BRADSHAWE: The commands of the court must be obeyed here. No answer will be given to the charge.

KING: Well, Sir!

It was with this regular royal harrumph that the second session concluded. Bradshawe had presided more impressively and the King had ended with a telling slip of the tongue. Charles was irritated and argumentative, involved now in the proceedings and anxious – against his own better judgment – to play the justice game. As he was taken down the stairs, he made a fatal mistake: he admitted his true feelings to his escorts, telling them he was untroubled by any of the thousands of deaths that had been laid to his charge, except for that of one man – the Earl of Strafford. This voluntary confession counted as admissible evidence of his remorseless state of mind: it was immediately reported to Cooke, and convinced him that this 'hard-hearted man' was not only guilty of 'so much precious Protestant blood shed in these three kingdoms' but would be happy to shed more in order to regain his prerogatives.[25] It was a turning point for the prosecutor, who had until now admired Charles's spirit and 'undaunted resolution' at the trial and had thought him redeemable.[26] The King's insouciance about the casualties suffered by both sides in the civil war also swayed the judges: it showed that so long as the King lived, the country would be embroiled in war.

Back at St James, Charles was concerned to publish the speech that Bradshawe had not allowed him to finish. His written reasons were quickly slipped to the clandestine royalist printers – probably by Bishop Juxon – and very soon appeared. They were for the most part predictable: You cannot impeach the King, since he is the source of law and can do no wrong. He did offer a defence, crafted more carefully in print than in court: 'The arms I took up were only to defend the fundamental laws of this Kingdom against those who have supposed my power has totally changed the ancient government.' His plea, in other words, was that he had acted in self-defence, at least in 1642. But self-defence is normally confined by law to the defence of one's physical self, one's family and one's home. Could it extend to the defence of one's prerogatives, or indeed one's kingdom?

The Third Session: Tuesday 23 January

This day began ominously for the King: the House of Commons passed a law that writs should no longer go out under his name and royal seal, but by reference merely to the judge who had issued them. And the wording of criminal indictments, which since time immemorial had always accused offenders of acting contrary to 'the peace of our Sovereign Lord the King, His Crown and Dignity' would be changed to accuse them, more rationally, of acting 'against the Peace, Justice and Council of England'. The great seal had already been altered to remove the King's emblems, and any trace of Scotland: it now featured a map of England and Ireland, with the cross of St George and the Irish harp. The flip-side had an engraving by Thomas Simon of the House of Commons in session, and the proud legend (suggested by Henry Marten, and added to the coinage) 'In the first year of freedom, by God's blessing restored'.

This was the first sign that Charles could not only be removed, but that he might not be replaced. None the less, he would be given one last chance to co-operate. The Lord President was instructed to make one final attempt to have the King recognise the court, and this attempt was to be triggered by the prosecutor's request to proceed to judgment if he did not offer a plea. If the King remained contumacious, then the clerk was to put the charge to him for the last time. But if the King agreed to make answer, he would be given a copy of the indictment and allowed an adjournment until Wednesday at 1 p.m. Otherwise, that would be the time when the court would proceed to judgment and sentence.

It is little wonder that the King looked melancholy and distracted when he was brought into Westminster Hall. Cooke was ready this time, to bring the King to the crunch: he leapt to his feet to make the speech which was later to hang him:[27]

My Lord, to put an end to this great delay of justice, I shall now humbly move your Lordship for speedy judgement against him. I might press your Lordships, because according to the known rules of the law of the land, if a prisoner shall stand mute or contumacious and shall not put in an effective plea – guilty or not guilty – to the charge against him whereby he may come to a fair trial, that operates as an implicit confession – it may be taken *pro confesso*. The House of Commons has declared that the charge is true – and its truth, my Lord, is as clear as crystal and as clear as the sun that shines at noon day. But if your Lordship and the court is not satisfied about that, then on the people of England's behalf, I have several witnesses to produce. And therefore I do humbly pray – and yet it is not so much I who pray, but the innocent blood that has been shed, the cry whereof is very great for justice and judgement – that speedy judgement be pronounced against the prisoner at the bar, according to justice.

As speeches go by prosecuting counsel in treason trials, this was remarkably lacking in venom: compare Coke against Ralegh or St John against Strafford. In demanding speedy justice Cooke was riding the hobby-horse he had mounted in the *Vindication* but with some reason, since the King had been avoiding justice for seven years and was now obviously temporising: no other defendant in a criminal court would be suffered to insist on these delays. Although the Solicitor-General referred to the pre-judgment by the Commons, he none the less offered to produce witnesses to prove the King's guilt beyond reasonable doubt. Given the agreement made by the judges a few minutes before in the Painted Chamber, Cooke's motion for judgment was intended as the trigger for the court to force the King for the last time to choose whether to plead (either 'not guilty' or 'guilty') or to continue in his contumacious refusal to recognise the court. As Cooke was later (and truly) to maintain, his application for judgment was *not* a demand for the court to enter a verdict of guilty, but rather a demand that the court should require the defendant to choose. If (as Cooke in fact desired) he chose to plead 'not guilty', then the prosecution would call its evidence and the King would have an opportunity to challenge it. That Cooke's motion for judgment was understood by all as a preliminary to putting the King to final election is clear from Phelps's minutes of the meeting in the Painted Chamber, which noted the resolution 'that the Lord President do inform the King, in case he shall continue contumacious, that he is to expect no further time; and that the Lord President therefore in the name of the court require his positive and final answer . . .'[28]

After Cooke's speech, that is precisely what Bradshawe did. More in control now, he picked up the 'speedy justice' slogan canvassed by the Solicitor-General:

Sir, in plain terms – for justice is no respecter of persons – you are to give your positive and final answer, in plain English, whether you are guilty or not guilty of these treasons laid to your charge.

There was a long pause. Charles had reached the point of no return. He could make a last objection to the legality of the court, or he might have his day in it – listen to Cooke's evidence, belittle it and then present a defence that would establish for posterity the justice of his cause. That option he rejected, and for all his protestations that his stand was one of principle, he must have made the tough calculation that in any forensic battle, he would come off worst. Cooke was in command of all his secret correspondence captured at Naseby and from various messengers over the years, which would reveal his ongoing duplicity and traitorous dealings with the Scots, with the Irish and with continental powers. He simply did not dare contest the charge. His best and indeed only realistic tactic was to get in as many attacks on the legitimacy of the court as he could before he was stopped.[29]

KING: For the charge, I value it not a rush. It is the liberty of the people of England that I stand for . . . [Bradshawe interrupts] by your favour, you ought not to interrupt me. There is no law that allows you to make your King your prisoner. I was negotiating a treaty with the two Houses of Parliament, then hurried along and brought hither. And therefore . . .

BRADSHAWE: Sir, you must know the pleasure of the court.

KING: By your favour, Sir.

BRADSHAWE: Nay, Sir, by *your* favour, you must hear the court, you may not be permitted to fall into those discourses. You appear as a delinquent, you have not acknowledged the authority of the court, but the court craves it not of you – but once more they command you to give your positive answer.

For three days, Charles had taken advantage of Bradshawe's polite reluctance to force the issue, turning every exchange into an opportunity to insult the court. The judge, looking down on the clerks' table, gave the loud command: 'Clerk, do your duty.' Broughton scrambled to his feet to put the charge – but not before the King had exclaimed with heavy irony: 'DUTY, Sir!' Charles was remorseless and defiant: the only 'duty' in Westminster Hall as far as he was concerned was owed to him. Asked yet again to plead to the charge, he shook his head and smiled insolently. 'Sir, you must excuse me.' Bradshawe's patience finally snapped:[30]

BRADSHAWE: Sir, this is the third time that you have publicly disowned this court. How far you have preserved the fundamental laws and privileges of the people, your actions speak louder than your words . . . you have written your meaning in bloody characters throughout the whole Kingdom. Clerk, record the default. And gentlemen, you that brought the prisoner, take him back again.

KING: I will only say this one word more to you . . .

BRADSHAWE: Sir, you have heard the pleasure of the court. Notwithstanding your refusal to understand it, you will now find that you are before a court of justice.

'Well Sir, I find I am before a power' was the King's sarcastic rejoinder as he was led away.

Both the judges and the King recognised that the die had been cast: the last opportunity for Charles to make his defence was now irretrievable. He had given the court no way out: by law, it had now to convict him. The judges processed back to the Painted Chamber, grim-faced and angry that Charles had denied them for a third time. This afternoon, they would not disperse. They met privately and marked the seriousness of the meeting by ordering that none should depart the chamber without asking special leave. They pledged to stay together until the King's fate could be determined.

The King himself was well aware that time had run out: as he was being escorted back to the Cotton House he swallowed a little pride – for the first time – and sent a message asking Hugh Peters to intercede with the court, as his emissary, to ask permission for him to see his chaplains. It must have caused Charles great pain to seek any sort of indulgence from the preacher he loathed, so he evidently feared that judgment was imminent. Peters burst self-importantly into the Painted Chamber to impart the request, only to be told that the King's spiritual welfare was a matter for the Commons. The judges were furious with the King for his offensive remarks but were more concerned by the fact that – as Cooke advised them – his refusal to plead would mean that the prosecution could not call its evidence. The common law required them to have the worst of all worlds: after three sessions in which Charles had insulted the court there would now be no opportunity to unveil the evidence of his responsibility for mass-murder, treason and tyranny. So they hit upon an unusual compromise:

> notwithstanding the said contumacy of the King and his refusal to plead, which in law amounts to standing mute and a tacit confession of the charge, and notwithstanding the notoriety of the facts charged, the court would nevertheless examine witnesses for the further and clearer satisfaction of their own judgement and consciences.[31]

This decision has often been interpreted as a device to stall for time: some historians speculate that it gave Cromwell the opportunity to persuade the commissioners to sentence the King to death, others that, on the contrary, it facilitated efforts behind the scenes to save him.[32] There is no need to impute a hidden agenda. Cooke, a stickler for due process, would have advised the judges that they could not hear his prosecution evidence as part of the trial, since the prisoner had been deemed to have confessed his guilt. There was, however, nothing to stop its being heard as part of a sentencing procedure – at a private session to satisfy their consciences that application of this *pro confesso* rule occasioned no injustice. It was unprecedented, but it did allow Cooke to take sworn statements from witnesses and present them to the judges. He recognised that it was an unsatisfactory expedient: it meant that the prosecution evidence against the King was not heard openly and did not become part of the public record. It would also mean, inevitably, that he could not make a closing speech.

Evidentiary Sessions: 24 and 25 January

The court convened in private on Wednesday morning in the Painted Chamber to elect a committee before whom the witness statements would be taken. It was a long day: Cooke summoned no fewer than thirty-three witnesses to prove that the King had been a commander who had breached the laws of war.[33] The prosecutor was particularly conscientious: the House of Lords was required to hand over documents for him to inspect and the army was ordered to produce from custody a royalist officer named Holder whom Cooke had heard could give evidence of the King's incitement of war-crimes. When asked about his conversations with the King, Holder begged the court's protection from being forced to incriminate himself. Ironically the right to silence, established by Bradshawe and Cooke in Lilburne's case, came to his rescue: Bradshawe ruled that Cooke's questions would force Holder to 'self-accuse' and therefore excused him from testifying.[34]

Many of Cooke's witnesses were royalist soldiers whose identification of the King leading his troops at various battles could not be disputed. Charles had been a highly visible presence, fully armed and with his sword drawn, urging his men on with stirring speeches ('Stand to me this day for my crown lies upon the point of the sword. If I lose this day I lose my honour and my crown for ever.'[35]) Witnesses depicted him in full command at Naseby and Copredy Bridge, at Edge Hill and Kenton and Newbury – all places referred to in the indictment. They usually added a description of the field after the battle, strewn with dead bodies. Cooke was able to prove that the King's preparations for war had begun as early as July 1642, and that his war crimes began soon afterwards. One eye-witness described the first act of plunder (the ransacking of civilian homes) committed on the King's orders at Hull Bridge and Beverley and produced a royal command that stopped the food supply to Hull, a town that on the King's orders was starved unlawfully into surrender.[36] Cooke called a number of witnesses from Nottingham who described the setting up of the King's standard and how his soldiers had extracted large sums of money from the inhabitants by threatening to plunder and fire the town.[37]

Much more serious were allegations that Charles had stood by and approved the beating and torturing of prisoners of war. Two witnesses claimed to have seen the King at Fowey in Cornwall, watching from his horse while his men stripped and stole from their prisoners, contrary to the surrender agreement and to the customary laws of warfare. One witness from Newark Fort, near Leicester, which had surrendered to the King and his forces in June 1645 on terms that no violence should befall its defenders, testified that 'the King's soldiers, contrary to the [surrender] articles, fell upon the [surrendered] soldiers – stripped, cut and wounded many of them'. They were rebuked by a royalist officer but the King 'on horseback in bright armour' ordered the brutality to continue with the words, 'I do not care if they cut them three times more for they are mine enemies.' This was testimony that directly implicated Charles in ordering the torture of prisoners of war.[38]

What Cooke was presenting to the court over these two days was evidence that Charles was guilty of waging war against Parliament, personally and enthusiastically, that he bore command responsibility for the war crimes of his soldiers and that he was responsible as an individual for ordering and approving the torture of prisoners and plunder of towns. Even more damaging were his secret letters, full of double dealings and attempts to procure military assistance from Catholic powers and from Ireland and from Scotland: this correspondence under his own hand would have been devastating if used to question him at Westminster Hall. There was damaging evidence from a Parliament agent, who had trapped Charles into making admissions about the support he had requested from the Irish.[39] The most damning testimony came from a barrister, Henry Gooch of Gray's Inn, who told of approaching the King during the Newport negotiations under the pretence of being a supporter. The King arranged for the Prince of Wales to commission Gooch in the royalist army in exile, and expressed his 'joy and affection' that so many of his subjects were prepared to fight a third civil war to restore him to power.[40]

The evidence, taken by Cooke in private before the committee on Wednesday, was read back in public in the Painted Chamber on Thursday when each witness attended to swear to the truth of his statement. The forty-six judges who sat through it to 'satisfy their consciences' had so little doubt after reading the captured correspondence that they closed the doors and resolved to proceed to discuss the sentence.[41] They provisionally decided – their resolutions were to be subject to confirmation by a full complement of commissioners the next day – that

1. This court will proceed to sentence of condemnation against Charles Stuart, King of England.
2. That the condemnation of the King shall be for a tyrant, traitor and murderer, likewise for being a public enemy to the Commonwealth of England.
3. This condemnation shall extend to death.

They proceeded to discuss the question of deposing the King – and indeed the Stuart line – but deferred this for discussion in the Commons. The sentence of death was to be drafted by a small committee – the lawyers Lisle, Say and Love, together with Ireton, Scot, Harrison and Marten, but the draft would 'leave a blank for the manner of his death'. Some thought that Charles should be deprived of his title of King once he had been convicted and before sentence, in which case he would face the commoner's death for treason, namely hanging, drawing and quartering. If he died as a king, he would be entitled to a relatively painless surgical exit from the world by beheading. It was a very important distinction: the difference between death with dignity and death by butchery.

Thursday had been another long day: the commissioners and their counsel deliberated well into the evening. The case was proven and the sentence agreed: the awesome consequence, namely the end of monarchical government in England, had for the first time to be squarely faced. Gooch's evidence had identified Charles the Prince of Wales as the alter-ego of Charles the King. There would be no point in executing Charles I if Charles II remained in command of his father's army and allegiances. The only long-term solution, which became obvious to Cooke by the end of this dramatic week, was that England should never again be burdened by a king. The form of government he had always promoted in his writings – constitutional monarchy – he could no longer support. He went back to Gray's Inn late that night, about 11 p.m., where he was recognised by a former pupil named Starkey who plucked at his sleeve. 'Mr Cooke, I hear you are up to your ears in this business?' 'No,' replied the barrister, 'I am serving the people.' 'I hear you charge the King for levying war against the Parliament – how can you rationally do this, when you have pulled out the Parliament to make way for this trial?' Cooke's reply was 'You will see strange things and you must wait upon God.' According to Starkey, he asked whether the King must suffer, to which the Solicitor-General replied, **'The King must die and monarchy must die with him.'**[42]

11

Farewell Sovereignty

The trial had cast a spell over London: the sense of awe observed in the audience at Westminster Hall was evident throughout the city. There had been no protests by the strong Presbyterian factions; no rescue attempts by cavaliers; no demonstrations in Westminster Hall. The commanding presence of the army cannot explain the numbing of the King's supporters, as if mesmerised by the sight of justice being done. It was not as if public allegiances had suddenly swung to the Independents, although some who had fled with uneasy consciences at Christmas were by now confident enough to return to Parliamentary duties. That astute lawyer Bulstrode Whitelocke was seen again in Westminster: as Lord Chancellor, he had the task of persuading the judges to issue the new style of writ, which omitted any reference to the King. 'In which matter the judges seemed not to be very forward to join with us'[1] he grumbled, after meeting them at Sergeant's Inn on 24 January. They were uncomfortable with the trial and were available to entertain a habeas corpus motion on behalf of the King, had his lawyers been instructed to make it.

In the city, there was a general sense of 'waiting upon God' and an expectation in many quarters that His verdict would be delivered through the court. The commissioners were not, however, finding God very easy to read. Forty-six had heard the evidence on Thursday and were sufficiently persuaded to resolve provisionally upon conviction and a sentence that 'shall extend to death' – a phraseology betraying their hope that the King might, even now, recognise the court. In that case, a sentence that 'extended to death' might not reach to its full extent. None the less, Ireton drafted a death sentence overnight for discussion on Friday, when sixty-two commissioners attended. It was confirmed, after what Phelps with infuriating brevity describes as 'several readings, debates and amendments'. They also agreed to have him brought again to Westminster Hall to receive the sentence, which meant – as they all recognised – that he would have one last chance to change his mind and save his life.

The court convened at 10 a.m. on Saturday in the Painted Chamber, to decide its tactics for the big day.[2] The sentence of conviction and death was again read and agreed. There was no dissent. It was the logical, legal and inevitable consequence of the King's refusal to plead to the charge. That it was not the *desired* consequence, at least by the majority of commissioners, is clear from their next two resolutions:

1) That in case the King shall submit to the jurisdiction of the court, and pray a copy of the charge, that then the court do withdraw and advise.

2) That in case the King shall move anything else worth the court's consideration, that the Lord President, upon the advice of his assistants, give orders for the court withdrawing to advise.

These resolutions give no hint of what the court's 'advice' would be in the event of a *volte-face* by Charles, but the first was specific and binding on Bradshawe, indicating that the judges would be prepared to hear his defence if the King was prepared to offer it – otherwise there would be no point in withdrawing. The second resolution required Bradshawe to consult with Lisle and Say, his lawyer MP assistants who were more politically savvy, to decide whether any new proposal made by the King was 'worth the court's consideration' – a reference to rumours that the King might come to court with some offer to relinquish the throne. The resolution assumed, wrongly as it turned out, that he would tell the court what proposal he had in mind. The commissioners were genuinely anxious to give Charles one last chance. If he remained truculent, however, the normal criminal court procedures would apply: upon conviction the presiding judge would deliver a homily, and the defendant would not be allowed a last word before sentence was passed. Bradshawe was asked to make remarks 'seasonal and suitable to the occasion'. One novel touch, appropriate given the number of judges, was that all should stand to their feet to signify their assent to the sentence.

The commissioners processed into Westminster Hall, Bradshawe having donned a scarlet robe to emphasise the seriousness of this session. Its purpose was anticipated by some members of the audience, who cried out 'Justice!' as the prisoner entered. This was recognised to be unseemly: after the formal cries for silence, Bradshawe ordered Axtell, the Captain of the Guard, to arrest anyone who created any further disturbance. The presiding judge stood and addressed the commissioners: 'Gentlemen, it is well known . . .' when at this point Charles interrupted. He had one last card to play, and was suddenly afraid that the game might be over.[3]

KING: I shall desire a word to be heard a little, and I hope I shall give no occasion for interruption.

THE PRESIDENT: Sir, you shall be heard in due time, but you are to hear the court first.

KING: Sir, I desire, it will be in order to what I believe the court will say, and therefore, Sir – a hasty judgment is not so soon recalled.

THE PRESIDENT: Sir, you shall be heard before the judgment be given and in the meantime you must forebear.

Charles was plainly nervous. Bradshawe had been instructed to hear him, but not before explaining to everyone that this would be an indulgence. 'Gentlemen, it is well known that the prisoner at the Bar has been several times brought before this court to make answer to a charge of treason and other high crimes, exhibited against him in the name of the people of England . . .'

At this point a masked lady in one of the galleries cried, 'It is a lie – not half the people.' Axtell muttered to his men 'What whore is that who disturbs the court?' and called out to her to hold her tongue, threatening to shoot if there were any further disturbance. The gallery – understandably – fell quiet and it was some minutes before Sergeant Dendy could reach the upper section by which time the masked woman – whether or not the same person who had interrupted the first session – had again disappeared.[4] Bradshawe was unruffled by the intervention, if indeed he was even aware of it: he went on to remind the court once again that the King was guilty of contempt for refusing to plead. The judges have considered of the charge, they have considered of the contumacy, and of that confession which in law does arise upon that contumacy: . . . they are resolved and are agreed upon a sentence to be pronounced against this prisoner. But in respect he does desire to be heard, before the sentence be read and pronounced, the court has resolved that they will hear him.

The only condition was that the King must not use the occasion to make a speech attacking, yet again, the lawfulness of the court. 'But Sir, if you have anything to say in defence of yourself concerning the matter charged, the court has commanded me to let you know they will hear you.'

There was an air of intense expectation. Today, the King seemed no longer defiant: it was as if his bluff at the previous sessions had been called and now he genuinely wanted to achieve a compromise to save his life or his posterity or both. His speech, however, came as an anti-climax:

I have something to say before sentence be given, that I may be heard in the Painted Chamber before the Lords and Commons . . . 'tis very well worth the hearing . . . I conjour you that you will grant me this hearing before any sentence be passed . . . it may be you have not heard of it beforehand; if you will, I will retire, and you may think of it . . .

Charles went on in this vein until he drew breath, which gave Bradshawe the chance for an ironic counterpoint: 'Sir, you have now spoken?' The King agreed that he had. But what he had said, Bradshawe pointed out censoriously, was exactly what he had promised not to say, namely 'a further declining of the jurisdiction of this court'. That was how the President interpreted the King's request to be heard before the Lords and Commons – a request to be released as prisoner at the bar and reunited with his Parliament. At this, Charles became rattled: he seems genuinely not to have thought through the implications of his move:

Pray excuse me, Sir, for my interruption, because you mistake me . . . I do not decline it, though I cannot acknowledge the jurisdiction of the court. Yet, Sir, in this give me leave to say, I would do it, though I did not acknowledge it in this, I do protest it is not the declining of

How history imagines John Cooke: a fictitious portrait from the
National Portrait Gallery.

A typical illustration from *Foxe's Book of Martyrs*: John Rogers, the protestant Vicar of

The traitor's death: hanging, drawing and quartering: the execution of Guy Fawkes and the gunpowder plotters, 1605. Note how the victim is dragged to execution backwards the hurdle: the smoke is from braziers heating the tongs for disembowelment.

Archbishop Laud dines on a Star Chamber delicacy: the ears of William Prynne.

'Black Tom Tyrant' Wentworth and a secretary, painted by Van Dyke in 1634, the year Cooke joined Wentworth's administration in Ireland.

A. Doctor Vsher, Lord Prim
te of Ireland,
B. the Sherifes of London,
C. the Earle of Strafford,
D. his kindred and Friends

Puritans on parade: the people of God turn out for Strafford's execution on Tower Hill May 1641, as observed by Wenceslas Hollar.

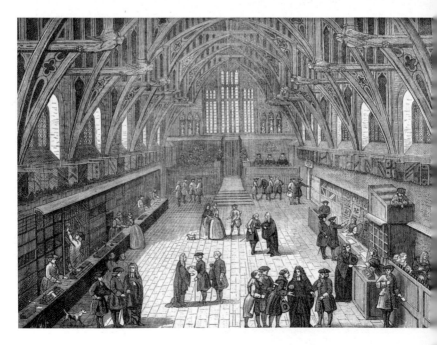

Westminster Hall in term time: the courts of King's Bench and Chancery are at the far end booksellers, and barristers pretending to be busy.

Title page of John Cooke's
first publication.

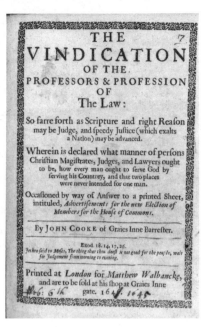

A barrister begs parliament for an
'angelical ordinance' to relieve the poor.

Cromwell: warts, middle-age spread and all.

General Thomas Fairfax:
the real 'Black Tom'.

The army council, 1647,
with Fairfax in command.

'Freeborn John' Lilburne at the Bar, quoting Coke's *Institutes*.

Charles between the bars: as seen in 1648.

Charles in the dock: an idealised drawing by Royalist painter Edward Bower, from a court-room sketch, probably on 22nd January: Charles clutches his speech notes but not his cane.

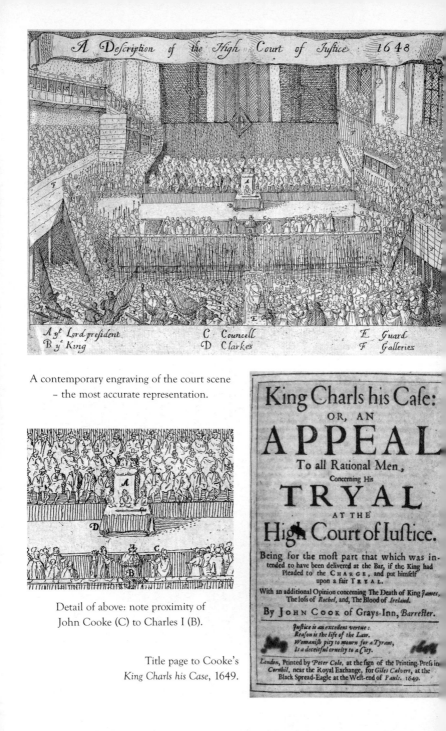

A Description of the High Court of Justice : 1648

A y.ᵉ Lord president   C   Councell   E   Guard
B y.ᵉ King   D   Clarkes   F   Galleries

A contemporary engraving of the court scene
– the most accurate representation.

Detail of above: note proximity of
John Cooke (C) to Charles I (B).

Title page to Cooke's
King Charls his Case, 1649.

King Charls his Case:
OR, AN
APPEAL
To all Rational Men,
Concerning His
TRYAL
AT THE
High Court of Iustice.

Being for the most part that which was intended to have been delivered at the Bar, if the King had
Pleaded to the CHARGE, and put himself
upon a fair TRYAL.

With an additional Opinion concerning The Death of King *James*,
The loss of *Rachel*, and, The Blood of *Ireland*.

By JOHN COOK of Grays-Inn, Barrester.

Justice is an excellent vertue:
Reason is the life of the Law.
Womanish pity to mourn for a Tyrant,
Is a deceitful cruelty to a City.

London, Printed by *Peter Cole,* at the sign of the Printing-Press in
Cornhil, near the Royal Exchange, for *Giles Calvert,* at the
Black Spread-Eagle at the West-end of *Pauls.* 1649.

it, since I say, if that I do say anything, but that that is for the peace
of the Kingdom . . .

Charles, for all this stammering incoherence, was clearly trying to have
it both ways – to maintain his refusal to acknowledge the court, yet in one
last attempt to restore his authority to request that it order a joint sitting of
Lords and Commons which he would address as King. He had already inti-
mated his wish through an intermediary – Peters had appeared in the Painted
Chamber on Tuesday afternoon and must have foreshadowed it then. As
Bradshawe next remarked, 'Sir, this is not altogether new that you have
moved to us, not altogether new to us, though the first time in person you
have offered it to the court.' He pointed out that it would mean further
delay in a trial which had been scheduled to start a week before; that the
King could have made his offer at any time during the previous sittings, that
he wanted 'another jurisdiction, and a co-ordinate jurisdiction' – namely the
High Court of Parliament itself, and 'that which you would offer there, whatever it is, must necessarily be in delay of the justice here'. The judges were
ready to deliver the verdict, but in deference to him they would retire to
consider whether to grant his request.

Bradshawe's decision to adjourn complied to the letter with the resolution passed in the Painted Chamber earlier that morning. Like most judges
required by law to adopt an inconvenient procedure for the benefit of an
uncooperative party, he lists the inconveniences before granting the indulgence. But one commissioner, John Downes, would later claim that at this
point he made an emotional appeal to his fellow commissioners: 'Have we
hearts of stone? Or are we men?' To which Cromwell, sitting in front of him,
turned around and hissed, 'What ails you? Are you mad? Can't you sit still
and be quiet?' Downes answered, 'Sir, I cannot be quiet' and at this point
by his own account jumped to his feet and addressed Bradshawe. 'I am not
satisfied to give my consent to this sentence, but have reasons to offer to
you against it, and therefore I desire that the court may adjourn to hear me.'
Downes's account makes no sense, because Bradshawe was not about to pass
sentence, he was about to adjourn.[5] Downes first made this claim in 1660,
to save himself from execution, and historians have accepted it uncritically,
all too anxious for colourful material to embroider the trial transcript. At
any event, with or without any intervention by Downes, an adjournment
was granted: the commissioners retired to the Court of Wards to consider

whether to proceed to sentence the King or whether to order that his offer, whatever it might turn out to be, should be entertained at a joint sitting of the Parliament.

For an hour or thereabouts, the judges debated the King's request.[6] Downes at this point did support the King, only to be brow-beaten by Cromwell as 'one peevish tenacious man'. 'Surely this gentleman knows that he has to deal with the hardest-hearted man upon the earth.'[7] This sounds authentic Cromwell: Downes was an unattractive figure who was perfectly willing to sign the execution warrant just two days later – a fact that undid him at his own trial. But he does appear to have been prompted by Cooke to make a further argument that sentence should not be passed until there had been a proper examination of the evidence.[8] This would have involved Cooke's calling in Westminster Hall the witnesses he had deposed in the Painted Chamber, and publicly producing the secret letters exposing the King's treacherous dealings: Charles would be present and in a position to comment on or contest them, a temptation he would be unlikely to resist. Nicholas Love, who also favoured this procedure, spoke against passing the death sentence, as did Colonel Harvey: both refused to sign the warrant.[9]

Cromwell and Ireton regarded the King's request as a tactic to delay the trial, perhaps until the anticipated invasion by Ormonde and the Prince of Wales. It would turn the clock back, and put the King into the negotiating seat he had occupied at Newport – the position that the Army Council deemed so dangerous for national security in December that it had purged the House of Commons. In 1660, when all responsibility had to be shifted to Cromwell, it would be alleged that he 'laughed and smiled and jeered in the court of wards,'[10] to deride those who wanted to give the King yet another chance, but the decision to turn down Charles's request was not reached by the force of Cromwell's character. The King could not sensibly demand an adjournment without telling the court what it was that he intended to offer: once granted the opportunity to address Parliament he could offer as much or as little as he wished – the Newport terms, for tedious example. So the commissioners determined that the King should be dealt with according to law and without further delay or aspersion on the court's authority.

The majority of the commissioners – 'jurors' as they had been described in the statute establishing the court – were not awed or persuaded by Oliver Cromwell. Like 'good men and true' then and now, they were convinced beyond reasonable doubt by what they had seen and heard of the defendant. It was the King's demeanour when confronted with Cooke's charge that made the fatal impression. Lucy Hutchinson explained that what decided the issue for her husband and most of his colleagues was the fact that when charged with the blood spilled on both sides 'he heard it with disdainful smiles, and looks and gestures which rather expressed sorrow' that the parliamentary side had not been annihilated. Charles had said loudly to his guards as they left court on 22 January that the only death that troubled him in the least was that of Strafford – evidence of heartlessness that so outraged the commissioners that they 'saw in him a disposition so bent to the ruin of all that opposed him' that there was no alternative but to proceed to execution 'with a good conscience for God and their country'.[11] That was certainly John Cooke's state of mind by the end of the trial – the King's 'confession' to his guards was a significant factor in changing his own mind about the King's fate.

The time had come for Charles to have his right to expeditious justice, whether he wanted it or not. That is how Bradshawe put it when the court re-assembled:[12]

BRADSHAWE: Sir, the return I have to you from the court is this: that they have been too much delayed by you already and this that you now offer has occasioned some little further delay. They are good words in the great old charter of England: 'To no one will we sell, to no one will we deny or delay right or justice'. There must be no delay . . . they are resolved to proceed to punishment and to judgment and that is their unanimous resolution.

Charles by now had only a tenuous grip on reality. He appeared surprised by the judge's decision to proceed with the sentence. He tried Bradshawe's patience by repeating his request, alternating condescension with wheedling, using an image borrowed from Shakespeare's hapless Richard II, who warned that God's punishment for lifting vassal hands against his head 'shall strike your children yet unborn and unbegot'.[13]

KING: I confess it is a delay but it is a delay very important for the peace of the Kingdom . . . a little delay of a day or two further may give peace whereas a hasty judgment may bring on that trouble and perpetual inconveniency to the Kingdom, that the child that is unborn may repent it: and therefore again, I do desire that I may be heard by the Lords and Commons in the Painted Chamber . . .

BRADSHAWE: Sir, I have received direction from the court.

KING: Well, Sir.

BRADSHAWE: . . . and they will proceed to sentence if you have nothing more to say.

KING: Sir, I have nothing more to say. But I shall desire that this may be entered – what I have said.

Even at this late stage, the court would have entertained a belated plea of 'not guilty', but Charles could not bring himself to recognise the court. He had not deigned to spell out the offer that he insisted would be so satisfactory that it would produce a lasting peace – an indication that it would have been nothing of the kind. He had behaved, throughout, as though he really did not think these lesser men – only a few of whom he could recollect meeting before – would dare to sentence their King to death. He was certainly not expecting Bradshawe to deliver anything by way of sentencing homily that would require an answer. But in this belief he underestimated the tough old lawyer whose tolerance had not been from slow-wittedness so much as a determination to be seen as conducting the trial fairly. It was now Bradshawe's moment, to justify the proceedings and the sentence, and he did so in a long speech (it took more than half an hour to deliver) which had passages of real force and substance.[14]

Bradshawe began with an emphatic denial that the King was above the law. For Charles to pit his 'single judgment' against the law made by the people of England through their elected representatives had been his fundamental error, for which courts of justice could call him to account. His office was one of trust, 'elective' in the sense that it required the continuing consent of the people, tacit so long as Parliament was meeting to redress their grievances. For all Charles's talk at his trial of the liberty of the people 'the great bulwark of the liberties of the people is the Parliament of England. And by subverting and rooting up that which your aim hath been to do, certainly at one blow you had confounded the liberties and the property of England.' Parliament represented the people and an attack on Parliament was an attack on the people. That the people were in consequence entitled to have the monarch tried, condemned and deposed Bradshawe set out to prove – in turn from history, political philosophy and law. His history was dodgy: he cited as 'precedents' the removal of Edward II and Richard II (neither of whom had been removed by legal process) and 'we will be bold to say that no Kingdom has yielded more plentiful experience than your native Kingdom of Scotland has done concerning the deposition and punishment of offending Kings'. This was a cheap shot, made cheaper by reference to the fate of Charles's own grandmother, Mary Queen of Scots. Many of the 109 kings and queens of Scotland to that date had indeed met sticky ends, but through brutal clan rivalries and power struggles rather than the decision of a court.

Where Bradshawe became more assured was in political philosophy: in a passage which predates 'social contract' philosophers like Locke and Rousseau by many decades, he identified the point at which the people might justifiably throw off their hereditary sovereign, namely when that sovereign broke his side of the bargain by failing to protect his subjects in return for their allegiance:

> For there is a contract and bargain made between the king and his people, and the oath is taken for the performance, and certainly, Sir, the bond is reciprocal, for as you are their liege Lord, so they are your liege subjects . . . the one tie, the one bond, is the bond of protection that is due from the sovereign, the other is the bond of subjection that is due from the subject. Sir, if this bond be once broken, farewell sovereignty!

It was a powerful point, and a neat harness of feudal theory to the concept of a contract between king and people. It set up the rhetorical question: 'Sir, whether you have been (as by your office you ought to be) a protector of England or a destroyer of England, let all England judge.' By this stage, Charles was becoming unnerved: when Bradshawe turned to Cooke's allegation that he was 'tyrant, traitor and murderer', he scoffed loudly ('Ha' is recorded) just as he had laughed when the charge was read on the first day. But Bradshawe explained that his arbitrary government was tyranny, his breach of trust was treason, and that 'all the bloody murders which have been committed since the time of the division between you and your people must be laid to your charge'. For the crime of murder, the common law of England and the law of God[15] laid down the sentence of death, and laid it down for everyone, kings not excepted. Bradshawe concluded, somewhat unnecessarily, by vowing defiance to all the royalist threats: he would trust in God (and, he might have added, in the special lead lining of his hat and the twenty officers protecting him around the clock). He turned avuncular (a common fault among judges at the end of sentencing homilies) and hoped that God would deliver the King from his blood guilt. By this point, Charles could bear this lecture no longer: Bradshawe's condemnation had stung him and he suddenly wanted to defend himself:

KING: I would desire only one word before you give sentence. And that is that you would hear me concerning these great imputations that you have laid to my charge.

BRADSHAWE: Sir, you must give me now leave to go on, for I am not far from your sentence and your time is now passed.

Bradshawe was on a roll. Pausing only for the acidic reflection that since 'you have not owned us as a court and you look upon us as a sort of people met together' the King could claim no right to address them:

Truly, Sir, we are not here to make law, but to apply law. We may not acquit the guilty. What sentence the law affirms to a traitor, tyrant, murderer and public enemy to the country, that sentence you are now to hear read unto you, and that is the sentence of the court.

Charles was crushed. Bradshawe was now in his element – he was, after all, a judge and used to tormenting convicted defendants with righteous put-downs. The King had been in turn arrogant, infuriating and contumacious: now he *was* an ordinary prisoner, with blood guilt heavy upon him and little time to wash it off before meeting his maker. He was obliged to suffer in silence a very long sentence, agreed by the court and read by Andrew Broughton which summarised Cooke's charge and recapitulated the defendant's refusal to plead, before reaching its dread ending:[16]

This court does adjudge that the said Charles Stuart, as tyrant, traitor, murderer and public enemy to the good people of this nation, shall be put to death by the severing of his head from his body.

Bradshawe rose with a formal incantation: 'The sentence read and now published is the act, sentence, judgment and resolution of the whole court.' The commissioners, at this prearranged signal, all stood up as an acknowledgement that it was unanimous. It took time for them to settle: as they did so a small and now stuttering voice was heard from the bar:[17]

KING: Will you hear me a word, Sir?

BRADSHAWE: Sir, you are not to be heard *after* sentence.

KING: No, Sir?

BRADSHAWE: No, Sir. Guard, withdraw your prisoner.

KING: I may speak after the sentence by your favour, Sir. I may speak after the sentence is over. By your favour – hold! – the sentence, Sir – I say, Sir, I do.

BRADSHAWE: Guard, take away the prisoner.

And so the King's trial ended, like many others, with the prisoner objecting as the guards take him down, out of sight and sound. Charles collected himself as he was being led away and flung a last few sarcastic words in the direction of the court reporters. 'I am not suffered for to speak. Expect what justice other people will have.'[18] Now he was and looked a convict: the soldiers in the Hall, hitherto well behaved, began to chant, 'Justice! Justice!' and some (recognising that justice had already been done) cried, 'Execution!' 'Poor soldiers,' Charles was reported to have said – and if he did, it reflected his underestimation of the New Model Army, 'for sixpence they would say as much for their commanders.' As he was escorted through passageways lined with soldiers some breathed tobacco smoke over him. Above him, his judges were processing back to the Painted Chamber for the final business of the day: to appoint five of their number – including Ireton and Harrison – to arrange the time and place for the execution.[19]

The King's trial had been conducted with a fairness and politeness that were unparalleled in criminal proceedings and which set an important precedent. The rule emphasised by Bradshawe – that the law was no respecter of persons – meant that the consideration he gave to the King should be applied in favour of meaner men when they came to trial. In a word, it meant the judges and prosecutors must show some respect for the wretched individual at the bar.

Charles was not, of course, wretched: he was engaged in a power play which would in due course make his family the executioner of his judges. His tactic was to confront them personally, rather than through legal counsel, although the best – Matthew Hale – was ready to appear for him. Significantly, Charles declined to instruct Hale, because he wanted to appear in all his dimmed glory, in charge of his fate, confronting his accusers alone. The presence of defending lawyers inevitably removes the spotlight from their client. (Centuries later, the first head of state to be tried in an international court would adopt the same tactic: Slobodan Milosevic ordered his lawyers to sit in the public gallery, so that television in Serbia would depict him as a solitary victim, alone against the world.) But Charles had seemed lonely rather than alone. He had not confounded lying witnesses, as had Strafford and Ralegh: his foils had been Cooke, with whom he had not engaged other than in occasional private whispers or public prods, and the ponderous but decent Bradshawe. He had attacked the court and scored well at the outset – when Cooke himself saluted the King's 'height of spirit and undaunted resolution' – but his increasingly desperate repetition of the same point made him seem bothered and, by the end, beaten.

The court, after all, had looked and acted like a court – a much fairer court, in public memory, than his own Star Chamber. There was no dispute that Parliament, the highest court, could create other courts. Charles defined 'Parliament' as the triumvirate of Lords, Commons and the King himself, whose consent (on this theory) would be required for his own trial. That would be an absurdity, although for any impeachment process the Lords would be needed as judges and they were nowhere to be seen at Westminster Hall. But the common law had for centuries recognised courts that had not been created by Parliament – the Star Chamber, for example, and other 'prerogative courts' in which the King's ministers were the judges, as well as the Church of England's complex system of ecclesiastical courts of quasi-criminal jurisdiction, and numerous local or customary tribunals (such as 'pie powder courts' attached to every market). The army had power to establish courts martial and both sides had carried on court-martialling enemies throughout the civil wars, and now the army had, in effect if not in form, relinquished that power to the House of Commons. That House, albeit truncated, was the *de facto* power in the land, and decided to give the King a trial rather than a summary court martial. Since the law protected men of noble birth from the verdict of a common jury, the Commons established a 'High Court of Justice' presided over by a judge, with a jury of the closest 'peers' they could find – men of influence as MPs, civil and business leaders, county officials and army officers. If treason was an offence that could, after the Strafford precedent, be committed by a king; if Charles as commander could be made responsible for war crimes committed by his troops; if the crime of 'tyranny' was justiciable – then a trial was in order, for which a court had to be established by the *de facto* authority – namely the authority that had supplanted his. The defendant, after all, was busy conspiring with Parliament's enemies to bring on the next aggressive stage of what was really an ongoing war, a state of national emergency. The King's trial might be unprecedented, but it was not for that reason unlawful.

This court put Charles on trial but it did not try him. That altogether more significant exercise the King prevented by refusing to plead. As far as Cooke was concerned, his reason for refusing to enter a defence was simple – he had no defence. Nor had he any mitigation, because he was entirely lacking in remorse. The King's conscience was not troubled by any of the bloodshed of the wars, but only by his responsibility for agreeing to Strafford's execution.[20] There can be no doubt that Charles really did believe himself innocent of any responsibility for the death-toll of the wars. He took a last brief opportunity, in his speech on the scaffold, to explain:

> . . . all the world knows I never did begin the war with the two Houses of Parliament . . . They began upon me . . . if anybody will look but to the dates of the commissions, their commissions and mine, and likewise to the declaration, will see clearly that they began these unhappy troubles, not I . . . I only say this, that an unjust sentence [meaning Strafford] that I suffered to take effect, is punished now by an unjust sentence upon me. So far I have said to show you that I am an innocent man.[21]

Cooke had called his first witness – William Cuthbert – to establish that the King was responsible for war crimes (plunder at Beverley and the starvation of Hull) as early as July 1642, before he formally declared war by setting up his standard at Nottingham. Charles claimed that Parliament levied war on him, and his standard was raised in self-defence, in putting down an unlawful rebellion. Cooke's answer was that the King withdrew to the provinces much earlier and recruited a fighting force to attack the national militia under the Earl of Essex. Even if the King had fought the first civil war to put down an insurrection, once a prisoner of Parliament he was guilty of inciting support for the second civil war by 'engaging' with the Scots in 1648 and for his secret urgings of Ormonde and Rupert and the Prince of Wales to prepare a further invasion. Moreover, he remained personally liable for war crimes committed to his knowledge by forces under his command, and it was for this reason that Cooke's evidence emphasised his responsibility for the crimes of plunder and starvation and for the torture of prisoners of war.

The weakness of the King's case as he explained it on the scaffold demonstrates why he was tactically sensible not to make it in the courtroom. His refusal to recognise the jurisdiction of the court served as a cover, which the judges failed to blow because they did not adopt procedures which would have brought on the adversary trial they so desired. The court adjourned – and adjourned and adjourned again – in the hope that the King would come out and fight. Instead, the judges should have given him no choice but to fight, by declaring that his refusal to plead was to be taken not as a confession of guilt but as a plea of 'not guilty'. It is anachronistic to criticise Cooke, the great legal reformer, for failing to urge this particular legal reform – it did not come about until 1827. He encouraged the judges to allow him to call his evidence in Westminster Hall, where the King could not have resisted the temptation to challenge it. It was his duty as prosecuting counsel to assist the court by explaining the forms of law it had to follow, and he also had a duty to his client, the Parliament, to present its case against the King most effectively, by urging that the charge must be taken *pro confesso*. As a result, there was really no 'trial' in any meaningful sense. All that happened was that the King objected to the court's jurisdiction, the court rejected his argument, and it proceeded to deliver sentence when and because he refused to enter a plea.

So disappointed was John Cooke with this result that he settled down to complete the 'speech' for the prosecution that he had not been permitted to deliver. He would prove in print what he had been denied the opportunity to prove in court, and more. Cooke decided to persuade the public not only that Charles deserved to die but that monarchy deserved to die with him.

King Charles, His Case was published a week after the King's execution: it contained the closing speech Cooke had intended to deliver 'if the King had pleaded to the charge and put himself on fair trial'.[22] After an opening insult ('Charles Stuart was a king whom God gave to England in his wrath and will take away out of his love for that country') he moved on to assert the King's command responsibility for the deaths incurred in the war. Tens of thousands of lives had been lost by his 'commands, commissions and procurements' or at least by omissions for which he might be held liable, since 'He that does not hinder the doing of evil, if it lies in his power to prevent it, is guilty of it as a commander thereof'. Charles he described as a 'hard-hearted man' who had confessed on 22 January that he cared only for the death of Strafford: he 'was no more affected with a list that was brought into Oxford of five or six thousand slain at Edge Hill than to read one of Ben Jonson's tragedies'. The real tragedy was that of Charles Stuart, a man 'beloved at home and feared abroad' who might have governed amicably with his Parliament, but instead was 'so proudly wedded to his conceits as maliciously to oppose his own private opinion against public judgment and reason of state, so as to attack the Parliament in pursuance of his lust for absolute power'.

Cooke repeated that kings were trusted with a power to govern that was limited by a common law that entrenched the people's right to a regular Parliament for the redress of their grievances. Charles's coronation oath bound him to preserve the peace and to observe the law: it reflected the political fact that 'all just power is now derived from and conferred by the people' who consent and voluntarily submit to a form of government. They may consent to a king, and even to hereditary kingship, but always retain the right to withdraw that consent, even if the hereditary monarch behaves himself. At this point, Cooke becomes much more radical than Bradshawe, who would only allow deposition of a king for breaching the feudal bond and failing to protect his people. Cooke would allow the people to rid themselves of monarchical government at any time, because it is not a form of government favoured by reason, nor by God, because their very existence tends to enslave the human spirit and create a courtier class. 'God permits this; he approves it not.'

Having established through biblical references God's dislike of the institution of monarchy, Cooke turns to the evidence against Charles on the count of tyranny. He instances his relentless desire for personal rule in 1628 by eliminating Parliament and cruelly imprisoning its champion Sir John Eliot and by sacking any judges whose decisions displeased him. His 'Machiavellian policy' was 'Call no Parliaments to question the injustice and corruption of judges, but make your own judges, and let them declare the law' as they did in the ship-money case, producing the perfect recipe for tyranny, namely that 'the King may take from the people in case of necessity and himself shall be the judge of that necessity'. In fine flourish, Cooke debunked the notion that the King's 'evil councillors' were to blame for his maladministration and injustice. Who elevated these evil ones to his counsel? The King, of course, who must be held accountable for the advice that he arranged for himself to be given by men like Laud and Strafford, the advocates of 'barbarous cruelties of brandings and nose slittings imposed on the Protestant martyrs'.[23] Nobody could pretend that Charles was led astray by evil counsellors if they read the letters found in his cabinet after Naseby, showing that the King was 'principal in all transactions of the state and the wisest about him but accessories'.

Cooke made short work of the King's defence that Parliament started the war. The King declared it by setting up his standard: he wanted an army under his absolute command, as well as the money to pay for it. He fought for the perquisites of tyranny: the power to call Parliaments when he pleased and to dissolve them when he wished, with his 'negative voice' to nullify anything they did, irrespective of approval from the Lords. But was this 'tyranny' a crime? Significantly, Cooke answers this question by invoking not only the fundamental law of England, but international law – 'the general law of all nations' – and natural law, 'written in every rational man's heart with the pen of a diamond, in capital letters and a character so legible that even he that runs may read'. The principle was simple:

When any man is entrusted with the sword for the protection and preservation of the people, if this man shall employ to their destruction that which was put into his hand for their safety, then by the law of that land he becomes an enemy to that people and deserves the most exemplary and severe punishment. This law – *if the King become a tyrant he shall die for it* – is the law of nature and the law of God, written in the fleshly tablets of men's hearts.[24]

Cooke's law against tyranny had a respectable pedigree in the laws of war, issued to the King's own army when it prepared to march on Scotland in 1640, which prohibited pillage and plunder and torture of prisoners.[25] The evidence implicated Charles in these atrocities. Although international lawyers had not gone so far as Cooke (and modern law) in imputing command responsibility to princes, Grotius held kings liable for wrongs they had known about and could have prevented. Erasmus had written extensively about the justification for regicide (in terms that Shakespeare applied to the account-ability of kings like Richard III and Macbeth) while Gentili, the Oxford Regius professor, had pointed out that 'unless we wish to make sovereigns exempt from the law and bound by no statutes and no precedents, there must also of necessity be someone to remind them of their duty and hold them in restraint'.[26] That 'someone' had to be a court, comprising judges empowerered to enforce the law against the King. Not every law – Cooke conceded the inconvenience of punishing a king for a single murder[27] – but for systematic breaches that resulted in the destruction of public lives and liberty. In this sense, 'tyranny' was a different crime to treason, which involved (if the Strafford precedent extended this far) an attack on sover-eign power in the realm, and the Militia Ordinance had vested in Parliament some of the King's sovereign power. This argument – that 'treason' now encompassed an attack on the state or on its settled institutions of govern-ment, which one such institution (the King) could commit by attacking another (the parliament) – sounds better in hindsight than it would if it had been challenged at the time by Matthew Hale.[28] The charge of tyranny, however, might carry a consequence more momentous than treason or murder: being against the law of nations and of nature, it would justify armed resistance, even invasion – what would now be termed 'humanitarian inter-vention'. As Gentili had put it: 'Look you, if men clearly sin against the laws of nature and of mankind, I believe that anyone whatsoever may check such men by force of arms'.[29]

For Cooke, tyranny was a crime committed by absolute rulers who became tyrants not just by virtue of the servititude their position inculcated, but by their fixed intention to govern without Parliament or an independent judi-ciary or any other democratic check on their power. Kings were not invari-ably tyrannical: monarchical government was tolerated by God and by the law of nations, so long as the monarch did not abuse his power – by, for example (and it was the example to hand), waging war on the people in order to destroy their vested political rights to an independent judiciary and to a regular Parliament for the redress of their grievances. When the ruler's oppression becomes systematic and widespread, the people were entitled to have him arrested and put on trial. If he could claim to have acted from incompetence or honest misjudgment as to the public good, he might be pardoned or permitted to abdicate in favour of an heir bound to observe constitutional limits. But if his misconduct had been motivated by a desire for absolute power, a just sentence would be death and disinheritance.

This was a revolutionary doctrine, far in advance of Bradshawe's cautious reasoning. It wove the laws of nations, God and England into a case for the overthrow and punishment of tyrants, no matter where or who they were. Cooke urged the export of this revolution 'to make him [Charles] an example to other Kingdoms for the times to come. That the kings of the earth may hear, and fear, and do no more wickedness.' In a postscript, written shortly after the execution, Cooke put down a famous marker that would haunt Oliver Cromwell over the next decade. The King's judges, he prophesied,

Have pronounced sentence not only against one tyrant but against tyranny itself. Therefore if any of them shall turn tyrant, or consent to set up any kind of tyranny by law, or suffer any unmerciful domineering over the consciences, persons and estates of the free people of this land, they have pronounced sentence against themselves.

The committee for executing the King found its first task was to provide him with solace: they received a message from Charles that 'seeing they had passed a sentence of death on him, and that his time might be nigh, might he see his children and have Doctor Juxon, Bishop of London, admitted to assist his private devotions?' The committee readily granted both requests, little realising how the children's visit would be turned into tear-jerking propaganda, or that Juxon would act as the King's press agent. But the commissioners were now consumed with kindness – they even allowed an emissary from the Prince of Wales – the enemy commander, exiled in The Hague – to visit. He found Charles unprepared for execution, clinging to the forlorn hope that his son would lead an invasion that might save him yet.[30] King Charles had sufficient presence of mind to send Rogue, his King Charles spaniel, away to his wife (contrary to royalist myth, the dog did not trot behind its master on his walk to the gallows) and sent a ring – 'an emerald set between two diamonds' – to a lady living off King Street in Westminster, subsequently identified as 'the King's laundress'.[31]

Meanwhile, Cromwell was overseeing the grim modalities of the King's execution. Charles spent Sunday with Bishop Juxon, a calming influence who helped steel him for martyrdom. The commissioners and soldiers needed steeling as well, and who better than Hugh Peters to inculcate a sense that God was still on their side? He obliged with a pulpit routine which likened the decision before the High Court of Justice to the choice offered to the people by Pontius Pilate: between the King (a.k.a. Barabbas, a murderer and oppressor of the people) compared with the soldiers in their red coats who were saviours of the people, and who risked being killed or maimed in a third civil war if the King were not executed. He also reprised Psalm 149, with its invocation to bring out the two-edged sword (i.e. the 'bright axe' kept in the Tower of London) to execute upon kings and nobles 'the judgment written'. Peters had a remarkable facility for bringing the Old Testament to life and making it relevant to contemporary issues in England: he added a text from Isaiah 14: 19–20 about a king 'cast out of thy grave like an abominable branch . . . because thou hast destroyed thy land, and slain thy people'.

Sabbath reflection on the enormity of executing the King made little impact on the determination of the commissioners. Their Monday morning meeting in the Painted Chamber produced no backsliding. On the contrary, their first decision was to have his head cut off in broad daylight 'in the open street before Whitehall' between 10 a.m. and 5 p.m. on Tuesday 30 January – the very next day. A warrant to this effect was produced – it had been drawn up several days before, and had already been signed by some of the judges. It was directed to Colonels Hacker, Hunks and Phayre who were to stage-manage the event, and a further order was directed to officials at the Tower of London to deliver 'the bright execution axe for executing male-factors' into the willing arms of Sergeant Dendy. No fewer than fifty-nine commissioners eventually signed the warrant although several MPs had to be rounded up by Cromwell, who intercepted them at the door of the House of Commons. Some were understandably unenthusiastic, but few took any objection in principle. One who did was Cooke's barrister friend Nicholas Love who had played a leading role in setting up the court but who now expressed firm opposition to the death sentence, as did William Heveningham: both men were present on the Monday and had no difficulty in declining Cromwell's request that they append their signature. The stories that Cromwell overbore many of the signatories ('I will have their hands now') should not be credited – they were first told in 1660 by men like Downes, desperate to save their own skins. For example, one story accepted for centuries was that Cromwell had frog-marched Richard Ingoldsby to the table, clutched his hand and forced his signature on the warrant. But examination of his signature shows no sign of force: the story was invented to protect Ingoldsby, who had assisted the Restoration.

On Monday morning, the judges confronted and accepted the awesome finality of their decision. A servant of Henry Marten claimed to have seen some face-painting in the Painted Chamber ('I did see a pen in Mr Cromwell's hand and he marked Mr Marten in his face with it and Mr Marten did the like to him'), an episode so bizarre that it may well be true and suggestive of some release of nervous tension at the conclusion of 'the great business'.[32] Most of the commissioners believed they were instruments of the law and of the will of God – the King's fate was an act of providence to which they willingly set their hand. General Fairfax was ambivalent about executing the man he had tried so often to kill on the battlefield, but consoled himself in verse:

> But if the Power Divine permitted this,
> His will's the law and ours must acquiesce.[33]

Little wonder that Fairfax was soon to hire a real poet, Andrew Marvell, to tutor his daughter. Notwithstanding his reservations about the death penalty, and the excitable outbursts attributed to his wife, the general played the straightest of bats throughout the trial, which owed much to his steadfastness – his adjutant delivered the daily orders from his Whitehall headquarters to the officers supervising events at Westminster Hall. The soldiers were unquestioningly loyal to Fairfax, their supreme commander, and not to Cromwell: they would have obeyed any order by Fairfax to halt the King's trial or execution. His 'command responsibility' was deliberately covered up at the regicide trials, and many histories still naively portray him as the innocent dupe of Cromwell. Fairfax had turned up for the first meeting of the court in the Painted Chamber but then absented himself to run the country. As acting head of state, he chaired a special meeting of the army council on Sunday evening (it had to be very special for them to meet on the Sabbath) to receive the ambassadors from the Dutch government, who had rushed to England to intercede for the King's life. He fobbed them off with the explanation that he could not intervene except with the approval of Parliament, which did not meet until the next day.

The Dutch government was too powerful and too dangerous to be insulted, so the Commons listened politely to their protestations – spoken in Dutch, which the MPs did not understand. The ambassadors, invited to have it translated, returned on Monday evening with a petition in English, which was very politely sent off to a committee for consideration. A protest from the Scots was ignored and a petition from the Presbyterian ministers of London was treated with contempt. The Commons did not even bother to open a letter from the Prince of Wales which was widely (but wrongly) believed to contain a signed blank sheet of paper on which they could name their terms for saving his father's life. The only force that could save the life of Charles I was General Fairfax, who was in thrall to the will of the Power Divine. He was also aware of the will of the great majority of his soldiers and officers, who wanted execution done on the man whom they blamed for the deaths of so many of their comrades. As supreme commander, he was all too conscious of the national security situation and the need for a resolution of 'the problem of the King' before the expected royalist invasion to restore him. And he could think of no other resolution.

The King, meanwhile, was preparing for death and for glory, with the sagacious assistance of Bishop Juxon. He was much helped by the kindness of his executioners. They had provided him with a companion – Sir Thomas Herbert – a rather dim parliamentary sympathiser who was sensible enough, after the Restoration, to prepare an account of the King's last days that was to ascribe saintliness to his conduct throughout them. He was allowed to say farewell to his children – Elizabeth (aged thirteen) and Henry (eight) – a heartrending occasion written up by Herbert and, more movingly, by Elizabeth herself (or by a skilful propagandist in her name – the authenticity of her memo has never been established). Her account contains a striking passage (also striking for being absent from Herbert's account) in which the King instructs his small son that 'You must not be a king so long as your brothers Charles and James do live: for they will cut off your brothers' heads (when they can catch them) and cut off your head too, at last; therefore I charge you, do not be made a king by them.' ('I will be torn to pieces first,' the child responded to this rather terrifying paternal farewell.) If not invented, it shows the depth of the King's opposition to the only parliamentary proposal which could have saved his life – namely his agreement (and necessarily that of his older sons, Charles and James) to allow little Henry to accede to the throne (under the tutelage of a 'Lord Protector') to reign as a limited constitutional monarch – Henry IX.

The most disastrous decision for long-term public relations was to have the King executed in public – on a black-draped scaffold outside the banqueting house in Whitehall. Perhaps they had Strafford's much celebrated execution in mind, but that was an occasion for popular rejoicing at the destruction of the evil councillor of a beloved King. The destruction of the beloved King was a different matter. Almost everything that was done conduced to his martyrdom. Troops of Horse Guards surrounded the funereally draped scaffold, on which someone (Peters, it was rumoured, although he convincingly denied it) had thoughtlessly decided to drive in some rails and manacles, to which the prisoner could be tethered in the event of any resistance.

The King played the martyr's part almost to perfection. The public nature of the occasion left eye-witnesses to his iconic last hours: his wearing of two shirts, lest his shivers from the cold seem like trembling with fear; the long walk through St James's Park ahead of a troop of drummers morbidly beating time; his steps to the scaffold through the Banqueting House with its Rubens ceiling which showed him as an infant, nursed by the goddess of wisdom. During the march through the park, the trees bare and the ground covered with frost, he requested Colonel Tomlinson to delay his burial because his son was coming back to England and would organise a proper funeral. This was an indication of his unworldliness, and that his delaying tactics at the trial were because he really thought that deliverance was at hand. On this day, it was Parliament that delayed, because it had the same concern: he was made to wait for several hours while it rushed through an Act making it treason for anyone to proclaim the Prince of Wales as Charles II, the new King of England. Charles I meanwhile took a glass of claret and a piece of bread to settle his nerves for the final walk to the gallows.

It was 2 p.m. when he stepped out onto the scaffold, a frail but undeniably noble presence now, set against the red-coated soldiers and the pantomime figures of the two executioners wrapped in outlandish dresses and wearing masks and ill-fitting wigs – one grey, the other flaxen – to disguise their identity for all time.[34] The bright axe was in pride of place, and when an army officer made to move it, Charles jested, 'Hurt not the axe that may hurt me.' His use of the conditional tense suggests he may have half-hoped for some *deus ex machina* – a golden chariot from the clouds as in his masques, or a last-minute reprieve from Fairfax – as he took out his notes and began his pre-execution address. He asserted his innocence and forgave 'all the world, and even those in particular that have been the chief causers of my death. Who they are God knows. I do not desire to know. I pray God forgive them.' He had been face to face with John Cooke and the judges in Westminster Hall, and his lack of knowledge of them had been the chief cause of his death. He spoilt the graciousness of his final speech by stubborn reassertion of his right to absolute rule: the paternalistic political philosophy by which he had lived and fought again and again hung heavily on his dying breath:

> For the people I must tell you, that their liberty and freedom consist in having of government, those laws by which their life and their goods may be most their own. It is not for having a share in government, Sirs: that is nothing pertaining to them. A subject and a sovereign are clean different things, and therefore, until they do that, I mean, that you do put the people in that liberty as I say, certainly they will never enjoy themselves.

The people had been warned: they would enjoy themselves under a king but never under their own representatives. 'I tell you that I am the Martyr of the people,' Charles declared to Bishop Juxon, who nodded and then prompted the denouement[35] by handing Charles his nightcap. The King put it on and said to the executioner, 'Does my hair trouble you?' The executioner and the bishop then helped him tuck his untidy locks under the nightcap and Charles turned to Dr Juxon for a final blessing:

KING: I have a good cause and a gracious God on my side.

DR JUXON: There is but one stage more. This stage is turbulent and troublesome. It is a short one. But you may consider it will soon carry you a very great way, it will carry you from earth to heaven and there you shall find to your great joy the prize. You haste to a crown of glory.

KING: I go from a corruptible to an incorruptible crown where no disturbance can be.

DR JUXON: You are exchanged from a temporal to an eternal crown, a good exchange.

Then the King took off his cloak and the blue sash with his silver medallion of St George, handing them to Juxon with the word 'Remember' (i.e. to give them to the Prince of Wales). He turned to the executioner; 'I shall say but very short prayers, and then thrust out my hands.' Then he stooped down, as if to look for the tip of his cane, but this time to lay his neck upon the block. After a short pause, he stretched out his hands, and the executioner at one blow severed his head from his body.

At this point, chroniclers of the scene invariably quote a doleful spectator, Philip Henry: 'At the instant when the blow was given there was such a dismal universal groan amongst the thousands of people that were within sight of it as it were with one consent, as he never heard before and desired he might never hear again.' Henry, then aged nineteen, was son to the most loyal servant of Charles I; he was writing many years later as a courtier of Charles II. Thousands of people did not in fact see the beheading – it took place on a low block, just six inches high, behind the black-draped railings of the scaffold. The 'dismal universal groan', essential to royalist myth-making, is mentioned by no other spectator, including the schoolboy voyeur Samuel Pepys.[36] The astonishing fact was that the execution, like the trial, went unopposed and uninterrupted. It was as if the country had failed to catch up with the events in Westminster: they heard of them unfolding, in a sort of awe. When the shock wore off it would be different. But on Tuesday 30 January the shops remained open, the public went about its business, the King was not immediately missed.

12

'Stone Dead Hath No Fellow'

'The fourth cervical vertebrae was found to be cut through its substance transversally, leaving the surfaces of the divided portions perfectly smooth and even, an appearance which could have been produced only by a heavy blow, inflicted with a very sharp instrument.'[1]

Thus did a very post (1813) post-mortem examination describe the King's neck after his embalmed body was discovered in a vault at Windsor Castle next to the remains of Henry VIII. The head of the corpse was loose and on inspection the dark brown hair at the back of the head had been cut soon after death 'to furnish memorials of the unhappy King' in the form of clipped locks for surreptitious sale. The blood of the royal martyr had an immediate value – soldiers at the scaffold allowed relic hunters to mop up the haemoglobin with handkerchiefs and to purchase pieces of the wooden flooring which had been spattered with royal gore. One soldier was quoted as saying: 'I would we had two or three more majesties to behead, if we could but make such use of them.'[2] There are several accounts of Cromwell inspecting the corpse of the King before its burial (muttering the epitaph 'cruel necessity') while Sir Purbeck Temple claimed to have given a half crown piece to a soldier to permit inspection of the body in order to describe it to Jane Whorwell, rumoured to be the King's mistress: 'I saw the head of the blessed martyr King . . . which smiled as perfectly as if it had been alive' – a smile which evidently faded by the time of the 1813 post-mortem.[3]

The army leaders were astute to avoid unnecessary publicity after the execution and it is likely that the lid of the King's coffin remained firmly shut after it left the embalmers. They refused Herbert's request for burial in King Henry VII's chapel in Westminster Abbey: Herbert relates that 'His request was denied, this reason being given, that probably it would attract infinite numbers of people of all sorts hither' which was judged unsafe and inconvenient.[4] So the royal chapel of St George in Windsor Castle was chosen and on the afternoon of 9 February a small procession of devoted retainers carried the coffin to its secret resting place. Herbert memorably relates – to the inspiration of many Victorian artists – that

> The sky was serene and clear, but presently it began to snow, and fell so fast, by the time they came to the West End of the royal chapel the black velvet pall was all white (the colour of innocency) being thick covered over with snow. So went the white King to his grave . . .

Other than snowing on the cortège, the skies did not fall after execution was done on Charles I. The King was dead, and Parliament had made it a capital offence to cry 'Long Live the King!' Few disobeyed – if they did, like one luckless Presbyterian minister, a Reverend Causton, they were sent to Messrs Cooke and Steele to consider prosecution for an offence against the new Treason Act.[5] The most astonishing consequence of the trial was that the revolution it accomplished met with no opposition. The cavaliers, whose personal courage was unquestionable, had made no move of any kind to rescue their endangered leader; the Presbyterian politicians and City fathers lifted neither finger nor voice against the republic while for a short time even the Levellers fell uncharacteristically silent. The judges and the great lawyers returned as soon as the trial was safely concluded, in order to jockey for places in the Republic. Steele, the Attorney-General, made a sufficiently speedy recovery to join Solicitor-General Cooke in prosecuting the Duke of Hamilton. The trial had not only effected the revolution, but had made it acceptable, at least for the time being, through its use of traditional procedures and the authority of its verdict.

The King's death was not the matter of political expediency it has subsequently appeared to many historians: it was perceived at the time as a matter of right and of justice. Charles Stuart was a defendant who deserved to die as punishment for his crimes, rather than for the kind of *realpolitik* reasons that had been used to justify the elimination of Strafford and Laud. Although the trial had been deficient as a fact-finding exercise because of the King's refusal to plead, Cooke had invoked the law's interpretation of that tactic as a confession which automatically triggered the conviction and execution. It was the inevitability of the verdict and sentence that impressed: this was the result of a law which was no respecter of persons – its consequences could not be avoided by wealth or power or station.

Since the court's proceedings had been solemn and the King had been given a fairer hearing than any other defendant charged with treason, this High Court of Justice appeared to live up to its name, certainly to Puritans who believed its result must have been ordained by God. Royalists could find no such solace in the outcome, other than as a punishment for their own sinful failure to stop it or even to protest against it. As one of their penitential poets put it,

> Though Pontius Bradshawe did in judgement sit,
> And Cooke dress hell-bred sophistry with wit,
> To drain the blood,
> Of Charles the good
> And strike the royal heart,
> Not by evidence but art.
> These were but the fire and wood!
> But who did bring?
> Or where's the lamb for a burnt-offering?
> Let every penitent loyalist now cry,
> T'was sinful England! and most sinful I.[6]

On the day they entombed 'the White King', his nemesis 'White Cooke' was hard at work: as Solicitor-General he had to prepare for the prosecutions of Hamilton and the lords captured at Colchester, and also advise the Commons about how to transform this ex-kingdom into a republic. His first task, on execution day itself, had been to dispatch a letter post-haste to all sheriffs in England, informing them that the sentence of the court had been carried out and ordering them to announce 'in all market towns and other public places' the Act passed that day *Prohibiting the Proclaiming of any person to be King of England or Ireland or the dominions thereof*. At about 3 a.m. the next morning he was woken to be told that the Duke of Hamilton had escaped from Windsor Castle. The Solicitor-General authorised the issue of a warrant for the duke (with a £500 reward) and a few hours later troops arrested a disguised Hamilton as he was trying to hire a carriage to Dover. (The duke, as inept in peace as in war, did not disguise his Scottish accent or hide his diamond ring.) The Commons, on hearing of his apprehension, determined that he should face a speedy trial and immediately appointed a new High Court of Justice under Judge Bradshawe to conduct it.[7]

This meant more work for the Solicitor-General, whom the Commons appointed on the same day to serve (with Oliver Cromwell) on a committee to revise the laws of the realm to conform with the exigencies of republican government.[8] But by this time, Cromwell had no shortage of expert lawyers: the grandees were back to claim power in the new commonwealth. That Tweedle Dum and Tweedle Dee of Cromwellian legal office, Thomas Widdrington and Bulstrode Whitelocke, became respectively Sergeant of the Commonwealth and Keeper of the Great Seal, from which positions they could head off most of the reforms of the legal profession which had been urged by John Cooke. They did not trust Cooke: he was a radical and an upstart, but he had done the state more recent and more dangerous service than they, so they bided their time.

The return of these conservative lawyers was paralleled by the return to the Commons of Independents like young Sir Henry Vane, who had supported a republic but objected to achieving it by executing the King, and over seventy 'secluded' MPs, mainly Presbyterians who were allowed back on condition that they disavowed their vote on 5 December to continue negotiations with the King. Their presence, with those who came back on the same condition later, made the 'Rump' of the Commons very much less of a rump – more a head and torso – of those MPs who had been elected to the Long Parliament. It also made the Commons a much more cautious and reactionary body than it had been in the weeks after Pride's Purge, when its hard core of Independent MPs oversaw the King's trial and execution. For the present, however, it served to provide reasonably broad support for the legislation advised by the Solicitor-General which turned the country into a republic.

The first task was to establish some form of executive government to replace the King and his Privy Council of ministers. The successor body was called a Council of State; a majority of members were MPs, but it also had five peers and three judges, including the chief justice, Oliver St John. John Bradshawe was appointed as its president – an indication of just how satisfactory his trial performance was regarded. The republican loyalty of its members was secured by an oath to 'adhere to this present Parliament . . . and to the maintenance and defence of its resolutions concerning the settling of the government of this nation for the future in way of a republic, without King or House of Lords'.[9]

It took another month before the republic was legislatively accomplished. On 17 March 1649, the Act abolishing the office of king was passed. Charles and his 'issue and posterity' and anyone else pretending to the title were declared incapable of accessing it and all the people of England and Ireland (but not Scotland) were 'discharged of all fealty, homage and allegiance' to the Stuarts, then or for ever. In language so reminiscent of *King Charles: His Case* that John Cooke must have had a hand in its drafting, the Act justified the extirpation of monarchy by reference to the English experience of it:

It is and has been found by experience, that the office of a king in this nation and Ireland, and to have the power thereof in any single person, is unnecessary, burdensome, and dangerous to the liberty, safety, and public interest of the people, and that for the most part use has been made of the legal power and prerogative to oppress and impoverish and enslave the subject; and that usually and naturally any one person in such power makes it his interest to encroach upon the just freedom and liberty of the people, and to promote the setting up of their own will and power above the laws, so that they might enslave these Kingdoms to their own lust; be it therefore an Act ordained by the present parliament, that the office of a king in this nation shall not henceforth reside in or be exercised by any one single person . . .[10]

The republic was declared in England without public opposition or significant support for any alternative form of government. But these were still dangerous days. The Scottish Parliament had already proclaimed Charles II as 'King of Great Britain' and Montrose – a more formidable fighter than Hamilton – was in arms in the new King's cause, whilst his navy, under Prince Rupert's command, was stooging around supportive Irish ports. The Rump promised to dissolve itself 'as soon as may possibly stand with the safety of the people' and to provide for regular elections on a wider franchise, but the people's safety (and the self-importance of the Rumpers) was to postpone them indefinitely. The House of Lords was abolished on 19 March: it was 'useless and dangerous' to continue a body which had so notably taken fright at the prospect of putting the King on trial. 'Where are my lords?' was the one question Bradshawe and Cooke could not answer: henceforth, it could not be asked – the only nobles who would play a part in government would be those elected to the Commons, and the Act expressly permitted them to stand. The Act declaring England to be a commonwealth made the House of Commons 'the supreme authority of this nation, the representatives of the people in Parliament'.

The King's trial had paved the way not only for a republic – inconceivable just a few months before – but for a meritocratic republic without political power diluted by an hereditary and unelected upper house. The extent of the franchise was still unclear, although there was significant support in the army for it to extend to all men who owned homes, paid poor relief and were not servants or employed workers – a democracy, in other words, of independent adult males, extending well beyond the narrow property franchise upon which previous Houses of Commons had been elected.

Laws were easy to alter, like the inscription on the great seal and coinage and the description of the high court – the Kings Bench quickly became the Upper Bench. More difficult was to replace the pro-monarchy prejudices in the hearts of the people – a change of loyalty which could only be accomplished by governing in a manner discernibly better and more endearing than the Stuarts. The commonwealth would need to achieve the reforms in law and worship that had been central to the Independent and army agenda. And it would need to entrench itself in public sentiment by making its own legends – about the guilt of Charles I, for a start, and the rightness of the proceedings that had brought him to justice.

So John Cooke was given every encouragement when he took the extraordinary step of publishing the speech he had intended to deliver to satisfy the court of the King's guilt. *King Charles: His Case* – i.e. the case against King Charles – was somewhat defensively subtitled '*An appeal to all rational men that love their God, justice and country more than honour, pleasure and money, concerning his trial at the High Court of Justice*'. It was, as we have seen, for the most part a rational argument that the monarch not only bore command responsibility for the mass-murder of his own people but had behaved like a tyrant from the beginning of his rule, bending judges to his will and wasting public champions like John Eliot in his determination to destroy Parliament. It was a hastily drawn but powerful indictment that was to reassure many Puritans in England and the American colonies of the rightness of the conviction. Its weakness was that its author, to justify the execution as well, interpolated some inflammatory material which had been excluded from the actual charge, such as the allegations about the King's responsibility for the loss of Protestant La Rochelle and his complicity in Buckingham's alleged poisoning of James I. He added a short introduction, magnifying the King's 'Machiavellian' crimes, and a postscript which addressed the objections to the court made by London's Presbyterian ministers. Courts are as courts do, Cooke argued: they are to be judged by the quality of the justice they dispense. The High Court acted like the highest court and conducted itself more fairly than the law required – for example, by examining witnesses for several days to satisfy the judges' conscience, although the prisoner had already convicted himself in law by refusing to plead. The Presbyterians who had objected to the trial were like 'foolish passengers that having been long at sea in dangerous storms, as they are entering into the quiet haven, to be mad with the pilot because he will not return into angry seas'.

It was to answer these 'dancing divines' and their MPs – the 'apostate scarecrows' like Prynne and Holles – that John Milton also took up his pen to publish, in the same week, *The Tenure of Kings and Magistrates* – a more coruscating polemic against 'the spleen of a frustrated faction' which had tried for years to kill Charles on the battlefield ('Directing their artillery without blame or prohibition to the very place where they saw him stand') yet now objected to his execution.[11] They had dared not judge him whilst they were converting his revenue and taking from it 'the warm experience of large gifts' but now that the power they played for had to be shared with others, they sought to save the very King they had so often attempted to kill – a tyrant who, heedless of the law or common good, had sought to reign for the benefit only of himself and his courtiers.

The commonwealth of England, argued into existence in the first weeks of February 1649 by Cooke's rhetoric and Milton's more elegant sarcasm, was a construct of justice and right reason, supported by the biblical view that kings were graven images – rivals rather than anointees of God. These arguments were calculated to appeal to rational minds, and although they conveniently persuaded men to serve under the new dispensation, they never lodged in their hearts or tugged at their emotions. Puritans felt gratitude that their congregations were no longer menaced by bishops or by the imposition of Kirk worship, but this was counter-balanced by an exasperation with some of the sects which crawled from underneath 'a world turned upside down'. Winstanley's 'Diggers' were a handful of communards, at first tolerated and then easily dispersed. The fabled sexual promiscuity of the 'Ranters' inspired a moral panic in Parliament and the newsbooks, but their followers were very few – unlike the Quakers, whose guidance from 'the light within' led them to defy authority and etiquette in a manner that spread genuine alarm later in the 1650s. The most influential sectarians were the 'Fifth monarchists' because their belief (based on the prophecies in the Book of Revelation) was that the second coming of Christ would be presaged by a thousand-year rule of the saints (the wisest and most godly men, who would reign supreme in church, Parliament and courts of law).

However, for the Presbyterians and many Protestants who still craved the Anglo-Catholic traditions of the Church of England, there was no cause for rejoicing. The republic brought no benefit, in worship or in power or in pocket, although under Cromwell at least there was peace at home and there would soon be triumphs over enemies abroad. Instead of reading Cooke and Milton, they consumed an underground best-seller, *Eikon Basilike* – a book about the devotions and sufferings of the holy martyr Charles I, in his final year of constant prayer for the souls of his people. It purported to be written by Charles, although it was in fact penned by John Gauden, another of Cooke's Wadham contemporaries. The contents of *'the King's Book'* (as everyone called it) had been discussed with Charles during his relative freedom at Newport, but Gauden had updated it with premonitions of the fate that had already overtaken him by the time of its publication.

The *King's Book* first appeared on the same day as *King Charles: His Case* and comprehensively outsold it, commencing that strain of iconography which identified the sufferings of Charles with the sufferings of Christ, their executions taking place after a trial which lacked legal authority, attended by soldiers and officials who insulted and reviled the holy figure.[12] The long-term impact of the *Eikon* was to sentimentalise the Stuarts as divinely appointed upholders of the Anglican faith: it worked the same spell as had *Foxe's Book of Martyrs* on a previous generation. Milton (with *Eikonaklasties*) and Cooke (with *Monarchy No Creature of God's Making*) would later return to the intellectual fray, but nothing they could write would extract the splinter of sentiment for a Christian king that *Eikon Basilike* lodged in so many ordinary English hearts. Call it superstition and servitude (as Milton did) and denounce it as incompatible both with reason and the word of God (as Cooke argued), the idea of the monarch promoted after the execution, as patron saint of a hierarchical system based on hereditary and breeding, played to one element of the English character – snobbery – that the commonwealth could never eradicate.[13]

Indeed, the most striking feature of royalist propaganda was the obsessive reference to the lowly birth or 'mechanical' trades of those who served the republic. It was enough for readers of their clandestine news-sheets to learn that a public officer or army colonel had been a draper or brewer or craftsman or – *horribile dictu* – a servant, to recognise that he was unfit for any office. In this milieu where 'democratic' was always a pejorative adjective, the potential strength of the new government – its broader base – was identified as its weakness. Status continued to govern character: persons of low breeding were necessarily persons of low worth. The royalist writers and printers, dodging the licensors with little difficulty and obvious relish, had no scruple in publishing venomous libels on these 'men of the middling classes', the plebeians of the republic.

Cooke could not hope to escape slander and it came quickly after the King's trial – in *Mercurius Elencticus* for the week ending 13 February. There, Cooke was denounced for his low birth and lack of money. His bar practice was said to be that of 'a matchmaker, or a helper to wives' – in effect, he was a marriage broker, who had wormed his way into the esteem of Strafford. He was falsely accused of decamping from Ireland with the money the earl had paid him to update the Irish statutes, and after conversion by the Jesuits in Rome had stayed in Europe, in fear of Strafford, until after his execution when he thought it safe to return to London. This 'mercury' was a malicious messenger: its author, George Wharton, was a royalist astrologer and libeller who vowed in the same edition that 'I should esteem it the best act that ever I did, if to quit the Kingdom of so damnable a traitor, I could but (by any means imaginable) let the blood out of that body which harbours so hellish a soul'. He was urging the assassination of Bradshawe. But Cooke would make an equally acceptable target.

It was not long before Wharton's ilk struck at the King's prosecutors. Dr Dorislaus had been appointed to Parliament's most important diplomatic post, that of ambassador to the United Dutch Dominion. In May, on the very night of his arrival at The Hague, a royalist death squad led by the son of a Welsh bishop broke into his apartment and stabbed him to death while he was taking supper. Although the Dutch, as fellow Protestants, were nominally friendly to the commonwealth, their government shared the general European horror (the Swiss excepted) at the King's execution and notably failed to arrest the assassins. Edmund Ludlow complained that 'Though this action was so infamous and contrary to the right of nations, yet the Dutch were not very forward to find out the criminals, in order to bring them to justice'[14] and Parliament sent an official complaint to the States-General. Clearly, Cooke's days of continental travel were over. There could be no place of safety for the man who had led the prosecution of the King, and the danger was emphasised the following year when the English ambassador to Spain, Anthony Ascham, was killed in a similar fashion, probably because he was confused with John Aske, the junior barrister who had assisted Cooke and Dorislaus and was soon elevated to the rank of sargeant and appointed to the High Court.[15] Dorislaus's corpse was brought back to England and given a state funeral, which became the butt of royalist venom and threats of further assassinations: *The Weeping Onion*, a doggerel sold on the streets, decried the pomp and public funds (£250) lavished on this 'alien reprobate' and imputed nerves to other targets:

> O for a messenger the House to tell
> And all the merry commoners of hell
> How Lenthall looks! How Whitelocke pales his face
> Who caught one *seal*, and lost that seal of grace!
> O how damned Bradshawe quivers as he comes
> And Fairfax groans. And Cromwell bites his thumbs.[16]

Cooke publicly defied his would-be murderers: 'It is for a Cain to be afraid that every man that meets him will slay him.'[17] He did not care whether he was killed by cavaliers or by consumption. 'I leave that to my heavenly father. If it be his will that I shall fall by the hand of violence, let him do what he pleases.' This was not empty defiance: Cooke was (and remained) utterly trusting to providence in respect of his own safety. But by now there were others to consider: not only Isaac his aged father, but his wife – Frances – whom he had married in 1646 once his practice had begun to flourish. The one place where they would be safe would be in the bosom of Cromwell's army, which was preparing to sail forth to subdue the unruly Irish. Soon, Cromwell would make him an offer.

For the present, in the hectic months after the execution, the Solicitor-General was immersed in trial work. Cooke was not a tub-thumping orator: his talent lay in creative application of the common law, and the trials of the courtiers gave this talent full rein in front of Lord President Bradshawe and the familiar faces (although not so many) of the commissioners who judged the King. He had four mighty lords to dispatch, all of whom can now be observed (unlike Cooke) gazing down upon visitors to the National Portrait Gallery. They ranged from Lord Goring, the most cruel and lawless of the royalist commanders, to the Earl of Holland, whose oscillation between the King and the Parliament was, he admitted frankly, contingent upon which side would give him the most money, because he believed poverty to be the greatest sin. The Duke of Hamilton, leader of the Scots invasion, was the main defendant, and then came Lord Capel, who like Holland and a fifth courtier, Sir John Owen, had reneged on earlier promises made to gain pardons and had led the royalists into the second civil war. Steele, the Attorney-General who had by now made a complete recovery, asked Cooke to take the lead in prosecuting Goring, Holland and Capel, and to assist him in the more difficult case of the Duke of Hamilton.

Cooke made short but interesting work of Goring, charging him in effect as a war criminal. Goring pleaded 'not guilty', so Cooke produced witnesses to testify that the defendant had ordered the torture of prisoners at Colchester, had burnt down hundreds of civilian homes and authorised the use of bullets boiled in poison. Goring admitted giving some of these orders, but he denied treason: he fought, he said, for peace – Cooke pointed out that his actions spoke louder than his words, and his actions infringed the laws of war accepted by both sides. Goring and the other peers tried to argue that their status carried various immunities from prosecution and that Magna Carta meant they could only be tried, quite literally, by 'peers'. Cooke, who was dogged by the tag 'plebeian' all his life, swept away these objections: the Act by which the court was established contained no exemption from its jurisdiction for those of high birth. In this he foreshadowed the approach of modern war crimes courts, which have declined to acknowledge immunities based on status or position, whether as head of state or minister of government. In one respect, however, Cooke's egalitarian logic went too far: he urged that in this republican age, noble defendants should now suffer the fate of common traitors and be hanged, drawn and quartered. At this, Capel blanched and almost fainted from shock. The court, however, drew the line at inflicting a commoner's death on noble lords: it decided they should die by the clean stroke of the bright axe. A gesture was made towards equality by vouchsafing this same aristocractic exit to Sir John Owen, the stout but common Welshman. Capel became celebrated for the excellence of the execution both of his portraiture (by Cornelius Johnson) and of his sentence: he disdained the comfort of a priest and declared loudly on the scaffold that Charles II was his King.

Where the prisoners taken at Colchester did have an arguable defence was that they had surrendered upon articles agreed with Fairfax which promised them 'quarter' for their life. The offer and grant of 'quarter' was a basic feature of the law of seventeenth-century warfare, accepted by all sides in the English civil wars.[18] A soldier who yielded and threw down his arms could not be slain, and had thereafter to be treated humanely as a prisoner of war. But did it operate as a full-blown pardon for all crimes of war he might previously have committed, or was it a temporary expedient that saved him from being killed either on the spot or after an army court-martial but did not prevent his subsequent prosecution for treason? This argument, too, is reflected in current debates over whether amnesties granted in peace settlements prevent prosecution for crimes against humanity. Cooke's answer was that military law operated in a different dimension to criminal law: the grant of 'quarter' was a right that operated only in the former context, where it protected the beneficiary from further attack and any court-martial. It did not prevent his subsequent prosecution for serious crime. The court accepted Cooke's submission: 'quarter' meant freedom from execution in or after the heat of battle, but not freedom from justice.

Capel fell back on the claim that he could not be tried for a capital offence other than by a jury. There was some historical force in this point – the old prerogative courts, such as the Star Chamber, could order defendants to be mutilated but not executed, and Capel's plea undoubtedly touched a nerve. It had been made on the advice of a most unlikely ally – John Lilburne no less, who had returned to London.[19] 'Where's my jury?' Capel expostulated, prompted by Freeborn John. 'I demand the sight of my jury, legally empanelled, as my right by law, without the verdict of whom I cannot in law be condemned . . . I hope you will not deny me the benefit of the law, which you pretend you have fought this seven years to maintain.' It was an unexpected volte-face: before Lilburne turned up to help him, Capel had been insisting that he could only be tried by fellow lords i.e. his 'peers'. For all the conventional legal talent available, it was the street radical, Cooke's old client, who gave the most cagey advice. The authorities noted the force of his argument for Capel, and when the army moved against Lilburne, a few months later, it allowed him, as a commoner, trial by jury – a decision Cromwell was to regret.

Cooke's insistence in these follow-up trials that military jurisdiction in the course of a war must not be allowed to subvert the jurisdiction of the common law remains of importance. Military and police authorities may offer expedient or unwise deals to prisoners guilty (it may subsequently turn out) of terrible offences, and Cooke's position, now accepted by international criminal law, was that such deals cannot prevent prosecution for certain heinous crimes that it is beyond the power of the military to overlook or forgive. In the event, however, the royalist commanders could not establish that their surrender at Colchester was induced by any promise of pardon. They had refused to capitulate at the beginning of the siege, when Fairfax offered them in return a safe passage out of the country, but had continued fighting until their men refused to fight any longer. Fairfax attended the trial in person to testify for the prosecution: he had been incensed at the arrogance of the defendants in wasting the lives of famished soldiers and townspeople, and had only accepted their belated surrender on terms that their men would be pardoned but they would be 'rendered to mercy'. When the officers had enquired what this might mean, they were told – in writing that Fairfax exhibited in court – that it meant he would be entitled to put them immediately to the sword, although he proposed to leave their fate in the hands of Parliament. Fairfax's attendance at court on 13 February, a fortnight after the King's execution, put paid to their defence, and incidentally signalled the general's support for the High Court of Justice.

The Duke of Hamilton had commanded the Scottish forces that invaded England: after defeat by Cromwell at Preston he had surrendered upon terms which he claimed precluded any subsequent trial or punishment. He also claimed that as a Scot born and bred he was an alien, owing no allegiance to the English nation or its Parliament, and hence could not be prosecuted for treason. This raised a difficult point of law.[20] Although prisoners were not allowed counsel to contest the *facts* of a treason charge, they were entitled to instruct barristers to raise any genuine point of *law* once the facts had been established. So the court granted the duke's request for counsel, as it would have done had Charles requested a lawyer, but none at first was prepared to accept the brief. Four senior barristers all found reason to decline, nervous that appearing for a traitor might bring reprisals, especially since they could only interview their client in the presence and hearing of his guards. This condition was lifted at the court's insistence, and the duke was then represented by a team led by Matthew Hale, who took the point that treason necessarily involved a breach of allegiance to a kingdom and since 'no man can be subject to two kingdoms', Hamilton's birth and title in Scotland prevented his owing allegiance to the kingdom of England. Steele and Cooke successfully replied that the duke had been made an English peer (the Earl of Cambridge) by Charles and had sat under that title in the House of Lords. Besides which, double allegiance was possible in the case of England and Scotland, given historical evidence that both nations were originally one, the treaties of friendship between them and the fact that under the Stuarts they had been ruled by the same person.

Hamilton's further argument, that he had surrendered on a promise of immunity, was supported by none other than Hugh Peters, who had been the intermediary. His understanding of the surrender treaty was that the duke would be safe not only from the soldiers but from any proceeding instituted by Parliament. Colonel Richard Lilburne, who had signed the treaty, said that he intended only to protect the duke from military justice and not from the justice of Parliament. Peters protested 'that much tenderness was to be used when the life of so eminent a person was concerned'[21] and that if the treaty had been intended to bear Colonel Lilburne's meaning, it should have been clearly expressed – to which Bradshawe responded dryly that 'you say well for the future, but it is now too late'. None the less, the duke forcibly urged his immunity, on the policy ground that if the surrender treaty were violated in his case then all wars would be 'downright butchery', because no soldier would trust a surrender settlement. This argument still resounds in criminal courts invited to override pardons that are given in order to free hostages or end civil wars: if these are worthless to terrorists and insurgents, will there be any incentive for them to stop the killing?[22] Steele and Cooke argued that the words of the surrender document were plain and in any event the army had no power to absolve prisoners from prosecution by the civil power, because the rule of law requires that serious criminal laws should not be dispensed with, certainly not by an army officer or even by a minister of state.

Cooke was not certain that the prosecution would prevail – if the surrender treaty really was ambiguous then the prisoner should have the benefit of it. So he came up with a further argument: Hamilton's escape from lawful custody had the effect of forfeiting the benefit of the pardon, because it was an implied condition of all pardons that they must be performed to the letter by their beneficiary, and the duke's unlawful escape extinguished the obligation of the state to keep its side of the bargain. Cooke's argument was greeted with great indignation by the duke and his party: they regarded it as a last-ditch attempt to shore up a weak prosecution case. Bradshawe, however, had no difficulty in finding Hamilton guilty: he was a rebel leader, who might have surrendered to the army on the promise that it would not shoot him, but that could not absolve him from treason. To the argument that no one would surrender on such a dubious promise, Cooke replied that it is generally better to live another day, or at least to die another way: in return for the sparing of his life the previous August, Hamilton's surrender had earned him nine months at Windsor, a fair trial, and the possibility of saving his life even after Bradshawe's sentence; the court postponed all the executions until Parliament could debate whether to have them carried out.

The trial of the King's courtiers had lasted, in fits and starts, for a month. Cooke performed more effectively than in the King's trial because the defendants raised real issues of law and fact which had been the subject of evidence and argument. The appearance of counsel – the renowned Matthew Hale – gave the proceedings a genuine adversary flavour and put Cooke and Steele on their mettle. The court strove to be fair and granted unheard-of indulgences to the prisoners. The Duke of Hamilton was permitted adjournments to gather evidence; he was allowed to instruct Hale in private; the Earl of Holland's illness was accepted as a reason why he should not stand trial until his doctors certified that he was well enough to cope. These novel civilities may have reflected a lingering respect for high-born defendants, but they set standards which could not easily be ignored by the ordinary criminal courts in this new republican era. Within the constraints of the current rules of evidence, which denied defendants the right to testify on oath or cross-examine, the High Court's proceedings were remarkably fair: no attempt was made to cover up the angry differences between Peters and Colonel Lilburne over the circumstances of the duke's surrender and the court's order that General Fairfax himself should attend was a sign of independence from the army. Its indulgence was not, of course, appreciated: Hamilton on the scaffold sneered at the low births of the commissioners and regretted being judged by a court 'a great part composed of men mechanic and unfit to be judges'.[23] It was typical for royalists to deride the tradesmen and plebeians of the New Model officer corps, but at Colchester these noble lords had preferred their own soldiers to starve to death rather than surrender. When they had to negotiate terms, the main point upon which they insisted was that they should be permitted to ride out in style on horses that should have been fed to their emaciated troops a week before.

Cooke, plebeian though he was, had proved his legal worth against Matthew Hale, the best legal mind of the time. His arguments have a contemporary resonance, in so far as the validity of pardons granted under pressure can no longer be allowed to bestow impunity for crimes against humanity. Cooke's point about the need to imply conditions into pardons is now accepted.[24] The proceedings had a less than satisfactory end, however, because there was no appeal in criminal cases other than to Parliament – and politicians cannot be trusted to deliver justice. Lord Goring, the most vicious of the defendants, was reprieved by the casting vote of the Speaker of the House – for no better reason, William Lenthall explained, than that he had once received favours from Goring and would now repay them by saving his life. When the House was similarly deadlocked over the fate of the Earl of Holland, on the other hand, the Speaker gave a casting vote against him – presumably having received no favours at his hands. But Holland, although a mercenary turncoat, had been of vital assistance at the outbreak of the civil war: in his unique position as 'groom of the stool' (assisting the King's defecations) he had organised defections to the parliamentary cause. For Bulstrode Whitelocke, the Speaker's behaviour was a salutary lesson in the need to keep politicians out of the business of justice:

> This may be a caution to us against the affectation of popularity, when you see the issue of it in this noble gentleman [Holland] who was as full of generosity and courtship to all sorts of persons, and readiness to help the oppressed, and to stand for the rights of the people, as any person of his quality in this nation. Yet this person was by representatives of the people given up to execution for treason: and another lord [Goring], who never made profession of being a friend to liberty, either civil or spiritual, and exceeded the Earl as much in his crimes

as he came short of him in his popularity, the life of this lord was spared.[25]

There were more political decisions. Sir John Owen was reprieved at Ireton's suggestion, because he was a commoner and a grant of mercy to him would emphasise that the aristocracy would find that high birth brought no favours in the courts of the commonwealth. Lord Capel was sent for execution on Cromwell's recommendation, not because he was a bad man but because he was feared as an exceedingly good one, whose conscience and sense of duty to the King would make him an implacable enemy of the republic.

What Cooke thought of these unprincipled decisions is not recorded: he probably shared Whitelocke's concern about 'the affectation of popularity' and the unfitness of both the people and their representatives for making sentencing decisions. Both lawyers wanted a justice system independent of government although Whitelocke, the son of an influential judge, desired the perpetuation of the system he knew and loved and had benefited from, whilst Cooke the poor husbandman's son understood the need for wide-ranging reforms. In the first year of the commonwealth, the Rump did effect two important reforms close to Cooke's heart; his hand may be detected in the statute which permitted imprisoned debtors to obtain release on habeas corpus unless the accusing creditors could produce some evidence of the debt, or if they could show that they were genuinely impoverished, and not deliberately withholding payment.[26] This legislation, passed in September 1649, did much to mitigate the worst injustice of the age – imprisonment on accusation of debt, from which Cooke's brother and brother-in-law had suffered. Another reform that had been passionately urged in the *Vindication* was accomplished the following year, by an Act requiring all court proceedings and judgments to be expressed in English and no longer in Norman French or Latin.

Law reform was not a priority in the early months of the republic: royalist opposition in England had been effectively suppressed but it was dangerously rampant in Ireland, where the Catholic and Protestant factions had actually joined together in a confederacy which was outnumbering and out-manoeuvring the small parliamentary army. Substantial reinforcements were required, then as ever an unpleasant prospect for English troops, who were now subjected to a fresh round of Leveller agitation. Lilburne wanted elections immediately; his pamphlets talked of dictatorship and asked the provocative question, 'We were before ruled by Kings, Lords and Commons; now by a General, Court Martial and a House of Commons: and we pray you, what is the difference?'[27] In April and May there were mutinous outbreaks which Fairfax, fully in command, put down forcefully. He had three Leveller leaders amongst the soldiers court-martialled and shot at dawn whilst their followers looked on, from the roof of Burford Church where they had been corralled. The general was an unyielding disciplinarian, crushing the mutineers (against Cromwell's preference for mercy) as firmly as he had dealt with the malignants at Colchester. It was his harshness – with soldiers who adored him – that overcame the Levellers, the 'enemy within'. Lilburne and other pamphleteers had been rounded up and sent to the Tower of London, and most of their followers expressed penitence after a lecture from Cromwell on godly behaviour.[28] Thereafter, the Levellers were spent as a political force. Lilburne himself had historic contributions yet to make, to criminal law but not to politics.

This man, whose exhortations had done so much to bring the King to trial, now found himself charged with treason – for stirring soldiers to mutiny against a Parliament that refused to dissolve. Although the Solicitor-General was in general agreement with Lilburne's democratic ideals, Cooke regarded his old client as irresponsible for pressing them with such personal vindictiveness against Cromwell and Fairfax at a time when the republic faced imminent threat of invasion, by Irish rebels and also by the Scots, whose Parliament had already declared Charles II their King. The Solicitor-General was instructed by the Council of State to prosecute Lilburne, although he was reluctant to act against a former client and doubted the wisdom of putting him on trial.[29] Fairfax wanted Lilburne eliminated, but the legal system was for the first time independent of the government. The judges demonstrated their independence by refusing the Attorney-General's demand that Lilburne be kept in the Tower, and allowed him bail over the summer on compassionate grounds, to look after his wife and children, struck down by smallpox. Cromwell, meanwhile, left for Ireland sure that Lilburne would be convicted. Everybody charged with treason always was convicted and he saw no reason why this traditional aspect of English legal life should not continue in his absence. But he reckoned without the courage and performing ability of 'Freeborn John' – a commoner, and therefore entitled to a jury of his 'peers' – his fellow commoners from London's East End.

The treason trial of John Lilburne in October 1649 must be ranked as one of the most significant criminal trials in legal history. In the course of a three-day disputation with the judges, this brilliant and radical autodidact renegotiated the meaning of due process, of what fair play for a defendant required. Indeed, Lilburne's historic achievement over all his court appearances was to turn the English criminal trial into an adversary process – hitherto, it had been largely inquisitorial: the defendant's guilt was assumed and he was given little chance to contest the evidence. Lilburne was a self-taught legal scholar but none the worse for that: a fine polemicist and an eloquent speaker, he had been a Star Chamber martyr, a courageous officer who had fought for Parliament and a popular favourite both of the army and the mob. He was not a defendant to trifle with, and the judges at his trial in October were well aware that they would be setting precedents for future treason trials. 'We are on trial for our lives too,' they reminded him, at the outset of the hearing.

Lilburne began with an eloquent demand that the court uphold 'the first fundamental liberty of an Englishman' that 'all courts of justice always ought to be free and open for all sorts of peaceable people to see, behold and hear, and have free access unto; and no man whatsoever ought to be tried in holes or corners, or in any place where the gates are shut and barred'. Judge Keble interrupted him with a smile: 'Mr Lilburne, look behind you, and see whether the door stands open or no.' The prisoner was somewhat deflated to see that it had just been opened, and hundreds of his supporters were filing onto the public benches even as he spoke. None the less, his outburst helped to establish the fundamental principle of open justice: the judges ruled that the court doors remain open at all times, 'that all the world may know with what candour and justice the court does proceed against you'.

Lilburne next mounted an attack on Bradshawe, for hypocrisy. The judge was now president of the council and in that capacity had summoned Lilburne to its sitting at Derby House:

I saw no accuser, no prosecutor, no accusation, no charge nor indictment; but Mr Bradshawe very seriously examined me to questions against my self: although I am confident he could not forget that himself and Mr John Cooke were my counsellors in February [1646] at the Bar of the House of Lords, where he did most vehemently condemn the lords of the Star Chamber's unjust and wicked dealing with English

freemen in censuring them for their refusing to answer questions
concerning themselves; and yet he dealt with me in the very steps that
formerly he had bitterly condemned in the Star Chamber lords; yea,
and there for refusing to answer his questions, committed me to prison
for treason.[30]

Bradshawe had been acting as investigator not a judge when he asked the
questions and Lilburne had not been jailed for refusing to answer (his fate
in the Star Chamber). But his protest was pointed, none the less, and the
court refused to permit the prosecutor, the new Attorney-General Edward
Prideaux, to force Lilburne to confirm that he was the author of the treasonable polemic. But this time, 'Freeborn John' was tripped up by his own
love of publicity: he had personally presented the pamphlet to the Attorney-
General a few months previously, with the boast: 'Here is a book that is
mine, the printing errors excepted – which are many.' Prideaux took a grim
delight in proving Lilburne's authorship by calling his young law clerk to
testify to the presentation. 'He looks a man of quality,' murmured one judge
as he surveyed James Nutley, friend and pupil to John Cooke, who gave
evidence against Lilburne as confidently as he would one day testify against
his own pupil master.

Lilburne was charged with treason under the new Act which had passed
the Commons on 17 May, incriminating those who subverted the government or incited mutiny in the army. While it was being read, the Attorney-
General stepped up to chat with one of the judges – a common feature in
criminal trials hitherto. Lilburne would have none of this and complained
bitterly:

LILBURNE: Hold a while, hold a while. Let there be no discourse but openly.
For my adversaries or persecutors whispering with the judges is contrary
to the law of England and extremely foul and dishonest play.

ATTORNEY-GENERAL: It is nothing concerning you, Mr Lilburne.

LILBURNE: By your favour, Mr Prideaux, that is more than I do know.

JUDGE THORPE: I tell you, Sir, the Attorney-General may talk with any
in the court, by law, as he did with me.

LILBURNE: I tell *you*, Sir, it is unjust, and not warrantable by law, for him to talk with the court or any of the judges thereof in my absence, or in hugger-mugger, or by private whisperings.[31]

Lilburne was confronting an English court with the unfairness of its traditional procedures – an unfairness that began to be recognised after the King's trial and those of his courtiers had shown some respect for defendants. He next challenged the rule that denied counsel to defendants on issues of fact. The Attorney-General pointed out that allowing barristers to contest the prosecution evidence would delay trials, and the court with some reluctance declined Lilburne's request although it permitted him to have a 'friend in court' sitting nearby, who was a solicitor named Spratt, the first of that profession ever to seek audience. His intervention on his client's behalf was firmly squashed ('What impudent fellow is that, who dares be so bold to speak in the court without being called to the bar?') but eventually the presiding judge accepted that Mr Spratt, the unsung precursor of solicitors' rights of audience (granted 350 years later), might be heard on points of law, once the facts had been established. Lilburne, of course, was bluffing: he had no intention to yield the limelight to any lawyer, but his arguments for his right to have counsel to contest issues of fact and cross-examine the witnesses read so powerfully (Lilburne, typically, edited and published the report of his own trial) that they were important in securing that reform, which came in the next century.

Lilburne's trial achieved the consolidation of such defence rights as could be extrapolated from the recent proceedings against the King and the courtiers, supplemented with further rights drawn from the republican values for which Parliament had fought, i.e. fairness and equality before the law. The prisoner was to be treated with a measure of dignity and humanity, and the judges showed a dawning sense of pride that by such principle, English law was, comparatively, much fairer than law in other countries: Keble boasted that it was 'the righteousest and most merciful law in the world – this we sit here to maintain and let all the world know it'. For all this, the defendant was plainly guilty of the offence created by the new Treason Act, which punished by death any published allegation that the government was unlawful: the defendant had described it as an 'army junto' run by 'tyrants, weasels and polecats'. Lilburne therefore invited the jury to usurp the traditional role of the judges by deciding what the law should be, rather than what facts had been proved. In this, as the judges splenetically pointed out, he was totally wrong. But he got across to the jury the idea that the law should permit free speech, and that his acquittal would enable it to achieve this purpose.

Lilburne was playing for his life: he knew that the army grandees whose troops he had incited to mutiny wanted him dead and that the judges, notwithstanding their fair procedural rulings, were time-serving at heart, and would in due course direct the jury to convict. He begged for an adjournment – just an hour, to relieve and refresh himself and collect his thoughts for his final speech. The judges were unimpressed and ordered him to hurry up: but Lilburne had one last precedent to create:

LILBURNE: Sir, if you will be so cruel as not to give me leave to withdraw to ease and refresh my body, I pray you let me do it in the court. Officer, I entreat you – help me to a chamber pot!

The judges sat in stunned silence as a chamber pot was fetched by the sheriff; then, as the official report notes, 'When the pot came, he made water and gave it to the foreman' – who presumably passed it around the jury.[32] It was Lilburne's last and most important precedent: courts must ensure the comfort of the prisoners at the bar throughout their trial.

When it came time to sum up, the judicial mask of fairness and politeness slipped – as it often does in English criminal trials. Keble sent the jury out: 'If you have fully apprehended the dangerous things plotted in these books of Mr Lilburne's, you will clearly find that never was the like treason hatched in England.' The jurors asked 'that they might have a butt of sack to refresh them' – a request for alcohol which was denied, as it has been to jurors ever since. They returned after an hour to acquit Lilburne on all counts, to the noisy acclamation of the packed Guildhall. He was conveyed back to the Tower, by soldiers who joined in the shouts of joy at his deliverance, and it was a fortnight before the Council of State judged it safe to discharge him. Cromwell, by now campaigning victoriously in Ireland, was astonished when he heard that Lilburne had been acquitted. Henceforth, the commonwealth would try its common traitors before a more reliable mechanism – High Courts of Justice.

They need not have worried: the Levellers were finished as a political force, and Lilburne acknowledged as much. He buckled down to the new tyranny (as he saw it) and tried to restore his fortunes. He continued his dispute with Haselrig over property in the north and settled in to a new occupation, running the first 'citizens advice bureau' from his home, conveniently situated in Old Bailey. He even applied to join an Inn of Court (the Inner Temple) to study as a barrister, but Prideaux churlishly led the clamour to refuse him admission.[33] In 1651 he made the mistake of returning to pamphleteering, albeit for his private interest, with a swingeing attack on Haselrig, but his enemy was an MP and he was held in contempt of Parliament. For this crime there was no trial by jury; Lilburne was fined and ordered into exile by Haselrig's MP friends. He departed, despondently, to the continent, following the path well-trodden by defeated English royalists.

The acquittal of John Lilburne may have irritated Cromwell, but it was the logical result of the revolution: justice and the Petition of Right had been a chief cause for which Parliament had fought. Lilburne repeatedly cited Cooke's *King Charles: His Case* as proof that governments which influenced judges were guilty of tyranny – this had been a crucial part of Cooke's indictment against Charles I. The consequence was twofold: judges must display their independence, and prisoners must be accorded certain rights to a fair trial: in particular, since the law was no respecter of persons, they were to enjoy the same respect that the King and the Duke of Hamilton were shown at their trials. From the same crucible in which the republic was forged in 1649 emerged a set of precedents which began a new tradition of fairness (or at least fairishness) to the defence: the criminal trial was beginning its turn from an 'inquisition for guilt' into a genuinely adversary procedure, in which the possibility of innocence would be ever present.

By the time Lilburne's trial took place, in late October, John Cooke had left for Ireland. He was still Solicitor-General on 30 June, when a House of Commons that was truly grateful for his services bestowed upon him the mastership of St Cross's Hospital at Winchester, the largest almshouse in England.[34] This was not a munificent reward for loyal work for the commonwealth: the master was entitled to keep some £200 per annum for himself after providing for the poor and those who ministered to them, and at Cooke's abstemious request the House of Commons ordered an 'augmentation' of the funds actually allocated to the paupers. This almshouse was renowned for relieving the poor by getting them sozzled: its 'wayfarers dole' comprised two and a half pints of wine to wash down a small loaf and its brewhouse ordered malt in much greater quantities than its bakery ordered wheat to make the daily bread.[35] The new master, so full of plans in his youth for curbing

223

drunkenness, was horrified to find himself running a glorified brewery, and soon turned off the taps. He quickly changed an institution which had been run in the interests of its clerics and a handful of aged paupers into a hospital which took in soldiers injured in the Irish and Scots wars.

The appointment was entirely appropriate given Cooke's interest in poor relief, although most previous masters had been clerics. The current guide-book (St Cross remains a sanctuary for elderly poor) complains about 'the forcible introduction of two lay masters, Lisle and Cooke, during the Commonwealth',[36] overlooking the facts that St Cross had survived Henry VIII's dissolution of religious charities only by proving that it was a lay foun-dation and that it was Cooke and Lisle, not their greedy clerical predeces-sors, who increased the proportion of its funds actually spent on the poor. The guidebook entry is typical of the ignorance about, and bias against, the regicides which is still apparent in English writing and thinking. In fact, Parliament's appointment of John Cooke, who really did care about the poor, should be compared with James I's appointment of his old tutor, who cared so little that he never once left Edinburgh to visit St Cross.[37]

This honour was the first of many lucrative public posts that Cooke might have expected to fall into his lap. He had for the past six months been inde-fatigable in working to create a republic – prosecuting its enemies and drafting its statutes. He was appointed by the House as a trustee for collecting the vast wealth and confiscated lands of the bishops, and paying it out to univer-sities, hospitals and 'godly ministers'.[38] He was appointed to investigate the mismanagement of Charterhouse Hospital[39] and to conduct an official enquiry in Guernsey.[40] A silver medal was struck in his honour by the master of the mint, Thomas Simon – a tiny engraving of the Solicitor General, surrounded by a laurel wreath – the only likeness of John Cooke that has survived (see p.1). Why then did he set sail for Ireland, in the wake of Cromwell and his army of invasion?

There is no doubt that he was now surrounded by lawyers who were much better connected and more conservative (for example, Edward Prideaux, the new Attorney-General) who with other cautious lawyers had been readmitted to the Commons once they had disavowed their December vote for contin-uing the Newport Treaty negotiations (an easy enough affirmation, once the King was no longer in a position to treat). These grandees distrusted Cooke, both for his low birth and for his past record of pamphleteering against their professional privileges, and Cooke must have sensed their opposition to his hopes for law reform. It is noteworthy that in midyear William Steele, who had failed the revolution at its most difficult moment, was made Recorder of London, and John Aske, Cooke's junior counsel, was elevated to the rank of Sergeant and then made a judge.[41] Cooke was passed over, either because he was considered too radical or at his own request. Remaining as Solicitor-General would mean accepting instructions to prosecute men like his old client Lilburne, with whom he had some sympathy. Then there was the question of security. Despite his public insouciance, the assassination of Isaac Dorislaus had been worrying enough for him to acquire a pistol to protect his wife and servants. His safety, and that of his family, would best be secured by the army, a large contingent of which was embarking for Ireland – a country he knew well from his days with Strafford.

There was a more important reason. Reassurance that he remained in a state of grace would come from an ability to act like a saint, and what could be more saintly than turning his back on London vainglory, and embarking on an expedition, as a missionary both for God and for justice, to a country full of heathen Catholics and rebellious royalists? The prospect for doing 'God's work' in Ireland was impressed upon him by Henry Ireton and then by Cromwell himself, who wanted a reliable judge to hand out retribution for the 1641 atrocities and then to reinvigorate the court system. Ireland was not an attractive prospect, but John Cooke was not a personally ambitious man and his law reform projects were being stalled by the conservatives. It occurred to Cooke that these reforms would have to be proved in practice before they would be countenanced in England, and 'West England' (as Ireland was optimistically called) might be the place where that proof could be demonstrated:

The lodestone that drew me over into Ireland was the great encouragement that I had from Cromwell and Ireton and many honourable persons in the army, who were pleased to say that Ireland was like a White Paper, apt to receive any good impression. Because the Lord had superseded the old courts here, it was hoped (by divine assistance) that such an expedient for a speedy and sure justice might have been settled; that though Ireland be but the younger sister yet England might have been learner and gainer by her.[42]

At some point in the summer of 1649, the Solicitor-General decided to abandon all ambitions for political or judicial office in England and to join

Cromwell's crusade to pacify and reconstruct Ireland. He spent some time in Winchester in September, signing leases and sorting out business at St Cross. Then, to the dismay of his wife's friends, he took Frances across the sea to Munster.

13

Impressions on White Paper

In the first months of the commonwealth, Ireland presented the gravest danger. The Duke of Ormond, himself a Protestant, commanded a substantial army comprising royalists, old English Catholics and native Irish Catholics, in alliance with an Ulster Catholic army led by O'Neil; they were joined by the most brutal of the parliamentary commanders, the Earl of Inchiquin, who defected when the King was put on trial. That left a parliamentary force in Dublin commanded by Michael Jones and another army under Sir Charles Coote in Connaught. The civil war years had seen these and other forces in varying alliances engaged in numerous battles, often marked by utter disregard for the rules of warfare – captured towns were frequently plundered, with non-combatants (women, children and old men) 'put to the sword'. Ormonde was commanded directly by Charles II, and Rupert's navy was based at Kinsale. The Council of State believed that waxing royalist power would mean an attack on of England from Ireland, unless England acted first. In March 1649, it had asked Cromwell to lead an invasion.

Cromwell hesitated for several weeks whilst he 'waited on God'. Like Fairfax, he was well aware of the danger from the combination of 'the Papists and the King's party' which might root out the Puritan settlements as violently as in 1641, when thousands of English Protestants had been massacred, and then use the country as a springboard for another war in England. Cromwell explained his eventual decision in terms that every Englishman of the era could understand: 'I had rather be overrun with a cavalierish interest than a Scots interest; I had rather be overrun with a Scotch interest than an Irish interest . . . for all the world knows of their barbarism.'[1] It was retribution for this barbarism that Cromwell believed was God's purpose: the atrocities of 1641 had never been requited and the conquest of Ireland would be the surest way to end impunity and bring the country to Protestant-led civilisation. After Leveller-inspired rebellion had been put down severely by Fairfax at Burford, Cromwell's agreement to lead the campaign gave the soldiers some reassurance. To avoid any suggestion of unfairness the choice of regiments to accompany him was made in a most unusual way: by a child, drawing the names of their colonels from a hat. The first name to be drawn was of Henry Ireton. Hence another of history's hypotheticals: what if the child's trembling hand had not drawn (and to a lamentably early death) the name of the only man after Cromwell capable of leading the Republic?

Travel from London to Dublin in 1649 could take up to a fortnight: a week by horse or carriage to Chester (the terminal for sea-passage to and from Dublin) or to Milford Haven (for Wexford and Cork) then a few more days (weather permitting) for the sea-crossing. It was not until August that Cromwell departed, having persuaded John Cooke to follow and play a part in post-war reconstruction and settlement, as a judge who would initially hold court in conquered areas and in due course deal with the perpetrators of the 1641 massacres. The Irish sea is not a placid prospect at the best of times: Hugh Peters reported that the general was 'as seasick as ever I saw a man in my life'.[2] At College Green,[3] still green around the gills from his rough sea-crossing, Cromwell spoke of his mission to propagate the gospel and deal with the 'barbarous and blood-thirsty Irish' who had perpetrated the 1641 massacres. In a less turbulent state a few days later, he issued a solemn declaration promising that none of his soldiers would 'do any wrong or violence' to any persons of any kind 'unless they be actually in arms or office with the enemy'. A few days later, marching north, he emphasised this promise Henry V style by executing two of his soldiers who had stolen some hens from a local farmer. On 3 September – always a portentous day for Oliver Cromwell – he reached a town called Drogheda.

Neither side had any illusion about the significance of this engagement. Ormonde's plan was to tie Cromwell down at Drogheda in a long-drawn-out siege, so that during the onset of the winter those two stalwart Irish defenders, 'Colonel Hunger and Major Sickness', would decimate the tenderstomached English invaders. Cromwell, for his part, methodically surrounded the town walls and sent its governor, the experienced royalist commander Sir Arthur Aston, an ultimatum to surrender 'to the end (that) effusion of blood may be prevented'. Answer came there none and Aston knew exactly what his defiance meant under the law of war, namely the right of the besieging army, once it breached the castle walls, to kill without mercy all its armed defenders.

That, in short, is exactly what happened a few days later. The English cannons cracked the town walls and Cromwell, with astonishing personal bravery, led his troops, like Henry V, once more into the breach. There is no reason to dispute his own, invariably candid, account of his orders to his men: 'being in the heat of the action, I forbade them to spare any that were in arms in the town, and I think that night they put to the sword about 2,000 men.' Civilians were not killed, but the next day officers who surrendered were executed together with one in ten of their surrendered soldiers. However fashionable it may be to accuse Cromwell of a 'war crime' in Drogheda, he stuck precisely to the rules of war as they were well understood by Aston and by Ormonde, who gambled their men's lives on a strategy of 'no surrender' that failed.[4] What was shocking about Cromwell's conduct at Drogheda was that he had fought according to these rules, and not according to the more humane understandings of them he displayed during the civil war – a war between English gentlemen.[5] Thus Whitelocke and Ludlow justified his harshness on the basis that it accorded with the law of war and was intended as a deterrent. Cromwell in his report to Parliament could not help giving his terror tactic the absolving character of retribution:

I am persuaded that this is a righteous judgement of God upon these barbarous wretches who have imbrued their hands in so much innocent blood, and that it will tend to prevent the effusion of blood for the future – which are the satisfactory grounds for such actions, which otherwise cannot but work remorse and regret.[6]

Cromwell persuaded himself easily enough, and doubtless many English people: his letter to the speaker was widely published. But he was not fighting the individuals responsible for the 1641 massacre, and these reprisals did nothing to stop the subsequent 'effusion of blood' – quite the contrary. The following month at Wexford hundreds of citizens were killed in overloaded boats as they tried to escape and at Clonmel a few months later the royalists took their revenge, trapping and exterminating some 2,000 of Cromwell's soldiers – his worst (indeed, his only) defeat. Cromwell acted reasonably at Drogheda in ordering 'no quarter' for armed enemies in the heat and turmoil of the battle, but his behaviour at dawn the next day, in a conquered and utterly devastated town, was a different matter. Cromwellian apologists praise him for sparing nine lives out of ten on the basis that commanders during the Thirty Years War would have killed all prisoners taken after a defiant siege, but this is to miss the point: Cromwell was not a continental commander, and his objective had been achieved without need for cruel executions.

These were times in which Englishmen of every political allegiance regarded Catholics as potential terrorists. The discovery of Guy Fawkes and the papist plot to blow up the Houses of Parliament on 5 November 1605 lived on in folk memory and was one celebration the Puritans did not ban. Irish Catholics were regarded as quite literally 'beyond the Pale' – they were collectively and indelibly responsible for the killings of 1641. For Cooke and his generation, Ireland was a permanent threat to security: the only long-term solution was to turn it into 'West England'. Post-war reconstruction would be achieved by planting Protestants like dragons' teeth throughout the land, and by transmigration – moving Catholic rebels to Connaught, the least fertile of Ireland's four provinces. But first, the rule of law had to be re-established, by punishing the crimes of 1641 and then operating a system of expeditious and effective justice for all.

To this end, John Cooke and his wife Frances arrived at Wexford shortly after it fell to Cromwell and on 1 January 1650 set sail for Cork in an old naval ship, the *Hector*. The ship made reasonable progress and by 4 January was half-way – Cooke could see the lights of Duncannon, the fort protecting Waterford Harbour – when the wind rose alarmingly. Early on Sunday morning the tempest struck and the sailors spent the day in desperate attempts to keep the ship off the rocks. In the evening, a vast wave split the foremast and the seas which washed over the stricken vessel left 5 feet of water in the hold. John and Frances huddled together in the main cabin with the other passengers, praying and lamenting as the boat shuddered in the darkness and its sailors shouted for all aboard to prepare for death.[7]

Cooke had no doubt about what was in store: 'My spirit fainted and my heart sank within me, the sorrows of death caught hold of me.' He grieved most for Frances, his 'poor dear heart' who was clutching him, 'my dearest friend upon earth', as the ship careened. But John was even more worried 'to think what my wife's friends would say in England, that I should bring her to Ireland to drown her'. He felt remorse for his servants too, but much of his grief was concerned with the political consequence of his own death: 'It almost split my heart to think what the malignants would say in England when they heard we were drowned.' They would claim it as God's vengeance upon him for murdering the King and for the first time there dawned upon him the awful thought that they might be right. Dorislaus had been assassinated and now he would be lost at sea: 'Such extraordinary violent deaths import the nature of some heavy judgment – as if the Lord had been displeased with us.'

He could not understand why he should be punished for coming to Ireland to do the Lord's service – 'What will thy enemies say', he upbraided his God, 'when the carcasses of thy people are given to be food for the fishes? It was for thy sake that we committed ourselves to the sea.' He tried to comfort his wife with the thought that God would not let them drown, for He had further work for them to do. This seemed most unlikely: as the waves crashed over the cabin, Frances tried to prepare him for death: 'We shall be made one with the father and the son, we shall be crowned with an incorruptible crown of glory' (she clung to the hope with which Bishop Juxon had comforted Charles on the scaffold). As others swayed and screamed in the turbulence, John and Frances solemnly took their leave of each other: when they kissed he felt the tears running down her cheeks and promised, 'These tears shall be wiped from our eyes in heaven.'

It may have been a kind of ecstasy that enveloped John Cooke as he concentrated his mind upon the joys of heaven, or it might simply have been dog-tiredness combined with the rolling of the ocean, but he felt an irrepressible drowsiness. He pinched himself to keep awake ('What! Be drowned in my sleep!') but could not fight off slumber. 'And in my sleep I dreamed', he subsequently recalled, 'of being in a large room with other mariners all beseeching that their ships would not perish that night in this storm.' A reassuringly Puritan young man, in 'sad-coloured clothes' and with snow white hair curled at the end beneath his broad-brimmed hat, explained that he was a servant of Jesus Christ – and he pointed to a glorious light shining from behind a curtain at the end of the room. 'What would you have?' the voice of Jesus asked, from behind the curtain. 'The lives of all in the ship,' replied Cooke. 'And what ship is that?' 'The *Hector*,' replied the dreamer. 'A bad name for those who profess belief in me,' said Jesus, his irony evincing a classical education. 'Unless you speak the word,' said Cooke, 'the sea will swallow us up.' 'But why are you not willing to die?' asked the Son of God, sternly. 'Because then I can't glorify you in the world,' replied the lawyer, used to thinking on his feet, even when asleep. But then he made the courtroom beginner's mistake of becoming emboldened by his own cleverness. He complained to the judge – of all mankind – that 'the Lord should surprise us, getting us into a ship at his call for his service, and then drown us'.

As he uttered this disrespectful remark, the light began to dim. Regretting instantly his doubting of divine purpose, Cooke threw himself down and begged for pity – unavailingly, until the young Puritan whispered that his complaint had been falsely premised – the tempest had been raised by Satan, not by God. Armed with this new information, Cooke begged Christ to hear him one last time: God may well allow Satan to play havoc on the 'children of disobedience' for their sins, but were not the children of obedience free from Satan's control? The light flared. 'Be not afraid. Your lives shall be saved.' Cooke asked for the goods in the ship to be saved as well and Christ consented, farewelling the lawyer with what might pass for divine wisdom (or mind-numbing banality): 'Go no more to sea in winter.'

Frantic elbowing from Frances awoke John – she wanted him conscious as they drowned. 'Peace, dear heart, and be quiet. We shall all be safe – Jesus Christ has promised our lives.' Captain Stokes was not impressed: the storm was getting worse and all hope had gone. 'I know God is very merciful and can do much,' he said, to humour his famous passenger. 'But this ship has five foot of water in the hold, which the pump cannot reach because it is blocked, and it is over twenty years old – it will shortly break asunder.' Cooke remained 'brimful of comfort' as the waves washed through the broken cabin windows and the ship seemed to founder. The sailors cried: 'Now we are gone.' 'Don't worry,' he shouted, 'we are as safe as if we were on dry land.' Frances, ever practical, suggested to Captain Stokes that the ship be lightened by throwing their heavy trunks overboard. Her husband would not allow it: he had made a deal with Christ and it included their baggage. Frances marvelled at his confidence, but Cooke's fears 'were so far above my hopes, as the rain descended and the floods came and the wind blew upon my soul, when we were like to have been split in pieces upon the rocks in the sea called "the three stags" I said I would cast my mind and body into the arms of my sweet saviour'.

To the amazement of the mariners, the *Hector* weathered the night and when she was blown towards the rocks a miraculous change of wind veered her out to sea again. Eventually, the ship staggered into harbour at Kinsale,[8] and both Frances and John set down the story of the dream and their deliverance. '*Mrs Cooke's Meditations*' were described as '*an humble thanksgiving to her Heavenly Father for granting her a new life, having considered herself dead, and her grave made in the bottom of the sea*'. John wrote an account of his dream, typically adding a didactic essay on other possible instances of 'divine light' provided through dreams. He was too much of a rationalist to claim he had really encountered Christ: he admitted that 'Usually dreams follow men's actual inclination' and that having meditated on the pity of Jesus throughout the Sunday as the storm grew worse, it was likely that any dream would feature a compassionate Christ. He offered it to the public none the less as a possible instance of divine communication, in which his spirit may have been translated to some metaphysical plane where Christ, attended by Puritans, was open to rational, even legal, argument. His booklet, entitled *A true relation of Mr Justice Cooke's passage by sea from Wexford to Kinsale and of the great storm and imminent danger that he and the others were in, with the wonderful appearance of the power and goodness of God in their deliverance, according as it was revealed to him in a dream*, went through several editions. It was circulated as devotional reading for the New Model soldiers in Ireland, and became the talk of many Puritan congregations back in London. The Lord had witnessed on behalf of the man responsible for taking the King's life, and if this was augury, it boded well for the republic.

It also augured well for their marriage. What the 'his and hers' accounts provide for modern readers is an affecting testimony to the love shared by John and Frances. The two had come to Ireland out of a missionary zeal to do God's work, and thanksgiving for their unexpected salvation made them redouble their efforts. Thereafter, on the Munster circuit between Dublin, Waterford and Cork, Justice Cooke would praise the Lord and proffer that cheap and speedy justice he believed that all legal systems should supply. His dream had been an epiphany which convinced him that he was one of the elect whose work had the stamp of divine approval: henceforth he would fear no evil. His pistol he thought the only possession lost at sea, but in conformity with Christ's promise that he should lose none of his belongings it was returned by a sailor upon landing – which he took as a sign that it would not be needed.

Shortly after the storm, Cooke's role in the 'civilising' mission became clear: Cromwell offered him the all-important post of chief justice of Munster, the largest and most settled of Ireland's provinces. He was not the first choice, which had lit upon John Sadler, a distinguished Cambridge academic. In an effort to entice him to Dublin, Cromwell offered the munificent salary of £1,000, recognising that inadequate pay for Irish judges in the past had deterred recruitment and encouraged corruption. The invitation which went out in his name to Sadler, written on 29 December, so encapsulates Cooke's language and hopes that it is likely he drafted it:

We have a great opportunity to set up, until the Parliament shall determine otherwise, a way of doing justice amongst the poor people which for the uprightness and cheapness of it, may be an exceedingly great gain to them, who have been accustomed to as much injustice, tyranny and oppression from their landlords, the great men, and those that should have done them right, as, I believe, any people in that which we call Christendom. Sir, if justice were freely and impartially administered here, the foregoing darkness and corruption would make it look so much the more glorious and beautiful . . .[9]

These prospects – and the pay that went with them – did not tempt Sadler. So instead the post went to Cooke himself at half the salary – £500 per annum – an indication of his willingness, in this 'second life' after the storm, to make personal sacrifices to do what he believed to be missionary work for God as well as for the commonwealth. He became chief justice of what had been a prerogative court of the president of Munster, who was now Henry Ireton: with his support Cooke began to work his miracle of summary justice. He decided over 600 cases in three months – a Guinness Book of Records average of seven decisions a day. Justice had suddenly – amazingly for most but alarmingly for a few – become fair and speedy and tenant-friendly. Cromwell was delighted and boasted to Ludlow that Chief Justice Cooke had 'determined more causes in a week, than Westminster Hall in a year' – and Westminster Hall housed all the civil courts of England.[10] The Munster Court mainly handled small claims (albeit claims not small to the impoverished tenants who made them) and could not decide title to land. None the less, Cooke's achievement in revitalising the justice system was spectacular. It came at a price, of course: he was accused of arbitrariness by those 'great men' his rulings disfavoured, and his zeal to protect the poor against their landlords earned him the enmity of powerful Protestant nobles and rack-renters.

In November 1651, Ireton died of fever whilst besieging Limerick. 'His heavenly father would not suffer him to die by the hand of an enemy', wrote Cooke, making the best of unfathomable providence. Ireton had been the prime mover in the King's trial and the intellectual force behind the republic: he was Cromwell's obvious (and only obvious) successor. Sir Charles Coote was not trusted to replace Ireton, least of all by Ireton himself, who had warned Cooke that the man would betray them if occasion arose to advantage himself. Charles Fleetwood, soon to become Cromwell's new son-in-law by marrying Ireton's widow, was eventually appointed Lord Deputy. Cooke worked well with him, as he tended to do with all veterans of the New Model Army. His pension arrangements were finalised in 1653 by act of parliament. In lieu of any pension, he received the freehold title to two houses in the town of Waterford, valued together at £208, some grazing land worth £245 at Kilbarry that also yielded wheat (twelve barrels of which went annually to the local hospital) and a farm at Barnahaly on which stood the crumbled remains of several castles.[11] These were hardly great estates, but they made him for the first time a man of some property.

There is evidence that Frances in these first years bore a child – a son, who died in infancy.[12] John coped with grief by throwing himself into his work, producing his major tract – *Monarchy No Creature of God's Making*, published both in Waterford and by his old publishers in London. As well as his presidency of the Munster Court he undertook assize work in Connaught and provided various public services in a country where he was the best lawyer – almost the only one – available to the state. For example, he was given the massive task of examining all the laws of England to decide whether and to what extent Parliament should apply them to Ireland. This was an important job, given the influx of English families 'planted' on land in Ireland forfeited by traitors and royalists.

Ireland was brought under Cromwellian heel by the end of 1650, when it became possible to exact retribution for the atrocities of 1641. These were crimes against humanity, even if the emphasis was on Protestant humanity, and to punish them was the first 'righteous cause' that Cromwell had given for the invasion: 'We are come to ask an account for the innocent blood that has been shed . . .' The extent of Protestant casualties in the Catholic insurrection had been exaggerated by the London papers, but not the nature of the injuries inflicted on the victims, often women and children, whose corpses were viciously mutilated, often *by* women and children.[13] The adjectives 'wild and barbarous' had perjoratively been applied to the native Irish by Elizabethan settlers like Sir Henry Wallop[14] who gave his surname to a form of smiting – 'There is no way to daunt these people', he averred, 'but by the edge of the sword.' But no other description could be applied to the behaviour of the insurrectionists, egged on by their priests, in 1641, when pregnant women had been impaled and children killed because 'nits make lice'.

For Cooke, these crimes were unforgivable: he ranked the 1641 atrocities with the Sicilian Vespers and the St Bartholomew Day massacres as the worst examples of mass-murder of innocents. He sat on a special 'High Court of Justice' which in three sittings is recorded to have convicted fifty-eight but acquitted thirty-nine – an acquittal rate (40 per cent) that is all the more surprising given the degree of English prejudice against defendants.[15] A record has survived of one trial – of Lord Muskerry, alleged to have approved of killings of civilians by men under his command. The court accepted defence evidence that he was not present and had afterwards wished to punish the perpetrators. After his acquittal the defendant paid heart-felt tribute to the fairness of his judges, who had 'leant to my favour rather than to my prejudice – in this court, on being sifted, I have come clear out of that blackness'.[16] Cooke directed that the prosecution must prove a killing was by the defendant's 'hand or command' and in the case of a commander like Muskerry, that he had actual knowledge of the crimes committed by his soldiers. In 1653 Cooke was appointed to chair a special tribunal to ensure that all the murder convictions fell within this limited definition.[17] There are many recent examples of defendants who have been unjustly held liable as accessories to political killings because of their support for the killer's cause:[18] it is remarkable to find a Puritan judge, in 1653, narrowing the definition of the crime in order to acquit Catholics.

In 1654 Justice Cooke was appointed both to the forfeited lands tribunal and to the tribunal to hear disputes arising out of the amnesty provisions of surrender agreements. He took on this extra work because he insisted that it be done by real judges, not 'Godly laymen'. He did not insist that judges should have read their law at university, but he vigorously opposed the radicals' idea that justice could be done by lay magistrates – a view the government supported in Ireland because it was cheap and anyway to attract real lawyers was difficult. 'The greatest misery to an innocent man is the ignorance of his judge' who, if untrained, would be 'all conscience but no science', and would not know what the rule of law required. In the preamble to *Monarchy No Creature of God's Making* Cooke had set out the qualities necessary for a good judge: *patience* (to hear all that can be said on both sides), *prudence* (to give satisfaction to the parties, each of whom will honestly believe that they are in the right), *justice* which respects the cause and not the person (untrained 'godly' judges would naturally pity the poor and give judgment in their favour, irrespective of the merits of the case) and *mercy* to deal tenderly with poor defendants after their case has been lost. Cooke plagiarised the ringing phrases of Job 29 to provide his own credo:

> If I have seen any perish for want of clothing, or any poor without covering; if I have lifted my hand against the fatherless or made gold my hope; if I rejoiced because of my wealth or at the destruction of my enemies; if I have allowed strangers to lodge in the street; if I did not minister speedy justice to the poor for the love of justice and to the rich for a small fee when I sat in open court so that every man might see and hear the reasons for my proceedings; if I have judged by the merit of the person and not the justice of the cause; if I have more esteemed birth than virtue and prefered greatness to piety; if my enemy's misery has been any pleasure to me; if I have thought myself better than my neighbours because I was richer; if I were ever overcome by threats, or corrupted by presents, to pervert judgement; if my constancy was ever shaken by a bribe; or if money had more power over my mind than reason; if I have not helped every man to his lands that had right to them without drawing tears to his eyes by tedious attendances . . . let my arm be broken by the hangman and heaven curse my lands; let the wheat which I sow reap but thistles . . .[19]

It was a fine catechism for a judge of any age, and Justice Cooke strove in his own conduct on the bench to live up to it. There is no evidence that he did other than justice according to his lights and did it speedily (but not peremptorily), cheaply (by fixing lawyers' fees) and fairly, given the legal rules and procedures with which he had to work. There is no doubt that he believed passionately in his work in Ireland – not only as God's work, but because it would pave the way for reform in England.

It is impossible at this remove to assess the quality of Cooke's judicial decisions – most private papers of those who worked for the Cromwellian system in Ireland were hurriedly destroyed at the Restoration and all official records of this period perished in the fire in the Four Courts in Dublin in 1922. The poor who benefited from Justice Cooke's rulings did not or could not write to express their thanks, although some surviving correspondence from the wealthy expresses a certain shock – if not outrage – at coming in front of a judge who was not biased in their favour. Lord Cork, greatest of the great landlords, was appalled that this new chief justice not only arranged for a barrister to assist an unrepresented defendant, but 'when the case was pleaded he [Cooke] did argue more for him than any of his counsel'.[20] His own well-paid barrister was so upset at finding a judge hostile to his noble client that 'he vowed he would never more plead in that court'. Lord Cork unconsciously provides a rather heartening vignette of a judge determined to ensure that poor defendants received justice when they came before him, but Cooke was making dangerous enemies. Another was Cork's cousin, Dean Michael Boyle, who claimed that Cooke would 'temper the wind to the shorn lamb', favouring the tenants that Boyle sued for debt.

As well as presiding over the Munster court, Cooke was always first choice for special commissions or inquiries. For example, he chaired a tribunal to decide which of the Protestant clergy – who had almost to a man supported the King against Parliament – were fit to resume their ministry. Cooke had always been tolerant of differences between Protestants and obviously enjoyed the work of disputing with Prebyterian ministers: 'I found much ingenuity in many of them and where they differ from us I take it to be on conscientious principle. I hope and daily pray that there might be better agreement between all honest and conscientious people who fear the Lord.'[21] But John and Frances lamented sorely the absence of 'godly ministers' in Munster and did their best to encourage those congregationalist preachers they knew back home to 'come over'. As late as 1652, the entire city of Waterford had no minister for its congregation, and a letter survives from its 'godly inhabitants' to one potential pastor, urging him to take up the position to a place 'which is likely to be a very comfortable English plantation in a short time' and where the congregation would include his old friend, Chief Justice Cooke. For all Cooke's pleasure at crossing intellectual swords with recusant ministers, he wanted to be led in worship by one of his own.[22]

Cooke's religious tolerance extended further than most English officials of his time: he was prepared to judge Catholics without discrimination so long as they did not 'seduce the people' or hold Mass publicly. In March 1650, Cromwell had issued his *Declaration for the Undeceiving of Deluded and Seduced People*, addressed to Catholic bishops who had urged their flocks to fight against him: 'You, unprovoked, put the English to the most unheard of and most barbarous massacre (without respect of sex or age) that ever the sun beheld', thundered Cromwell. Notwithstanding his determination to punish that crime, 'I meddle not with any man's conscience . . . as for the people, what thoughts they have in matters of religion in their own breasts, I cannot reach; but think it my duty, if they walk honestly and peaceably, not to cause them in the least to suffer for the same . . .'

As chief justice of the main province, Cooke had to make this promise of non-discrimination good; for example, when deciding cases between English and Irish, or in assessing evidence from Catholics. He admitted that this was one of his greatest difficulties, but over English objections he permitted Irish witnesses to swear on 'Lady Psalters' (books about the Virgin) or to take oaths 'by St Patrick' – and in this way he accepted that they were binding themselves to tell the truth. However, when the public gallery was full of Catholics he was unable to resist the temptation to lecture them condescendingly about

the ridiculousness of their bread God in the transubstantiation . . . that priests and friars are cheats and thieves robbing poor deluded simple people; that their priests by their law are not to marry but by their custom do not live chaste; their pretended miracles are mere impostures, and the only miracle about the Catholic religion is that priests who must have no wives yet have many children; friars have no money yet the best wine-cellars . . .

Cooke deluded himself that his sermonising was gratefully received ('They, perceiving it is spoken in love, intentionally for their own good, are not angry'). But he would not have made many conversions.[23]

The chief justice took on a prodigious case-load, in the belief that Ireland was a 'white paper' upon which he could impress a speedy system of cheap and incorruptible justice which would serve as an example for England. He would often lecture soldiers and settlers upon this favourite theme. But as John Percivale, a local landowner and occasional litigant in Cooke's court, explained to an English cousin, there were different ways in which Ireland might be thought a *tabula rasa*:

> I cannot be so much your enemy as to wish you here. Such is the miserableness of this place, I can compare it to nothing but the first chaos, or as Justice Cooke called it, at the late meeting of the officers, a white paper. Indeed, poor Ireland has lost much blood and I cannot wonder it shall be pale-faced now, and it may be called paper in that it may be quickly set on fire with faction – but that 'tis white paper ready to have anything writ on it that the State shall think fit – that is denied by some.[24]

None the less, Cooke continued to see Ireland through rose-tinted glasses, as the blank paper on which he was writing a new system of justice which would provide a lesson for London. At the end of 1650, his first year in Munster, he penned a petition to the House of Commons explaining how his reforms could change England's appalling legal landscape, where 'Satan laughed to see murderers escape through a mistake in the indictment; where poor illiterate men were hanged for stealing corn to feed a starving family; where men with estates or titles would laugh at their creditors and poor men be locked up for the rest of their lives for incurring debts they could never pay from prison'.[25] He had taken his court (he sat with two 'gownsmen', i.e. barristers) on circuit around the province, bringing justice to the people rather than forcing them to come with their witnesses to Dublin. He had attacked corruption by drastically reducing the number of court officials, and had reduced legal fees ('There is seldom more than 20 shillings spent in a cause by all parties', he boasted, 'unless it be in counsel's fees' – which he fixed at a low but reasonable level). He explained to Parliament that his court fused law and equity jurisdictions, thus preventing the interminable delays and tactical ploys experienced in London when cases brought in the wrong division were struck out and had to begin all over again. Because the judges were full-time, without the short 'terms' kept by English lawyers, cases were heard as soon as they were ready, rather than at a distant fixed date when indulged judges returned from their overlong vacations.

Most importantly, in civil cases his court did not imprison debtors, but instead ordered them to pay the debt by instalments. It was this system that Cooke fervently recommended to Parliament: although the people in Munster were 'extremely indigent, there not being scarce a tenth part of the money here that is in England, debts are I believe ten times better paid' because he had abandoned the pernicious system of arresting men for debt (from which his own brother and brother-in-law had suffered). His work in Ireland could show the way: instead of throwing debtors into prison and reducing their wives and children to beggary, the debtor came to Cooke's court and offered to pay by instalments: under judicial guidance a jury of his neighbours fixed the amount and the dates of payment, as they reckoned him to be able to meet.

Cooke's petition was received by the Council of State on Christmas Eve 1650. It was referred to the committee for Irish affairs, since there was no real resolve in the barrister-infested Commons to progress in England this great work for which so many who believed in the commonwealth had fought and expected. Cooke was shocked to find that law reform was more difficult than abolishing tyranny, and that lawyers would struggle as hard as bishops to protect their own interests.[26] Parliament might slough his petition off to a committee, but he would continue to set examples in Munster.

Cooke made the most determined attempt to cut through the miasma of technicalities that bedevilled lawsuits in England and Ireland, frequently resulting in actions which bumped along for twenty years or so on a roller-coaster of hazardous pleading. It was all too easy for a malicious plaintiff to harass an innocent defendant and for a bad debtor, by being first to sue, to have his creditor falsely arrested. Cooke's own description of the legal system that he found in Ireland was of a morass of injustice, delay and oppression. He was particularly struck by the phenomenon of the absentee English landowner, and by the injustice that victims who wished to sue them must get leave, at great expense, to serve the writ on them in London: 'it is no small mischief that men that have estates in Ireland may live in England and pay no debts.'[27] Those accused for debt, even wrongly, were thrown into prison – 'penniless, friendless and for the most part graceless': if they died there without funds, the guards could have dice made of their bones, and sell the dice to pay for their keep.

Although he was now a judge and well into his forties, John Cooke still had the passion of his pamphleteering days as a young barrister: he maintained his rage against the oppression of the poor by 'old courts and tedious formalities' and by a system in which court officials served the rich who paid them bribes. In this system, honest causes were won by a miracle ('sometimes, a blind man may tread upon a hare and catch her').[28] Cooke inveighed against the enemies of reform – both the reactionary formalists who wanted to keep traditions for no better reason than that they were traditions and the realists who feared that any change would endanger property. He was keen to point out that cheap and speedy justice provided for the protection of property. It was the law's obsession with form over substance that endangered property, and even life – as when murderers were set free because their names were misspelled on indictments (this was a particular bug-bear of Cooke's and must have been a not infrequent occurrence). The judges of England and Ireland had been at fault. 'The love of fees has so blinded their eyes'[29] that these judges, heedless of the public interest, had created and sold court offices like horses in Smithfield.

> They have appointed twenty or forty offices and places in the court, where the business might better be done by three or four honest clerks . . . Every case must run through so many officers' hands, and everyone must pluck a fleece from the clients – until that be done, the judge could not allow a cause to end, for fear of displeasing his officers.[30]

This indictment of the traditional courts in Ireland was written after five years' experience. It was all too true of the courts in 'our beloved England' where 'the sons of Zeruiah are very strong . . . stones in the building are not easily removed'. John Cooke had hoped to set an example in Munster, and was troubled by criticism. 'Good precious men . . . tell me I argue for arbitrariness and that they would rather live in Turkey than to be left to the discretion of a judge.' Cooke tried to explain that the vice of arbitrariness was really found in judges ignorant of law and learning, whose decisions turned on which party they liked (or which had bribed them): the arbitrary judge was he who 'judges persons not causes'.[31] Law was not a set of 'lesbian rules, flexible upon any importunity' but 'an exercise of inflexible rectitude to help every man to his right . . . that no honest causes shall suffer for want of good management'. This was Cooke's credo as a judge, strictly applying the law whomsoever benefited, but ensuring that the poor had counsel in difficult cases and intervening on their side when he deemed it necessary for justice. Doing justice had become an uncompromising passion, and in 1654 he had given up the mastership of St Cross to concentrate full-time on Irish lawgiving. His resignation the following year would come from the depths of a despairing heart.

14

The Protectorate

And now the Irish are ashamed
To see themselves in one year tamed . . .
But thou, the wars and Fortune's son,
March indefatigably on.

(Andrew Marvell, 'Horatian Ode')

Cromwell had been recalled from Ireland in May 1650, to confront a new threat from Scotland which had welcomed Charles II as its King once the young man – with his father's disingenuousness – took the Solemn League and Covenant, pretending to bind himself to Presbyterianism for ever. They agreed to invade England and restore the monarchy, in return for the monarch's promise to impose Presbyterianism by force of law. To sweeten this pill, Charles announced from his exiled court in Breda a general amnesty for all who had fought or judged his father, with only three exceptions: Cromwell (naturally), Bradshawe (now president of the Council of State) and Cooke.[1] Cromwell had an army and Bradshawe was still heavily protected in Whitehall, but Cooke in Munster – sitting in open courts, lecturing Catholics, praying in congregations – was always vulnerable. After surviving the storm he took no special precautions: his response to being made a target of royalist terror was to write *Monarchy No Creature of God's Making*, a provocative argument that (as the title page claimed) 'The execution of the late King was one of the fattest sacrifices that ever Queen Justice had'.

Fairfax, the army's leader, had resigned in June 1650, pleading exhaustion and a dislike of killing fellow protestants – which excused his reluctance to fight a war against the Scots that he doubted could be won. This left Cromwell

...ow the King's execution really looked: above the black drapes, Charles speaks to Juxon, while the axe-man, with false beard and mask, waits.

Charles as blessed martyr and icon: front page of the *samizat* bestseller *Eikon Basilike*.

Crimes against humanity: how a Puritan tract depicted the 1641 atrocities committed by Irish Catholics against English protestants in Ireland.

A TRUE
RELATION
OF
Mr. Iohn Cook's

Paſſage by Sea from *Wexford* to *Kin-ſale* in that great Storm *Ianuary* 5.

Wherein is Related the Strangeneſs of the Storm, and the Frame of his Spirit in it.

ALSO

The Viſion that he ſaw in his ſleep, and how it was Revealed that he ſhould be preſerved, which came to paſs very miraculouſly.

LIKEWISE

A Relation of a Dream of a Prote-ſtant Lady in Poland, which is in part come to paſs, the Remainder being to begin this year 1 6 5 0.

Apr. 12 **All written by himſelf.**

Printed at *Cork*, and Re-printed at *London*, and are to be ſold by *T. Brewſter* and *G. Moule* at the three Bibles in *Pauls* Church-Yard neer the Weſt-End of *Pauls*, 1 6 5 0.
1649

Justice Cooke's account of his near death experience in the great storm, January 1650.
Thomas Brewster sold the work in London.

'The ranters ranting', the cult that takes Calvinism
to its logical conclusion.

'Take away that bauble'. Cromwell boots out the Rump parliament, April 1653.

Man of law and man of God: John Bradshawe and Hugh Peters, by Sir Peter Lely.

John Lambert,
the republic's lost leader.

Edmund Ludlow –
the voice from the watchtower.

George Monck –

Charles II, who turned out to want more

Lord Clarendon, aka Edward Hyde,

Sir Orlando Bridgeman –
'the King can do no wrong'.

The Sessions House in Old Bailey.
This 1720 drawing shows the court rebuilt after the great fire, but with the

A contemporaneous illustration of the execution of two regicides – presumably
Peters on the gibbet whilst Cooke's body is chopped into four quarters.

Tyrannicides: the pantheon of republican martyrs (and Oliver Cromwell).

in command of a coming conflict in which the two sides were separated only by that narrow distinction between the authoritarian Calvinism of the Presbyterian Kirk and the more tolerant Calvinism of the English Congregationalists. 'I beseech you, in the bowels of Christ, think it possible you may be mistaken', Cromwell begged the bigoted Kirkmen as he marched north. But they were constipated by their solemn covenant, and undismayed by the coming of war's and Fortune's son, whose small and sickly army they trapped at Dunbar. As 3 September dawned, no one could have thought an English victory possible. But this was Cromwell's lucky day, and Colonel John Lambert (his second-in-command) provided the plan for an astounding military success, in which the Scottish army was decimated. As usual, Cromwell gave all the credit to God. In this hour of his greatest military victory, Cromwell communicated it to the Commons with a plea – virtually an order – to get on with the godly business of law reform: 'Relieve the oppressed, hear the groans of the poor prisoners in England, be pleased to reform the abuses of all professions; and if there be anyone that makes many poor to make a few rich – that suits not a Commonwealth.'

This was exactly what John Cooke had been saying for the past five years. It was the authentic voice of radical Puritanism which came from Cromwell at moments of high emotion. The lawyer-fed Rump could not ignore it: they set up a committee chaired by Matthew Hale to find 'the speediest way to reform mischiefs that grow from the delays, the changeableness and the irregularities in the proceedings in the law'. Cooke was heartened by the establishment of the Hale committee, which included some of his old friends like Hugh Peters and William Steele. His experiments in Munster could serve as their template.

The Scots were beaten but unbowed. They crowned Charles II at Scone in January 1651 and put him in charge of what was left of their army. He invaded England later in the year, expecting the country to rise in his support. But the country did no such thing: on the contrary, the commonwealth at this point commanded general support and even loyalty. The nation was fed up after a decade of civil war and rightly judged that only Cromwell could guarantee peace. He played an astute waiting game, leaving General Monck (the former royalist who had, after his defection, become a solid parliamentary commander) in Scotland to subdue the lowlands and cut off Charles's retreat, whilst forces under his two doughty colonels – John Lambert on one side and Thomas Harrison on the other – shadowed Charles through middle

England, intercepting his supplies and inhibiting any show of support. He reached Worcester, where Cromwell was waiting – and waiting for the dawn of another 3 September.

In 1651, once again, it proved Cromwell's lucky day, although the result of the battle of Worcester was never really in doubt. Charles II fled: round-head soldiers failed to spot him, in the upper branches of an oak tree outside Boscobel. His second in command, the Earl of Derby, was court-martialled and executed – an indication of Charles' fate, had he been captured. He was entrusted to an underground Catholic network used by Jesuit priests, and smuggled along this lifeline to an apparently hopeless exile in France. In the meantime, all London turned out to cheer General Cromwell's return from Worcester, much as they might cheer the return of a king.

But for all his might as leader of the army and his moral force in the Commons, Cromwell was frustrated by the Rump's lack of progress. It failed to arrange fresh elections or to do away with titles and monopolies, although its failure to reform the law infuriated him most. The Hale commission had reported with a raft of proposals which might almost have been lifted from Cooke's *Vindication:* imprisonment for debt should be abolished; law fused with equity; all land holdings should be registered and new county courts established at the main provisional centres. But there were thirty-three lawyer MPs who sat regularly in the Commons, comprising half of the House, and they managed to obstruct every attempt to implement the report. The most influential of them – Whitelocke and Widdrington, Lenthall and St John – were firmly opposed to any reform that could threaten professional privileges.[2]

Cromwell's army had petitioned the Rump to hold fresh elections, implement Hale and get on with abolishing corrupt officials and ungodly minis-ters, but to no avail. So on 1 April 1653 Oliver Cromwell led his troops into the House of Commons: 'Take away this bauble,' he ordered of the precious mace which symbolised parliamentary sovereignty and had once rested on the table of the High Court of Justice alongside Cooke's charge. 'You are no Parliament,' he shouted, listing their failure to provide speedy justice and their protection of the legal profession amongst their chief sins. He then marched to Whitehall to inform the Council of State, where President Bradshawe responded with as much forlorn dignity as the circum-stances permitted. 'Sir, we have heard what you did at the House this morning and before many hours all England will hear of it. But Sir, you are mistaken to think that the Parliament is dissolved, for no power under heaven can dissolve them but themselves; therefore take you notice of that.' Commonwealthsmen like Bradshawe and Ludlow and Vane could never forgive this action, but John Cooke was in two minds: he rode the old Munster circuit, torn between allegiance to Parliament and support for Cromwell's attack on the MPs who were blocking the law reforms to which he had dedicated his life.

Cromwell quickly issued a declaration justifying the forcible dissolution of a body whose 'lack of progress' and desire for self-perpetuation had caused so much grief to 'the good and well affected'. The Rump would be replaced by a caretaker Parliament which would 'encourage and countenance all God's people, reform the law and administer justice impartially; hoping thereby the people might forget monarchy'.[3] It was unfairly but immortally characterised by royalists as 'Barebone's Parliament' after one of its more godly members, the Puritan preacher Praise-God Barebone. Some of these radical army-appointed MPs talked ignorantly about how law might be practised without lawyers, and proposed to abolish Chancery (the equity court) and to express all law in a short statutory code. This was precisely the puerile radicalism that Cooke had attacked in the *Vindication*. And as if to prove that the present system, despite its flaws, could still do justice if operated fairly, who should return to London to put it to the test but 'Freeborn John'.

After Lilburne was banished for contempt of Parliament for his libels on Haselrig, he had joined the refugee English abroad, unwisely but inevitably consorting with royalists. He was anxious to befriend them lest he be 'Dorislaused' (as he put it) for his part in urging the King's trial. The Commons had decreed his death should he come back to England, but Lilburne plausibly argued that its dissolution had ended his liability for contempt of the House. He was arrested, none the less, and his old supporters came out onto the streets, including 6,000 women who signed a petition presented by their leader, the formidable Mrs Chidley, to a trembling Praise-God Barebone. Meanwhile, and despite his imprisonment, Lilburne managed to publish A *Juryman's Judgement* – an exhortation to his future jury to acquit him. Cromwell was up to Lilburne's tricks and this time had a few of his own: on the eve of Lilburne's trial there appeared in print the testimony of government agents who had been tracking his meetings with royalist exiles. These revelations lost him some sympathy, but his supporters still crowded into court to applaud his jousts with the judges.

Lilburne's capacity to make legal history was undimmed. He invited the jury to pass judgment on the morality of the act of banishment rather than the more embarrassing factual question of whether he had breached it. The statute had set the stakes too high by decreeing death should he return, and the jury's verdict was a condemnation of the intemperate legislators: 'John Lilburne is not guilty of any crime worthy of death'. There were the usual rejoicings, even amongst his guards, but he was taken back to the Tower while the Council of State turned itself into the Star Chamber: it called each juror before it to demand an explanation. But the jurors had all met at the Windmill Tavern and agreed on their answer: 'I gave the verdict with a clear conscience and I refuse to answer any questions about it.'[4] It was an unparalleled act of defiance: John Lilburne's juries carved out a new role for that body as an independent protector of the citizen against the state.

Barebone's Parliament was an experiment which took only six months to fail. It ended in December in a mass resignation of its army-sponsored MPs, orchestrated by the officers to make way for Oliver Cromwell to become Lord Protector of England (and of Scotland and Ireland), under an Instrument of Government. This remarkable document, drafted by John Lambert, was Britain's first (and only) written constitution. It was also the first law to embody the bedrock principles of a modern democracy, under which 'the Commonwealth of England, Scotland and Wales' would be governed by a Head of State and Executive Council which could not tax or make war or legislate without Parliamentary consent. It sought to preclude any form of dictatorship: legislative authority resided in 'the people assembled in Parliament' elected every three years by all male citizens in England and Wales who were worth £200, unless they were English royalists (banned from voting for nine years) or Roman Catholics or Irish rebels (permanently disenfranchised). Legislation had to be presented for the Lord Protector's consent, but he had no 'negative voice': if he did not consent within a month or satisfy Parliament that it should reconsider the proposal, then the bill would become law. Parliament had to approve appointments of senior judges, who were to have security of tenure for life, independent of the government, i.e. of the Protector and his council. Any law which interfered with religious doctrine or worship was unconstitutional 'provided the liberty be not extended to popery or prelacy, nor to such as, under the profession of Christ, hold forth and practise licentiousness'. The English could go to heaven in their own way, without the help of Catholic priests, Anglican bishops or 'ranters' who thought that since salvation was pre-ordained, they might as well enjoy themselves with as much sex and alcohol as possible. The Lord Protector was empowered to award honours, but he could not grant pardons for murder or for treason. He was, in effect, President for Life, but crucially, his office 'shall be elective and not hereditary', and on his death the Council must meet immediately and not disband until they elect his successor.[5]

Diehard republicans deplored the protectorate, which they viewed as a monarchy in all but name, and never forgave Cromwell for engineering it. John Cooke, however, continued to accept commissions and was sufficiently trusted to undertake the delicate task of apprehending his friend Ludlow and obtaining his undertaking to present himself to Cromwell (now 'His Highness') at Whitehall. Cooke continued in great demand: he presided over a court of claims in Dublin, and an assize court in Cork where there is a record of his granting costs to an army lieutenant against a colonel – evidence that he did not decide disputes by the rank of the disputants. He was solicited to give legal opinions to the government on the confused issues of law arising from the rights of 'adventurers' (who advanced money to the army in return for a right to forfeited land) and the legal consequences of amnesties and surrender agreements.

One important new face in Ireland in 1655 was that of Major-General Henry Cromwell, the younger son of the Protector. Cooke welcomed him with a plea to do something about the state of Irish prisons. Henry, however, did not share the zeal for law reform that obsessed his father's Puritan generation. The young man (he was twenty-seven) preferred to associate with the old English landowners who distrusted their radical chief justice, with his propensity to rule in favour of their tenants. In one letter to Thurloe (Cromwell's Secretary of State) Henry appears irritated that 'Judge Cooke refused to act' on a rumour that an alleged murderer had been accepted under a false name as a member of the Protector's Life Guards. It sounds an unlikely story and Cooke obviously so regarded it: Henry thought it should have been investigated, and he reminded Thurloe of the need to find other judges prepared to work in Ireland.[6] Egged on by his landowner friends, Henry was probably behind the protectorate's decision to close down the Munster court and bring back the Upper Bench, a set of four courts (including a separate court for equity) which would be permanently based in Dublin. On 13 June 1655 the council appointed John Cooke to be a judge of this new court – it must automatically have assumed that he would accept one of the foremost positions of profit and honour in the land. But two months later, in a long and passionate dispatch to Fleetwood, Cooke sent in his resignation. He explained that his conscience would not permit him to accept a position that was antipathetic to all he believed in and had struggled to achieve.

Cooke poured out his heart about the vices of the system that was being reintroduced. The old forms of pleading, the split between law and equity, the proliferation of court officials, all on the take, the inbuilt bias in favour of rich litigants, the harassment of debtors, the opportunities for manipulation by malicious plaintiffs – all the evils and the tedious formalities he hoped had been 'interred in the sepulchre of monarchy'.[7] He lamented the lack of progress in his beloved England: 'so long as I saw any hopes of law reform I went on cheerfully . . . if I should now continue the old oppression, I should be the most egregious dissembler that ever sat on a bench.' The court to which he had been appointed 'had power only to imprison and torment its suitors, not to open prison doors or relieve the oppressed . . . for any man to be called "Justice" – who by the course of the court where he sits cannot do justice to any man – is but a ridiculous utopian fantasy'.[8]

John Cooke's resignation letter was pamphlet-length, and leaves an indelible description of the morass that was justice in Ireland – and in England – in the mid-seventeenth century. It is impossible to read it without recognising his utter sincerity and the fury of his disillusionment at the failure of reform. His resignation involved real sacrifice: he was approaching fifty years of age, and lacked the connections to rebuild his career in an England that had moved on since 1649, and by no means in a direction he approved. His thoughts turned to retirement:

> I wish I could find out some Protestant monastery where I might, with my dear relations and some of the people of God, bid adieu to the world which crucified Lord Jesus Christ, and spend the remainder of my days in prayers and tears which have been counted the Christian's best weapons.[9]

But the state could not spare him just yet. The large-scale confiscation of rebel lands with the subsequent sale or letting of this newly acquired state property, and the harsh business of 'transplanting' Irish families to Connaught provided ready means of unlawful enrichment for commissioners entrusted with the task and the council was determined to stamp out corruption. In

February 1656 Cooke agreed to sit at Athlone, together with Sir Charles Coote, to investigate allegations of malpractice and unlawful oppression of the Irish.[10] This was a delicate task, since it meant curbing the greed of Parliament's supporters and rectifying the grievances of Catholics and royalists, but Cooke's reputation for impartiality and honesty made him the best choice to balance the less judicious Coote.

He was also appointed to decide claims under the Act of Settlement, which protected from forfeiture those who could prove 'constant good affection' to Parliament during and after the Catholic rebellion of 1641. Records of his commission when it sat at Mallow from July to September 1656 show that Cooke was exercised by the harshness of the test, which would be failed by claimants who had saved Protestants from butchery in 1641 but had subsequently accommodated to Catholic or royalist occupying forces. In such cases, he was obliged to rule that 'doing nothing was insufficient to prove constant good affection, which must appear by outward signal to demonstrate the affection of the heart, and not in sitting still'. This excluded men who had supported parliamentary forces but had then stayed with Inchiquin after his defection to the King: they feared reprisals from fellow Catholics if sent to Connaught. 'They would rather be sent to the plantations in Barbados,' their counsel explained, urging the judge to do them equity. 'We must proceed according to law' was Cooke's regretful reply. He was upset by the wailing in the courtroom when he rejected the claim, and he immediately wrote to the council explaining how the harshness of the law was discrediting justice, by requiring rejection of all claims. He had carefully distinguished those claimants who had come nearest to showing 'constant good affection' – and hoped that executive discretion might be exercised in their favour.[11]

Cooke was inwardly dismayed by this 'face of rigour' that the law, unmitigated by equity, required him to show which still echoes in Ireland with the phrase 'to hell with Connaught'. (This bitter legacy meant that the impression of radical republicanism that Cooke's generation left on the white parchment could never be acknowledged. Wolfe Tone and others reinvented it – as Irish nationalism – in the eighteenth century.) His frustration was further exemplified by the case of the Duke of Ormond's mother, Viscountess Thurles, who protected several English families in 1641 and had assisted English Protestants over the years since. Cooke found her 'a very deserving person', but unfortunately the good lady had chosen to live under enemy protection. The test of 'constant good affection' would bar her claim, so instead of ruling against her he reported the merits of her case to the council. Buck-passing to politicians was preferable, in Cooke's mind, to twisting the law.[12] He also served in this period as an assize judge for Cork and as recorder of Waterford, the town where he lived and worshipped.

Worship, as ever, was much on his mind, in a province where Congregationalist ministers were still few in number and had to compete not only with shadowy priests but with proselytising Presbyterians, who established a weekly lecture at Cork in 1656 and intended to exclude all the 'unordained' Congregationalists. So in his charge to the City's grand jury in August – an occasion for the senior judge to animadvert on the state of the nation – he urged ecumenical 'unity and love between all honest and peaceable men' and the rejection of 'over bold' preachers who 'disown and vilify their brethren'. But next day, when he gate-crashed the lecture, he heard a zealous young Presbyterian excoriating 'with many bitter expressions, those that differ from him in doctrinal discipline'. He wrote immediately to Henry Cromwell, who had become Lord Deputy in all but name after Fleetwood returned to England. Typically, Cooke did not ask for the lecture to be banned: his solomonic solution was that a Presbyterian lecturer alternate with a Congregationalist, 'which will be a great encouragement to all Godly persons'.[13]

For more than a year after his resignation from the Upper Bench, Cooke was still doing the state much service even though the state itself had changed dramatically since he had been its Solicitor-General. He was out of touch with the coming men in London, like Edward Montagu at the Admiralty, and with the 'comeback' men like Sir Anthony Ashley Cooper and Arthur Annesley, 'secluded' by Pride's Purge but now powerful MPs in protectorate parliaments. Cooke was pleased when Matthew Hale was appointed to the bench – although a royalist who had defended the Duke of Hamilton,[14] this legal genius had championed many of Cooke's reform suggestions. He supported Cromwell's decision to readmit the Jews, banished from the realm since 1290: their conversion to Christianity was mentioned in the Book of Revelations as a portent that the millennium – the thousand-year rule of the saints prior to the second coming of Christ – was near.[15] Cooke's loyalty to Cromwell never wavered: his friends Ludlow and Bradshawe had been carpeted for their antagonism to the protectorate, but Cooke had always set the law and God far above politics. So long as Oliver refused the throne and held out hope of godly government and law reform, Cooke was willing to serve him.

By 1657, after three years of the protectorate, Cromwell was undeniably secure. Notwithstanding some frenetic plotting by the Sealed Knot, a royalist underground infiltrated by Thurloe, uprisings such as Penruddock's in 1655 were pathetic affairs and juries did not hesitate to convict the ringleaders. There was little public sympathy at this stage for Charles II, although Cromwell lost some support when he installed major-generals to rule as 'Lord Deputies' in the counties. They were obeyed, but not gladly, as they closed down alehouses and cut down maypoles and tried to effect Cromwell's 'reformation of manners' by prohibiting cock fights and bear-baiting and by arresting drunkards and bawds. But by cutting loose his old commonwealthsmen (he called them 'Levellers who had found a finer name'[16]), by sounding and acting royal ('We would keep up the nobility and the gentry'), by excluding more elected MPs than Colonel Pride (mostly for some disrespect to himself or to the army) and by distancing himself from Lambert, now his only credible successor, he was playing into the hands of the reactionaries and the closet royalists. When the second protectorate Parliament met in September 1656, Cromwell urged it to end abominations in criminal justice such as 'to hang a man for six pence, threpence, I know not what; to hang for a trifle and pardon murder'. Protectorate MPs were conservative, and ignored his request that MPs intrude some humanity into the law: one of his Parliament's first actions was to constitute itself a court and to sentence the Quaker James Naylor to the very similar torture of branding and whipping and tongue-boring with which Charles I had scandalised the godly by inflicting upon Prynne and Bastwick.

John Cooke brought Frances back to England in early 1657. He was much in demand for tribunal work in Ireland, but his wife had developed a consumptive illness and his father, Isaac, was old and sick in Leicestershire. Moreover, Cooke wanted to see Cromwell – the Lord Protector who needed protection from the conservative lawyers and MPs who were now trying to make him king. Cromwell was first offered the crown by Speaker Lenthall at the end of March and he equivocated for several months – the great lawyers like Whitelocke and St John had urged him to accept. They had been advising him, ever since 1651, that any settlement must have 'something of monarchy' in it, and now they produced a 'Humble Petition and Advice' which would replace the 'Instrument of Government' by re-establishing an Upper House and some royal prerogatives. Most of his colleagues from 1649 – Bradshawe, Ludlow, Harrison and Marten – had fallen from his favour, but his faithful Solicitor-General visited, to remind him that monarchy was no creature of God's making.

Historians offer different reasons why Cromwell eventually refused the crown – the opposition of his officers; a true sense of humility; or even to win a poet's praise:

> He seems a king by long succession born,
> And yet the same to be a king does scorn.[17]

It is more likely that he was persuaded to keep the republican faith by John Cooke's heady brew of God's word and 'right reason'. 'Whether they be good or bad', Cooke had argued, 'kings are the people's idols, creatures of their own making.'[18] They were sought after by irrational people, in 'nations delighting rather in servitude than freedom'.[19] Cooke had demonstrated, in an argument lodged in Cromwell's soul, that God had never approved the office, but suffered it so the people could be punished for their sins when kings gave way to the temptation to become tyrants. 'Hereditary kingdoms have no footsteps in scripture' any more than do Popes. Machiavelli's *Prince*, that exemplar of absolute monarchs, would keep no promises if they turned to his disadvantage.[20] That was the sort of man Cromwell would become if he took the crown, and his acceptance would be a sign that he was not one of the elect. Unlike his republican comrades, Cooke supported a 'Lord Protector' who served as what would today be described as President, restrainable by Parliament and accountable to the law. God approved rational and just governments – what Cooke termed an 'elective aristocracy'. It was rational for the wise to govern the ignorant – it was absurd to have a system where the hereditary head of state might be a child or an idiot. But he warned that the trappings of monarchy were vainglory: 'Reason abhors it and God approves it not.' This was the basis upon which they had sent Charles I to the scaffold: Cromwell dared not deny it by metamorphosing into Oliver I, father of Richard IV.

Cromwell did not refuse the crown because of army opposition or political caution, much less from genuine humility. He refused it because he feared for his afterlife and he was persuaded that for Puritans there could only be one King, now and for ever. Earthly crowns are not worn by saints, Cooke warned, and if a seeming saint covets such adornment, then maybe he is not a saint after all. Cromwell announced that he would serve the state 'not as a king but as a constable'. He would not follow the Stuart kings, for 'God has seemed providentially not only to strike at the family but at the name'.[21] Fine words

– but his office of constable was defined by a revised 'Humble Petition' which gave him an Upper House, most of the attributes of kingship and, fatally, the right to nominate his successor. About this time (June 1657), he fell out with John Lambert who refused to take an oath to support this new constitution. He was a force for free thought, having supported James Naylor against the tide of intolerance, and was the only leader who might have been capable of keeping the army, the parliament and the people in some form of equilibrium.

Cooke's advice to Cromwell about Irish justice was equally uncompromising. He wrote to Henry Cromwell in December 1657 congratulating him on his recent accession to the lord deputyship ('May the Irish harp be kept in good tune') explaining that he had been in London in attendance on the Lord Protector over the last few months. He delicately mentioned that they had discussed 'the reviving of a presidency court for Munster, to have law and equity, as formerly'. This had become an obsession, and the Protector seems to have indulged him in it, whilst insisting that the final decision would rest with Henry and the council in Dublin. Cooke promised to return to Ireland (as he had apparently been urged – he says 'commanded' – by the Protector) in March 1658 and to attend upon Henry then, although not in any public capacity 'for I dare not for all the world divide between law and equity'. The young lord deputy would not have understood this passion for fusion, but Cooke was one of the few good judges prepared to work in Ireland, and his price for that service was a court that combined both jurisdictions. It was a strange issue on which to take such an uncompromising stand – the merits of combining of law and equity being a subject for a debate between lawyers lasting for centuries but of no interest and indeed of no comprehension to anyone else. (Fusion eventually happened in England, in 1873, with the advantages that Cooke claimed; in New South Wales, incredibly, it did not happen until 1970). Cooke did not return to Ireland the following March, as he had promised both Cromwells, but for an altogether more understandable reason.

The year 1658 was a black one for him, as it was to prove for them. First, his beloved father Isaac died and then the tuberculosis consuming Frances became much worse. She could not travel, and John would not leave her – he nursed her until her death.[22] This was the year he did spend 'with my dear relations . . . in prayers and tears which are the Christian's best weapons' – and they must have been his, in coping with the loss of the two great human loves of his life – the father who had shared his chamber and his aspirations, and the wife with whom he had weathered the storm.

Whilst in mourning in Leicestershire, Cooke would have heard the news from London of the death of Robert Blake, his contemporary from student days at Wadham, the great admiral who had vanquished first the Dutch and then the Spanish fleet. He would have heard about the new Parliament, opened by prayers from Hugh Peters but with a new Upper House full of the great lawyers – now dubbed 'Lords' – who opposed reform.[23] He would have been furious to read the tract *Killing No Murder* which urged Cromwell's assassination, with deliberate echoes of Cooke's argument against tyranny in *King Charles: His Case*. Members of the Sealed Knot were put on trial in June 1658 for making preparations to assist invasion by the King's forces. Cromwell distrusted juries after his experience with Lilburne, so he established another High Court of Justice under the presidency of John Lisle (now a Chancery judge), who had assisted Bradshawe at the King's trial. One conspirator – John Mordaunt – was acquitted, on Lisle's casting vote.[24] The evidence established that he was probably guilty, but probability, as Lisle pointed out, was no longer sufficient. The evidence against the other two was overwhelming, but although both were commoners, they were permitted to enjoy (for want of a better word) an easy and speedy death by beheading. For all that it may be odd to modern ears to find dignity in a death sentence, the horror and the lengthy and excruciating pain of hanging, drawing and quartering made the axe-man a merciful alternative.

John Cooke and his family, like everyone else in Leicestershire, cowered in cellars or under beds when the country was hit on 3 September – which had always been Cromwell's lucky day – with a storm of unbelievable ferocity. Andrew Marvell, who had moved on from the Fairfaxes to become assistant to Milton, the Latin (i.e. Foreign) Secretary to the Council of State, describes its fearful progress:

> First the great Thunder was shot off, and sent
> The signal from the starry battlement:
> The winds receive it, and its force outdo,
> As practising how they could thunder too:
> Out of the binder's hand the sheaves they tore,
> And thrash'd the harvest in the airy floor;
> Or of huge trees, whose growth with his did rise,
> The deep foundations open'd to the skies.

> Then heavy showers the winged tempests lead
> And pour the deluge o'er the chaos' head.[25]

By the time the storm subsided, the Lord Protector was dead. For Marvell, who would guide the steps of the blind Milton at Cromwell's funeral, it had been the tumult of the universe as his wasting spirit left the earth for heaven. A darker rumour, that the storm had been Satan returning to claim his soul, was credited by too many for his successor's comfort. Like the hereditary monarch he had refused all entreaties to become, Cromwell had appointed his elder son to succeed him.

Part III

Restoration

15

Tumbledown Dick

Primogeniture – succession of the eldest son, the key to security of large family estates – was a principle the English did not question. The traditional expression of joy by bonfires and bell-ringing, on Richard Cromwell's proclamation as Protector, was genuine enough. Charles, the alternative heir, ill-naturedly bided his time, not yet occupying the thoughts of any significant number of his countrymen. The conspiratorial web spun by the venomless spiders of the 'Sealed Knot' had by 1658 been thoroughly infiltrated by Thurloe, Cromwell's cabinet secretary. Thurloe proved the ablest of public servants, combining administrative *nous* with a spymaster's cunning. His task was to protect the protectorate, to hold the country together and demonstrate that the form of government instituted in 1654 was not just the personal fiefdom of one mighty individual, but a system that worked even when inherited by a pleasant nonentity.

It was not the royalists from whom Richard would need protection, but the republicans, who took fresh heart from the death of the man they saw as having betrayed their revolution. Sir Henry Vane had already used the phrase 'the Good Old Cause' to provide a slogan for Haselrig and Scot and Ludlow and Bradshawe and Marten and all the restless, resurgent Rumpers, the 'Class of 49'. The slogan had a resonance among many middle-ranking army officers, who could not forget why they had fought the civil war, and whose power base was in London, commanded by Richard's brother-in-law Fleetwood and his uncle Desborough. Richard might be their relation by marriage, but so far as these army grandees were concerned he was not 'one of us' – he had never commanded a regiment. General Lambert had been cashiered by Cromwell for insubordination, but this architect of the victory at Dunbar and draftsman of the Instrument of Government had a touch of brilliance that outshone other candidates for leadership. But which way would Lambert jump? Not to the royalists, who had made repeated overtures, even offering Charles II's hand in marriage with his daughter, Mary. Only time would tell, and in the meantime Thurloe had to make do with Richard, already lampooned on the streets as 'Tumbledown Dick'.

Thurloe also had to run the country – the 'three nations' that had not yet called themselves Great Britain. Scotland, at least, seemed pacified and unproblematic, under the competent heel of General Monck. This experienced soldier, first and instinctively a royalist, represented the kind of man that Cromwell ended up by cultivating and advancing, both in the army and the law: solid, self-seeking conservatives who were very good at their jobs, but fearful of innovation and reform. They were, however, loyal to the establishment of which they were part – so long as it was likely to stay established. Ireland was, as ever, more problematic, although young Henry Cromwell was showing political ability, unlike his elder brother. Ireland's perennial problem was its lack of indigenous legal and administrative talent. 'It is a most difficult thing to get any person of quality to go from hence to Ireland . . .', lamented Thurloe in a letter to Henry in January 1659.[1] The immediate problem was the Upper Bench: Chief Justice Pepys (uncle of the diarist) had just died and there was already a vacancy for another judge. The only obvious candidate had resigned as a matter of conscience back in 1655. But John Cooke had been talking to Richard Cromwell, and his mind had changed.

Both men had recently lost fathers to whom they were close, and they met in November – probably at Oliver's funeral at Westminster Abbey. Cooke was still remembered as a hero of the revolution: a silver medal had been struck in his honour and he was placed (with Cromwell and Bradshawe) in the regicidal triumvirate whom Charles II could never forgive. He had done the state signal service in Munster, where few of its lawyers were prepared to venture. He had not become identified with anti-protectorate republicans, and had maintained good relations with Oliver Cromwell who had directed him to return to work in Munster in 1658. His agreement then had been on condition that he would not serve on the Upper Bench until law was fused with equity. What changed his mind? The appointment of his old friend William Steele as its Chancellor, in charge of the Equity division, may have somewhat allayed his concerns. Or he may have needed the money – and there is a hint of this in his first letter of acceptance, written to Henry on 1 February 1659, which notes that the Protector had agreed that despite his absence he could receive his salary for the previous year.[2] But John Cooke had never gone against his conscience for the sake of money, and emphasises that his acceptance had to be subject to 'whether my poor weak wife be able to travel or not'.[3] Frances was in the last stage of tubercular illness, and her only journey now – as her husband must have realised – would be to the grave. She must have expired in that bitter winter, shortly after Cooke had signalled to Henry his willingness to accept the appointment. Her death freed him for more work in Ireland – a place, he told Henry, 'which I love best of any upon earth, God having cast my lot there'.

It was a delicate situation, however, for Henry Cromwell was not his unalloyed admirer. There is irritation in Henry's letter to his brother, the Protector, in January, warning that 'a total failure of justice' would ensue unless a fit judge were appointed to the Upper Bench. He noted testily that Richard had recently commissioned Justice Cooke 'yet he has not since that time been in this nation, and that, when he had the like commission formerly, he was not satisfied to act therein'.[4] Cooke arranged for a mutual friend to deliver a glowing reference, written by Richard himself, and wrote again to Henry, explaining that he could not return earlier, owing to his father's death and his wife's consumption, but promising that 'my future diligence may in some measure make recompense for my too long absence, which I beseech your Lordship to pardon and excuse'.[5] It is likely that he left Leicestershire shortly after the simple burial service for Frances, and took his place on the Upper Bench at the beginning of the Easter term, 1659. There was time, however, to talk and pray with Mary Chawnor, a member of their congregation whose companionship had helped him through the deaths of Isaac and Frances. By the year's end, she joined him in Ireland and became his second wife.[6]

Cooke had never been interested in playing politics and his departure spared him the unedifying sight of the backstabbing and power-jostling that enveloped Richard Cromwell's new Parliament. Haselrig led the old Independents in a powerful attack on the protectorate. He pointed out (with some historical force) that the problem with the Humble Petition and Advice was that it required one man to be the judge of necessity – the vice of the ship-money decision. This republican onslaught was supported by elements in the army and by religious independents: Congregationalists, Baptists and the increasing number of Quakers. Richard could still count on the protectorate's general popularity and reputation for stability – his father's legacy – although after four years the institution had set down no firm roots. But Fleetwood came under pressure from his middle ranks as a result of clever manoeuvring by Haselrig. So the son-in-law decided to pull the carpet from under the son. On 21 April Fleetwood forced Richard to dissolve Parliament. A council of officers – led by Fleetwood and Desborough and including Lambert – formed a provisional government, ignoring Richard and negotiating directly with the Parliamentarians they most respected – Vane and Ludlow – for a way out of the impasse. They wanted law reform, a guarantee of respect from Parliament, and a golden handshake for Richard Cromwell to go quietly.

These Christian soldiers then hit upon the notion that the way forward to democracy was to reconvene the Rump – that 'Long Parliament' first elected in 1642, purged in 1648 and dissolved by Cromwell in 1653. The sense of this decision has eluded historians – nostalgia must have played a part, and an inability to think of anything better. It was a step backwards and not forwards, but there was no time to be lost. In May they all reconvened: the good old boys summoned to deliver the Good Old Cause. Bradshawe, dying from the ravages of malaria ('the ague', common in England at the time), was brought back to the Council, and Cooke's old friend Ludlow was dispatched to govern Ireland in place of Henry Cromwell, who resigned out of brotherly solidarity with Richard. This political upheaval awoke the dozy conspirators of the Sealed Knot, who planned summer uprisings with John Mordaunt actively recruiting for the King. He had some success amongst the Presbyterian gentry, who had supported the protectorate under the Cromwells but were dismayed by the return of their old Puritan foes in the Rump and prepared to join a rebellion to urge the return of a 'free parliament' – i.e. the House of Commons before it was purged by Colonel Pride. The rising itself, under Sir George Booth, was an uncoordinated disaster, easily put down by Lambert. Booth escaped in the disguise of a lady's maid, only to be arrested at an inn when he aroused suspicions by arranging to have a shave. He was taken to the Tower, to await his trial for treason.

The Rumpers thought themselves secure. But they had made the mistake of dispensing with Thurloe's services, so that consummate public servant was not around in the autumn to read the danger signals, notably the Presbyterian disaffection, the 'moral panic' amongst the gentry over the Rump's toleration of Quakers, and the siren slogan now heard from all sides – a demand for a 'full and free Parliament'. Fresh elections on the old and narrow franchise would produce many MPs who might prefer to bring back the King. It may have been about this time – August 1659 – that the royalists managed to hook their biggest fish. Their secret offers of vast wealth and additional titles had fallen on the deaf ears of Fairfax (who had wealth and titles enough, as well as severe gout) and Lambert, a godly republican at heart. But for the somewhat plebeian General Monck – unlettered, married to his cook, a good soldier without political principles or philosophy – the offer of a dukedom and the massive sum of £100,000 each year for the rest of his life may have been an irresistible bribe to rejoin those for whom he had fought in the first place. Cromwell's death and Fairfax's abdication had freed him of under-takings given to them personally when they recruited him after Nantwich, and he had always been a royalist at heart – he claimed to have in his genes a touch of the Plantagenets. The evidence that he succumbed at this point is strong but not conclusive. At any event, Monck soon began to rid his force of republicans and remodel his troops, all the while assuring Haselrig and Scot, leaders of the Rump, that he would support them in their increasingly hot quarrels with Fleetwood and the army officers in London.

The Rump needed to keep the army on side and prepare a workable exit strategy for its own dissolution and fresh elections on a wider franchise, having produced a proper constitution which would entrench the fundamentals of the revolution and block any enthusiasm in the new Commons for a return to monarchical government. But Haselrig, to whom most blame for the collapse of the republic must attach, was obsessed with making the military subservient to the civil power – a foolish point to press whilst Parliament was dependent upon military support. On the army side, Fleetwood owed his advance to nepotism (the son-in-law also rises) and was devoid of political imagination while Desborough was a dunderhead: they were understandably angered by Parliament's provocations, but they did disastrously overreact.

What happened, in short, was that into George Monck's unpredictable hands, Haselrig delivered England. Emboldened by Monck's secret promise that he would support the Rump against the London army, Haselrig led Parliament in a vote to cashier Lambert, Desborough and other senior officers.

The London army responded by cashiering the Rump: it dissolved Parliament and set up a 'Committee of Safety' to run the country. By breaking with Parliament, the legitimate authority supported (however lukewarmly) by many officers, tradesmen and professionals, Fleetwood and the army leaders split their own ranks: eventually their Committee of Safety found loyalty only from the more extreme republicans (mainly Baptists and Quakers) and from *realpolitik* politicians like Ludlow and Vane and Whitelocke who saw a quasi-military dictatorship as the lesser evil, for the time being, to a freely elected Parliament which would bring back the King. Neither side at this point had a leader capable of greatness. Lambert alone had Cromwellian potential, and in November the Committee of Safety sent him north to confront General Monck, who had been putting his army on a war footing and was now, thanks to the purblind Haselrig, the real power in the land. He was preparing to fight – but in whose interests other than his own?

The only possible beneficiary was in Brussels. Charles II heard of these developments from Edward Hyde, who had been tirelessly corresponding (under the pseudonym Sarah Fairfax) with a network of agents in England, Scotland and Ireland. They were as mystified as everyone else over the turn of events, but it boded well for those Cooke called 'the malignants' – the bad old cause. Bradshawe died, declaring that he would convict Charles again if he had to,[7] and he was buried at Westminster Abbey with much pomp and heraldry. But his funeral, in November, saw the first outbreak of 'jeering books' and ballads sold in the London streets, savagely celebrating the death of a 'king-killing murderer' and an 'infernal saint'. It was the first sign that underneath the rock of the republic a vengeful monster was waiting to tear public men to pieces.

These were dog days, the saddest, John Cooke reflected, that he could remember in the 'poor shaken and shattered' nations, which were slipping towards anarchy. The law courts in both countries adjourned until consti-tutional authority became clear; there were street demonstrations for a free Parliament and London goldsmiths moved their gold offshore.[8] A new consti-tution, Cooke thought, was the only way forward now, through the thickets of religious differences which would never be settled. He accompanied his good friend Colonel Ludlow to the boat that would take him back to England to mediate between the Rump and the Committee of Safety – he was a member of both.[9] Afterwards, it has been conjectured that Cooke penned a public broadsheet, headed simply 'MAGNA CHARTA' and signed 'J. C.'.[10]

It called upon the authorities to appoint seventy of the most experienced, righteous and tolerant men to form a great council, which would in turn elect twenty-one members to form a council of state to run the government and defend the country. Its most important work would be to draw up 'substantial laws relating to liberty and freedom' which would become 'fundamentals' incapable of alteration by representatives in Parliament. This idea was, in effect, for a Bill of Rights – a set of constitutional guarantees which the courts would uphold by striking down, as null and void, any antipathetic legislation passed by MPs. Cooke, if the pamphleteer, was long before his time – Britain did not adopt a Bill of Rights for another 350 years and even now it is not entrenched against the whim of Parliamentary majorities. The broadsheet had other interesting proposals about the appointment of poor persons of good character as Justices of the Peace (a radical notion at a time when this powerful office was reserved for the wealthiest men in each parish) and the use of judges and JPs as mediators, attempting to resolve disputes before they came to public trial (a reform introduced by the Court Practice Rules in 2000). Most fundamentally, this Magna Charta offered a paraphrase of clause 29 of Magna Carta:

That none of the freeborn people of these nations shall be arrested, imprisoned, banished, condemned or sentenced to the loss of life, limb, estate or liberty, or be in any other way molested or distracted, after a very short fixed time, but by a lawful judgement of his peers or by virtue of and according to some known approved or published law or laws of these nations.

The drafting was pedantic, but the principle was hallowed. The time was soon coming when it would not avail John Cooke. The Committee of Safety was unpopular and the Rump was sitting indignantly in exile at Portsmouth. Their respective leaders, Fleetwood and Haselrig, had to find, and urgently, a respectable means of governing the republic and entrenching its values. Otherwise – as 'J C' warned – the 'relics and props of corrupt monarchy' were waiting to take their place.

In the meantime, for a nation weary of post-Cromwellian politicking and civil strife, General Monck appeared on the horizon as a *deus ex machina*. He faced down Lambert when their forces met at Berwick in December: Lambert's men preferred to talk rather than fight with their numerically superior old colleagues. Monck's talk at this point was simply to demand the restoration of the Rump and the abolition of the Committee of Safety – an impeccably constitutional position supported by Montague, who had been allowed to go into retirement after the suspicion (all too true) that he had 'gone over'. So had Sir Charles Coote – whom Ireton never trusted – and Lord Broghill (Roger Boyle) son of the Earl of Cork and an instinctive royalist. They began to isolate the Committee of Safety supporters in the Irish army ranks. Their coup against Ludlow and the committee in Dublin and other major towns in December resulted in a declaration in favour of 'the Rump', but in the streets the cry was for fresh elections for a 'free Parliament' – which as wise men knew (but nobody said) would bring back the King. When news of the Dublin coup reached Edinburgh on 26 December, Monck saluted it with cannons and sent his congratulations.[11] Army officers in Dublin condemned Ludlow – their absent commander-in-chief, who set sail for Ireland immediately, to dispute the allegations and to reclaim command.

In England, meanwhile, astute supporters of the 'Good Old Cause' started to worry. Already, straws were in the wind: John Evelyn, that well-connected royalist, contacted his old schoolfriend Colonel Morley, the Lieutenant of the Tower, inviting him to join a conspiracy to bring in the King. (Morley declined: he could not believe that Monck would turn traitor.[12]) Chief Justice Oliver St John, always most anxious about his own safety, began to make overtures to known royalist agents and to profess his support for a 'free Parliament'.[13] Whitelocke, the most self-preserving of the great lawyers, let into the secret by his Presbyterian friends that Monck planned to bring back the King, rushed to Fleetwood to suggest that they should both make immediate overtures to Charles II, so that they and not Monck would get the credit for his restoration. Fleetwood was not so base as to agree, although by this time his Committee of Safety had so little support that he had no alternative but to disband it and bring back Parliament.

So it was that the Rump, with all the flouncing tragi-comedy of an aged actress making her positively last appearance at a Christmas panto, began its final run. Haselrig, deluded to the end, was beside himself with excitement – 'very jocund and high' (according to Whitelocke) as he addressed the restored MPs on 29 December, persuading them to remove all the officers who had been loyal to Lambert – which was exactly what Monck wanted. The Rump, assured by Haselrig of his loyalty, declared Monck the commander-in-chief of all armies in England and Scotland and dismissed

Lambert, the only officer who could conceivably defeat him. Parliament did not invite him to enter England, or approve his march to London. But George Monck was coming, whether they were ready or not.

Monck's progress took a month – in a politic manoeuvre he diverted to Yorkshire to obtain Fairfax's blessing. The gout-ridden general gave it: his daughter, to Cromwell's disapprobation, had married the second Duke of Buckingham, a Stuart stalwart like his father, but he was kept out of sight while the general declared his support for a 'free Parliament'. It was important for Monck's double bluff to keep most people guessing about his real intentions and the excitement was palpable in London in January as the King's restoration – unthinkable a few weeks before – became a whispered possibility and then, on contemplation, perhaps the best prospect of security, so long as it could be engineered without another civil war. The city council, meanwhile, was threatening a tax strike, the Parliament had not healed its fight with Fleetwood, and its speaker, Lenthall, was on politic sick leave. A street ballad said it all and everyone was singing it:

> Monck under a hood, not understood,
> The city pulls in their horns;
> The speaker is out and sick of the gout
> And the Parliament sits upon thorns.[14]

Absence had made most hearts grow fonder of the Stuarts: Charles II was an unknown quality but more impressive in prospect as a ruler than Haselrig or Richard Cromwell, now out of his wits and deeply in debt, wandering about Whitehall (where he could give his creditors the slip) lamenting 'Who should a man trust, if he may not trust to a brother or an uncle?'[15] London's intellectuals still fervently debated the ideal shape of a republic at the Rota Club, held at the Turks Head coffee house near Westminster Pier,[16] but the real question was whether Charles II could be brought back as a constitutional rather than an absolute monarch – in other words, how the hard-fought democratic gains of the past eighteen years could be preserved in a constitution with 'something of monarchy' in it. But amid the delusions of Haselrig, the equivocation of Lambert and the stealth of Monck, this question was barely faced – until it was too late to prevent everything of monarchy.

Monck arrived in London with his army in early February and took only a few days to weigh the Rump. Any second thoughts about supporting it were quickly dispelled by its behaviour, at first by ordering him to arrest the city councillors who were urging a tax strike (which he did, prompting Haselrig's exultation 'All is our own. He will be honest') and then by proposing to take away his supreme command and forcing him to share it with a number of MPs, including Haselrig. Even if Monck had not sold out already, this threat to his own position would have been the last straw. His plan was exquisitely ironic: to restore autocracy through a democratic process. Restoring the Rump had merely been his first stage. Step Two would be to bring back the MPs 'secluded' by Pride's Purge; Step Three: to rely on these secluded members to make safe appointments to all positions of power; and then Step Four: to have the Parliament call fresh elections on the old franchise, which limited the vote to landholders and gentry. Step Five: the new Parliament with its predicted Presbyterian pro-royalist majority would invite Charles II back as King. The assumption – at least of the Presbyterian worthies who connived to achieve this result – was that Charles II would accept the terms they had negotiated with his father at Newport. They did not realise that the popular momentum they had started might end with the election of a royalist majority, in favour of an unconditional restoration.

On 11 February, the general told the Lord Mayor of his intention to have the secluded members readmitted, and the news spread like wildfire. Young Sam Pepys, whose fortunes stood to rise because he was nephew to Montague, excitably describes the roasting of the Rump:

> In Cheapside there was a great many bonfires, and Bow bells and all the bells in all the churches as we went home were a-ringing, it being about ten o'clock. But the common joy that was everywhere to be seen! At Strand Bridge I could at one view tell 31 fires. In King Street, there were rumps tied upon sticks and carried up and down. The butchers at the Maypole in the Strand rang a peal with their knives when they were going to sacrifice their rump. On Ludgate Hill there was one turning of the spit, that had a rump tied upon it, and another basting of it. Indeed, it was past imagination, both the greatness and the suddenness of it. At one end of the street, you would think there was a whole lane of fire, and so hot that we were fain to keep still on the further side nearly for heat.[17]

After this night of the long knives, there could be no doubt that the Rump was skewered. Civic leaders had decided that Restoration was best for business, and wealthy merchants had paid for all the rumps that hungry Londoners joyfully roasted and then devoured. Monck acted by pre-arrangement with Speaker Lenthall, his health suddenly restored, introducing into Parliament some eighty or so of the MPs excluded by Pride's Purge. This operation, on 21 February, was skilfully handled: the Rumpers did not know what hit them. (They thought that the soldiers had gathered at the door of the Commons that morning to keep the secluded members out, rather than to let them in.[18]) Once readmitted, these presbyterian MPs outnumbered the hardcore republicans. They appointed a new Council of State, mainly of royalist-inclining Presbyterians, set Monck in full command, put Montague back at the Navy, released George Booth from the Tower and put Lambert there in his place. Then they dissolved, having issued writs for elections to produce a new 'Convention Parliament'[19] in late April, which everyone expected would vote to bring back the King on the Newport terms. His health was openly drunk and the royal standard – the lion and unicorn – was brought out from behind many a fireplace and openly displayed.[20] The Rota Club wound itself up, since there was no point in further debate – the republic was a lost cause. Indeed, it was a dangerous cause, as the appearance of nasty little handbills presaged. Some merely listed the names of the judges present at the sentencing of 'King Charles of blessed memory'; others gave the names and the addresses of the thirty-three witnesses that John Cooke had called to testify in the Painted Chamber hearings.[21] There was no explanation – the message was all too clear.

Monck presided over the frantic jockeying for the expected royal favour. There would be royal disfavour as well, and servants of the commonwealth and the protectorate began to burn their papers, cover their tracks and make plans to leave the country. Pepys noticed 'strange thing – how I was already courted by the people' at the Admiralty, even before his relative, Montague, was confirmed as admiral.[22] Colonel Morley changed his mind and begged John Evelyn to help him to a pardon: he was put in touch with John Mordaunt (soon to be Viscount Mordaunt) who provided one for £1,000. Oxbridge-educated moderates like Pepys and Montague sneered at Monck – 'a dull heavy man', 'a thick-skulled fellow';[23] but he outsmarted them all with guile and instinct and authority. They were to blame him for betraying the Presbyterian cause of constitutional monarchy, which involved bringing the

King back on the Newport terms. Monck upset their expectations by refusing to disqualify any candidates, thus permitting the election of many cavaliers – even those who had borne arms against Parliament – who outnumbered the Presbyterians when the Convention Parliament met, and wanted the King back almost unconditionally, on the terms his father had conceded following Strafford's execution in 1641.

The penny finally dropped for Haselrig – two pennies in fact. He asked Monck, after he brought back the secluded members, whether he would honour his repeated promises to be loyal to the Commonwealth. Monck replied with a sneer, 'How could he [Haselrig] expect anything from him whom he had endeavoured to make less than he was before he reached London?'[24] He contemptuously offered to save Haselrig's life for tuppence if he promised to retire from all public office. Haselrig quickly agreed: he withdrew his candidature for the new Parliament, and dispatched two pennies in a letter reminding the general of his promise (Monck, fork-tongued as ever, delivered on his life but not his liberty – he would die in prison).[25] With Haselrig's capitulation, the 'Good Old Cause' was good no longer – indeed it was bad for anyone who valued their life at more than tuppence. A few honourable men stayed and fought as best they knew how – Ludlow and Scot by standing for the new Parliament. Thomas Harrison refused all offers to flee abroad, being 'so fully satisfied of the justice of his cause' that he waited calmly at home for his arrest.[26]

Lambert, ingenious as ever, escaped from the Tower one night in early April, sliding down from his window on a silk ladder provided by Joan, a sympathetic chambermaid, who dressed in his night-shirt and cap and bade goodnight to the warder in a deep voice.[27] As soon as he was free, Lambert raised the republican banner for a final stand, symbolically at Edge Hill where it had all begun. But thanks in part to Haselrig's sacking and scattering of Lambert's supporters in the army, Monck's forces were so superior to the 'Lambertines', as they were derisively called, that any stand could only be symbolic. Monck showed a sense of humour, or at least of irony: to meet and beat Lambert he dispatched a large force under Colonel Dick Ingoldsby, who in 1649 had been one of the King's most enthusiastic judges, but was now willing to fight for his life (in order to save it) against his former comrades. On 22 April Lambert surrendered after firing one symbolic shot. At the age of 41, this remarkable man was marched away to an imprisonment which would last for the rest of his long life.[28]

16

Endgame

Amidst all the excitement following Monck's arrival in London, news from Dublin was barely noticed when it arrived weeks late through the winter storms. So it is impossible precisely to date the extraordinary event (one report has it as early as 10 February) that signalled the decision of the Irish Protestant establishment to declare for the King. That event was the unlawful arrest of Justice Cooke.

From Easter 1659, Cooke had sat on the Upper Bench until its sittings were suspended in September. Thereafter, he served where required – he was recorder of Waterford and received various commissions from the council deputed to run Ireland by the Rump and later by the Committee of Safety. His last job, in November, was to peruse a consignment of books intercepted by customs, to determine whether any were seditious or blasphemous. He reported within a fortnight, having read thirty of them, that they betrayed 'an erroneous untoward spirit, denying any external reverence to magistrates, condemning ministers as anti-Christian hirelings and dumb dogs, expressing much bitterness against all manner of learning . . . and many popish and other erroneous tenets opinions contrary to sound doctrine'.[1] It is sad to find any one of Milton's circle making his living as a censor, vainly trying to keep Catholic opinion out of Ireland. By this time, with Bradshawe dead as well as Cromwell, Cooke was the only remaining member of that triumvirate named by Charles II in his wrath as incapable of forgiveness. The nearer the Restoration, the greater John Cooke's value as a dish that might be carved fit for a new king.

The danger to Cooke became greater in December, when supporters of the Committee of Safety (i.e. those who would cling most firmly to a republic) were forced out in the Dublin coup and the new council of officers led by Sir Charles Coote sought to impeach Ludlow. The absent commander made haste to return and anchored off Dublin on 31 December. Fearing capture, Ludlow sailed south to the fort of Duncannon, manned by loyal officers, and remained there for three weeks while his leading supporters – including Colonel Phayre and Miles Corbet – were held prisoners in Dublin Castle. Cooke realised all too well that the agenda of Broghill and Coote was 'to put the army in a prepared readiness to receive Charles Stuart at a week's warning', although that 'must not yet be mentioned: the design must be first to bring in the excluded members from 1648, and then – ding dong bells – will come in kings, lords and commons'.[2] This he wrote, presciently but anonymously, in a pamphlet entitled *A Sober Vindication of Lieutenant-General Ludlow* which his publisher at St Paul's had out on the streets in early February. Ludlow had been attacked for favouring sectarians – Baptists and Quakers – but 'a sectary is a name they give to the godly and to Parliament's best friends'. Cooke begged – too late – for unity against the 'common enemy', the bishops and their cavaliers, who were masterful propagandists with their demeaning references to 'the Rump' and their siren slogan 'a free Parliament' by which they hoped to bring in the King. Ironically, Cooke had begun his public career by debunking pamphleteers who take refuge in anonymity, but Mary, his new wife, was pregnant, and the danger of the times made him fear for his family. He should have kept silent, but the old urge to say what he thought was right overcame caution. He signed himself as *Philanthropus* ('one that loves the commonwealth as his own life').

Now was the time for John Cooke to fly the country, and he knew it. William Steele had taken ship for the continent, and Miles Corbet, on escaping from Dublin Castle, followed him. There were boats leaving for New England, and a well-trodden path to safety in Geneva. But Cooke scorned to run away: once again, he would 'wait on God'. He would not have long to wait.

By February 1660, Coote was in control in Dublin and had already been in secret communication with the King, as well as with Monck. His own Restoration agenda, after despatching Ludlow, was to have the King come first to Ireland, receive a rapturous welcome, and progress on to London – with Coote at all times by his triumphant side. (The plan was rejected by

Hyde, who knew only too well that Englishmen refused to believe that any good could ever come out of Ireland.)

Sir Charles Coote was a man who never bothered over much with conscience or propriety and it occurred to him that within his grasp was a prize worth the unlawful taking. John Cooke – with whom he had often sat on tribunals and special commissions – would certainly earn him the King's pardon. Coote had in the past been a scourge of the King's supporters in Ireland, hanging royalist commanders, killing bishops, scorching earth and profiting vastly from confiscated estates. He needed now to demonstrate a new-found loyalty. So in early February he sent a friendly message asking Judge Cooke to wait upon him at Dublin. Cooke delayed, spending several days with Mary at Waterford, agonising over whether to go or to stay – or to go to America. Fatally, he went as far as Monkstown, on the outskirts of the city, where Coote sent a troop of cavalry to arrest him and hold him in the dungeon at Dublin Castle. There was no Upper Bench in session in Dublin to grant habeas corpus to its most senior member. Lord Broghill, now emerging as the real power in Ireland was not minded to help the Chief Justice who had sided with tenants against his father, the Earl of Cork. Besides, his sister had married Lord Goring's son in a match the family had expected to bring wealth and status. After Cooke's prosecution of Goring in 1649 (see p211) the family estates had been forfeited.

Justice Cooke was Coote's biggest prize and was soon followed by others: he double-crossed his supporter Sir Hardress Waller, a signatory to the King's death warrant and arrested Colonel Hercules Hunks and Robert Phayre, who had been bidden to execute it; and captured two of the judges at the King's trial, John Jones and Matthew Tomlinson. News of these arrests soon reached the royal court at Brussels: 'In Ireland they play Rex', a royalist agent wrote breathlessly to Hyde, 'Cooke and five more are close prisoners in Dublin'.[3] The royalists had every reason to distrust Coote, and thought at first he was playing a double game. There was panic that Ireland 'outgoes our pace' and there could be complications if Coote and Broghill (who had summoned an Irish Parliament and addressed it in favour of restoration) jumped the gun being primed so delicately by Monck in London. So the Council of State directed them to send Cooke and the others under close guard to England.[4] Cooke's immediate execution might disaffect Monck's officers and alarm wavering supporters of the Restoration. So Judge Cooke's fate was put on hold until the new Parliament could meet.

The counter-revolution was under way. After a decade when their cause appeared hopeless, Charles and his courtiers, living on borrowed money in Brussels, were bewildered at this sudden improvement in their fortunes. Now Edward Hyde came into his own: he organised the removal of the court from Brussels (then under the control of Spain, England's historic enemy) to neutral Breda, in Holland; by early April he had drafted the Declaration of Breda, and a number of royal letters to accompany it addressed in turn to Monck, the Commons, the Lords and the City Council. At this time, the royal party could not judge its own strength: elections were underway and it had no expectation of winning them and no idea that it would win them spectacularly. The royal party wanted to come in at all costs, if need be under the Newport conditions, and was even prepared – but only if absolutely necessary – to forgo all revenge. It did not believe, then, that it would be in a position to execute its enemies: the object of the Breda letters was to overcome resistance by promising that there was no intention of settling old scores. 'We wish that the memory of what is passed may be buried to the world', said Charles with pretended magnanimity in his letter to the council and the officers of the army. To the newly elected House of Commons, the King offered reconciliation on their own terms:

> If you desire security for those who in these calamitous times either wilfully or weakly have transgressed . . . we have left you to provide for their security and indemnity in such a way as you shall think just and reasonable . . .[5]

To the City of London, the King was explicit in his desire 'to obtain peace . . . without effusion of blood'. The city should know 'how far we are from the desire of revenge'.[6]

To its own surprise, the King's party won the election: cavalier MPs outnumbered Presbyterians in the Convention Parliament, which met at the end of April. They wanted their King back and back Charles wanted to come – preferably, without any conditions at all. When some Presbyterians and moderate royalists, led by Matthew Hale, tried to impose the Newport Treaty conditions, Monck put his foot down: the security situation made it essential that there should be no conditions upon which opposition could fasten. Hyde, on hearing of Monck's ploy to beat off Hale, roared with delight, whilst Montague shook with rage when he realised how the Prebyterians had been duped.[7] The King, once again, was to be sole judge of what national security required. After the letters from Breda came a Declaration, also drafted by Hyde, and it was a diplomatic master stroke. Addressed 'To all our loving subjects, of what degree or quality soever', it sought 'a quiet and peaceable possession of our right'. Everyone who within forty days declared 'loyalty and obedience of good subjects' was to be pardoned, 'excepting only such persons as shall hereafter be excepted by Parliament'. As for the thorny question of return of confiscated estates, just satisfaction 'shall be determined in Parliament'. But all soldiers in the service of General Monck should receive in full their arrears of pay.[8]

That was it. Never was regime change accomplished so artfully yet so effortlessly. The King promised nothing, except a vague 'liberty for tender consciences' and to pay the soldiers who followed Monck. The winner would take all: Charles II would 'enjoy what is ours', leaving Parliament to settle the vexed question of religion on the basis of tolerance (i.e. for Anglicans and their bishops, not necessarily for sects like Quakers and apparently not for Catholics). Parliament would also resolve the vexed issue of confiscated land – but since MPs would benefit, nothing could be more satisfying to them. Most craftily of all, the buck was passed to Parliament to decide how many human sacrifices to offer up to the divinely ordained, hereditary and more or less absolute King Charles II. The Declaration of Breda called for 'the Restoration of King, peers and people to their just, ancient and fundamental rights': on 1 May it was read and adopted by acclamation in both Houses, followed by a unanimous vote that all books advocating republican government should be 'brought into the House and burned'.[9]

The emollient promises of the Breda letters had come from the King's perceived necessity rather than from the King's heart. Taken literally, the Declaration of Breda meant that Parliament might apply the preferred amnesty to everyone, John Cooke included. But by the time it was read, the situation had changed. The cavaliers controlled the Commons and Lambert's defeat had deprived the republicans of any military base. They were now at the King's mercy: all he had to do, if he wanted revenge, was to ignore his Breda letters.

It did not take long to set in motion the machinery for this breach of trust. In mid-May the new House of Commons ordered that all who had sat in judgment on Charles I (they were now openly and officially called regicides) should be seized: several were apprehended trying to flee from Dover. At this stage, before the King's return, it was assumed that only seven regicides need be put on trial, selected from the most publicly unrepentant: Thomas Harrison headed every list. Moreover, the number of MPs could be reduced by targeting the court's officials, so a few days later Cooke was added, together with Broughton (the clerk who had read out his charge) and Dendy, the sergeant-at-arms. But the appetite for retribution grew as the opportunity to take it increased. The cavalier MPs wanted much wider vengeance – one of their number, John Lenthall, actually suggested that all who had borne arms against the King should be prosecuted, which would have meant tens of thousands of traitors, including many fellow MPs (who duly reprimanded him) and the turncoat Lords. Lenthall's royalist zeal would even have executed his own father, William, the former Speaker, who had just sent a bribe of £3,000 to Charles in the hope of keeping his position as Master of the Rolls (the King kept the money, but told him the office was promised to another).[10] On 6 June (just one week after his entry into London) Charles II proclaimed no fewer than forty-nine named regicides, as

> being deeply guilty of that most detestable and bloody treason, in sitting upon and giving judgement against the life of our royal father . . . the persons beforenamed shall within 14 days next after the publishing of this our royal proclamation personally appear and render themselves to our speaker under pain of being exempt from any pardon or indemnity both for their respective lives and estates.

This proclamation was deliberately devious. It declared that all the named persons were guilty of treason (so much for their prospect of a fair trial), but then plainly indicated that they would be pardoned if they surrendered within the next fortnight. Nineteen of them did so, in reliance upon this interpretation, including General Fleetwood, John Downes and Henry Marten, only to be told they would be tried for treason: they would be sentenced to death, but would not be executed unless Parliament so determined.[11] But Cooke was never admitted to this class, because he had not surrendered to the Speaker. The reason he had not surrendered was that he was not at liberty to do so: he was imprisoned in Dublin and then delivered under close escort to the Tower of London: on June 6th, the day of the proclamation, he was under guard at Chester, en route to London.

The Restoration was here to stay, and now it was party time. The celebrations had been more or less continuous since May Day, and they culminated on 29 May with the triumphant return to London of Charles II. John Evelyn stood in the Strand to behold it:

This was [the King's] birthday and with a triumph of above 20,000 horse and foot, brandishing their swords, and shouting with inexpressible joy; the ways strewed with flowers, the bells ringing, the streets hung with tapestry, fountains running with wine; the mayor, aldermen and all the companies, in their liveries, chains of gold, and banners; lords and nobles, clad in cloth of silver, gold, and velvet; the windows and balconies, all set with ladies; trumpets, music and myriads of people flocking, even so far as from Rochester, so as they were seven hours in passing [through] the city, even from two in the afternoon until nine at night.[12]

The world really was turning upside down for God-fearing republicans: the big question was: who would be pitched out of it? The republican Admiral Lawson was quick to drink the King's health and become 'as officious, poor man, as any spaniel can be'.[13] He survived (against Pepys's predictions), demoted to the command of one ship. Oliver St John jumped aboard the first boat to Holland so he could come back beside the King, which saved his neck but not his job: he was too much of a timeserver for even the royalists to permit him to serve them.[14] Thurloe was charged with treason, although he managed – to the happiness of history – to save the state papers from burning by hiding them in the roof of Lincoln's Inn Chapel, where they were discovered decades later. New titles and appointments cascaded from the royal prerogative: George Monck was soon able to style himself *'George, Duke of Albermarle, Earl of Torrington, Baron Monck of Potheridge, Beauchamp and Teyes, Captain General and Commander-in-Chief of all His Majesty's forces in the three kingdoms, Master of His Majesty's horse; knight of the most noble order of the Garter; Privy Councillor and Lieutenant of the Kingdom of Ireland'*. Power-brokers like John Mordaunt, now a viscount, were plied with bribes. Corruption, which Cromwell had always held in reasonable check, flourished as never before. Lady Monck proved so avaricious at charging placemen for their places that she insisted that the former royal coach-maker, whose patent was still valid, should pay her £500 to be appointed to the position he already held.[15] Bishop Burnet, a confirmed royalist, was deeply shocked at the brazenness of the man to whom he owed his cassock: 'Monck was ravenous as well as his wife. They asked and sold all that was within their reach.'[16] Royalist propagandists were needed to cover up the corruption and spin-doctor the new dispensation, so Marchmont

Needham was sacked as editor of Parliament's newspaper *Mercurius Politicus*, and replaced by Henry Muddiman – an 'arch rogue' as Pepys described him, who had unashamedly written for the Rump and would henceforth slant the news for Charles II. The most crucial 'conversions' to royalty – of Presbyterian grandees like Holles and Annesley and Ashley Cooper – came not from conviction but from self-interest: monarchy was embraced for reasons of insurance rather than affection.

This was a time when public men would make any sacrifice to protect their lives and estates. That a few men were prepared to die for the republic was the real wonder. Some were motivated by religion: the Fifth-monarchist Thomas Harrison, for example, was waiting patiently and prayerfully for the King's troopers: death would deliver him to glory. Edmund Ludlow was awed but also irked by his religiosity: he thought it was the duty of the godly to flee persecution rather than 'expose themselves to the merciless cruelty of their bloody enemies'.[17] He had been amongst the forty-nine listed in the proclamation, so he turned himself in to the Speaker within fourteen days and arranged bail, but soon realised that his fate had been sealed. He broke bail and went into hiding: in September, the King proclaimed a large reward for his apprehension. John Cooke, from his cell in the Tower, offered to die in Ludlow's place: he would plead guilty and suffer execution if all proceedings were dropped against the colonel. The council declined to entertain this novel idea of a trial (and execution) by substitute – no doubt it suspected Cooke's reason was (as he privately admitted) that Ludlow was a better man to continue the fight for their 'good old cause'. The colonel laid low for a while in London, then slipped across the Channel and made his way to the safe shores of Lake Geneva.

Cooke must have realised his days were numbered. He had been unlawfully held prisoner in Dublin Castle for several months while the Irish Parliament, called by Coote and Broghill, raged on: it ended on 1 May by declaring 'those most inhumane, unparalled and barbarous proceedings' against Charles I to be 'the foulest murder and highest assassination'.[18] This declaration was designed to provide some retrospective justification for the arrest of Cooke, whom Coote was holding as hostage until his own fortune was secure.[19] He delayed implementing the council's order until confirmation that he had returned to royal favour: on 18 May, Cooke and the other prisoners finally left for London. Before his departure Cooke was brought before the recorder of Dublin, John Bisse, and examined over his part in the

King's death.[20] By this time, other captured regicides were confessing and avoiding, seeking to minimise their role in the hope of saving their lives. But John Cooke was the barrister who had established the right of silence and he declined to answer any of the questions put to incriminate him, or even to sign the record of his examination.[21] His blank deposition was dispatched for Parliament to consider, before his arrival in London, as to whether he should be put on trial for treason.

John Cooke travelled under guard but with his new wife for company, arriving to face jeering crowds in Chester. He had been told that Parliament would pay his passage to London, but his guards now insisted that he pay them for horses and accommodation, else they would make him and Mary travel on foot. But he did not even have £20: he had been in prison for three months and had not been able to sell cattle to raise money for their passage and it was now too late: on 24 May the Convention Parliament in Ireland ordered sequestriation of his estate. He had to borrow to enable them to continue the journey on horseback.[22] He gave no thought to escape: at first, he wrote to a friend, it was a relief to be out of Ireland, where 'those that will not swear or get drunk, but have family prayers, are accounted fanatics', but he was unprepared for the royalist hysteria that was sweeping England and 'the thousand curses we had between Chester and London'. Cooke finally arrived at the capital on 18 June, with Colonel Hercules Hunks, Lieutenant-Colonel Robert Phayre and William Hulet, a soldier suspected of being the King's executioner. They were paraded through the streets in an open cart, and then placed in a barge for the doleful entry to the Tower through 'Traitor's Gate'.

Cooke was a close prisoner over the summer, kept in leg irons and chains and allowed no visitors other than three commissioners who interrogated him to discover whether he knew anything about the identity of the King's executioner. Mary stayed in London with the family of Colonel Ludlow. She went to the Tower each day, asking in vain for admittance, until her husband spied her from his cell window and cried, 'Go home to our friends, dear lamb. I am well, blessed be God; they cannot keep the comforter from me.' When the jailer, fed up with being pestered by Mary, threatened to have him removed to Newgate – the disease-ridden jail for common prisoners next to the Old Bailey – Cooke shrugged: 'If the way to the new Jerusalem be through Newgate, blessed be God for Newgate.'[23] He managed to snatch an occasional word with Thomas Harrison, who occupied a nearby cell and radiated his own spiritual comfort. Cooke had never believed in the Fifth monarchy but it cheered him to think that 'all who are called forth to testify for Christ prove courageous . . . we live by faith and not by fight'. He managed in time to smuggle out messages to Mary, telling her jocularly to save money by not spending any on dressing in black for his funeral, since by that time his soul would be enveloped in saintly white. 'I am full of spiritual joy and trust God to make what bargain for me he pleases, for he knows the appointed time of my composition and dissolution.'[24]

The appointed time drew on apace. In June the Houses began to argue in earnest over the identities of those who would be denied 'Immunity and Oblivion'. These debates went on until the end of August and the final decisions had little to do with evidence – they were based on personal loyalties, money and family connections. Lenthall avoided 'exception' thanks to his son's exuberant royalism, and regicides like Tomlinson (commended by Charles I) and Ingoldsby (who had 'gone over' to the royalists and put down Lambert's revolt) and Cromwellian stalwarts like George Downing were protected by their royalist or Presbyterian friends. Even Lieutenant-Colonel Phayre, executor of the warrant for the King's death and Cooke's fellow traveller from Dublin, was saved from certain death by a lucky marriage with the daughter of Sir Thomas Herbert, who interceded on his behalf. But John Cooke, who had neither judged nor executed the King, could claim no such connections: he had played no part in Parliament as an MP; had insufficient money and estate for bribes, and could not rely on class or gentry connections. His fellow lawyers were not prepared to help him: as Ludlow explained, 'The malice towards this gentleman was very great from those of his own robe . . . for that he constantly pressed for a reformation of what was amiss in the laws.'[25] Cooke would be given no credit for his years of judicial service, either: the King was a regular guest at the Blackfriars mansion of the Earl of Cork, who could not forgive the chief justice who had ruled in favour of his tenants.[26] In Ireland, the vultures were gathering over the farm of a man marked for death: as early as 29 May, the day of the King's return to London, the Dean of Cloyne asked Sir John Percivale to help him obtain Cooke's land in Barnehay. Dripping with hypocrisy, the dean pretended that 'he is not much inclinable to be trading in such affairs' but the land 'lies conveniently for his near residence upon this parish'.[27]

The Parliamentary debate over John Cooke's life was a mere formality. On 6 June, Mr Annesley informed the House that he had received the record of the interrogation of 'Jo. Cooke Esq, a prisoner in the castle of Dublin'. The next day, the record of the interrogation of the judge who claimed his own right to silence was read to the House and it resolved – without any recorded debate or dissension – 'that John Cooke Esq be excepted out of the Act of General Pardon and Oblivion, for life and estate'. (This meant that Cooke was liable to execution and forfeiture of all his lands and goods, and the Dean of Cloyne could rub his hands in greedy expectation).[28] The Commons could hardly wait to pass the next resolution, accepting the King's gracious pardon for all its present members.[29]

The debates over other regicides continued for three months, much to the King's irritation: three times he had to address Parliament and ask them to hurry up, whilst thanking them 'for your justice towards those, the immediate murderers of my father'. Prynne, now back with a vengeance in Parliament, took the lead in calling for the death of as many republicans as possible, including all who had acted as prosecuting counsel in any high court of justice;[30] Matthew Hale led the MPs who wanted to limit the scapegoats and save the lives of those who had voluntarily surrendered. The lords were less forgiving, and there were casualties in the battles between the two Houses – Adrian Scroope, for example, was twice voted a pardon by the Commons, but rejected each time by the Lords. Clarendon explained that the royal proclamation of 6 June (requiring surrender 'under pain of being exempt from any pardon') did not *mean* that those who surrendered would be pardoned. The republicans remained dangerous, and must be eliminated – besides, he said, no one would stay loyal to a king so weak that he forgave all offences. Clarendon guided several joint sessions to a compromise – the Act would bestow a general pardon, subject to exceptions for the most dangerous republicans, who would lose all civil rights. Those who were also regicides would be liable to trial and execution for treason.[31] Following these intemperate debates with special interest was the newly appointed Solicitor-General, Heneage Finch, the MP for Canterbury. He was the son of Charles I's cowardly Speaker and nephew of Chief Justice John Finch of ship-money infamy who had just returned from exile. It would fall to him to prosecute those whom Parliament decided to condemn.

Parliament also determined which of the great 'commonwealthsmen' should keep their lives but none the less lose their lands, be barred from public office and remain liable, at the King's pleasure, to indefinite imprisonment. Here the great lawyers, who had disappeared in droves during the

King's trial but had taken what benefit they could from its aftermath, came up for judgment. Lenthall now lost out (by 215 votes to 126), as did Oliver St John; Whitelocke, who had been frantically pulling royalist strings since the beginning of the year, narrowly (by 176 to 134) kept his property and his civil rights. Clarendon delivered the King's promise that despite some cavalier MPs urging that 'they must die for the Kingdom, rather than for the King', John Lambert and Sir Henry Vane would be spared because they had not been involved in the King's trial.

The *Act of Free and General Pardon, Indemnity and Oblivion* was finally passed on 29 August. It excluded the forty-nine regicides named in the King's proclamation, together with the two unnamed persons 'who being disguised by frocks and vizors, did appear upon the scaffold'. The Act presumed guilt in uncompromising terms:

All which persons for their execrable treason in sentencing to death, or signing the instrument for the horrid murder, or being instrumental in taking away the life of our late sovereign lord, Charles I, of glorious memory are left to be proceeded against as traitors to his late Majesty according to the laws of England and are out of this present Act wholly excepted and foreprized.

Noting that the nineteen who had surrendered within a fortnight of the proclamation 'did pretend thereby to some favour, upon some considered doubtful words in the said proclamation' the Act of Oblivion directed that this 'favour' should be to have their sentence of death confirmed by Parliament – and the mood of the members of this Parliament, cavaliers and Presbyterians alike, was merciless. It was signified by Article XXXVII: 'Except also out of this present Act Oliver Cromwell deceased, Henry Ireton deceased, John Bradshawe deceased and Thomas Pride deceased'. This inexcusable clause was inserted so as to permit an act of revenge both macabre and puerile: to desecrate their graves, dig up their bodies and hang high their skeletons. Notwithstanding the King's promises, from Breda onwards, of reconciliation and forgiveness, his party had a pathological determination to exact retribution for the trial of Charles I. Historians praise the Act of Oblivion for its 'moderation' in focusing on the regicides rather than other supporters of Cromwell's regime, but this is to overlook the disproportionality of that focus. Parliament not only permitted desecration of the dead bodies of England's former leaders; it selected certain of its own servants and members as victims to propitiate the King.

The new Speaker of the House (the turncoat lawyer Harbottle Grimstone) offered this legislation to the King much as a priest would offer libation to a pagan god: its list was 'a long black prodigious dismal roll and catalogue of malefactors . . . we deal not with men, but monsters, guilty of blood, precious blood, royal blood, never to be remembered without tears'. This hardly presaged a fair trial, but a fair trial for the regicides was never in prospect. Restoration propaganda showed Charles I as an iconic, Christ-like figure, whose blessed qualities had been inherited by his son (a veil was drawn – on pain of prosecution – over any true account of Charles II in his debauched exile years). What the state needed now was a show trial, in which the new King's puissance would be on show: those who had once dared to dim the divinely ordained light would be torn to pieces, for public edification and entertainment.

And public entertainment was back. It was the age of miracles, when fetes and fairs and freaks and festivities were suddenly all the rage, as John Evelyn describes:

I saw in Southwark, at St Margaret's fair, monkeys and apes dance, and do other feats of activity, on the high rope; they were gallantly clad *à la mode*, went upright, saluted the company, bowing and pulling off their hats, they saluted one another with as good a grace as if instructed by a dancing master; they turned heels over head with a basket having eggs in it, without breaking any; also, with lighted candles in their hands, and on their heads, without extinguishing them, and with vessels of water without spilling a drop. I also saw an Italian wench dance, and perform all the tricks on the high rope, to admiration: all the court went to see her. Likewise, here was a man who took up a piece of iron cannon of about 400 lb [pounds] weight with the hair of his head only.[32]

Charles spent his first regal summer feasting, hunting and ennobling. His appetite was prodigious, as was his lust (somewhat contained in these early days, as he tried to live up to the propaganda about his chastity). His memory was good: Bishop Juxon was made Archbishop of Canterbury; John Gauden, Cooke's Wadham contemporary who had ghost-written *The King's Book*, was made Bishop of Exeter. 'At this time the bishops begin to be very high and in great power', John Rugg notes with alarm. Rugg, a Covent Garden barber, was reassured to hear that 'his majesty and many of the nobility were at the bull and bear-baiting in the tiltyard, as it seems an ancient custom in times of peace in England, in the King's peace'.[33] The ceremony that really proved the Stuarts were back was that of 'touching for the King's evil' which Charles II immediately revived.[34] It was a ritual mix of custom and superstition, in which the King touched the scrofulatic necks of those who recognised him as 'the true light that came into the world', and who received a gold coin – an angel – for reporting an immediate detumescence in their glands.[35] It was the apotheosis of kingship, making a magic that Parliament had abominated and abolished back in the 1640s. It was a time of wonder and splendour for the new aristocracy and a moment of marvel and miracle for the poor. As for the poor champions of the people's cause in the Tower of London, John Cooke's letter to a friend (probably Ludlow) shows him making the best of his bad luck.

'Let never any Christian fear a prison' is his jaunty beginning, 'it being the only place where (wanting other books) a man may best study the book of knowledge of himself, having a long vacation from all business.' Hard as it was not to feel the unfairness of his persecution, he now understood that he was in a state of grace, with 'a sweet certificate from heaven for the pardon of sin'.[36] Grace enabled him to face death: 'What need you care, if they say *Behold the head of a traitor* when your better part is in heaven?' Martin Luther regretted, as he lay dying in his bed, that he had not actually suffered torture or prison for Christ's cause – all the more reason for Cooke to rejoice that he, 'one of the meanest lawyers in Westminster Hall', had been chosen as a sacrifice. He refused to contemplate escape: 'it is accounted shameful to soldiers to run from their colours but it is more odious for advocates to prevaricate and betray the client's cause.'

Cooke conceded: 'I am reasoning myself against sense into a willingness to die.' He could find a few rational reasons: 'The axe or the halter [the rope around the neck on the scaffold] will be less pain than the pangs of childbirth' – which was true enough in 1660. There was likely to be a flood of persecution and 'it is a mercy to be taken away from the evil to come'. Moreover, at fifty-two he was old anyway: 'I can expect to do little more for God. I am three parts dead (seventy being divided into four), the shades of evening are upon me and aches and pains are inseparable companions.' But these reasons were insufficient to overcome death's terror: he owned to frequent 'fainting fits and despondencies; the spirit blows where it likes'. At these times he needed the cheer of Harrison and the prayers of his friends, and to believe that he was of the elect. 'We shall judge our judges', he exulted. Cooke would not judge kindly the 'men of Keilah', led by Charles Coote, who delivered him up 'for the Parliament to sacrifice us', or the Presbyterian MPs 'for whose privileges we ventured our all and who cannot condemn us without giving judgment against themselves'. Unlike these hypocrites, he would keep the faith: 'The cause for which I am in bonds is as good as ever it was . . . being for truth, holiness and righteousness for our liberties as men and as Christians.'[37] Cooke had at this stage not heard any plan for his trial, although he understood that 'they' – Hyde and the cabal presently around the King – regarded him as the worst of the surviving regicides because he had been the evil genius behind the prosecution. But he would not beg for his life:

> Let us not entertain damps of despondencies. My rejoicing is in a good God, a good Cause, a good Conscience . . . men's law at Westminster will be adjudged treason in heaven . . . We are not traitors or murderers or fanatics but true Christians and good Commonwealthsmen, fixed and constant in the principles of sanctity, truth, justice and mercy, which the Parliament and army declared and engaged for, and to that noble principle of preferring the universality before particularity. We fought for the public good and would have enfranchised the people and secured the welfare of the whole groaning creation, if the nation had not more delighted in servitude than in freedom.[38]

17

'They All Seem Dismayed . . .'

The Act of Oblivion identified the men liable to lose their lives for involvement in the trial of Charles I. A few had already fled to the Puritan colonies of Virginia and Massachusetts while others had found asylum in the republic of Geneva or the Low Countries. But nineteen had surrendered on the promise of the King's proclamation of 6 June while some major targets – notably Cooke and Harrison – were already in custody. The sight of Cooke and the other prisoners from Ireland being taken to the Tower on 18 June began a hue and cry for Hugh Peters, who was excepted from the Act that very day but hidden by a Quaker family in Southwark: he was eventually apprehended, hiding under their bed. That made twenty-nine regicides available for trial.

The cavaliers wanted revenge, and execution after a trial process would serve that purpose well. But the architects of the Restoration – Hyde and the landed nobility – required a spectacle that would protect their own posterity, both by eliminating dangerous republicans and by deterring any future leaders from challenging the settled prerogatives of the King and his courtiers. Their talk about the trial as a just reckoning for the 'horrific' murder of his 'sacred' majesty, was a way of selling it to a public made credulous by Cromwell's encouragement to think in terms of providence, and hence more easily persuaded that the Restoration was a signal that God was, after all, on the side of monarchy. For an entire class that would henceforth derive its power and its perquisites from the restored King, this 'trial' was the opportunity to entrench monarchy in the common law of England, by having all judges declare that any serious act of opposition was a capital felony without prospect of defence.

To lower the law so that the King would always be above it, reliance was placed upon a new set of judges. Despite Cromwell's admirable dispassion in judicial appointments – he did not hesitate to promote fine lawyers like Matthew Hale, despite their royalist sympathies – the protectorate bench was not trusted by the new regime. The King could hardly wait to create Orlando Bridgeman his first new peer, as chief baron of the Exchequer, in effect the nation's chief justice. He had practised mainly in property law, where his ability at protecting great estates was such that even now he is hailed as 'the father of modern conveyancers'.[1] His loyalty to Charles – father and son – had been unswerving, as befitted the son of a bishop. Knighted by Charles I for supporting Strafford, he had defended Laud, served the King at Oxford and led his legal team at Newport. Despite his 'malignant' tendency he was permitted to practise during the interregnum: although some restrictions were placed on his court appearances they did not stop him from making a large fortune, or from spying for Hyde.[2]

Bridgeman was relied upon to provide intellectual leadership since the other Restoration judges were placemen, with the exception of Matthew Hale (who kept his place, although he was so embarrassed at the regicide proceedings that he said not a word in their entire course). Sir Robert Foster was a fanatical royalist who had defended ship money and had hastened to Oxford in 1642 to serve the King. Sir Thomas Malet, old and garrulous, had been Solicitor-General to the Queen and his son had been killed fighting as a cavalier. Sir Robert Hyde, cousin to Edward, had also joined the King at Oxford and sheltered Charles II on his flight from Worcester: his loyalty was clear and his Restoration reward, a knighthood and judgeship, was automatic. Thomas Twisden was a staunch loyalist who in 1656 had acted, with the prosecution junior William Wyndham, for a merchant, George Cony, who instructed them to challenge the legality of a protectorate customs duty as incompatible with Magna Carta. Cromwell was furious – 'Your magna farta cannot control actions taken for the safety of the Commonwealth' – and had them committed to the Tower, whereupon they secured their release by abandoning their clients and apologising profusely for accepting their brief. They were criticised for unprofessional conduct: even Hackney cabmen, the new competitors with

Thames boatmen, acknowledged a duty to accept all paying customers.[3]

With judges of this ilk, the result of the regicide trial was a foregone conclusion, especially since they were to sit with a number of non-judicial commissioners who were scions of the new establishment. These included the all-powerful Lord Chancellor (Hyde, now elevated as Earl of Clarendon), Monck (now Duke of Albemarle), Manchester and Montague (now Earl of Sandwich) together with other Presbyterian grandees who were soon to be ennobled – Denzil Holles, Ashley Cooper, Arthur Annesley, Harbottle Grimstone and several of the King's Secretaries of State. This extraordinary cast from the past included the Duke of Ormond and Lord Finch – the architect of the ship-money verdict. Other than the cowed Matthew Hale, there was not a man of principle or jurist of independence among the thirty-four commissioners. Fifteen of them were Presbyterian turncoats who had fought against both Charles I and Charles II, and were now more anxious than anyone to offer up the defendants in expiation. There was only one problem: royalist propaganda against Cromwell's 'High Courts of Injustice' had been sustained and feverish, and it was an article of faith among royalists that their like would not be seen in England again. Thanks to Lilburne, the only tribunal trusted to deliver a popular verdict was a jury: the regime had now to devise a means of controlling this body and incorporating it into the trial of men proclaimed by Act of Parliament to be 'deeply guilty of that most detestable and bloody treason'.

The solution was to summon only jurors who had been carefully vetted for loyalty. This required co-operation from the sheriff, but the office was occupied by William Love, a man of integrity with independent religious sympathies (he was later expelled from the cavalier Parliament for criticising the Book of Common Prayer). So there was some delay, until elections for new sheriffs in September brought in more pliable officials.[4] The art of jury-packing, subsequently honed by Tory sheriffs, was not, of course, publicised – but ten years later the Mayor of London, Samuel Starling, gave the game away. He had sat as a judge at the trial of two Quakers, William Penn and William Mead, whose jury refused to convict despite his threats ('You factious fellow,' Starling screamed at one juror, 'I will cut off your nose'). When criticised for this conduct, he responded incautiously by boasting how in 1660 he had been 'esteemed for his loyalty a fit person to be of the jury upon the King's judges and had passed upon no less than 18 of those assassinating traitors'. It turns out that Starling, a barrister, had been selected for the jury panel to try the regicides because of his previous refusal to take the oath of fidelity to the Commonwealth, thus disabling himself from practising.[5] It may be assumed that other jurors had made similar sacrifices for their royalist beliefs before being esteemed sufficiently loyal to vindicate those beliefs by convicting all the defendants. It is a tribute to the assiduity of the new sheriff and his officers that only once in all the trials did the jurors even bother to retire before delivering 'guilty' verdicts.

The regicide trial required careful legal choreography: having rigged the jury, the regime now had to rig the law. Throughout September and early October, Orlando Bridgeman presided over meetings between the professional judges – notably Foster, Hyde and Malet – and the prosecutors, which took place at Serjeants' Inn just off Fleet Street. The prosecutors were the Attorney-General, Sir Geoffrey Palmer (a member of the King's legal team at Newport), Sir Heneage Finch and William Wyndham. They were joined by John Kelying, instructed as special counsel for the King, and Sir Edward Turner for the Duke of York, both appearing on behalf of relatives of the victim, something never permitted in English criminal trials before or since. These secret meetings at Serjeants' Inn were improper, even in 1660. In 1649, Cooke and Dorislaus had openly attended minuted meetings of the King's judges and advised them on procedure, but had not sought to have them alter the law behind the defendant's back. A few months later, Lilburne's complaint that his prosecutors must not be 'hugger-mugger' with his judges had been conceded. The Serjeants' Inn meetings were only revealed years later when Kelying, by then promoted to chief justice, thought that posterity might be interested in his notes of the decisions that were taken about the law. Those decisions were quite sufficient to make the issue of guilt and innocence a formality, because they did not permit of innocence.

At these meetings, the judges helped the prosecutors to frame the indictment so that it would survive any defence argument. They advised against charging the defendants with murdering the King, because this would create difficulties for convicting those who had not sat as judges, especially the prosecuting counsel (Cooke), the guards (Axtell and Hacker) and the hated preacher, Hugh Peters. Instead, the charge should be for treason by 'compassing and imagining' the King's death, which meant no more than doing or saying something that might conduce to it.[6] But treason was a mindset that had to be proved by a course of conduct, i.e. by an 'overt act', and in law such an act had to be proved by sworn testimony from two witnesses.

So they decided, without hearing argument, to abolish this ancient rule that served as the only safeguard for defendants at treason trials. Since the judges dared not openly abolish a long-standing rule of law, they determined instead to pretend that the 'two witnesses' rule remained, but that it was satisfied if one witness testified to one overt act and another witness testified to another overt act. This was intellectually dishonest, because the historic purpose of the 'two witnesses' rule was to require corroboration before any single overt act could amount to treason.

It was further decided that the rules of evidence should be discarded in order to ensure that all defendants were convicted. For example, it had always been a strict rule of criminal procedure that 'particulars' of any conduct alleged to amount to the crime should be given in the indictment – so that defendants could not be taken by surprise by sudden accusations. In this case, however, the judges resolved to admit any prosecution evidence of any act 'which tends to the compassing of the King's death' irrespective of whether it was charged or even mentioned in the indictment. The judges, in other words, were promising the prosecutors, before the trials, to abandon the rule which permitted the admission only of relevant evidence, and to permit them to throw at the defendants whatever mud came into their hands – a decision that had to be reversed by Parliament after the demise of James II.[7]

The judges and prosecutors were particularly concerned about the ability of the new sheriff to 'vet' for loyalty all the jurors who might be required, since each defendant by ancient right was entitled to challenge up to thirty-five. If there had to be separate trials for twenty-nine defendants, that would mean vetting hundreds of jurors and would make the exercise impractical. So another departure from law was authorised, namely that only one panel – of eighty-six vetted jurors – would be summoned, and that it should not be an objection to any juror at a later trial that he had already convicted another defendant on the same indictment, however similar the facts. This ploy was unscrupulous and unlawful: men charged on the same indictment who are tried separately must always be allowed a dozen fresh jurors, otherwise the prejudice is impossible to combat: the jurors who have already convicted are no longer 'good men and true'. But the King's judges were taking no chances.[8]

At the Old Bailey, the recorder of London would normally be expected to address the grand jury, preside over the trial and deliver the sentencing homilies. But the recorder, Sir William Wilde, was not exactly 'one of us'.

Although a royalist, he was the son of a vintner (birth now mattered a great deal) and was not as bright as Bridgeman the bishop's son nor as unscrupulous in his dedication to the cause. So Lord Chancellor Clarendon (Edward Hyde) insisted that Bridgeman preside. The judges decided that the indictment must end with Latin phrases beloved by lawyers down the centuries: the Cromwellian reform which abolished legal Latin would be reversed.[9] All defendants who had not yet been apprehended were to be 'attainted by outlawry' – a medieval procedure which made it a capital offence not to turn up for trial. (The three regicides captured in Holland in 1662 were in consequence executed without a trial.)

John Cooke knew nothing of these manoeuvres, although from the fact that other regicides were brought to join Harrison and himself in the Tower he deduced that his hour of trial was nigh. He was still smarting from the unlawfulness of his arrest and was thrown into occasional despondency at the awfulness of the death that awaited him – he had no doubts that the cavaliers would revive 'drawing and quartering'. But in communications to Mary he was anxious to appear cheerful. 'Tell Sister Jones', he wrote with reference to an exceptionally pious member of their congregation, 'that she but keeps two or three Sabbaths in one week: but in prison, every day is a Sabbath. I smile to think they cannot stop me from preaching – I preach every day to myself.' He urged the 'soul-melting consideration' that they might attain heaven, '. . . a sinless, sorrowless, temptationless, oppressionless, sickless, timeless and endless estate . . . I leave you and our dear child in the arms of He who sits in heaven on the right hand of the Father: we need not fear what man can do unto us.'[10] Mary was still lodging at the London home of their friend Edmund Ludlow, the stout parliamentarian whose fate Cooke rightly saw as a barometer for his own. When he heard that Ludlow was back at home after giving sureties to the Speaker of the House that he would attend if summoned, he felt reassured. When he heard that Ludlow had fled, he knew his own fate was sealed. If they had come for Ludlow, then they would come for Cooke.[11]

In the stink of his cell on these drawn-out summer days, John Cooke gave increasing thought to the allegations that would be levelled against his fellow prisoners. Although the opportunity to talk together in the Tower was limited, they could pass messages through helpful warders and speak at brief meetings in the corridors, and it was to Justice Cooke they all turned for legal advice. They were not minded to go meekly to the slaughter, but they would need the assistance of counsel to face the pantheon of royalist lawyers and judges.

The show trial opened, without their presence or even knowledge, on 9 October, when a grand jury was summoned to decide whether the prosecution evidence was sufficient to send them to trial. This ceremony took place at Hicks' Hall in John Street, Islington, a large building donated for public use by a wealthy merchant. It was a down-market venue for the thirty-four noble commissioners summonsed to sit on the bench for 'the trial of the pretended judges of his late sacred majesty'. Twenty-one grand jurors were sworn, all rock-solid royalists – nine of them were knights, having inherited the title or received it from Charles I, the man into whose murder they were sworn to enquire. Amongst them, ironically, was the dissolute poet Sir Charles Sedley, who was to make his own contribution to English criminal history three years later, when a drunken party on his Covent Garden balcony ended, according to a law report, by his 'pulling down his breeches and excrementalising on the crowd below'. The King's judges decided that they, and not the lax church courts, should punish any act that was 'against public morality' and fined Sedley, who left the court complaining that he was 'the first man to pay for shitting'.[12] His task as a grand juror was to listen to the law of treason expounded by the Lord Chief Baron, and then to confer in secret with the prosecutors in order to return a *billa vera* – a true bill – against those prisoners who appeared from the evidence to have breached that law.

Bridgeman's speech set out the legal basis for Stuart absolutism: the King could do no wrong. Moreover, as wearer of what Bridgeman called 'the imperial crown', Charles I was so untouchable that the mere *thought* of touching him – by putting his person under any force or constraint – was treason. That thought, i.e. that 'imagining or compassing', was proved by an 'overt act' sworn to by two witnesses or else (the Serjeants' Inn twist) by two or more overt acts described by one witness each. Once treason was proved in this way, there was no defence at all, whether of necessity or duress or self-defence. Since the King was above the law, he could never be put on trial by any authority, so – this was fundamental to Bridgeman's direction – it would be unlawful for the Commons and Lords to establish any court to try the King or to impeach or attaint him. It followed that it could not be lawful for the House of Commons – a purged House of Commons at that – to do it alone. Since the prisoners were proposing to argue that they had acted by order of the only authority in the country at the time, namely the House of

Commons, Bridgeman's speech rejected their defence before it was even raised. The flavour of his charge to the grand jury is captured in these excerpts:[13]

Gentlemen,

This commission is into a special occasion, the execrable murder of the blessed King who is now a saint in heaven, King Charles I . . . by the statute of Edward III (1351) it is made high treason to compass and imagine the death of the King . . . in the case of a king, his life is so precious that intent alone is treason. What is imagining or compassing? Truly, it is anything which shows what the imagination is. Words, in many cases, are evidence of the imagination – they are evidence of the heart.

I must deliver you the plain and true law: that no authority, not the people collectively or by their representatives, have any coercive power over the King of England. The King is immediate from God and has no superior – he is our sovereign Lord, and sovereign means he is supreme . . . the imperial crown is not subject to any human tribunal or judicature whatsoever . . .

The King can do no wrong: that is a rule of law, it is frequently found in our law books, Lord Coke's and many others. If he can do no wrong, he cannot be punished for any wrong. The King has the infirmities and weaknesses of a man, but he cannot do any injury – he must do it by ministers, who if they do wrong, although by his command, are punishable. As to the person of the King, he is not to be touched: 'Touch not mine anointed'. The King is immediately under God, accounting for his power to none but God.

Bridgeman was winding the clock back to the days of absolute monarchy, reversing all the constitutional gains of the last half-century.[14] He placed medieval theology at the core of England's constitution by his statement that the King was a sacred personage accountable to God alone. He misstated the law of treason, too, which had hitherto required proof of an overt act both tending and intended to overthrow the monarch and not of acts showing no more than hostile intent. (Spoken words, for example, had never been regarded as sufficient for a conviction of high treason: the rule was that

'bare words may make a heretic, but not a traitor'.)[15] But it would be idle
for the defendants to object that Bridgeman was wrong in law: 'In this case
they are all guilty,' he told the grand jury. 'Their first consultation was
treason.' His closing direction was, quite literally, bloodcurdling:

> You are now to enquire of blood, of Royal blood, of sacred blood, blood
> like that of the saints . . . this blood cries for vengeance and it will
> not be appeased without a bloody sacrifice . . . Remember this: you are
> persons of honour and know the obligation of an oath. He that conceals
> or favours the guilt of blood, takes it upon himself. Willfully, know-
> ingly, takes it upon himself.

The grand jurors had been warned: if they refused to indict men so patently
guilty of shedding the King's blood they would themselves be guilty of treason.
Bridgeman ended his charge with a fervent 'God Save the King' and the
jury chorused 'Amen'. Bridgeman had sent a chilling warning to all who had
collaborated with Cromwell. As one of the government lawyers who
had attended Hicks Hall reported back to Samuel Pepys, 'In Sir Oliver (sic)
Bridgeman's charge, he did wholly rip up the injustice of law against the
King from the beginning, and so it much reflects upon all the Long
Parliament; that though the King hath pardoned them, yet they must hereby
confess that the King does look upon them as traitors.'[16] The jury were
quickly convinced by the prosecutors to return a 'true bill',[17] and the court
adjourned until 9 a.m. the next day, when the prisoners would be arraigned
at the Old Bailey.

The defendants were all being held in solitary confinement in the Tower.
At about 9 p.m., warders told them the news that the grand jury had sent
them to trial for high treason, and that they would be required in the morning
to plead to the indictment (which so far they had not seen). At 6 a.m., they
were roused and herded into several large coaches, and driven under heavily
armed escort to their new accommodation at Newgate Prison, adjacent to
the 'Sessions House' in the Old Bailey. It was built of stone, but like most
criminal courts of the period, the front was left open to the elements. Keeping
them in the fresh air would reduce the risk that judges would catch their
prison diseases. Prisoners stood there in a 'pen' waiting to be sent up the
steps to the 'bar' – a railing across the body of the courtroom, facing the
row of judges. At about 9 a.m. the prisoners were marshalled at Newgate

and herded across the street to the pen, shuffling in their fetters and leg-irons. In court, the commissioners had already assembled, and some of the spectators who had jeered the prisoners as their coaches arrived at Newgate had taken their seats in the public gallery.

There was a buzz of excited anticipation as the regicides were brought up, one at a time, to the bar of the court.[18] Sir Hardress Waller was first: he had been one of the King's judges but had supported Coote's coup in Dublin, and the government believed he could be pressured into a plea of guilty – he had been told that this was the only way to save his large estate and possibly his life. Next was Thomas Harrison, demonised by royalists ever since he had brought the King on his last journey from Hurst Castle to Windsor. He was now seriously ill from a fever caught in prison but was notoriously unrepentant. It was determined that an example should be made of him: his signature was on the King's death warrant, so he could have no defence against the treason charge. Nor could the other unrepentant judges – Scroop, Clement, Scot, Carew and Jones – whose trials were slated to follow in quick succession. The purpose of selecting these regicides for the first easy cases was to settle the legal rulings and spread a little terror by executions before the more difficult trials – of Cooke and Peters and Axtell.

John Cooke advised his fellow prisoners that they had a right to counsel to argue any point of law arising on their trial: they should explain that they had been in solitary confinement and had not yet seen the indictment. They would need counsel to argue that the court had no jurisdiction to try them because in 1649 they had acted under a commission from Parliament, and Parliament's orders could not be questioned or invalidated in a court of law. This was the defence Cooke had devised for all of the regicides; it was self-evidently a point of law which entitled the prisoners to counsel. But the court had other ideas. In an opening scene that begs comparison with the patience displayed by Bradshawe at the opening of the King's trial, Bridgeman bullied Sir Hardress Waller into a plea of guilty. In 1649, when the King had refused to plead, he was given five days to make up his mind. Waller was given less than five minutes:[19]

CLERK OF THE COURT: How say you, Sir Hardress Waller? Are you guilty of that treason whereof you stand indicted, or not guilty?

WALLER: My Lords, I dare not say 'not guilty' but since in this business we have no counsel and no advice and are not able to speak as to matters of law . . .

BRIDGEMAN: I am loathe to interrupt you but this is the course. You have heard the indictment read and the course is you must plead guilty or not guilty. There is no medium. That is the law. Are you guilty? Or not guilty?

WALLER: I may confess myself guilty of some particulars in that indictment but not of all otherwise I shall wound my conscience.

BRIDGEMAN: No man standing at the bar in the condition you are, must make any other answer to the indictment than 'guilty' or 'not guilty'. It is the common case of all men. Either guilty or not guilty.

WALLER: My Lord, I do desire some time to consider it for it comes as a great surprise.

BRIDGEMAN: You have had enough time to consider it. You must follow the directions of the court. Are you guilty or not guilty? You must not thus discourse about being surprised for such discourse is contrary to proceedings of this nature.

Bridgeman then invoked the *pro confesso* rule – plead or be deemed guilty – to pressure a plea from this confused defendant:

BRIDGEMAN: There are but three things to be considered. Either you must say guilty, which is a confession and there remains nothing further but judgment. If you say not guilty, then you shall be heard. Judgment will pass if you stand mute which is as if you had confessed.

WALLER: In as much as I have said I dare not say 'not guilty' I must therefore say 'guilty'.

The next prisoner, Thomas Harrison, was made of sterner stuff:

HARRISON: My Lord, I have been kept a close prisoner for nearly three months so that nobody might have access to me. Do you now call on me to give a legal answer, not knowing of my trial till 9 p.m. last night, and brought away from the Tower to this place at 6 o'clock this morning?

BRIDGEMAN: You must give your exact answer, guilty or not guilty. You cannot say it is sudden or unprovided. You spend our time in vain. You trouble the court.

HARRISON: I desire to be advised about the law. This is a special case.

At this point, Finch the Solicitor-General made a sarcastic intervention which drew laughter from the crowd. 'I beseech your Lordship to make him plead. Perhaps he knows his case so well that he thinks it would be as cheap to defy the court as to submit to it.' It was a cheap shot, the first of many that Finch would level at men he was dispatching to the gallows. In groups of three or four they were put up from the pen, and allowed to say nothing but 'guilty' or 'not guilty'. After Waller, only Major General George Fleetwood (cousin to Charles Fleetwood) pleaded 'guilty'. John Cooke was prisoner number 25. His arraignment went brusquely:

CLERK: John Cooke, hold up your hand. How say you? Are you guilty of the treason whereof you stand indicted or not guilty?

COOKE: I humbly conceive that this is now time to move for counsel to argue a matter of law.

BRIDGEMAN: You know too well the manner of the court. Are you guilty or not guilty?

COOKE: Not guilty.

The pleas were all taken within the hour, although there was some resistance from Henry Marten, who objected that his name was not in the indictment:

BRIDGEMAN: How is his name written?

CLERK: It is Henry Martin.

MARTEN: Henry Martin? My name is not so. It is Harry Marten.

BRIDGEMAN: The difference of the sound is very little. You are known by the name of Martin.

MARTEN: I humbly submit that all penal statutes ought to be understood
literally.

Cooke had suggested that Marten take the point – it had been one of
his repeated complaints that guilty prisoners were let off on exactly such
technicalities. This time, however, Bridgeman ordered that the trial proceed
because the two names sounded the same. He made no effort to stop the
crowd roaring abuse when Hugh Peters – the most hated of the defendants
– was hauled up from the pen to make his plea. When he failed to give
the correct answer to the clerk's formal question 'How would you be tried?'
(he said 'By the word of God' instead of 'By God and the country') the
audience fell about with laughter. Most of the prisoners were old, and now
sick from jail fever: they seemed cowed and bewildered by the power that
had gripped them so suddenly and put them back in the public spotlight
for a few moments.

The last defendant hauled up from the pen was Daniel Axtell, the soldier
who had commanded the guard at the King's trial but had never served in
any decision-making capacity and should never have been included in the
indictment. Others had meekly accepted the court's improper refusal to allow
them counsel before they were forced to plead, but Axtell showed something of the spirit of the late John Lilburne: 'I desire to have the freedom
of an Englishman, which is my right by law and inheritance. I have a point
of law to offer . . . and I pray that counsel be assigned me.' The point of law
was significant, but Bridgeman incanted: 'No man can justify treason. If the
matter be justifiable, it is not treason. If treason, it is not justifiable.' This
was the catch-22 upon which lawyers were denied to all the prisoners: they
were ordered to plead immediately, either guilty or not guilty, else they would
be deemed to have confessed. Samuel Pepys at dinner that evening heard
the talk of the town: the regicides had made their first public appearance
and 'they all seemed to be dismayed and would all be condemned without
question'.[20]

The shared dismay of the morning turned to a resigned camaraderie
amongst the prisoners by the evening. In the Tower they had been in solitary confinement but in Newgate, although hobbling in chains, they could
mingle and plan and pray together; they could meet their families and talk
to ordinary prisoners. In the heightened atmosphere, spiritual fervour was
intense, although Cooke was not unmindful of the consequences for his prop-

erty: unlike Harrison, who cheerfully told his wife that he only had a Bible to leave her, Cooke had a smallholding in Ireland and he fretted lest it 'be taken away from my poor wife and child'. He told friends that his greatest desire was that his baby daughter, Freelove, should have a Puritan upbringing. Those who paid their way into the visiting yard at Newgate found him full of Christian cheer: 'little do my enemies think what a friendly service they do me, to hasten me to my father's kingdom.' Cynicism came from the ordinary prisoners, most of whom were robbers. They were unimpressed by Cooke's piety, pointing out that Jesuit priests had gone to their execution just as cheerfully. They knew he was a judge, and they attacked him for punishing robbers. (In prison, law enforcers are invariably abused by ordinary felons.) 'I have relieved many of you so far as by law I could, because the worst of men should have justice,' replied Cooke in his own defence. 'I dare not wrong any man for I know I shall meet them at the bar on the Day of Judgment.'

At 7 a.m. on Thursday 11 October, Thomas Harrison went on trial.[21] He knew some of the jurymen all too well, and challenged those he knew were biased: soon he had exhausted his thirty-five challenges. Solicitor-General Finch opened the prosecution case by explaining to the jury that the law against treason was based on the theory that kings were 'God's vice-regents on earth . . . their subjects stand accountable to them for the very thoughts of their hearts – and it's the thought of the heart which makes the treason; the overt act is but the evidence of it'. Finch gave the jury a potted royalist history of the process by which 'this blessed King, this glorious saint' was tried and condemned – 'I had almost said, crucified'. At the very news of the execution 'many poor subjects at home and some Protestants in foreign nations, fell down dead'. As the prosecutor finished the audience began to hum – a rising wall of sound to presage the defendant's death. But Bridgeman would not allow melodrama. 'Gentlemen, this humming is not at all becoming . . . it is more fitting for a stage play than for a court of justice.'

Harrison was not intimidated. In his opening remarks, he pointed out – almost proudly – that the execution was 'not a thing done in a corner'. He asked the jury to remember something that Finch dared not mention: 'You know what a contest has been in these nations for many years. Various members of the bench were formally as active . . .' But the court cut him short. 'This is not to the business,' Bridgeman interrupted. The jury must not be reminded of the civil war, let alone of the fact that half the judges had then opposed the King. Harrison turned to the argument that he acted by order of Parliament, the highest court in the land, whose orders could not be questioned in this or any other court. The indictment alleged that the regicides had been 'inspired by the devil' to usurp the King's authority, but 'I say, this was done rather in fear of the Lord . . .' At this, Bridgeman's anger could no longer be contained and his mask of politeness slipped:

'Away with him. Know where you are, Sir. You are in an assembly of Christians. Will you make God the author of your treasons and murders? Take heed where you are. Christians must not hear this!'

Harrison asked again for counsel, to argue the legal point that the House of Commons was in January 1649 the *de facto* government and could establish a court to try the King. 'This is a new treason for which he deserves to die,' protested Finch. 'The King is not accountable to any coercive power.' Any argument to the contrary would itself be treasonable, and no barrister could be permitted to make it. The court agreed, and Finch called his evidence proving that Harrison had sat on the court and signed the death warrant and had forcibly taken the King from Hurst Castle to Windsor. At one meeting in the Painted Chamber he had urged Cooke to elaborate the charge – 'Let us blacken him what we can' were Harrison's words, said crown witness James Nutley, then a young barrister assisting Cooke.

The prosecutor closed with an attack on Pride's Purge. This caused a shifting and shuffling among some of the commissioners: the prosecutor was telling *their* story, and although they were meant to be sitting as judges, they were going to have their say. Arthur Annesley interrupted first: 'I do still more willingly speak to this business . . . I was one of that corrupt majority (as they called it) that were put out of the House . . . all those who had a mind for peace, who minded their duty and trust, were seized on by this gentleman [he pointed at Harrison] and his fellows.' Denzil Holles waved his fist and raised his voice at the defendant. 'You do very well know that this horrid, detestable act could never be perfected until you had broken the Parliament . . . so do not make Parliament the author of your black crimes . . . your plea is overruled.'

The judges were turning into witnesses, and then into prosecutors. Even the professional judges descended into the arena, vilifying the defendant in front of the jury. Old Justice Malet muttered sadly: 'Sir, what have you done? You have taken away him that was our father.' Justice Hyde shouted: 'Your plea is naught, illegal and ought not to be allowed.' Sir William Wilde, the recorder passed over for the better-connected Baron Bridgeman, became impatient for a conviction: 'I beseech you, my Lord, direct the jury for their verdict. This gentleman forgets their barbarity – they would not even hear their King.' These comments were made in front of the jury, who were left in no doubt about the verdict the judges expected. To ram it home, Bridgeman stopped Harrison from asserting that the King had started the war, and turned to the jury:

Methinks he should be sent to bedlam, till he comes to the gallows to render an account for this. This must not be suffered. It is a new impeachment of the King, to justify their treasons against his late majesty.

The counsel for the Duke of York, in effect, for the royal family, stood up for the first time. There was a hush, as Sir Edward Turner addressed the crowded bench.

My Lords, this man [he pointed to Harrison] has the plague all over him. It is a pity any should stand near him for he will infect them. Let us say to him, as they used to write over a house infected by plague, 'The Lord have mercy upon him' and so let the officer take him away.

The fact that King's counsel was permitted to make malicious jokes about the ill-health of the defendants added another dimension of prejudice to the general viciousness that pervaded these proceedings. As an added terror, the hangman (carrying the rope and halter in his arms) stood in the well of the court opposite the prisoner, who was forced to make his defence while staring at the brawny arms and steely countenance of his executioner. Bridgeman, for all his artificial politeness, fully endorsed this behaviour, and even picked up Turner's cruel point, telling Harrison: 'The end of your speech is nothing, but to infect the people.' Harrison replied with some dignity: 'You are uncharitable in that. I have been kept six months a close prisoner and could not prepare myself for this trial with the help of counsel.' But the court had suffered this defendant for over an hour, and it was time for Bridgeman to bring down the curtain.

'Imagination alone is treason by law,' he told the jury in a short summing-up. It was proved by overt acts, and Harrison had confessed to participation in the meetings of the High Court and to conducting the King from Hurst Castle, and such forcible constraint over the sovereign was treason. 'The evidence is so clear and pregnant that I think you need not go out.' The jury took the hint: without bothering to move from their seats they all nodded and their foreman – the royalist Sir Thomas Allen – loudly declared: 'The prisoner is guilty.' Finch jumped to his feet to ask that sentence be passed on Harrison immediately – an improper request, because the convicted prisoner was always entitled to at least a day's grace so he or his counsel could prepare a motion 'in arrest of judgement' – asking that further consideration should be given to points of law which could vitiate the conviction. But Bridgeman had been rehearsing his dread sentence, directing the butchery of the body by hanging, drawing and quartering, and decided it should now ring out on Harrison.

It was a sentence which Bridgeman would intone repeatedly over the next week. On Friday, juries convicted five former MPs, selected as unrepentant representatives of the Parliamentarians who had the impudence to judge their King.[22] Adrian Scroop had served in various parliamentary capacities – sitting with Monck and Broghill as a commissioner for Scotland, for example. John Carew, of wealth and position in Cornwall, had served both the commonwealth and the protectorate as a member of the Council of State, as had Gregory Clement. Colonel John Jones had been a Welsh MP leading troops for Parliament in England and later Ireland where, as a commissioner since 1650, he had worked closely with John Cooke. His added attraction as a scapegoat was the fact that he was related to Oliver Cromwell. Thomas Scot, the London alderman and MP, had twice fled the country to avoid royalist revenge – on the first occasion his ship was seized by pirates who robbed him and put him ashore in Hampshire. His friends subscribed for his second sea passage on a vessel which made an unscheduled landfall on Spanish territory, where he was again seized. As good luck this time would have it, the governor had been the Spanish ambassador to England during the commonwealth and had admired Scot, whom he immediately set at liberty. But on hearing of Charles II's proclamation and assuming that he could save his life by surrendering within forty days, Scot returned to England voluntarily, where he was imprisoned and now put on trial for his life. In this court, there was no chance that he would be three times lucky.

The first juror to be 'called to the book to be sworn' in Scroop's trial was none other than Sir Thomas Allen, the foreman of the jury which the previous day had convicted Harrison. Scroop made the obvious point – that those jurors who had already convicted a defendant should not be called again, but received Bridgeman's acerbic response: 'This is nothing to you.' He ruled that Scroop's attempt to explain his actions was an aggravation of his treason – a point seized upon by Lord Finch, who interjected. 'You shelter yourself under a command of the House of Commons, but let me tell you and all the world, that if the House of Commons (let it have been never so complete) had given a command, it had been a thing no ways justifiable.' Finch's own impeachment in 1642, for corruptly serving the King's interest in the ship-money case, had been by overwhelming vote in both Houses, and it was a measure of the backsliding of the time that men like Denzil Holles, who had been among the first to accuse him then, could sit comfortably beside him now, condemning former comrades to death. Scroop faced down Holles and Montague and Annesley and all the other turn-coat judges. 'If I have been misled, I am not the only one . . . I could say (although it does not become me to say) that [he looked at the bench] I see a great many faces that at this time were misled as well as myself.' The fifteen judges who had fought for Parliament, most of them now wearing the ermine robes of their very recent peerages, stared back at him unflinchingly: hypocrisy was not yet an embarrassment to public men.

Scroop was convicted after Bridgeman had told the jury that they need not bother to retire. He was pulled down into the pen, to be replaced by John Carew. The first juror called – allegedly at random, but he had been the first called in every case – was Sir Thomas Allen. After Finch's opening address, the audience began the death hum, but Carew fought bravely for the right to tell the truth about who started the war:

'I desire to have time to speak about how it was begun or else how shall I be able to make my defence? I shall declare the grounds upon which the Parliament did proceed . . .'

But the judges would not allow it: Carew could not be suffered even to mention that the King had made war on the Parliament. But some of them insisted on reliving their own roles in the old parliamentary caucuses: Arthur Annesley jumped in to condemn Carew for opposing him that notorious night in the Commons on 5 December 1648, when they debated whether the Treaty of Newport offered any grounds for peace. Carew made an objection, all the more effective for its understatement:

305

'I am a stranger to many of these things you have offered, and this is strange. You give evidence, sitting as a judge.'

Bridgeman should have silenced Annesley: instead, he launched into a pithy summation with the usual sting in its tail: 'I think you need not stir from where you are, members of the jury, but I leave that to you.' After a momentary consultation the 'guilty' verdict was delivered and Carew was hauled down to the pen, to be replaced by Thomas Scot. His trial was to be the highlight of the day and the crowd had already begun to whisper at the sight of the familiar face – and body now stooped with age – of William Lenthall, the Speaker who had once defied Charles I with a momentous claim to parliamentary privilege. Now, in an attempt to retrieve his fortune, Lenthall had come to court to destroy that very privilege. He was called as a prosecution witness to testify that the previous March, on the last day of the Long Parliament, Scot had told the House that he was proud of his part in the judging of Charles I – so proud, in fact, that he would wish it engraved on his tombstone.[23]

SCOT: You speak of words that I have uttered in Parliament. I do humbly insist on this, that I am not to answer any allegation of this nature. It is a high breach of privilege.

SOLICITOR GENERAL (FINCH): There is no privilege of Parliament for treason.

BRIDGEMAN: I would have you understand that in case a man should commit an act of treason, be it in what place so ever, there is no hiding place or sanctuary for treason.

Bridgeman ruled that MPs could be put to death for words spoken in the House of Commons; evidence of their 'traitor's heart'. There would be no privilege of free speech in Parliament until 1689, when his ruling was reversed by the Bill of Rights.

Scot pleaded that by surrendering within forty days he had earned the pardon promised by the King's proclamation. 'Pardon' was an ancient and legitimate plea, often advanced at criminal trials by defendants claiming to be beneficiaries: evidence was heard and the issue decided, as a matter of law, by the judges. But Bridgeman now played a trick on Scot, telling him that most regrettably he had raised this issue too late – it was a point of law which had to be taken before he pleaded, or not at all. This was a breath-taking ruling, for Bridgeman himself had *refused* to hear any argument – even a request for counsel – before these defendants had pleaded. He shut out a legitimate argument that should have saved the defendant's life, covering the deceit with a promise to Scot and Scroop that the warrant for their execution should not issue 'till consideration be had how far you are within the compass of that proclamation'. Bridgeman was a member of the cabal advising the King; he knew that both men had been marked down for execution, and that the promise of a pardon would in their cases be dishonoured. At the end of this long and doleful day, all five defendants were brought to the bar to hear their collective death sentence for the murder of 'a prince whom we who had the honour personally to attend knew was of such unparalleled parts and virtue'.

The prisoners trooped back to Newgate late on Friday night, to find that Thomas Harrison's execution warrant had already been issued. He was taken down to the dungeon to prepare himself for the ordeal, crying out, 'This is nothing to what Christ has undergone for me.' The five newly convicted men had no doubt that their turn would shortly come: they reproached themselves for naivety in believing the King's proclamation. Cooke listened to their accounts – he had heard the proceedings only imperfectly from the pen – and determined to take a different course. He would not disavow the regicide, but would not be caught out in 'new treason' by attempting to justify it. As he had lived by the law so he would hazard his life on its application to his case. He would respect the court, its procedures, and even its judges, and make a defence which would stand up to future scrutiny, at least among his own profession. The prosecution would have to prove he was 'instrumental' in the King's execution, so he would take his stand on the principle that a barrister has a duty to accept any brief to appear in a court in which he is entitled to practise, without suffering for the cause of those who instruct him. With this professional principle for his shield, John Cooke stepped up to the bar of the Old Bailey, at 7 a.m. on the morning of Saturday 13 October.

18

The Trial of John Cooke

Trials are not meant to begin with a joke and certainly not a joke by the defendant. 'I desire to challenge none of my jurors, other to enquire about their profession,' he said. 'I do not want to meet with any butchers just yet.' This reminder of the fate which a guilty verdict would bring amused the large audience – and annoyed Bridgeman, who later struck the remark from the official record.[1] Most of the jurors had already convicted co-defendants in the previous trials, so Cooke asked 'Because my life depends upon their indifferency, I beseech your lordship to demand of the sheriff whether any of them are pre-engaged [i.e. to the royalist cause]. I hope they are not and for that reason I have not challenged any.' Bridgeman, who knew all about the vetting that had produced ultra-loyal jurors, dissembled politely: 'Sir, the officer reads their names out of his papers. I suppose he does not pick and choose them. I would not have him, and I am sure he will not, do you any wrong in that particular.'

Finch opened the case for the prosecution. The prisoner stood at the bar

as a wicked instrument who with his own hand subscribed and exhibited a charge of high treason, a scandalous libel against our sovereign . . . he would not suffer his Majesty to speak in his defence, but said he spun out delays and asked that the charge might be taken as if he had confessed it – he pressed the court that judgement might be given against the King.

To all this the defendant had an answer, but Finch ended with an unexpected allegation: that Cooke had once said: 'The King must die and monarchy with him.' 'There in truth', said the prosecutor, 'was the treason and the cause of that fatal blow which fell upon the King.'

Cooke was nonplussed, but had no time to dwell on this new allegation. The first witness was called – James Nutley, the law student who had been his pupil at the time of the King's trial. Nutley had refreshed his memory from the transcript, and gave an accurate recitation of the course of the proceedings: the reading of Cooke's charge by the clerk and the King's responses; Cooke's eventual request – pressed several times – that the charge be taken *pro confesso*. Nutley added that on 20 January he had been in the Painted Chamber and observed the charge being formally written on parchment by a scrivener named Price: Cooke was standing in the vicinity, presumably dictating it. The scroll was shown to Nutley and he identified Cooke's signature. Finch asked: 'What discourse have you had at any time with the prisoner at the bar concerning this impeachment?' Nutley was a barrister and by now a seasoned crown witness, but either out of compassion for his old tutor or in order to minimise his own previous republican commitment, Nutley threw a life-line to the defendant:

Truly my Lord, I knew the gentleman well. I was well acquainted with him and for the satisfaction of my own conscience (for I was very tender in the business and sorry he was engaged in it) I went to him and did desire him to desist. I had discourse with him, for I was then a young student in the Temple and had a little knowledge in the laws. I desired him to consider the dangerous consequences of such a proceeding. I did it with tears in my eyes, for I had a very good respect to the gentleman for his profession's sake, being learned therein. Truly my Lord he did answer me thus. 'I acknowledge it as a very base business, but they put it upon me. I cannot avoid it, you see, they put it upon me.'

Cooke realised that Nutley could be pushed further, to give more emphasis to the fact that he had been acting under a professional duty, and could not properly have refused the brief. Although cross-examination was not allowed, he asked the court's permission to put some questions. He asked whether Nutley could recall what he (Cooke) had told him about the court's intentions in putting the King on trial. The answer was helpful:

NUTLEY: My Lords, I do remember that I often had conferences with the defendant. I desired him to desist from the business, considering the dangerous consequences of it. Truly my Lord, I do well remember that he did say he did hope they did not intend to take away the King's life. I said, 'If they go about any such thing, please use your utmost endeavour to preserve his life.' He said, 'I did labour to that purpose, but they tell me they only intend to bring him to submit to the Parliament.'

COOKE: It is said that I demanded judgment of the King's life. Mr Nutley, I ask you whether I used the words 'judgment against his life' or whether I only demanded judgment?

NUTLEY: My Lords, I cannot possibly remember to that syllable. But judgement was demanded . . . if you please give me leave to add this one word more, my Lord, I did hear him say at the time, and he showed me a paper that contained an order of the court that did direct the very words that he should use when he came to deliver the charge.

COOKE: So I was directed by those gentlemen as to the very words I should speak?

BRIDGEMAN: We are satisfied in that. The witness says that you showed him an order by which you were directed.

This was an important concession: Bridgeman accepted that Cooke was acting under instructions, and had been directed by the court to charge the King in the name of the Commons and the people of England. Nutley had volunteered that Cooke was under the impression that it was not the purpose of the proceedings to have the King sentenced to death. And as for the allegation that Cooke pressed for the court's judgment against the King, this witness left open the possibility (it was indeed a fact) that Cooke had asked the court only to deliver judgment – which might in theory have been 'not guilty' and might well (there had been a number of commissioners in favour) have been for an adjournment, so the King could make his offer to Parliament. Nutley was the first witness for the prosecution, but had been helpful to the defence in suggesting that Cooke was innocent of malice.

Other witnesses testified that Cooke had requested that the charge be taken *pro confesso*, had pressed 'very earnestly' for judgement and had complained about the King's delaying tactics. They told how the King had hit Cooke on the shoulder with his cane – clearly a memorable moment – and that the Solicitor-General looked back at him 'with a great deal of indignation'. There was nothing to show that Cooke had gone beyond his instructions or had been activated by malice in carrying them out. A soldier named Burden, whom Cooke had called as a witness in the Painted Chamber proceedings to show that the King had been an active field commander, gave evidence but this too was supportive of Cooke's defence that he had only asked the court 'to proceed according to justice'. When yet another witness agreed that Cooke's request to the court had not been for it to convict the King, but that all proceedings should be 'agreeable to justice', Bridgeman could contain himself no longer: 'Read the last article of that charge to the jury,' he snapped at the clerk.

> And John Cooke does, for the said treasons and crimes, on the behalf of the people of England, impeach Charles Stuart as a tyrant, traitor, murderer, public and implacable enemy to the Commonwealth of England, and prays that . . . judgment may be hereupon had as shall be agreeable to justice.

It was a doom-laden moment. The words 'tyrant, traitor, murderer' echoed through the courtroom, to remind the jury that Cooke had used them of a man who could not be referred to nowadays without the prefix 'blessed' or 'sacred'. Their eyes would have narrowed as they surveyed the author of these libels, the prisoner at the bar: the point about his asking only that the proceedings be 'agreeable to justice' was entirely lost. 'Mr Cooke,' said Bridgeman, doubtless with a crocodile smile, 'will you have any witness examined touching the question you last asked?' Cooke gave up: Bridgeman had terminated his best point, and with prejudice. The King's laughter in Westminster Hall, when this part of the charge was read, had returned to haunt his prosecutor.

But Cooke's own prosecutor had thus far failed to establish that he had done more than follow the instructions in his brief – to draft the charge and to present the case against the King. He had done no more than his duty as counsel retained for a fee, and there was no evidence of malice or of his 'traitor's heart'. This came from a surprise witness, one George Starkey, whose name had not been on the list of prosecution witnesses filed at the grand jury proceedings just five days before.[2] Starkey testified that he 'owed all my knowledge in the laws' to Cooke, who had tutored him at Gray's Inn 'at the beginning of the Long Parliament' – i.e. in 1641. Cooke, he claimed, was then in debt and needed to make money by teaching students. Starkey said that he had remained friendly with Cooke, who at Inn dinners had spoken so critically of Pride's Purge ('I think they are all mad') that he assumed Cooke was attending Westminster Hall out of curiosity, until hearing of his starring role as Solicitor-General. Then came the incriminating part of the testimony, about a conversation one evening during the King's trial:

> Mr Cooke came to Gray's Inn about 10 or 11 o'clock at night. I was walking in the court before my chamber with another gentleman, and did see him pass out of the house to go back again. I called after him, 'Master Cooke', upon that he turned back and met me. I took him by the hand and said, 'I hear you are up to your ears in this business.' 'No,' he said, 'I am serving the people.' 'Truly,' said I, 'I believe there are a thousand to one will not give you thanks.' He answered me – 'You will see strange things and you must wait upon God.' I did ask him, but first he said this of himself: 'He was as gracious and wise a prince as any was in the world . . .' I did by the way enquire what he thought concerning the King, whether he must suffer or not. He told me, 'He must die and monarchy must die with him.'

Cooke seemed taken completely by surprise: he asked when this alleged conversation took place – whether it was before or after the King's sentence. Starkey could not say, but thought that the chance meeting had taken place shortly before the sentencing. John Cooke denied the conversation: it had taken place, if at all, ten years previously and the witness was obviously fabricating at least some of its detail. Starkey was produced at the last minute to bolster a weak case and he made his royalist bias clear later in the day by testifying against Hugh Peters. He spoke then of living in this period with his family at Windsor and not at Gray's Inn. However, his account of the conversation did reflect Cooke's state of mind shortly after the trial, when he wrote *King Charles: His Case* – a work the prosecution did not rely upon both because it post-dated the crime, and because they did not wish to give it publicity.

Starkey's evidence had been called to prove an 'overt act', i.e. the uttering of words which proved malice, but only one witness, Starkey himself, had sworn to it. There was 'another gentleman' present and he had not been called to confirm it. Cooke naively believed the jury would be told to disregard Starkey's evidence because of the 'two witnesses' rule: he was unaware of the Serjeants' Inn meeting, at which the judges had agreed with the prosecutors to change this rule, for the very purpose of ensuring his conviction.

The prosecution case ended, and since prisoners were not at this time allowed to testify in their own defence, Cooke launched into his closing address. He began with a deliberately disingenuous tribute to his judges and to English justice: in other kingdoms, men accused of treason were 'served like John the Baptist' – i.e. summarily beheaded – but here 'I have a fair trial with judges of the law who are upon their oaths to do equal right and justice between the King and every prisoner concerning matters of life and death'. This was not an admission that his trial was fair – it was far from over at this point – but a challenge to the court, at the outset of his defence, to try him fairly.[3] This was a vain hope – he went on to remind the commissioners that they were on their honour to save his life if there was any law that would do so – blithely unaware that the judges had already changed the law. The evidence, Cooke said, did not establish that he had been 'instrumental' in the King's death and he relied upon 'the naked truth which Mr Nutley has in a great part spoken'. He had been assigned as counsel for the government, and he could not be held criminally responsible for his instructions: there was no malice or wicked intention in acting within his sphere as a barrister. He was instructed to lay the charge and to ask for judgment: this could not amount to treason, because the court was free to accept or reject his submission. His only request was that the allegations be tried 'according to justice', i.e. according to the rule of law.

A barrister, Cooke insisted, cannot be held responsible for the fate of the prisoner he prosecutes. He has no power at all, merely a duty: 'the counsellor is to make the best of his client's cause, then to leave it to the court.' He had not played any part in establishing the court and he could call many witnesses to confirm that there was not, before the sentence, any fixed intention declared by any of the judges to put Charles to death. The prosecution had to prove malice and 'that I did nothing maliciously I hope will appear in this – what I then spoke, it was for my fee. I may be called *avaricious* but not *malicious*. I hope the jury will take this into consideration: I had no power to act judicially – I was not magisterial, but ministerial.' In this role he could not have been instrumental in the King's death: 'His Majesty being a prisoner without any hand of mine, I giving advice according to what was dictated to me to bring him to that trial whereby he might have been acquitted and so set at liberty – I hope that will not be said to be instrumental.'

It was a vain hope. But calmly and logically, although at risk of his life, John Cooke was articulating for the first time what has now become the bedrock principle of the English bar: the duty of counsel to accept any brief that is offered with an appropriate fee and to make the best argument he can for his client's cause, irrespective of the danger to himself or to his reputation. Even the press seemed to understand the point: it reported the next day that Cooke 'appealed to all barristers as to whether they had not very often pleaded in a cause, where they could have wished with all their hearts that the verdict had gone against them.'[4]

Centuries later, two more celebrated (and better-connected) lawyers were to dress this argument in finer language, and win the profession's accolade for originating the 'cab rank' rule. Lord Erskine, who accepted the brief to defend Tom Paine for writing *The Rights of Man*, said 'the liberties of England are at an end' if barristers could be permitted to refuse an unpopular brief. All that Erskine lost was his retainer to advise the Prince of Wales.[5] His famous speech is never published in full because it is an epic of self-adulation, in which the barrister boasts so much about his own virtue that he omits to offer any defence of Tom Paine, who had the foresight to flee to France.

Lord Brougham, who accepted the brief in 1820 to defend Queen Caroline against the King's allegations of adultery, waxed even more portentous:

> An advocate, by the sacred duty which he owes his client, knows in the discharge of that office but one person in the world, that client and none other . . . he must not regard the alarm, the suffering, the torment, the destruction which he may bring upon any other. He must go on, reckless of the consequences . . . even if his fate it should unhappily be, to involve his country in confusion for his client's protection.[6]

Brougham, a wealthy liberal lawyer like Erskine, was appearing without any danger to himself in a case that could only advance his political career. These self-promoting whigs making high-flown statements in utter safety bear no comparison with John Cooke, a defendant clinging to the principle for his very life, defending himself in the face of hanging judges, a rigged jury and a hate-filled public gallery. By the time he began his final speech the public hangman – absent from court in the morning – had taken up his position opposite the prisoner. His rope was draped around his shoulders and his tunic was flecked with blood. He had, just an hour before, cut Thomas Harrison into four pieces.

John Cooke continued, unfrightened and unfazed – uninterrupted (it was a tribute to his advocacy that in this, alone of all the regicide trials, no judge other than Bridgeman said a word). Cooke had to answer the prosecution argument that he knew from the outset that the High Court of Justice was (as described in the Act of Oblivion) 'tyrannical and unlawful'. Cooke riposted that

> a tyrannical and unlawful court is a court *de facto* although not *de jure*. If a court be not a just and lawful court, none the less it is a court. This was a court: officers attended it, they said they had authority for counsel to be appointed and to act within his sphere and according to his instructions . . . There was, then, no other authority: authority was *de facto*, otherwise it would not have been lawful for any man to exercise a profession during such a power, and I hope that barristers might exercise their profession as well as others. I was within my sphere acting as a barrister.

Cooke had a good statutory basis for this argument. The *de facto* Act of Henry VII in 1495 was still in force, providing a defence for those who acted in accordance with established authority, even if that authority had as yet no legal basis. The provisional authority envisaged by the Act was that of a king who had not yet been crowned, or a usurper who was on the throne for the time being and possibly for a long time, but the principle applied equally to a power that had already established itself as the supreme and only power in the land. That was the reality in January 1649: the army had installed the Rump as the sole authority and with army backing it went on to govern until dissolved by Cromwell in 1653. By that time, the authority of the Commonwealth was recognised throughout Europe. As Lord Campbell, a lord chancellor in the mid-nineteenth century, observed of the Regicide prosecution:

No satisfactory answer could be given to the plea that Parliament was then *de facto* the supreme power of the state, and that it could be as little treason to act under its authority as under the authority of a usurper on the throne – which is expressly declared by the statute of Henry VII *not* to be treason, and it was miserable sophistry to which the court was obliged to resort that, as there was no one else acknowledged as the King of England, Charles II, while in exile, must be considered *de facto* as well as *de jure*.[7]

Cooke advanced other arguments. He maintained that words alone could not constitute treason, but Bridgeman countered that treacherous words were the best evidence of a traitor's heart. He urged that on true construction of the Act of Oblivion the words 'or being instrumental', in the phrase 'sentencing, signing or being instrumental' had to be construed in a temporal sense as referring to those involved in the execution, which came after the sentencing and after the signing of the death warrant. This was an ingenious grammatical construction, but Bridgeman was right this time to point out that Parliament had not intended it.[8] It was a nice legal point, of a kind that barristers can never resist taking, but it gave Finch – a robust jury advocate – the cue for a crushing retort, delivered while pointing at the prisoner: 'He that brought the axe from the Tower was not more instrumental than he.'

Cooke did make a good point that he was within the promise of the Declaration of Breda since although imprisoned in Ireland at the time, and not therefore capable of surrendering, he had petitioned to have the benefit of the declaration. Bridgeman repeated his erroneous ruling that the declaration was non-justiciable: it binds the King 'in honour and in conscience but not in point of law'. As to Starkey's evidence that he had said of the King 'He must die and monarchy must die with him' – words relied upon heavily by the prosecution in closing – Cooke argued that the 'overt act' rule required two witnesses, and Starkey's companion had not testified. Cooke was right, but the judges had secretly agreed at Serjeants' Inn to change this rule, so Bridgeman would direct the jury in due course that they should rely on Starkey's uncorroborated testimony.

John Cooke was a mild-mannered and somewhat intellectual lawyer: it was impossible for him to summon up the rhetorical devices which more knock-about counsel use to arouse jury sympathy. There was, of course, no sympathy in this court to begin with, and Cooke's defence was based on a professional ethic that was not widely understood, even among the profession of the 'long robe'. His peroration was a summary of his best arguments mixed with a crude plea that there could be no urgency about putting him to death:

> Now gentlemen of the jury, I must leave it to your consciences whether you believe that I had a hand in the King's death when I did write only what others did dictate to me and when I spoke only for my fee . . . When I was in Ireland I had an opportunity to flee and I might have done so had I thought I was guilty. My name was in his Majesty's proclamation, but I was a prisoner for four months and for that reason I could not surrender myself – I did not hide. Humane justice never punishes for expiation but only for prevention – when there is danger that the like crime may be committed again. Now all things are settled and there is no danger at all: there can never come such a case as this again. I say that I acted as a counsel and had no malicious intent. Mr Nutley bore testimony that I told him there was no intention to put his Majesty to death. I did say that I desired the court to do justice, what they decided to do was the court's act, not mine.

There must have been a tangible feeling in the courtroom, when Cooke rested his case, that he had raised real doubts about his guilt. This may be inferred from the grudging admiration in the next day's official news report. Whilst the royal propagandist – probably Henry Muddiman – notes the impossibility 'of any defence for such horrid wickedness, yet to do him (Cooke) right, we must need say, he answered as well as possible in such a foul case.'[9] But that was before the summing up.

Bridgeman called for silence: it was now time to refute a case made with skill and moderation, and which had given the judges no excuse to accuse him of further treason. Cooke's closing address had taken over an hour to deliver: the four speakers who followed were twice that length. Finch began with sarcasm: 'If this defendant could not be convicted except by evidence that would render him speechless, then they would stay for a very long time.' Cooke, he complained, had spoken like a lawyer, making the best arguments his case would bear – indeed, the prisoner was 'a lawyer of great understanding and of good parts' but 'it is a great aggravation to his crime that he who knew the law so well should so much transgress it'. Finch had no answer to Cooke's central argument that no malice could be implied from his acceptance of the brief, other than to pontificate that 'no man can have a lawful calling to pursue the life of a king and the law implies malice'. Cooke's defence was not insolent like the other defendants' but it still amounted 'with honesty and good manners, to justification of high treason'. His charge had been exhibited in the name of the people of England, but

> I hope you meet here to tell this nation and all the world that the people of England had no hand in that charge. Do but consider how this prisoner at the bar has hunted the life of the King. How he did fish out and examine evidence about whether the King set up his standard at Nottingham, whether he was at such a place and such a place. To what end is all this but with design of blood? Is it not plainly proved to you by witnesses how he did exhibit the charge, press it, aggravate it, desired it might be taken *pro confesso*, was afflicted with the delays – how angry he was when he was interrupted! What does he do at last when the thing had gone far? He speaks that which is the only truth I have yet heard from him, *He must die and monarchy must die with him* – from which event may the good Lord deliver us.

It was clever rhetoric: by convicting Cooke, the jury as representatives of the people of England would disassociate themselves from any part in the killing of Charles I. If they acquitted Cooke, they would share in his treason. To emphasise this message the Duke of York's own counsel, who represented the royal family, rose to make a final speech as well. He had no right to do so but this court was not going to stop him, and his intervention was prejudicial in the extreme to the prisoner. He warned the jury against Cooke's 'skill and cunning', and told them in terms that 'the charge, the pressing for judgment, the request for *pro confesso* – every step in this tragedy was treason'. As for his claim that 'I acted as a counsellor for my fee' – that was 'the fee that Judas had, the thirty pieces of silver, that made him hang himself'. Now the jury must hang this Judas.

This was dramatic advocacy, but it still did not meet Cooke's defence – as Wadham Wyndham, the prosecution's junior counsel (and its best lawyer) realised. Concerned that Finch's bluster had failed to nail the defendant, he jumped to his feet. 'The chief argument the prisoner shelters himself under is his profession – which gives a blast to all of us of the long robe.' Wyndham himself had betrayed his profession by his cowardly apology to Cromwell for accepting George Cony's brief, but he continued: 'a counsellor carrying himself within the compass of his profession is not answerable but if he exceeds the bounds of his profession, then so far from sheltering him it amounts to an aggravation.' What were the 'bounds' that Cooke had exceeded? Wyndham explained, correctly, that if a barrister advises how to kill a man, then he becomes accessory to the murder. Cooke, however, had been asked to advise how to end the impunity of a head of state responsible for mass-murder – although Wyndham did not think of it that way. Advising how to prosecute a king was simply beyond the imaginable bounds of any barrister's duty. 'Mr Cooke is as much a traitor as the man in the frock who did the execution.'

This was not much better than Turner or Finch: these prosecutors were having difficulty in pinning the crime of treason on their predecessor. All eyes turned to Orlando Bridgeman: could he deliver the *coup de grâce*? For the next hour and a half he unleashed a sustained and ferocious diatribe, telling the jury time and again that Cooke was guilty of high treason. There was no pretence of fairness: Bridgeman would allow no possibility of an acquittal and no possibility that the death sentence might be commuted. He purported to deal only with the evidence, but between the lines of his lengthy summation could be read the clearest belief of the King's judges – and they were all there, nodding in agreement – that John Cooke had been the evil legal genius behind the King's trial and was 'up to his neck in this business' much more than the evidence revealed. 'It appears you were privy to this before the proclamation [of the King's trial],' Bridgeman let slip at one point, indicating the court's suspicion – there was no testimony to support it – that Cooke had advised Cromwell long before his brief arrived on 10 January. Backhandedly, he saluted Cooke's qualities – 'Truly I do know myself, this gentleman to be a man of great parts in his profession.' Although the lives of Cromwell's legal grandees – Whitelocke, St John, Lenthall and the like – had all been spared, John Cooke was different: he was as clever as they, but of lowly birth, and he had a radicalism that could not be suffered, either in the legal profession or in the politics of the nation.

Cooke's radicalism derived from his passion for equal justice, a concept that men like Clarendon and Bridgeman could not comprehend. They tried to write him off as a religious fanatic – Bridgeman seized on the phrase Starkey attributed to him: 'You will see strange things, and you must wait upon God' as a means of explaining Cooke: 'These words *waiting on God* – people use them nowadays when they would do some horrid impiety, which has been the sin of too many. It is canting language,' he told the jury.[10] But Cooke was not a fanatic: he was a radical lawyer who had taken the law's promise of equal justice to its logical conclusion, by applying it to the most powerful in the land.

Bridgeman began, continued and ended by directing the jury that every separate step that Cooke had taken as prosecutor of the King – preferring the charge, requesting justice, criticising the King's delaying tactics, asking that the charge be taken *pro confesso*, and so on – was in each and every case an overt act which proved his guilt of treason. He scuppered Cooke's defence by refusing to accept that the court was a court, the prosecutor a prosecutor or the King a defendant:

> If there were nothing else in this case, that a man in a paper should call the King 'traitor, tyrant, murderer and implacable enemy' as there his words are – he delivered this paper and it was read – if this be not an overt act of imagining and compassing the King's death I do not know what an overt act is. [To Cooke] You positively demanded judgement against the blessed King . . . Mr Cooke, it is no excuse to say you hoped or believed they would not take away the King's life.

Bridgeman told the jury that Cooke's defence was no defence at all. The other defendants were impudent or ignorant: that this prisoner was a learned lawyer made his offence much worse than theirs. If counsel speaks treason from the bar on his client's instructions, he goes outside his professional duty. At the end of the day there could be no possible defence, simply because the King was unprosecutable: 'No court whatsoever could have any power over a king in a coercive way, as to his person.'[11] He drew the jury's attention to Starkey's evidence that Cooke had said of the King 'He must die and monarchy must die with him' and directed the jury to rely upon this as an overt act, although attested by only one witness – 'One witness, if you believe him, is as good as twenty witnesses because other overt acts are proved by other witnesses.'[12] The Lord Chief Baron was in no danger of correction from an appeal court, because there was no appeal. Every senior judge in the country was now on the bench of the Old Bailey, nodding as if by prearrangement with this jurisprudential ambush, plotted at Serjeants' Inn. 'If you have any more to say I will hear you, if not I must conclude to the jury [turning to them]: you hear the evidence is clear for compassing and imagining the death of the King.'

John Cooke had a little more to say, namely that if the judges were going to set aside all the acts and authorities of the Parliament 'whereby I did truly and conscientiously act, and look upon us as so many men got together without authority . . . I humbly make bold to say I have not received satisfaction in my judgment'.[13] Bridgeman was implacable – Cooke was now making his case worse by falling back on the authority of the Rump and complaining about the unfairness of the summing-up. 'Acting by the colour of that pretended authority was, so far from any extenuation, an aggravation of the treason.' Bridgeman repeated all the steps taken by Cooke as Solicitor-General, and said for the last time, shaking his head as judges do, 'If these be not overt acts of compassing and imagining the death of the King I do not know what are.'[14] He added for form's sake 'It must be left to you members of the jury' but 'I think you need not go from your bench.'

The jury, as always, took the hint. After a hurried consultation, they indicated they were agreed. The court ushers called for silence. Cooke was ordered to raise his right hand while the foreman was directed to 'Look upon the prisoner at the bar: how say you? Is he guilty of treason in manner and form as he stands indicted or not guilty?'

The foreman, Sir Jeremy Whitchcott, said: 'Guilty' and the judge said: 'Look to him, Keeper' as the warders grabbed the defendant and took him down to the pen. As the jury left their places, Sir Jeremy – a royalist barrister[15] soon to be made Baron Whitchcott for services like this – was ushered to the seats reserved for prosecution witnesses, since he was to give evidence for the crown against the next defendant, Hugh Peters.[16]

John Cooke was taken down to the pen at the back of the court, open to the chill autumn afternoon. He had lived by and for the law and now he would die by the law – as declared by judges who had changed it in order to convict him. There was no appeal: Bridgeman would deliver the death sentence later in the afternoon, as soon as Peters was convicted, although before it was pronounced Cooke would have one last brief opportunity to raise points of law. He had often inveighed against legal technicalities which set murderers free because of the misspelling of their names on court documents, and he had noticed that in the Act of Oblivion he had been referred to as 'I Cooke' – confused with the Christian name of his late father Isaac. His heavenly father having failed, could his natural father save him now? Or would he be a hypocrite to take the point? He had several hours to think about it, standing in the cold pen while Peters's trial engaged the court.

Poor Hugh Peters was not the man he once was. A manic depressive, this was, unsurprisingly, one of his days of deepest depression. He had been waiting in the pen since 7 a.m. for Cooke's trial to conclude and now, in mid-afternoon, he was dragged into the spotlight. He was sick and confused and a throat infection made him barely audible. He challenged none of the jurors although four of them had sat on Cooke's jury and the others had all by this stage been 'blooded' by having convicted at least one regicide. In his glory days as Cromwell's chaplain, Peters had been a person of influence and respect. The prosecution witnesses told of his sermons in December 1648 and January 1649, on the text *to bind their kings with chains*, when he likened Charles I to Barabbas and urged that the choice was between his death or that of the soldiers who would die in a third civil war. These sermons counted as 'overt acts', although the prosecution suggested that there was something more sinister to the preacher: he had been 'sent over' by the Puritan clergy in Virginia, allegedly to promote 'reformation' in England, but they had secretly instructed him to foment a republican revolution.

Peters's voice was so hoarse that he had to be brought closer to the judges' bench to make his denials. The prosecution had no evidence that Peters had 'compassed' the King's death, until George Starkey returned to the witness box in order providentially to provide it, just as he had against Cooke. In December 1648, he claimed he was staying at his father's house in Windsor where Henry Ireton was quartered and to which Peters frequently resorted and would say (conveniently, within young Starkey's hearing) that the King was a tyrant and the office of monarchy was dangerous when it was not useless. On one occasion, when Starkey's loyal father said a grace at mealtime with a special request that 'God Save the King', the cleric responded: 'Old gentleman, your idol will not live long.' After Starkey, there came evidence that Peters had congratulated Cooke at the close of the first day of the trial on a 'most glorious beginning of the work', and Sir Jeremy Whitchcott, who doubled both as a juror and as a prosecution witness, told his fellow jurors how Peters likened the High Court of Justice to that tribunal of the saints which would sit with the returned Jesus Christ in judgment on humankind when the world ended. In this tribunal, however, eloquence deserted Hugh Peters: his questions were feckless and his final speech almost incoherent, ending in pathos as he produced a sheet of testimonials from royalist lords whose lives or families he had saved. 'We do not question you for what good you have done, but for the evil you have done,' said Bridgeman coldly, waving them away.

Peters in his life, as in his death, alternated courage with cowardice: on this, his own day of human judgment, he seemed incapable of inciting anyone to do anything. As the evening drew on he merely shrugged as witnesses recounted how from the pulpit he had vilified the late and blessed King. Only one allegation stirred him to angry and convincing denial – that of an army porter who suggested that Peters might have been the hangman's disguised assistant. The judges were genuinely interested in solving the riddle of the executioner's identity and permitted the defendant to call Cornelius Glover, his former servant now working for the post-office. Glover swore that on the day of the King's trial Peters was 'melancholy sick, as he used to be' and remained in bed. The prosecution could not contradict Glover, now a confirmed royalist, and backed away from the allegation that Peters was involved on the scaffold – he was, after all, involved in almost everything else, as preacher, inciter, religious adviser and general busybody. Finch summed up all the occasions on which Peters had been seen consulting or heard praying for the King's trial and execution, then verbally twisted the knife that was soon to gut the prisoner.

What man could more contrive the death of the King than this miserable priest? The honour of the pulpit is to be vindicated and the death of this man will preach better than his life did. It may be a means to convert many a miserable person whom the preaching of this person has seduced, for many have come here and said they did it in the fear of the Lord and now you see who taught them. I hope you will make an example of this carnal prophet.

A 'miserable priest' he certainly was, but a 'carnal prophet'? This unkindest cut of all referred to a rumour amongst the faithful that he had been unfaithful to his wife, a rumour that Peters was most anxious to deny in his last days on earth. The jury instantly agreed on their verdict of 'guilty'. The hour was very late, daylight had disappeared from the open wall and the overhead skylight, and rows of candles illuminated the judges' bench and the clerk's table. Judges in this period would frequently sit until midnight to conclude a case and there was one further formality: to pronounce the sentence of death on both men who had been convicted this day. So John Cooke was brought up from the pen, to stand alongside Peters and receive his sentence. The clerk intoned the familiar preamble:

'John Cooke, hold up your hand. Do you have anything to say as to why the court should not pronounce judgment for you to die according to law?'

Cooke took a deep breath and made the very objection that he had so often criticised other judges for upholding – the individual excepted out of the Act of Oblivion was 'I Cooke' and not John Cooke. Bridgeman brushed the point aside. So he tried another technicality – the overt acts for which he had been convicted had not been particularised. This had been a serious defect in the indictment against all the regicides, but the judge and prosecutors had resolved at their meetings in Serjeants' Inn that the rule requiring particulars – an elemental protection for the defendant against being taken by surprise – would not apply. 'This cannot help you,' snapped Bridgeman, anxious to finish. Cooke repeated his point that he had acted professionally, but Bridgeman's patience was now at an end. 'The profession of a lawyer will not excuse treason – this has been overruled and is overruled again.' Cooke was at the end of his tether – he began to stutter out a final point – that the House of Commons had *de facto* authority – but Bridgeman shook his head. 'This is all passed and overruled.' 'Then I have no more' were John Cooke's final words in a court of law. All that was left was the sentence. The Lord Chief Baron peered down through the gloom at the two men he was to eviscerate:

I shall not need to tell you what it is to die. You are men of liberal education. You have had time, a great deal of time, to think of it and therefore I shall spare my labour of telling you about that eternity you are to enter. You know very well it is the law of this nation that no one House or even both Houses of Parliament have any coercive power over the King, much less to put him to death, and you know that the imprisoning of the King is treason. You know, both of you, this undoubted truth – the rule of law is that the King can do no wrong in the estimation of the law . . .

He then intoned the death sentence:

You shall be drawn upon a hurdle to the place of execution and there you shall be hung by the neck and being alive shall be cut down, and your privy members to be cut off, your entrails to be taken out of your body and (you living) the same to be burnt before your eyes, and your head to be cut off, your body to be divided into four quarters and your head and quarters to be disposed of at the pleasure of the King's Majesty. The Lord have mercy upon your souls.

The usher cried for the court to adjourn, ending with a loud 'God Bless King Charles'. The two condemned men, Cooke and Peters, were chained to each other and led by guards, whose torches lit the gloom, through the pen and across the street to Newgate prison.

19

A Trembling Walk with God

In Newgate on Saturday night, all the talk was of the courage of Colonel Harrison, who had been executed that morning at Charing Cross. He had gone to his death with a bravado that had astonished many of the crowd, who had thought to deride him and enjoy his humiliation. 'Where is your Good Old Cause now?' someone jeered. 'It is here,' he announced with a smile as he clamped his manacled hands to his breast, 'and I am going to seal it with my blood.' He went up the gallows ladder with a spring in his step, 'looking as cheerfully as any man could do in that condition', so Pepys, who was present, reported.[1] His scaffold speech – a ritual allowed to all traitors – exulted that he, a 'poor base vile worm' should be accounted worthy to suffer:

> I have served a good Lord and Creator; he has covered my head many times in the day of battle: by God I have leapt over a wall, by God I have run through a troop, and by God I will go through this death and He will make it easy for me. Now into thy hands, O Lord Jesus, I commit my spirit.

With these fighting words Cromwell's fine colonel jumped from the ladder, as he had jumped into the breach of castle walls: when his prancing in thin air seemed to stop, the hangman cut the rope and Harrison collapsed on to the scaffold. They picked him up and pulled their red-hot instruments out of the brazier and wrenched the bowels out of his fundament to burn them in front of his eyes which opened and with what seemed to the crowd to be superhuman strength (although it was probably a muscular spasm) he hit the hangman around the ears before doubling up and dying. Harrison's Fifth monarchy beliefs about the imminence of the second coming gave him extraordinary valour in facing death. John Carew, who shared them, told Cooke and Peters on their return to Newgate that his turn would be next, and he asked them to pray that he could share Harrison's strength. Members of his family were begging him to repent and petition for a reprieve but 'death is nothing to me, let them quarter my body none so much, God will bring all these pieces together'. It was with semi-mystical psychological boosts of this sort that the regicides occupied their minds, but the horrible reality must at moments have struck all of them with terror.

None more so than Hugh Peters, who was very far from a state of grace. He confided to Cooke his fear that he could not go through the coming ordeal without breaking down. He was the weak link among men who were well aware of the importance to the cause in England and abroad that they should die as martyrs to it without betraying fear or despair. Cooke asked the two Anglican divines sent to minister to the condemned prisoners to intercede with the King to grant Peters a stay of execution: his depressive condition made him unfit to die. The ministers agreed, although they were shocked that Cooke remained so loyal to his old friend, whom he extolled as once 'the brightest example of holiness'. How could he 'vindicate and defend this wretch', the future Archbishop of York asked the next Dean of St Paul's, as they left Newgate, shaking their heads over the object of Cooke's Christian charity.[2]

On what they knew would be their last Sabbath on earth, the convicted men were visited in Newgate by family and friends, who reported that Cooke had taken the lead in devising consoling perspectives on their plight. When one tried to comfort him with the thought that life was brief anyway, he replied, 'Why say that? This might be suitable talk if I was sick from a fever, but we must talk at a higher level now. If I had the choice, I would choose this death rather than death from fever, which is painful for days but here a man is well when he goes up the ladder and is out of all pain in a quarter of an hour.' To other visitors, he played the joker: 'We are going to heaven, and we are leaving *you* in the storm.'[3]

This may have provided some relief on a day that must otherwise have been sad beyond measure. Children visited their fathers and the prison yard resounded to their sobs. Taking one of Adrian Scroop's weeping daughters by the hand, Colonel Jones said tenderly, 'You are weeping for your father, but if he were to become King of France tomorrow, and you had to stay here, would you weep? He is going to reign with the King of Kings, in everlasting glory.' Jones meant it and may have convinced the girl. To others, he could display a talent for irony: 'The sledge that will carry me to execution is like Elijah's fiery chariot, except that it goes through Fleet Street.'

It was a busy day: the Newgate keepers were well paid by well-wishers taking their leave of men who, for all the displays of public hatred, were part of loving congregations whose members were not ashamed to visit them and report their good cheer. 'Company so exhausts me that I can write no more', said Cooke at the end of an uncharacteristically short letter to his brother-in-law. He reported his own trial in one bitter but accurate sentence: the court decided that everything done by Parliament since 1642 was treason, and they were to be the scapegoats for it. He was angry at the unfairness, but not consumed by it: if anything it rekindled the twin Puritan passions – the belief in God and in liberty – that had carried them through the revolution, and carried the revolution through. By dying like the saints in Foxe's *Book of Martyrs*, they would prove to others, and most importantly to themselves, that they were of 'the elect'. Buoyed up by their faith and in an ecstasy of anticipation, they were martyrs in waiting who did not have long to wait.

The sled came for John Carew, as he predicted, on Monday morning. The prisoners yet to be tried had already trooped past his dungeon at dawn, shouting farewells as they went to the Old Bailey. It was a cold and wet morning and the sheriff was late but Carew was smiling as his fetters and chains were removed and he could lead his guards down the Newgate steps to the sledge, a platform drawn by horses to which the prisoner, facing upwards and backwards, was tethered. Carew was cursed and spat upon as he was dragged through Ludgate, Fleet Street and the Strand to Charing Cross. It began to rain as he mounted the ladder but his final speech was defiant and his final prayer exultant, inflaming the Fifth monarchy men who had gathered around the scaffold to see him off. Their republicanism was grounded upon the simple proposition that there could be no King other than King Jesus. The barbaric execution, far from deterring regicide, in their case actually encouraged it. They went direct from the scaffold to their meeting hall in Coleman Street, and planned an armed uprising for 6 January, the anniversary of the Ordinance for the King's trial. (Some fifty Fifth Monarchy men were killed, or later executed like their heroes: an early reminder that capital punishment incites rather than deters political crime.)

Meanwhile, back in the Old Bailey, Colonel Daniel Axtell was proving the doughtiest forensic fighter of them all, thanks to his advice from a certain 'learned judge' – undoubtedly, Judge Cooke. Sunday had not been spent entirely in prayer, but also in arming Axtell for a legal battle that others had lost too easily. He had first become friendly with John Cooke in Ireland, where his administrative abilities had been recognised by Cromwell and he had been made governor of Kilkenny. He was loathed by royalists because of the avidity of his seizures of their properties in Ireland and by the Presbyterian grandees because he had presented the army's petition against their 'rotten members' back in 1648. Two of the men he had then accused of corruption were now his judges – Denzil Holles and Arthur Annesley.

Axtell was not guilty of high treason. He had, under orders from Fairfax, commanded the soldiers who kept order in Westminster Hall. He had threatened a masked lady, who had shouted from a gallery that Oliver Cromwell was a traitor, but as he rightly said, 'If a lady will talk impertinently, it is no treason to bid her hold her tongue.' He encouraged the soldiers to chant 'Justice' as the King was led away on the first day and 'Execution' when he was led away on the last, but these shouts were made after the court had risen. He had sent a troop of horse to collect Brandon, the common hangman, on the day of the King's execution, but he was still acting under Fairfax's orders. The prosecution pardoned Hercules Hunks in return for giving evidence that Axtell had urged him to sign the execution warrant, but Axtell denied it and the court refused his request that the other two witnesses be called to contradict Hunks, although Hacker was only a few yards away in the pen of the court (since he was next to be tried) and Phayre was in the Tower.[4]

General Fairfax – the regicide commander – had his true role covered up by the prosecution. He was a national hero and he had supported the restoration of Charles II when Monck met him *en route* to London. So it became a central tenet of royalist faith that all blame for the King's trial rested with Cromwell, who must therefore be assumed to have duped or detained General Fairfax. To assist this rewriting of history, Clarendon identified Lady Fairfax as the masked lady who shouted 'Nol Cromwell is a traitor!' at the King's trial. Whether the masked lady was indeed the General's wife is not at all clear: witnesses at Axtell's trial, including the owner of the gallery who sold her the ticket, did not identify her as Lady Fairfax other than by rumour.[5] Axtell, commanding the guard in the body of the court, certainly did not think the interjector was his General's wife – a woman he must have known well. He had looked up and growled, 'Who is that whore who disturbs the court?' and ordered his men to raise their muskets. They lowered them when it became apparent that there was no threat. Axtell sent Sergeant Dendy to make some enquiries at the house which led to the gallery. From a fair reading of all the evidence, Axtell did a reasonable job of keeping order in a potentially dangerous situation. The prosecution case, however, was simply that he commanded the guard which coerced the King, and on that basis alone was guilty of treason.

Axtell's defence, crafted by Cooke, was that the army in which he had served obediently throughout the King's trial was lawfully raised by Parliament in 1642, led first by the Earl of Essex and subsequently – and at all material times – by Lord General Thomas Fairfax. The Long Parliament had raised this army by vote of both Commons and Lords; it was an authority which throughout the civil war had been obeyed in England and recognised by foreign states: its leader was General Fairfax, who gave Axtell his daily orders to keep decorum in the courtroom. As Axtell put it,

> I am only charged for being an officer in the army – if that be so great a crime, I conceive I am not more guilty than the Earl of Essex or Fairfax or the Earl of Manchester or his Excellency Lord Monck who acted by the same authority . . .

At last: a defendant had stuck it to his judges, and they had no answer. Manchester and Monck, sitting on the bench in front of him, had on Bridgeman's rulings been traitors. Fairfax had been an arch-traitor, defeating and capturing the King and authorising his trial and execution. Axtell was not going along with the cover-up: he protested that he would have been cashiered for disobeying orders, and probably shot – Fairfax was a harsh disciplinarian, as his merciless executions after the Cork Bush Field and Burford mutinies had shown. But Annesley and Holles rose to his provocative mention of their own hypocrisy. Annesley, an MP excluded by Pride's Purge, shouted that the Presbyterians would have brought the nation peace by negotiating the Newport Treaty, but for Axtell's army 'whose trade it was to live by war – when they had felt too much of the sweet of war they would not suffer the people to enjoy peace'.[6] This was an outrageous allegation – the army had acted, rightly or wrongly, to prevent a third civil war, and not to enjoy the 'sweet' of further bloodshed.

Annesley was sitting as a judge, looking down at a wretched prisoner, but malice from the past rose in his gorge: 'You cannot forget that you yourself were one of the army members that came to offer accusations against the majority of the Commons, calling them "rotten members".' Denzil Holles became apoplectic at the memory: '. . . you came to the bar of the House – I think it was you yourself, Axtell – and charged eleven of us as rotten members. These men were forced away. You know your general had no commission to do this – it was a violation of your general's commission.'[7] Holles let the cat out of the bag, just for one second: General Fairfax was really to blame. There was coughing and shuffling on the bench, and Bridgeman quickly intervened to change the subject. But there was no doubt that some judges wanted Axtell convicted, not for killing the King but for accusing Holles and Annesley of corruption. Bridgeman told the jurors it was really an open-and-shut case. 'They met in a traitorous assembly about the King's death. I shall say no more: you need not I think go from the bar.' They did not.

Axtell was replaced by Colonel Hacker, who had been directed to super-vise the execution by a warrant, and had made the mistake of holding on to it as a keepsake. His wife, thinking to help her husband, handed it in to the House of Lords – just in time for it to be used to convict him. Hacker scarcely bothered to defend himself: his case was similar to that of Axtell, so there really was no point. The prosecution pardoned Colonel Tomlinson in return for evidence against Hacker, but his testimony disappointed icono-graphers who wanted to liken Charles's suffering at the hands of soldiers to that of Christ bullied by the centurians: Tomlinson said that the only incon-venience the King had suffered was that they smoked tobacco in the royal apartments. What had not been discovered, despite a lengthy search, was the warrant Hacker himself had signed appointing the executioner, and he stoutly refused to remember its addressee. Arthur Annesley and Secretary of State Morris, who were sitting as judges, had examined him in the Tower, and both were called to testify to his confession that he had appointed the two executioners and to his obviously false claim that he could not remember any names.[7] Even by the standards of this court, it was grotesque for judges to step down from the bench to give sworn evidence against the prisoner they were trying. The jury were directed to convict, which they did without bothering to deliberate.[8]

Axtell and Hacker knew the secret the government was desperate to discover: the names of the two masked men, wearing ill-fitting frocks and false grey beards, who had executed the King. The obvious candidate for axe man was Richard Brandon, the public hangman who died back in June 1649, having executed Strafford and Laud and Hamilton. He had confessed to his wife and friends that he beheaded the King. But royalists were unconvinced: their spies had heard Axtell say 'We would not employ persons of low spirits that we did not know' and rumours abounded that Cromwell, Peters, Joyce or Pride – or even John Cooke – had undertaken the momentous task, which is why Annesley and Morris had interrogated Cooke and other prisoners in the Tower. Their suspicions eventually settled upon William Hulet, a sergeant in Colonel Hewson's regiment, who was the next prisoner called up to the bar to be tried.[9]

It was at this point that a dramatic change came over the bloody assize: it briefly metamorphosed into a fair trial, of a man in whose guilt and innocence there was genuine interest and real doubt. The prosecution proved that on the day before the King's death, Colonel Hewson offered £100 and promotion to any of his officers who would act as executioner: all refused, but subsequently Hulet was promoted and Hewson would jokingly call him 'Father Grey-Beard'. This was circumstantial evidence – little more than regimental gossip. The judges allowed evidence in Hulet's defence, that Brandon had been brought to Whitehall on the morning of 30 January with his 'instruments'. Shortly after the execution, troopers delivered him to a boat which took him across the Thames and the hangman 'shook every joint of him' when asked by the boatman whether he had wielded the axe. Bridgeman summed up the conflicting evidence with scrupulous fairness and for the first and only time in these trials actually asked the jury to retire to consider their verdict. It was 'guilty' of course – the jurors were programmed to convict everyone – but the judges were unconvinced and Hulet was subsequently pardoned, in the hope that evidence might later emerge to confirm the rumours of a more notorious beheadsman.

The identity of Charles I's executioner has caused almost as much speculation as the identity of Jack the Ripper. But for those familiar with that obnoxious character the English hangman, it is inconceivable that

Brandon would have refused a duty that crowned his career. He had been born to the grisly trade and was immersed in its arcane rituals. The army brought him to Whitehall that morning because it wanted the execution to go off without a hitch: Brandon could (and did) execute it faultlessley, while a botched beheading would signify to the groundlings that 'the great business' had been wrong from the start. In case Brandon refused to go through with it, there had to be a back-up soldier trusted to take over and complete the job, and in all probability Hulet was the army understudy, the executioner's disguised assistant. His alibi (that he was under arrest at the time because he had refused scaffold duty) was not credible in light of his subsequent promotion. The axe-man performed with an expertise that could not have been attained without practice: Brandon knew to tuck the King's hair down under his cap and to bend for forgiveness. His assistant, however, behaved exactly as a soldier who hated Charles would act – grabbing the head and waving it aloft, and forgetting the traditional cry ('Behold the head of a traitor') because he had never made it before. Hacker and Axtell knew the truth and could have traded it for their lives: to protect a very ordinary soldier, they remained tight-lipped.

At Newgate that evening, the regicides were wondering which of them would be next for the scaffold. They would know soon enough: the warden had two death warrants for the morrow and he read them – first to Hugh Peters, who collapsed in despair, and then to John Cooke. They were shackled together and taken down to the dungeon, where condemned men had to spend their last night and where they were permitted to write their last letters. Freelove was a baby: she would read it years later, from a father whose love she would not remember and who would be allowed no grave at which she could mourn, but whose infamy she would bear as 'daughter of the regicide'. Puritans usually hid emotions behind Polonius-like precepts: John Cooke's last letter to his daughter was short and sweet:

My Dear Sweet Child,

Let thy name, Freelove, put thee in mind of the freelove of God in giving thee to me and thy dear mother, and know that thou art the child of one whom God counted worthy to suffer for his sake . . . I pray thee never learn any pride, but be humble and meek and courteous and wait upon God's ordinances . . . be sure to marry a man that is gracious and fears God; be sure to prefer grace before wealth and parts – for a little with the fear of God is better than great riches with an ungodly man . . . never marry without the consent of thy dear mother if she be living. In all thy actions have an eye to eternity and never do anything against the light of thy own conscience. Know that thy dear father is gone to heaven to thy dear brother and be sure so to live that by God's grace thou mayest follow after . . .

Freelove's father now had little time. Hugh Peters was more than 'melancholy sick' – he was in mortal terror. So Cooke tried to cheer him with a biblical text (Hosea 13: 14: 'I will ransom them from the power of the grave; I will redeem them from death'). When he woke, after a few hours' sleep, Cooke put on a show of jollity as he welcomed the jailer, Mr Loman, and the guards, talking of the 'angels who in a few hours will take over your office and escort me to eternity. Come brother Peters, let us knock at heaven's gates this morning.'[10] But Peters had found a different kind of spiritual consolation – a bottle containing alcoholic spirit, from which he hoped to imbibe the courage he would need for the journey to whatever gate awaited his soul: his body, he knew, would be impaled on Aldersgate.

Mary came to the prison early on Tuesday: the doors of the dungeon were open to the family before the sled arrived. She laid her head upon his bosom and sobbed uncontrollably. 'My dear lamb,' John said tenderly, 'let us not part in a shower. Here, our comforts have been mixed with a chequerwork of troubles, but in heaven all tears shall be wiped from our eyes.'[11]

Lawyers don't cry, in any event. His chains and manacles were struck off when the sheriff arrived to take him down the steps to the waiting sled. It had a pole stuck on the back, to which Thomas Harrison's severed and bloody head was attached. Cooke was strapped down backwards on the straw, so that he faced the grisly visage. Peters was placed on a separate sledge, but he looked distracted and sottish, gnawing his gloves and toying with pieces of straw.[12] It was a chill and blustery October day – so cold and wet in the pen of the Old Bailey that the prisoners waiting there petitioned the court that they might return to Newgate until called for trial. The sleds bumped over the cobbled stones – the point of this drag along Fleet Street was so that the backs of lowborn traitors should be bruised and bloodied before they arrived at the railings of Charing Cross, where the gibbet had been erected. There, a large crowd had gathered to see this double entertainment: they jeered and laughed at Hugh Peters, and called for him to go up the scaffold first, but Cooke insisted that his friend needed more time to prepare for the ordeal. With one look at the preacher, the sheriff agreed. So it was the lawyer who was taken first to the scaffold, and shown the axe and the fiery brazier in which the tongs and elongated iron corkscrews were glowing red-hot. Peters was tethered to the railings while Cooke went up a short ladder to the gallows platform. The hangman fitted the halter loosely around his neck: he was allowed a final speech and prayers before it would be tightened and he would be required to step off. With the rope around his neck and the sheriff by his side, the barrister made his final speech.[13]

He began with a short prayer, seeking God's blessing on a poor servant in 'this valley of derision', and His blessing upon England and all other nations. Then he said, 'Mr Sheriff and gentlemen, I desire to speak a few words, briefly . . .' Whenever lawyers promise to speak briefly they are not to be believed, and John Cooke spoke at great length. Conventionally, he pardoned those who had brought him to this pass, in a passage that royalist spin-doctors were later to seize upon to pretend he was penitent:

> I have no malice in my heart against any man or woman living upon the face of the earth; neither against the jury that found me guilty nor the court that passed sentence. I desire freely to forgive everyone from the bottom of my heart. Truly, I say, as to the King's Majesty, I have not any hard thoughts concerning him: my prayers shall be for him, that his throne may be upheld by truth and by mercy.

There was acid in his forgiveness, however, as he continued:

> But I must needs say, that poor we have been bought and sold by our brethren, as Joseph was. Brother has betrayed brother unto death – that scripture is in a great measure fulfilled. I desire for my own part to kiss the rod and I do desire (if it may please the King's Majesty) that no more blood may be shed after mine: it may be the Lord will put it into his own breast.

(He then indicated Peters on the scaffold below.)

Here is a poor brother coming. I am afraid that he is not fit to die at this time. I could wish that his Majesty might show some mercy.

It was a poignant moment: Cooke's compassion touched even the hack propagandist Henry Muddiman.[14] Peters, tethered to the scaffold rail, was wild-eyed and stupid, gulping at his alcohol bottle. The moment passed as the sheriff brusquely interrupted Cooke's solicitude: 'Leave that out. The King has clemency enough for everyone but his father's murderers.' Cooke took the hint. 'Then I shall proceed to say something about my profession and faith, founded upon the rock of Jesus Christ . . .' This was too much for the sheriff: there could be no divine justification for treason. 'You must not use such expressions.' Cooke replied with as much dignity as a man with a rope around his neck could muster: 'It has not been the manner of Englishmen to insult a dying man, nor even in other countries, amongst the Turks and heathens . . .'

But to avoid argument, he turned to members of his old congregation in Gray's Inn, some of whom he had spied in the crowd. Ever one for citing precedents, he referred them to two obscure verses in the Book of Philippians – the sheriff did not realise that Cooke was urging them in Bible code to keep faith in the Good Old Cause (*If I be offered upon the sacrifice and service of your faith, I joy, and rejoice with you all. For the same cause also do ye joy, and rejoice with me*).[15]

Cooke had to speak carefully. He expressed the acceptable wish that 'the Lord keep England from popery and from superstition and from profanity, and may there not be an inundation of the anti-Christ in the land'. He forgave his debtors 'those few pence that are owing to me' but then spoke of his clear conscience – at which the sheriff shook his head and told him to leave it out. Cooke turned to him angrily:

'Sir, I pray take notice. I think I am the first man to be hanged for demanding justice, therefore I hope you will not interrupt again. If you will believe the words of a dying man, let me say, as I must give account, that I have nothing lying upon my conscience.'

He then turned to his friends in the crowd: 'I have a poor wife and child – commend me to them.' He made a heartfelt plea to the King and Parliament not to forfeit his estate or the estates of the other regicides and to deal justly with the claims of his wife. He asked again that all the other condemned defendants be reprieved, and that he let his death be a 'living sacrifice' for them. He made a short motion to the court of final appeal, namely 'Jesus Christ, before whom I hope to appear'. He then turned to the sheriff: 'I have nothing else to plead. I shall speak a few words to the Lord in prayer and shall not trouble you further.'

Lawyers do not speak 'a few words', even to the Lord. But as he stood with the rope around his neck, the crowd must have felt for the loneliness of the longwinded barrister. The sheriff was used to lengthy prayers and respected a man's final address to God – he would not interrupt again. His prisoner began conventionally, asking for strength to bear the burden of suffering and hoping to be numbered amongst the elect on the great day of judgment. He was a ship about to enter harbour after a long voyage – 'I would not go back again for all the world.'

It was a coded way of saying that he had no regrets. Then, came the last words the barrister was ever to speak:

Lord, let it be well with England, hear me for my poor friends and rela-tions, for my poor wife and child, and for Ireland . . . I believe that an army of martyrs would willingly come from heaven to suffer in such a cause as this that I come here to suffer for . . . O that the Lord would grant that no more might suffer. So, dear and blessed Father, I come into the bosom of thy love, and desire to enter into that glory which is endless and boundless, through Jesus Christ.

John Cooke looked up at clouds heavy with rain, and stepped into thin air. The rope pulled tight about his neck and he briefly blacked out, but the hangman quickly cut the rope and his body crumpled on to the ground. The assistants took the tongs and pincers and one held a flaming torch. John Cooke was quickly stripped and bent over backwards, as his genitals were cut off with a sharp knife. He was held up, conscious, while they were dangled in front of his goggling eyes before the hangman threw them into a bucket. The captain of the guard, egged on by the crowd, ordered that the cowering Peters be untied and brought forward, forced to watch the disembowelling. 'Come, Mr Peters: how do you like this work?' laughed the hangman. His assistants pulled on the halter that brought the judge forward: the hangman inserted the molten knife and expertly twisted out the lining of the inner bowel: Cooke was then bent backwards again to watch as his entrails were put to the torch.

The executioner would normally at this point end the excruciating suffering by cutting out the heart but this executioner wanted Peters to observe Cooke in conscious agony for as long as possible. The stench became sickening as the yards of bowel were slowly burned – ladies clasped scented handkerchiefs to their noses as the wind carried the smell to the residential apartments overlooking the gallows. Eventually, Cooke expired: his heart was cut out and exhibited, still pumping, to the approving crowd, the executioner holding it high around the scaffold on his knife before casting it into the bucket. Then the body was beheaded in dumb show, the dead head falling at the stroke of the axe and being held aloft by an assistant shouting: 'Behold, the head of a traitor!' It was thrown in a separate bucket (the King had plans for this head) and then the body, laid out on a trestle, was expertly chopped with a cleaver into four pieces – lengthways and then horizontally – to provide four 'quarters' – two arms and two legs each with a torso base, for impalement on the spikes of the city gatehouse.

Charles II was in no mood to show the mercy that Cooke had beseeched in his dying speech. He was there, says John Evelyn, and Cooke may even have caught sight of him as he pleaded for the lives of Peters and his fellow prisoners.[16] The crowd was already baying for Hugh Peters. But now, according to some reports, a minor miracle occurred: the preacher summoned up the mental capacity to face the ordeal, inspired by his friend's courage and by the bestiality of the executioners. He turned to the sheriff – 'You have here slain one of the servants of God before my eyes, to terrify me, but God has given me strength' – and he went up the ladder unaided. He said a few inaudible words in prayer, and was seen to smile as he stepped off the scaffold.[17]

Meanwhile, back at the Old Bailey, it was mop-up time. A change had come over the proceedings, now that ten regicides had been convicted and were in the process of execution: those remaining were mainly MPs who had surrendered in reliance upon the King's proclamation, and the court now invited them to plead guilty on the promise that executions would be suspended until a further order by Parliament. Colonel Harvey, who had opposed the King's execution, was permitted to call a witness – a Presbyterian minister – who confirmed his opposition and the court promised to pass on to the King his petition for mercy 'on behalf of myself, my wife and thirteen children'. John Downes made a similar claim, although the prosecutor sarcastically remarked that he had none the less signed the death warrant and asked the court to cut short his self-pitying plea in mitigation. It was more congenial for judges to hear defendants confess and apologise, with a short statement that they had been 'over awed' by Cromwell. Even more acceptable was the demoralised blubbering of George Fleetwood, one of Cromwell's briefly despotic Major Generals, who was the only defendant to cry.

One prisoner who refused the plea-bargain was the irrepressible Harry Marten.[18] His defence was that he had acted unmaliciously, to which Finch replied that he would prove Marten acted merrily. 'That does not imply malice,' the defendant rejoined, and listened with equanimity to the story of his face-painting jest with Cromwell as they signed the warrant. Marten adopted a light touch: accused of being an incorrigible regicide, he said that on the contrary, he would wish every drop of Charles I's blood were back in his body if only a similar miracle could restore the bodies of all the Englishmen slain during the civil wars. As for the purged House of Commons, the court might not think it a lawful body but everyone else did, at home and abroad. He adopted Cooke's argument that its *de facto* authority was legitimated by the statute of Henry VII. And anyway – a novel and interesting point, this: he had not been involved in killing the King, because Charles was not King at the time – he had been a non-monarch, indeed a prisoner, ever since his surrender to the Scots. Now all Henry Marten wished for was a peaceful life, and he was very happy to be reigned over by Charles II, who had 'the best title under heaven' because he had been invited to take it up by Parliament, the true representative of the people of England.

Marten was an extraordinary man. The first republican and the only agnostic among God-obsessed public men, now, it seemed, he had become a loyal constitutional monarchist. Finch smelled a rat: 'He has accepted the King, but thinks his title comes from acknowledgement by the people – and anyone could obtain that sort of title!' Marten refused to repent, and despite conviction for his key role in the King's trial he escaped the hangman. As a true humanitarian he had opposed severe punishments for cavaliers when he was in power, and so they spared his life, allowing him to spend the rest of it in Chepstow Prison.

Four more of the convicted regicides were 'turned off' (the official euphemism) at a public bloodbath at Charing Cross on the following day. On this occasion, however, the crowd was unsettled and seemed sympathetic. The sheriff, who had been admonished for allowing Cooke and Harrison too much freedom of final speech, was booed when he intervened to stop Tom Scot's explanation that he joined the parliamentary cause 'because I saw liberties and religion in danger, I saw the approaches of popery . . .' Scot upbraided the sheriff: 'I shall say no more but this, that it is a very mean and bad cause that will not hear the words of a dying man.' He then launched into an extremely long prayer in which he managed to incorporate all the points he had intended to make in his speech – namely that he had managed to escape to Europe, but God had called him back to suffer for His sake in a cause for which he was entirely unrepentant. The sheriff interrupted again, and the crowd became angry – it was verging on blasphemy to stop a dying man's final prayer. It was noticed, too, that the hangman was in some distress: he could only get through his grisly task by swigging from a bottle of alcohol passed up to him on the ladder. Colonel Jones made a modest speech, and his last prayer was short and dignified, for which he was sincerely thanked by the unhappy sheriff. Colonel Scroop, the last to be disembowelled, gave a powerful oration, urging the crowd to leave judgment to God – with whom he seemed so much at ease that his dying agonies were received with more tears than jeers.

The next day, to everyone's surprise, there were no executions. Samuel Pepys, his appetite whetted by watching the execution of Thomas Harrison, went early to Newgate to observe the expected exit of two more of Cromwell's brave colonels, Axtell and Hacker, but was told they had been reprieved for a day.[19] In fact, the government was having second thoughts: the courage of the 'black regicides' in bearing the cruellest death the state could devise was the talk of the town. Comparisons were being made with the Anglican saints who defied bloody Queen Mary. Harrison had set a noble example and Scot and Cooke in particular had made memorable ends, if in the latter's case a most malodorous one. That gave rise to another, very practical, reason for postponement.

In the words of a contemporary report, after the execution of Cooke and Peters on Tuesday, 'The stench of their burnt bowels had so putrefied the air, as the inhabitants thereabouts petitioned his majesty that there might be no more executed in that place'.[20] Charing Cross, chosen as the place of execution so that the regicides would gaze their last down Whitehall to the Banqueting House, the scene of their crime, was overlooked by residential buildings. The residents who complained were well connected, and the executions of Axtell and Hacker were delayed until arrangements could be made to hang them at Tyburn (near modern-day Marble Arch). It was ironic that John Cooke, whose proposals for more humane administration of justice were so rarely implemented during his own life, should achieve by the barbaric manner of his death this early example of environmental law reform.

On Thursday, the King met his advisers to decide what to do with the dead regicides – eight of them, including Cooke, were now in five pieces (four 'quarters' and a head) placed in storage to await the royal command. The bodyparts had been thrown into buckets and paraded through the city on the sled, to delight royalists like John Evelyn: 'I saw not their execution, but met their quarters, mangled, and cut, and reeking, as they were brought from the gallows in baskets on the hurdle. Oh, the miraculous providence of God!'[21] Their hearts and privates, having been displayed triumphantly to the mob, had no further use: they were tossed into a bucket and later fed to stray dogs at Aldersgate. But the King spent some little time considering how to display their remains to his best advantage: he chose the head of John Cooke, as the man responsible for the trial, and Thomas Harrison, who had conveyed the King to it, as those most appropriate for public opprobrium. He personally ordered that both heads should be fastened onto poles which were fixed above the entrance at the north end of Westminster Hall. The head of Hugh Peters was in similar fashion exhibited on London Bridge.[22] Their quarters were impaled on spikes at the four gates into the city along with those of the other regicides.

The King's 'commands' were speedily implemented: two days later Pepys 'saw the limbs of some of our new traitors set upon Aldersgate, which was a sad sight to see' – even for a man who that morning 'going down into my cellar put my foot into a great heap of turds',[23] a common enough occurrence in this insanitary city. The following day – Sunday – Pepys attended a sermon followed by lunch with his boss Montague (now Lord Sandwich) who had been in a 'melancholy humour' all week – understandably, since he had spent it sitting on the bench at the Old Bailey while Bridgeman dispatched men he had fought alongside at Naseby and Marston Moor. (Montague never said a word throughout the trials, and the experience sent him into a depression from which he never recovered his religious faith.) Pepys went on to Westminster Abbey where he met some friends from the office and, in these newly liberated times, went with them on an extended pub-crawl. On his way to The Crown in Palace Yard, he stopped to inspect a friend's new home and was taken to see the view from its turret. It over-looked Westminster Hall and – lo and behold – 'there is Cooke's head set up for a traitor, and Harrison's on the other side. From here I could see them plainly, as also a very fair prospect about London.'[24] This is the last recorded sighting of John Cooke: his head mounted above the great gate of the hall where he had once demanded justice on the head of state.

20

Long Live the King

John Cooke had been put to death for daring to prosecute the King. Many men in the country had been guilty of treason, as defined by Bridgeman, for taking up arms against Charles I and thereafter adhering to forms of government which forcibly excluded Charles II. The Act of Indemnity and Oblivion bestowed a blanket amnesty: the new regime would protect and even elevate those who had turned their coats in time. This indulgence was necessary to smooth the Restoration and to encourage future obedience. But the Act of Oblivion was an act of expediency, not of reconciliation. The royalists could never forget and could only selectively forgive those who had deprived them of their power and perquisites, of their happiness and hereditaments, for eighteen long years, in which they had at first been cooped up at Oxford and then forced to choose between lonely exile and sullen submission to modestly bred colonels and lawyers and preachers. The regicide trial served as an outlet for this deep-seated desire for vengeance (a motive masked by its legal formalities) and as a means of deterring any future assault on the prerogatives of the monarch.

Soon the King and his advisers became concerned at signs that the exercise was turning counterproductive.[1] They decided, after the executions of Axtell and Hacker, to bring no more regicides to the public scaffold for the time being. Axtell had been popular for rounding up Catholics responsible for the massacres in Ireland, and Hacker moved many to tears by his short but dignified speech, made with the rope around his neck, explaining that

343

he joined the parliamentary cause because he believed it to be right and that his conscience was clear – as he went to a higher court: 'I do not doubt but to have the sentence reversed.' The two men had stood, in Tyburn fashion, on a horse-drawn cart rather than a scaffold: when the Sheriff gave the signal for it to move off from under them the driver at first refused, saying that he would rather forfeit his cart and horse than have a hand in hanging such men. When Tench, the carpenter who had nailed the tethering posts to the King's scaffold, was apprehended at the end of November he was secretly tried and immediately beheaded: although patently innocent of treason, he was guilty in royalist eyes of a crime tantamount to sacrilege.[2] In January, fifteen survivors of the Fifth monarchy rebellion were hurriedly hanged, and their heads were impaled on the spikes of the gate at London Bridge to keep Hugh Peters company. Their quarters, boiled at Newgate, were impaled upon other gates to the city alongside the carved-up carcasses of the regicides.

The desire for vengeance was still unsatiated. The decomposed bodies of Bradshawe, Cromwell and Ireton were dug up from their graves on 30 January 1661 (the anniversary of the King's execution) and hanged at Tyburn. This pantomime was carried out in front of an enormous crowd – Pepys noted that the ladies of the court were all in attendance.[3] The bodies were first taken to the Old Bailey, where one of the King's judges solemnly condemned the corpses, still in their shrouds, propped up against the bar. They were then strapped to sledges and dragged through the streets to the gallows. 'The curses of the people went along with them', reported Wharton, the astrologer who had defamed Cooke in 1649 but who was now Sir George, the respected correspondent for *Mercurius Publicus*, the King's newspaper. 'When the three carcasses were at Tyburn they were pulled out of their coffins and hanged at the several angles of that triple tree, till the sun was set, after which they were taken down and their heads cut off, their loathsome trunks thrown into a deep hole under the gallows.'[4]

This ceremonial desecration took place after a morning spent in 'solemn fasting sermons and prayers at every parish church', singing newly composed psalms to the glory of kings and bishops:

> Angels look down, and joy to see
> Like that above, a monarchy.[5]

It was followed by macabre exhumations of Parliament's chief heroes: the skeletons of John Pym; of Admiral Blake who had died in the course of his great naval victory over the Dutch; of Colonel Dean, killed while helping Blake famously to defeat Tromp back in 1652; of Thomas May, the Parliamentary historian; of William Strode, one of the 'gang of Five' MPs who had defied Charles I; of Cooke's co-counsel Isaac Dorislaus; and of all the commonwealth colonels and admirals and MPs and preachers whose bones could be uprooted by frenzied cavaliers. Even, and most viciously, those of Cromwell's mother and daughter. The carcasses were briefly exhibited to ghoulish crowds and then thrown into a common pit in the yard of St Margaret's church at Westminster.[6] In this fashion did the sovereign, in the first year of his Restoration, seek to bury in a mass grave all memory of the sovereignty of Parliament. The King ordered the hangman to set the several heads of Cromwell, Bradshawe and Ireton upon poles, to be erected on top of Westminster Hall alongside the heads of Cooke and Harrison.

Having wreaked this vengeance on the dead, the King's men turned to hunt down the living – those regicides who had escaped to friendlier countries. Some disappeared, and had to be hanged in effigy (Pepys noticed a portrait of Colonel Hewson hanging on a gallows at Cheapside). Colonel Okey reached safety in the Low Countries, and obtained a personal assurance from the English ambassador to Holland that he and Colonel Barkstead would be untroubled if they made a visit to The Hague. Since this ambassador, George Downing, had once been a fervently republican chaplain to Okey's regiment and owed his advancement as MP and diplomat largely to the colonel, they felt safe in accepting his word. But Downing, with a treachery unparalleled even in these times, burst through their door with an armed force and captured them as they were dining with fellow regicide Miles Corbet. In 1662 the English government prevailed upon the Dutch to ignore international law and repatriate all three political refugees. Their trial was a formality, for all surviving regicides had been 'outlawed' by Act of Parliament: once positively identified, they were taken directly to the gallows. To the government's dismay they were accompanied by an army of friends and supporters, some of whom had to be dragged off the fatal cart before it could be drawn away to leave the three dangling. Corbet had made a memorable speech, explaining that in the Commons he had opposed putting the King on trial but had been so convinced by the evidence that he voted in favour of the sentence. He added, pointedly, that the 'immoralities, lewdness and corruption' encouraged by the Restoration 'were no inconsiderable justification of the proceedings against Charles I'.[7] Later, when it was learnt that pieces of Okey's mangled body had been released to his family for burial, an estimated 20,000 well-wishers turned up for the funeral – so many that the sheriff seized the coffin and had it buried by night in the safety of the Tower.

After this, it became state policy to employ assassins to hunt down the fugitives. In 1664 at Lausanne they murdered John Lisle. He was a master of the Middle Temple who had assisted Bradshawe at the King's trial and had himself presided over the High Court of Justice which on his casting vote had acquitted the royalist recruiter John (now Baron) Mordaunt. The Swiss cantonal governments, unlike the perfidious Dutch, genuinely welcomed Protestant asylum-seekers: they stepped up protection of Ludlow, Broughton (the clerk who had read out Cooke's charge), Phelps, Love and Cawley, who in due course died in their beds at Vevey, beside the serene shore of Lake Geneva. There St Martin's church continues to afford their bodies the dignity and commemoration denied by their own country.[8]

Regicides who had taken ship for the American colonies could receive no official protection, although many family members sought refuge there and were well looked after. (Thomas Harrison's genes, for example, were transmitted to the eighth, ninth and twenty-third Presidents of the United States.) Colonels Goffe and Whaley were sympathetically received by the people of Boston, where they worshipped openly and attended civic functions. When a local loyalist accused them as killers of the King, the magistrates showed whose side they were on: they arrested the accuser. But such tolerance in the King's dominions could not be suffered for long: warrants were issued for their arrest and in 1664 commissioners arrived from London to take them into custody. So they headed for the hills, hiding in a cave and then living for many years in concealment outside the town of Hadley, a hundred miles from Boston. In 1675 Hadley became the target for a massed Indian attack: surrounded and outnumbered, its citizens were confused and in despair, until

suddenly a grave elderly person appeared in their midst, in his mien and dress differing from the rest of the people. He not only encouraged them to defend themselves, but put himself at their head, rallied, instructed and led them on to encounter the enemy, who by this means were repulsed. As suddenly, the deliverer of Hadley disappeared – the people utterly unable to account for this strange phenomenon.[9]

Colonel Goffe, so legend has it, had taught them the tactics of the New Model Army – as effective against arrows and tomahawks as they had proven against Prince Rupert's cavalry.

Some of the better-connected regicide supporters were permitted to purchase their pardons. John Milton had done as much to justify the King's trial as Cooke and Peters; imprisoned in October 1660, he was saved by the intercession of his barrister brother, a close friend of the Duke of York, and by royalist masque-master William Davenant, reputedly William Shakespeare's illegitimate son, against the advice of Heneage Finch, who said that the poet 'deserved hanging'.[10] Clarendon was unconcerned about coffee-house intellectuals and he spared James Harrington, author of *Oceana*, the blueprint for a British republic, and the members of his Rota Club. The real danger, he brooded, would come from men of practical genius, especially Lambert and Vane – both under secure imprisonment. His problem in taking their lives was that the Parliament had petitioned the King in a merciful moment in mid-1660 to spare them and he had personally reported to the House of Lords that the King had assented to this request. It would be an astounding breach of faith to renege on that promise, but the courage Clarendon had displayed over his long exile was replaced by perfidy when in power. Besides, his own daughter had married the King's brother, James, the heir to the throne, and he was determined to protect his royal grand-paternity. In April 1662, Vane and Lambert were brought to trial. Lambert, a general who always knew when he was beaten, threw himself on the mercy of the court. He was locked away, in solitary confinement in island prisons where, over the twenty-one years until his death, the draftsman of England's first and only constitution slowly lost his mind. Sir Harry Vane, however, was of a different metal.

Vane had not been a regicide – on the contrary, he had firmly opposed both Pride's Purge and the King's execution, and had publicly broken with Cromwell over his dissolution of the Rump. (Vane was on his feet at the moment when Cromwell brought the House down and had suffered his unfair but immortal rebuke: 'O Sir Henry Vane! Sir Henry Vane! The Lord deliver me from Sir Henry Vane!') Understandably, he had held no office during the protectorate, preferring to write about God and republicanism, and to campaign for what he was the first to term 'the Good Old Cause'. He had enjoyed an illustrious career, beginning with his governorship of Massachusetts and then his election to the Long Parliament, in which he had produced the evidence that secured Strafford's conviction and later played whip to the Independent group of MPs, outwitting the Presbyterian faction under Holles, whose impeachment he had been the first to move. He returned to parliamentary duties just a few hours after the King's execution and served the commonwealth as its most formidable administrator – his control of naval business was the key to Blake's triumphs over the Dutch. His return to power in 1659 – he was first a leader of the Rump and then recruited by Fleetwood to the short-lived Committee of Safety – showed that he was the best man left alive to command the allegiance of all the anti-Stuart factions. So Clarendon decided that he had to die, irrespective of the King's promise to Parliament.

The problem was how to convict a man who had not in any way coerced Charles I. For treason to be committed against a king, that monarch had to be in actual possession of the crown and not merely entitled to it. But the unprincipled Restoration judges ruled that Charles II became King the moment his father's neck was severed and all who had supported the republic thereafter were traitors. The ingenious Judge Wyndham (the smart junior prosecutor of Cooke, now elevated to the bench) decided that every Parliament dissolved automatically on the death of the monarch and therefore nothing done or spoken by members of any Parliament since 30 January 1649 could be protected by privilege or provide a defence to those who had obeyed its orders for 'keeping out' the new King.

Vane was popular and to obtain his conviction required another major exercise in jury manipulation. The prosecution was horrified to find on the list of names for the first jury panel a number of political moderates, so they directed the sheriff to summon a new panel composed of 'vetted' royalists. Vane was refused time to summon his witnesses: he was told that the jury 'were to be kept without meat, drink, fire or candle' until their verdict, so no delay could be countenanced. Even so, the jury took a record half-hour before all its members would agree to a 'guilty' verdict, and that was only after the Solicitor-General told them that 'the prisoner must be sacrificed for the nation'. Charles, on the principle that the safety of the King was the supreme law, ignored his parliamentary promise: 'certainly Vane is too dangerous a man to let live if we can honestly put him out of the way', he wrote to Clarendon.[11] Vane was dishonestly put out of the way, by an execution which served as a doubly symbolic whirligig of royalist revenge: it took place on Tower Hill (the place of Strafford's death) and on the anniversary of the battle of Naseby. Vane wore a fine black suit and a scarlet waistcoat for his last public appearance, and manifested contempt for the King and his judges throughout the ordeal.

In other cases in 1662, these pliant judges declared that it was treason merely to attend a meeting which discussed how to revert to republican government,[12] and the crime of misprision (covering-up) of treason not to report any rumour of republican action to the Council of State or the nearest Justice of the Peace.[13] To underline the illegality of republicanism the statutes for the trial of Charles I and for the commonwealth were solemnly burned by the common hangman in Westminster Hall, while the courts were in session. There were regular humiliation rituals for public enjoyment, as remaining regicides were brought from the Tower for mock executions at Tyburn, then paraded to Parliament to plead for their lives. The cavaliers court-martialled at Colchester, Lucas and Lisle, were given lavish state funerals, while Cooke's Scots equivalent, the lawyer Archibald Johnston who had drafted the Solemn League and Covenant, was 'hung high' on a twenty-two-foot gibbet.[14]

Clarendon wanted to keep republican diehards in prison indefinitely, but Magna Carta endowed everyone in England with the right to challenge the legality of his detention by habeas corpus. So Clarendon hit on a devious plan: he *would* keep the 'enemy combatants' in custody for ever, but not in England – instead, on offshore islands like Jersey and the Isle of Man. Clarendon's device was regarded as despicable at the time – it was one of the reasons for his dismissal, and it led Parliament in 1679 to pass the Habeas Corpus Act, which gave 'the great writ' extra-territorial affect. Centuries later, the Bush administration followed Clarendon's thinking and established Guantanamo Bay. In 2004 the US Supreme Court drew on shared precedents from the seventeenth century and applied the 1679 Act to insist upon due process for detainees.[15]

All this while, John Cooke's head remained on Westminster Hall. The starlings had plucked through the embalmed flesh of his cheeks, their deposits on his skull giving him, viewed from a distance, the white cap always worn by solicitors in court. The skeletal stretch of his mouth had not, however, stopped talking. Four editions of an underground publication, *Speeches and Prayers of the Regicides*, in which his letters and scaffold address featured prominently, surreptitiously circulated among the faithful at prayer meetings and in taverns. The royalist regime had instituted a strict censorship: its official newspaper, *Mercurius Publicus*, had not reported the defiant speeches and prayers from the scaffold. Now Roger L'Estrange, 'surveyor of the press' (a witch-finder General with powers to seize unlicensed presses and arrest dissident journalists and printers) went after John Cooke's posthumous publishers.

Meanwhile, a licensed transcript of the *Trials of the Black Regicides*, edited by Bridgeman himself, with the assistance of Finch's notes, was rushed out to satisfy readers about the legality of the proceedings.[16] It declared itself as *An exact and most impartial account of the murtherers of his late sacred majesty* and was anything but impartial (the title page promised *a summary of the dark and horrid decrees of those caballists, preparatory to that Hellish act*). Nor was it exact. Sections of Cooke's speech were omitted[17] and there were many implausible promises of fair play attributed to Bridgeman and probably inserted by the editor – Bridgeman himself.[18] Its most curious omission was that it did not report the speeches and prayers of the regicides on the scaffold, such speeches being at the time routinely appended to accounts of the trials of traitors. The reason provided was wholly unconvincing: '. . . as they were made in a crowd and therefore not possible to be taken exactly, so it was thought fit rather to say nothing than to give an untrue account thereof: choosing rather to appear lame, than to be supported with imperfect assistances.' Here, Bridgeman protested too much. The only reason why 'it was thought fit rather to say nothing' was because to say anything about the bravery of these dying men would give too much credence to their cause.

Suspected publishers of the *Speeches and Prayers of the Regicides* were arrested after a thorough investigation by L'Estrange: they were held in prison for many months before being brought to trial at the Old Bailey in 1663, charged with sedition. The presiding judge was Hyde, Clarendon's cousin, who had been on the bench at Cooke's trial and who was much less skilled than Bridgeman at hiding his bias. 'Tie him up, executioner!' he roared as the first guilty verdict was brought down. His sentencing homily was short: 'I speak it from my soul – I think we have the greatest happiness in the world under so gracious and good a king. I shall not waste time in preparing you for death – I see a grave person whose office it is [the hangman, as usual, stood in front of the prisoner] and I leave it to him.' 'I humbly beg mercy,' said the convicted printer. 'I am a poor man and have three children. I never read a word of it. I most humbly beg your Lordship to intercede for me.' To which the judge replied. 'I would not intercede for my own father in this case, if he were still alive.'[19]

The most seditious passages singled out by the prosecution were taken from a letter Cooke wrote from the Tower ('the cause, for which I am in bonds, is as good as ever it was . . .') and his final speech from the scaffold. Thomas Brewster, a bookseller, made the best defence he could in the circumstances:

BREWSTER: I did not do it maliciously or with any design against the government.

LORD HYDE: The thing speaks for itself.

BREWSTER: Booksellers do not usually read what they sell.

HYDE: Have you any more? If you have, say it.

BREWSTER: My Lord, these are the sayings of dying men, commonly printed without opposition.

HYDE: Never!

BREWSTER: I can instance many. The bookseller only cares about getting his penny. This book declares to the world that as they lived such desperate lives, so they died – so it might show the world the justice of their punishment and provide a benefit rather than sedition.

Hyde was immune to the bookseller's argument for free speech. He was, however, determined to vilify Justice Cooke in his summing up:

Such a barbarous transcendent wretch that murdered his prince, without the least colour of justice! To declare that he 'rejoiced in his bonds' and that 'the martyrs would willingly come from heaven to suffer for it' – horrid blasphemy! What can you have more to encourage and incite the people to the killing of kings and murdering their lawful prince! To publish it all over England – this is to fill all the king's subjects with the justification of that horrid murder. I will be so bold to say, not so horrid a villainy has been done upon the face of the earth since the crucifying of our saviour. To print and publish this is sedition . . . If men would be so vile to be as wicked at their deaths as they had been in their lives . . . is that a justification to publish them because they are the words of a dying man? God forbid.[20]

The bookseller was duly found guilty, although the jurors took a long time and were obviously unhappy. Hyde sentenced Brewster to the pillory and then to 'imprisonment at the King's pleasure' (he died there a few months later)[21] and warned that it was an offence 'to publish that which is a reproach to the King, to his government, to the church, nay to a particular person'. The King's judges had now refashioned the law of sedition as well as that of treason to eradicate any favourable memory of those who had fought against royal absolutism. For the next three decades, it was impossible to display any sympathy for the regicides – it was dangerous even to have possession of their works. So far as the law could manage, they were to be cast down the memory hole of English history.

The case of Brewster the bookseller was significant for John Cooke's memory in this respect: the prosecution did not allege that his 'letter from the Tower' in *Speeches and Prayers* was a forgery, or that the booklet gave an inaccurate account of his speech from the scaffold. Given that the government blamed the publication for inciting rebellion, this would certainly have been its case if the indefatigable L'Estrange had uncovered any evidence of fabrication. It may therefore be assumed that John Cooke went to his death much as this publication depicted, steadfast in the belief that he had served the will of God and the cause of liberty. He died as he had lived, the quintessential 'commonwealthsman', who 'fought for the public good, and would have enfranchised the people and secured the welfare of the whole groaning creation, if the nation had not more delighted in servitude than in freedom'. In these words, Cooke wrote the epitaph for the lawyers and the colonels, the Puritans and the preachers who had dared to act on the belief that no man was above the law.

John Cooke's final prayers had been for his wife and child. The intensity of Mary's emotions and the extent of her sufferings over John's horrible death can only be imagined. On the scaffold his heartfelt plea was that they should not be dispossessed of his small estate, over which royalist vultures like the Dean of Cork had been hovering for some months. But notwithstanding the precedents to which he referred – the commonwealth's legislation permitted cavaliers to keep much of their property – all possessions of a traitor were forfeit to the King and this rule was now applied with full force. Charles II found that regicide land came in very useful as a means of rewarding those who had served his family in and out of office. The Dean was not in that category, so Cooke's land and possessions were given by the King personally to Sir George Lane, as a reward for clerking his father's privy council and for serving the loyalist cause in Ireland with Ormonde.[22] Cooke's property was not extensive but it was gone from Mary, and from Freelove, for ever.[23] They were not permitted to mourn in London – when Cooke's quarters were eventually taken down from Aldersgate they were flung into the common grave in St Margaret's church, behind Westminster Abbey. The law of treason was designed to ensure that nothing remained of a traitor – not even his remains.

Freelove grew up in the enfolding protection of her people – the people of God – in Northampton, and in 1678 she married John Gunthorpe, a London goldsmith, and emigrated to Antigua. There, Gunthorpe flourished as Provost Marshall and an MP in the island's legislature, although Freelove's paternity did not go unremarked by his enemies. She bore him sons who continued his example of prosperity and public duty – her line of descendants in due course would include a Chief Justice (of Trinidad) and even a Bishop, and is now scattered prolifically, mainly in the US.

Vane's death, and the wasting away of the republic's leaders in far-flung fortresses, caused the Good Old Cause to grow older but in some respects better: the catastrophic defeat by the Dutch in 1667, as a result of the corruption and incompetence that flourished in the navy under Monck and Montague, made people yearn for the days when it was in the safe hands of Vane and Blake. That national disgrace came hard on the heels of the great plague that devastated the country and the great fire that burned down half of London – including Hicks' Hall, St Bride's church and the Sessions House at the Old Bailey. Those who had seen Marston Moor and Naseby as God's judgment on monarchy now believed they were suffering for the sin of restoring it. From this point the English crown takes on an abiding characteristic, as a subject of public amusement. It was with England's defeat in the second Dutch war that rudeness about the royals became commonplace:

> As Nero once, with harp in hand surveyed
> His flaming Rome, and, as that burned, he played,
> So our great prince, when the Dutch fleet arrived,
> Saw his ships burn and, as they burned, he swived.
> So kind he was in our extremist need,
> He would those flames extinguish with his seed.[24]

It was in 1667 too that judges lost their independence, becoming once more subject to dismissal at royal pleasure. Malign creatures of the King like

Jeffreys and Scroggs slimed their way onto the bench after Clarendon was banished – the victim of a plot which involved one of the King's mistresses. But it would take another two decades for England to rid itself of Stuart Kings, a release that owed more to fears of their Catholicism than to the heady Puritan combination of God and liberty that had triumphed in 1649. The new protagonists were Whigs and Tories, although the regicide flame was briefly held aloft by Algernon Sidney, who in his youth had refused Cromwell's invitation to join the High Court of Justice but now described its sentence on Charles I as 'the justiest and bravest action that ever was done in England'. He revered Cooke, and suffered his own treason trial in 1683. The main evidence against him was some personal jottings found in a notebook seized from his study: he argued that it was 'the right of mankind to write in their closets what they please for their own memory and so no man can be answerable for it unless they publish it'[25] but Jeffreys ruled that they proved his traitor's heart. Sidney was duly convicted and disembowelled, providing the crowd at his execution with a brave performance dedicated to his heroes, the regicide martyrs.

Jeffreys went on to run the 'bloody assizes' after Monmouth's attempted rising in 1685, where the vilest of his many vile deeds was to put to death Alice Lisle – John Lisle's seventy-year-old deaf widow – merely for feeding a starving soldier.[26] By this time, Lambert had died in prison and Henry Marten in poverty. Milton, eyeless in Gaza, left in his last work – *Samson Agonistes* – coded references to his own agony about the regicide trials of 1660 – 'the unjust tribunals, under change of times' which had left its victims' carcasses 'to dogs and fowls a prey'. But there was one regicide still alive to welcome the 'glorious revolution' of 1689. Edmund Ludlow, at the age of seventy-three, returned to London for a few months, but was such a magnet for 'old rebels and republicans'[27] that the House of Commons revived his attainder for the murder of Charles I and once again he was forced to flee to Geneva. The inability to tolerate one of the greatest living Englishmen was an apt comment on the constitutional milksoppery of the 'glorious revolution'. Its Bill of Rights entrenched the privileges of politicians rather than the liberty of the subject, and in due course – by the Act of Settlement of 1700 – the seal was set on a white Anglo-German Protestant monarchy, which inherited through feudal primogeniture (discriminating in favour of male descendants) from Sophia, the Electress of Hanover, who was the daughter of Elizabeth, sister of Charles I. Catholics were (and still are) absolutely excluded from succeeding to the throne.

Epilogue

And it may be said of him, without flattery, that he was of a most upright and conscientious spirit, one who did justice yet loved mercy; an affectionate and tender husband, a loving and careful father, a true and faithful friend; a lamb in prosperity, a lion in adversity, of meek and lowly spirit in the things of his own concern, courageous and bold in what concerned the glory of God and the good of his country.

(Edmund Ludlow on John Cooke[1])

Charles I refused to plead in Bradshawe's court, as he would have refused in any other, because of belief in his impunity: acts of state and of heads of state were beyond the reach of any legal system. That position was adopted in October 1648 by the continental kingdoms which ratified the Treaty of Westphalia, the basis of modern international law, and it would remain the position until 30 September 1946 when the judgment of the allied military tribunal at Nuremberg declared that rulers were responsible for crimes against humanity. The King's refusal to submit to the law entailed his conviction and had the constitutional effect of securing those rights which the Long Parliament had declared but which had remained uncertain so long as there was no settlement with the King. The axe that beheaded Charles confirmed at its stroke the principles of parliamentary sovereignty, judicial independence, no taxation without representation, no detention without trial – as G.M. Trevelyan concludes: 'Never perhaps in any century have such rapid advances been made towards freedom.'[2]

The years of the republic were devoted more to defending these freedoms than to enjoying them. Parliament – even the Rump – remained a reactionary body, the lawyers who had led the fight for constitutional liberty being backward in supporting any reform which might affect their own property or status. Cromwell's protectorate put down no roots in English hearts: the edifice collapsed when its flimsy institutions and unpopular leaders felt the bootheel of General Monck. It had provided stability whilst Cromwell was at its helm, but subsequently its erratic and increasingly chaotic course made restoration the alternative that best promised security in future.

The new regime lost no time in self-celebration. The censorship system that denied to the 'black' regicides even their dying voices was paralleled by praise singing and pantomime celebration of Charles II, and pamphlets demonising Cromwell and all his works. Records of the commonwealth disappeared or were destroyed, disloyal correspondence was burned, the 'People of God' went to ground. It was the Vicar of Bray's time: memories became self-protectingly selective and memoirs published from 1660 onwards cannot be trusted to remember with honesty what happened after the start of the civil war. Typical of the time was George Downing, the army chaplain who advocated king-killing and later served as Cromwell's ambassador to Europe, now remorseless in hunting down his old comrades-in-arms. In New England, where Downing was remembered as one of the first Harvard graduates, his very name became a synonym for treachery. But in London, this colonial Quisling was quickly baronetted and became the King's financial adviser and a massively wealthy property developer. Perhaps it is a measure of the English inability to recognize the achievements of its republicans that the name of the man who betrayed them (and human nature) still graces the street from which the nation is governed.

After the settlement of constitutional monarchy in 1689, the retrospective battlelines were drawn over both the trial of the regicides and the trial of the King. The royalist textbook, Clarendon's *History of the Rebellion*, was most influential, due to its elegance of style and its author's supposed familiarity with the subject – notwithstanding that Edward Hyde had more scores to settle than anyone else. Understandably, from his perspective, the King's trial was an abomination: he cannot even bring himself to write the name of John Cooke, and refers to the 'choice of some lawyers (eminent for nothing but their obscurity, and that they were men scarce known or heard of in the profession) to perform the offices of the Attorney-General and Solicitor-General for the State'. Bradshawe he described with typical snobbery as 'a vulgar spirit, acquainted only with a very moderate fortune'.[3] Clarendon does not discuss the regicide trials, which he attended as a commissioner only on the first day but manipulated behind the scenes. The author of the rival work, *The Memoirs of Edmund Ludlow*, is haunted by the unfairness of the proceedings and the barbarity of the sentences, and is full of praise for Cooke, who was a soul-mate. But there was no republican party to champion Ludlow: his memoirs were appropriated by Whig propagandists and heavily edited, removing much of the detail of the regicide trials, and eviscerating the Puritan religiosity which permeated the original. Cooke's undelivered closing speech, *King Charles: His Case*, was republished in 1691, earning Cooke more posthumous vilification from royalists,[4] and it was appended to later editions of Ludlow's *Memoirs*.

Whigs were liberals, entranced by the civil war and the victory of Parliament but embarrassed by the execution of the King, which was put down to 'cruel necessity' and quickly passed over – as, in consequence, was the trial of the regicides. This attitude was partly induced by political consid-erations: English liberals are nervous at the best of times and it was polit-ical suicide (and under George III might have been sedition) to be perceived as supportive of king-killing. But there is something deeper here, which can almost be ascribed to a collective mental block, and even radicals like John Wilkes shared it: they all date English liberty to 1689, and dare not own up to any sympathy with the ideas of 1649. For most Whigs, even after elevating Cromwell to hero status in the nineteenth century, the episode remained highly distasteful, to be glossed over by reference to Charles James Fox's aphorism about the right to resist – 'A principle which we should wish kings never to forget, and their subjects seldom to remember'.

Later historians mainly conceded the political progressiveness of the republic whilst deploring the trial as a 'high crime' or at least as the product of religious fanaticism. The execution was invariably perceived as counter-productive – 'It gave to his person a sacredness which had never before appertained to it'.[5] Only Catherine Macauley ventured a justification, on the rather vague basis of society's 'Right of self-preservation . . . from the lawless power and enterprises of the tyrant'.[6] Thomas Carlyle described it as perhaps the most daring action ever taken in history – which may well be true – although he was the hagiographer who lauded Cromwell's acts of 'surgery' at Drogheda. It took Gardiner's late nineteenth-century study of the period in all its complexities to restore some sense of perspective, but even this great historian became confused about the King's trial. He says that

Cooke 'threw his case away by relying on legal not political arguments',[7] although the whole point of a trial is that its prosecutor *should* rely on legal not political arguments.

By the start of the twentieth century, the statute of 1660 which required the Church of England to say special prayers in every church on the anniversary of the King's execution (30 January) and to celebrate the day of his son's restoration (29 May) had finally been repealed. MPs had even agreed to erect a statue of the Lord Protector outside the Houses of Parliament which he had so often dissolved. But all was not forgiven. Empire loyalists in the states that were joining together to make Australia insisted that the new country should be described as a 'Federation' rather than a 'Commonwealth' because the latter carried 'revolutionary connotations'.[8] In 1911, the decision of Winston Churchill (first Lord of the Admiralty and an admirer of Cromwell) to name a new battleship after the Lord Protector was vetoed by King George V on the grounds that an 'offensive oxymoron' – namely *His Majesty's Ship Oliver Cromwell* – should have no place in the royal navy.[9] The mental block the British have in understanding what the regicides did for them is symbolised by the BBC's *Great Britons* series which in 2002 invited the public to rank the top ten British heroes. Incredibly, Cromwell's advocate – a history professor – could not begin to justify the King's trial ('Oh dear, Oh dear . . . shocking, shocking') so it was little wonder that Cromwell came last, behind such 'greater' Britons as John Lennon, Princess Diana and Isambard Brunel.

The inability of the English to celebrate or even to grasp the achievement of 1649 is most clearly demonstrated by its school history curriculum. At the formative age of 13, children are taught (in the words of the government's education website) to 'focus on 1649 as a year of reckoning – as the winners of the civil war demonstrated their power over the losers.'[10] This odd notion that 1649 rather than 1660 is the year for revenge is taught through three 'violent incidents', namely 'the sombre scene at Whitehall as Charles I is beheaded in public, the drama of the Burford church as leaders of the Leveller mutiny are shot dead by firing squad and the killing of Irish Catholic civilians at Drogheda'. The true facts are that Catholic civilians were not killed at Drogheda; only three of several thousand army rebels were executed (against Cromwell's wishes) after a lawful court martial at Burford; the scene at Whitehall was solemn but not necessarily sombre and the public could not see the actual execution. The republican revolution, unlike that in France more than a century later, was achieved by shedding no blood other than the King's. However, British children must use these 'violent incidents' to answer the question 'Should the king share power with parliament?' In the 21st century, just as in the mid-17th century, they might be asked whether the king should have any power at all. However, the UK government does not encourage teenagers to think about the advantages of a republic. Most countries teach their children well about their national triumphs: Britain's educators must be unique in hiding from them the truth about the nation's *annus mirabilis*.

John Cooke has always been lost in Cromwell's shadow. He usually rates only one mention in books about the period, as having read his charge against the King, although this was done by Broughton the court's clerk. It was not until the 1970s that any significant analysis of Cooke's contribution to law reform in England[11] and Ireland[12] emerged. Christopher Hill has noticed his wider significance as a radical visionary, and A. L. Rowse (in an otherwise silly book about the regicides) gives him 'the credit of being a genuine reformer' and praises both his work in Ireland and his criticisms of the legal profession in England.[13] G. E. Aylmer, the expert on public service in the period, notes Cooke's uniqueness as 'the epitome of honest independency and frustrated reforming zeal'.[14]

Other modern writers have taken their cue from Clarendon, who is manifestly unreliable when describing rival lawyers and persons of low birth (Cooke was both). Antonia Fraser misdescribes how 'A charge against the King was then read by John Cooke, a man of no particular reputation',[15] and Sarah Barber thinks him 'a hack lawyer from Leicestershire'. She mentions his account of the storm, when 'Cooke's feverish dream had him screaming into the dark "I am not a parricide: I did not kill my father"' – a scream that Dr Barber may herself have dreamt, since it does not occur in either John's or Frances's account of the event.[16] Popular historians are apt to embellish his body-language. 'John Cooke the prosecutor shouted, blustered and argued' says Derek Wilson;[17] he stares the King 'fervently' in the face while reading the charge, says Christopher Hibbert.[18] Cooke did not read the charge and we have no contemporary description of his demeanour, which seems to have been mild – by repute 'he was of a somewhat feeble frame and retiring manner'.[19] Ask the National Portrait Gallery for pictures of the Solicitor General who prosecuted the King and it produces royalist propaganda drawings made in the nineteenth century that look nothing like him. In fact, the only likeness of John Cooke is a tiny engraved medal struck by Thomas Simon in 1649, the year of his triumph, used as the frontispiece to this book. The British Museum misdates it as 1660, the year of his disgrace. In the movie *Cromwell*, made in 1966 by Richard Attenborough, Cooke at last gets to deliver his final speech by way of some souped-up sentences from *King Charles: His Case*. This was forgivable dramatic licence: not so a bizarre twist in a 2005 television reconstruction of the regicide proceedings, when Cooke at the end of his trial thanks the court for its fairness – the very opposite of what happened at the Old Bailey on October 13, 1660.[20]

Ironically, since none of John Cooke's pamphlets have been republished in modern times, his first wife's meditations on the storm have recently featured in an anthology of women's writings, *Lay By Your Needles*.[21] Frances may not have done much sewing (she had a servant) but her decision that 'my heart and tongue shall not only praise Him but with my pen also will I stir up myself' now give her feminist credentials. This is anachronistic, of course – not even the wildest republican promoted the notion of votes for women, while Lilburne exploited them as shock troops to discomfort Parliamentarians ('Strange that women should petition' murmured one Puritan MP to a Leveller gentlewoman who pressed him in April 1649 to have Lilburne released from prison. He received the curt response: 'Sir, that which is strange is not therefore unlawful. It was strange that you cut off the King's head, yet I suppose you will justify it.').[22] Frances Cooke's place, which she knew, was to tend her husband and to praise the Lord: Puritan women were permitted equality in access to heaven, but not in access to Parliament. Only when affairs of state became affairs with the head of state did women wield political influence – as Clarendon found out when the King's mistress engineered his dismissal and disgrace. (He farewelled Barbara Villiers, in her moment of triumph, with the parting shot: 'Remember, Madam, *you will grow old*.')

John Cooke's visionary suggestions for reforms of law and medicine and public administration have mostly come to pass. There is still time for his own profession to deliver on his exhortations, however: a revival of his proposal that barristers should make it a professional obligation to donate 10 per cent of their time to *pro bono* work was greeted with stony silence at a recent conference of the English bar. As for Cooke's old Inn, Gray's, it has avoided any mention of him for 350 years, ever since its benchers ordered the seizure of his chambers in July 1660 – presuming his guilt some months before his trial. Like the other Inns of Court, it now glories in its royal connections, and boasts the future Charles III as an honorary bencher.

The instruction in Cooke's brief was to devise a lawful means of ending the impunity of a tyrant who happened to be a king. The republic came as a practical rather than a logical consequence of the trial: the Puritans who invoked God's wrath on kings succeeded largely because there was no viable royal alternative. That was also the case in revolutionary France where the trial of Charles I assumed importance for all parties involved in the trial of Louis XVI. His lawyers advised him to adopt Charles's tactic of denying juris-diction, since the constitution guaranteed his inviolability, but Louis doggedly insisted upon establishing his innocence. This regicide trial was more akin to Strafford's attainder by Parliament – the King was unanimously convicted by a national assembly that had already declared his guilt. The vote to have him executed was close – Tom Paine, an honorary delegate, urged them to exile the King to America, where he might be reformed and become a democrat. Marat accused Paine of being a Quaker, Robespierre said humanity could not pardon mass-murdering despots, and St Just adopted Cooke's argument: all kings were tyrants, and this king must die so monarchy would die with him. Jacobin censorship ensured that Louis did not become a Charles-like martyr: they even directed drummers to interrupt his speech from the guillotine.[23]

It was not until the twentieth century that Head of State immunity was challenged, by a British government at Versailles determined to deliver on Lloyd George's promise to 'Hang the Kaiser' for ordering the unprovoked invasion of Belgium and unrestricted submarine warfare.[24] But the USA insisted that sovereign impunity was central to Westphalian international law: the Kaiser remained in Holland, unhanged, as a guest of the Dutch government until his death in 1941. Had he been tried and punished, Hitler might have been given pause.

In 1945 the trial of Charles I cast a shadow over the US plans to put the Nazis on trial. Churchill, an admirer of Cromwell, believed the trial had been a mistake: the King had exploited it to secure his own martyrdom. That, he feared, was exactly what Hitler would do if put on public trial. So he proposed the same procedure used in 1662 against Downing's victims, Okey, Barkstead and Corbet: the top Nazis would be 'outlawed' by name and once captured would be executed as soon as their identity could be verified. Truman and his legal adviser, Justice Robert Jackson, objected: summary executions would not sit easy on the American conscience or be remembered by our children with pride. The only course is to determine the innocence or guilt of the accused after a hearing as dispassionate as the times and horrors we deal with will permit and upon a record that will leave our reasons and motives clear.[25]

So there was a deadlock over whether the Nazi leaders should be put on trial at all. Stalin had the casting vote, and he loved show trials – so long as every defendant was shot at the end. From this unpromising beginning, the Nazi leaders went to Nuremberg to face a new jurisdiction – that of international criminal law.

Herman Goering at first ordered his co-defendants to say only three words to their judges – the defiant catch-cry of one of Goethe's warrior heroes, loosely translated as 'kiss my arse'[27]. But as the pre-trial months passed, the Nazi leaders were inveigled by the fairness of Anglo-American trial procedures into playing the justice game.[26] It was because they entered so fully into the adversarial dynamics of the traditional criminal trial, testing the prosecution evidence and undergoing cross-examination, that the ensuing judgment at Nuremberg has the stamp of historical authority. It was this kind of judgment, of course, that Charles had skilfully pre-empted by challenging the court's jurisdiction and refusing all temptations to enter a defence. Goering cheated the hangman by taking poison: Charles, 'the royal actor', would not for all the world have missed performing on the scaffold stage.

For the half-century following Nuremberg, tyrants of all types lived happily ever after their tyrannies. Although the US Supreme Court in 1946 confirmed Cooke's 'command responsibility' principle in relation to Japanese generals who connived at the war crimes of their troops, the allies covered up the responsibility of Emperor Hirohito for Japanese aggression. There was no accountability for Stalin, nor for other mass-murdering heads of state like Pol Pot and Emporer Bokassa and His Excellency Idi Amin V.C. and bar. It was not until General Pinochet's arrest in London in 1998 that an English court would again consider the scope of sovereign immunity, finding in the law of nations the basis for ruling that former heads of state who order the torture of prisoners – one of Cooke's allegations against Charles I – must face trial. There was increasing acceptance, at the turn into the twenty-first century, that sovereign immunity would be lost if the sovereign bore command responsibility for a particularly heinous class of offence – a 'crime against humanity' – such as genocide or widespread torture, or plundering innocent civilians. Slobodan Milosevic became in 2001 the first head of state since Charles I to face a panel of judges, at a court in The Hague set up by the UN Security Council.

Milosevic opened with the King Charles gambit, refusing to plead on the ground that the court had been unlawfully established. The English presiding judge, Richard May, did not make Bradshawe's mistake of taking the plea *pro confesso*: he treated it as 'not guilty' and appointed an *amicus* team to take legal points on Milosevic's behalf. The defendant instructed his own lawyers but had them sit in the gallery so that he could appear in court like Charles, isolated and alone, and made rabble-rousing addresses which played well on television to his supporters back in Serbia. The proceedings encountered many difficulties before they were abandoned upon his death: the court had approved an overlong indictment so the prosecution lasted for three years; it attempted at one point to foist barristers upon the defendant against his will; it was thrown into some disarray by the defendant's self-induced ill-health. The problems that were encountered in trying to try Milosevic lend a kinder view to the way similar problems had to be approached by Cooke and Bradshawe back in 1649.

As for Saddam Hussein, there is no one who better fits the allegations of tyranny in Cooke's charge against the King. When he first appeared in court after his arrest, his language (in translation) was identical to that of Charles: 'By what authority do you put me on trial?' This was a good question, since he had been overthrown by a US invasion generally held by international lawyers to be unlawful. The US set up a rump Parliament (the interim administration) which in turn appointed a High Court of Justice (the Iraqi Special Tribunal) empowered to send him to the scaffold for making war on his own people, albeit with poisoned gas rather than poisoned bullets. The Shia-dominated government and the Bush administration seem determined that Saddam will die like Charles I, on a gallows in some dusty square packed with soldiers. A brave face at his execution, and this tyrant too will achieve martyrdom.

Meanwhile, former tyrants still live happily ever after while others strut their local stage – in North Korea and Turkmenistan, in Burma and the Congo. The world has plenty of prerogative-happy crown princes and emirs, sultans and kings and presidents-for-life. Nominally democratic republics without effective consitutional safeguards for civil liberties soon develop the oppression and corruption that are features of tyranny-lite. Running a despotic government which commits widespread human rights violations is not currently condemned by the law of nations. (The Taliban would still be the lawful government of Afghanistan, had it not committed the error of harbouring Osama bin Laden.) However much Kofi Annan talks about the need to end impunity, tyranny is not a criminal offence.

The ultimate goal of the modern human rights movement must be to eliminate rulers, be they hereditary monarchs, military dictators, high priests or political despots who comprehensively violate the fundamental liberties of their subjects.[27] In today's world, that could only be achieved by a UN convention against tyranny, which would invalidate provisions in national constitutions preventing the prosecution of leaders for crimes committed while in office and would nullify, once and for all, amnesties and immunities traditionally accorded to those who wield the power of the state. It might go further, and establish an international tribunal empowered to examine the record of particular governments to decide whether their violations of fundamental rights are so systematic and widespread as to justify a finding of tyranny. That finding would serve both as a warning and as a warrant – a warning to change, or else to face the prospect of regime change, if necessary by a war the legitimacy of which could not be in doubt. The moral rightness of overthrowing Saddam Hussein and the wrongfulness in law of the means used to accomplish it, serves to emphasise the lasting importance of John Cooke's tyrannicide brief.

Chronology

Opening of the Long Parliament (November)

1641	March	Strafford's trial
	July	Court of Star Chamber abolished
	November	Rebellion in Ireland: slaughter of Protestants
	December	Grand Remonstrance
1642	4 January	Charles attempts to arrest Pym and other MPs
	10 January	The King flees London
	15 January	Parliament establishes judicial independence
	February	Militia Bill becomes law without royal assent
	June	The Nineteen Propositions, and the King's answer
	22 August	Charles declares war on Parliament by raising his standard outside Nottingham Castle
	October	Battle of Edgehill (a draw)
1643	June	Death of John Hampden
	July	Fall of Bristol (Royalist victory)
	September	Parliamentary alliance with Scottish covenanters
	October	Battle of Winceby (Cromwell's first victory)
	December	Death of John Pym
1644	January	Scots army enters England
	July	Battle of Marston Moor (parliamentary victory)
1645	January	Execution of Laud
	April	Self-denying Ordinance (Cromwell excepted). Fairfax made commander-in-chief of the New Model Army.
	June	Battle of Naseby (definitive parliamentary victory)
	September	Siege of Basing House
1646	6 February	Publication of *Vindication of the Professors and Profession of Law*
	12 February	Cooke and Bradshawe represent John Lilburne
	April–May	King surrenders to Scots at Newark

	July	The Newcastle propositions
	August	The King's first answers to the propositions
	September	Cooke marries Frances Cutler, St Olave's Church, London
	October	House of Commons resolves to maintain New Model Army for only six months
1647	January	Scots sell the King to Parliament and withdraw
	February	The King at Holmby House
		What the Independents Will Have
	May	Parliament moves to disband the Army
	June	Fairfax's regiment refuses to disband; Joyce takes the King into army custody
	August	Army enters London. *A Union of Hearts*.
	September	Independents secure city government
	October	Putney debates
	November	King escapes from Hampton Court, detained on Isle of Wight (Carisbrooke Castle)
		Cork Bush Field mutiny
	December	'Engagement' between the King and Scots
1648	January	Vote of No Addresses
	February	*The Poor Man's Case*
	July	Second Civil War: Scots army under Hamilton invades England
	August	Cromwell vanquishes Scots; Hamilton captured
		Royalists surrender to Fairfax at Colchester
	September	Parliament begins negotiations with the King at Newport
	October	Murder of Colonel Rainborough;
		Treaty of Westphalia ends the Thirty Years War on the continent.
	November	*Remonstrance* of the army
	1 December	The King is moved to Hurst Castle
	5 December	Parliament rejects *Remonstrance*, determines to treat with the King

6 December	Pride's Purge
16 December	Army Council orders that the King be brought to Windsor
23 December	Commons passes Ordinance for trial of the King

1649	1 January	House of Lords rejects Ordinance
	6 January	Commons passes Ordinance, this time as an Act of Parliament
	8 January (Monday)	
		Judges of the High Court convene in the Painted Chamber
	10 January (Wednesday)	
		High Court appoints Bradshawe as President, Steel, Cooke, Dorislaus and Aske as prosecutors
	15 January (Monday)	
		Cooke produces first draft of charge against the King
	20 January (Saturday)	
		Cooke signs and presents charge at the opening of the King's trial in Westminster Hall
	22 January (Monday)	
		Second session of trial
	23 January (Tuesday)	
		Third session of trial
	24–25 January	Cooke examines witnesses
	27 January (Saturday)	
		Charles I sentenced to death.
	30 January	Execution of Charles I
	9 February	King's burial at Windsor Castle
		King Charles: His Case. Also the King's Book (*Eikon Basilke*)
		Opening of trials of Duke of Hamilton and other courtiers
	13 February	John Milton, *The Tenure of King and Magistrates, Mercurius Elencticus* No. 56
	9 March	Hamilton, Holland and Capel executed
	17 March	Act abolishing the office of King
	19 March	Act abolishing the House of Lords

2 May	Assassination of Dorislaus
19 May	Act declaring England to be a Commonwealth
May	Leveller revolt in Army put down at Burford
June	Cooke appointed Master of St Cross Hospital
August–October	
	Cromwell's campaign in Ireland: storming of Drogheda and Wexford
24–26 October	
	Trial of John Lilburne

1650	1–5 January	John and Frances Cooke survive the storm at sea. *A True Relation of the Sea Voyage.*
	March	Cooke appointed Chief Justice of Munster
	May	Cromwell leaves Ireland; Henry Ireton appointed Lord Deputy
	June	Fairfax resigns; Cromwell appointed Lord General
	3 September	Cromwell defeats Scots at Dunbar

1651	3 September	Cromwell defeats Charles II at Worcester
	November	Death of Henry Ireton

1652	January	Committee on law reform, chaired by Matthew Hale
	February	*Monarchy No Creature of God's Making.*
	July	Settlement of Ireland Act
	6 August	Charles II offers amnesty to all, excepting Cromwell, Bradshawe and Cooke

1653	April	Cromwell dissolves the Rump
	July	Barebone's Parliament
	August	Lilburne's last trial
	September	Irish Satisfaction Act: Cooke given lands in Cork in lieu of pension
	December	Instrument of Government: Cromwell installed as Lord Protector

1654		Fleetwood made Lord Deputy in Ireland
		Opening of Protectorate Parliament

1655	January	Cooke made Recorder of Waterford
	June	Council appoints Cooke as judge of the Upper Bench
	August	Cooke writes to Fleetwood resigning judicial commission to the Upper Bench
	September	Cromwell appoints major-generals to rule counties
1656	August	Ludlow, Bradshawe and Vane carpeted by Council of State for opposing Protectorate
1657	April	Cooke returns to England
		Cromwell refuses the crown
	November	Henry Cromwell appointed Lord Deputy of Ireland
1658	September	Death of Cromwell; Richard becomes Lord Protector
1659	April	Army dissolves Protectorate Parliament
	May	Richard Cromwell resigns
		'Rump' of Long Parliament reconvenes
	July	Ludlow appointed commander-in-chief for Ireland
	August	Royalist rising led by Sir George Booth, put down by Lambert
	October	Death of Bradshawe
		Army expels Rump and sets up Committee of Safety
	26 December	Rump returns
1660	1 January	Monck enters England
	10 February	First report of Cooke's arrest
	11 February	'Roasting of the Rump': Londoners celebrate after Monck's meeting with City Council
	21 February	Return of MPs 'secluded' by Pride's Purge
	March	Long Parliament dissolves for elections
	April	Lambert surrenders
		Convention Parliament opens
	1 May	Declaration of Breda
	8 May	Charles II proclaimed King of England
		Cooke's deposition taken in Dublin Castle

19 May	Cooke departs under guard for England
29 May	King enters London
7 June	Parliament excepts Cooke from pardon
29 August	Act of Oblivion
September	Pre-trial meetings between judges and prosecutors at Serjeants' Inn

9 October (Tuesday)
Regicides committed for trial

10 October (Wednesday)
Opening day at Old Bailey

11 October (Thursday)
Trial and conviction of Harrison

12 October (Friday)
Trials and convictions of Scroop, Scot, Clement, Carew and Jones

13 October (Saturday)
Cooke and Peters tried, convicted and sentenced
Harrison executed

15 October (Monday)
Trials and convictions of Daniel Axtell, Colonel Hacker, William Hulet. John Carew executed

16 October (Tuesday)
John Cooke and Hugh Peters hanged, drawn and quartered at Charing Cross. Trials of all remaining regicides

17 October (Wednesday)
Scot, Clement, Scroop and Jones executed

19 October (Friday)
Axtell and Hacker executed at Tyburn

1661	January	Fifth Monarchy rebellion
		Desecration of corpses of Cromwell, Bradshawe and Ireton

1662	Execution of Corbet, Barkstead and Okey
	Trials of Lambert and Vane, execution of Vane
1663	Prosecution of Brewster for *Speeches and Prayers of the Regicides*

Notes on Sources

John Cooke's writings survive among the Thomason tracts – an exhaustive collection of the pamphlet literature of the period – in the British Library, the Bodleian and elsewhere. The *Vindication of the Professors and Profession of Law* (1646) was reprinted in 1652, by which time Cooke was Cromwell's chief justice in Munster and his reform proposals were highly relevant to the newly established Hale commission. The work provides a unique critical account of the law in practice and as practised in London at the time of the civil war. *King Charles: His Case*, intended, as its subtitle explains, 'to have been delivered at the bar, if the King had pleaded to the charge, and put himself upon a fair trial', was republished as an appendix to the second and subsequent editions of Edmund Ludlow's *Memoirs*. Cooke's earliest writing that survives – his letter to Strafford in 1641 – was transcribed by William Knowler and first published by Professor Firth: the original has disappeared, but there can be no doubt about its authenticity (neither royalists nor republicans could gain from depicting John Cooke as a Straffordian).

Cooke's long resignation letter to Fleetwood, written in August 1655, survives in the Bodleian Library (RAWL.A.189) and was published in full by Edward MacLysaght in *Irish Life in the Seventeenth Century* (Cork University Press, 1950) as a commentary upon the legal system. Cooke's letters to Henry Cromwell survive in Thurloe's collection of state papers. Some doubt attends the attribution of *Magna Charta*, a broadsheet acquired by Thomason in December 1659 from a shop at Temple Bar. Its contents lend some support to Professor Prest's *DNB* conjecture that its author 'JC' was in fact John Cooke. I am more confident of his authorship of *A Sober Vindication*, which was published anonymously early in 1600: it bears Cooke's stylistic hallmarks and was printed by Giles Calvert, his former publisher. Ludlow (who must have known) tells us that Cooke wrote such a vindication but adds – perhaps for his own comfort – that his enemies never discovered Cooke's authorship.

My account of the King's trial draws upon standard sources: Gilbert Mabbott's *A Perfect Narrative* (the most detailed contemporary report, republished in Volume IV of *State Trials*); the official transcript (sometimes inaccurately called *Bradshawe's Journal*) that was presented to Parliament in December 1650 and is now in the Public Records office; the minutes taken by John Phelps of the Painted Chamber meetings, found (amongst extraneous royalist comment) in Nalson, *A True Copy of the Journal of the High Court of Justice for the Trial of King Charles I* (1648); John Rushworth's version of the trial (edited by Roger Lockyer for the Folio Society, 1974) and various contemporary newsbooks. The commitment to open justice meant that these proceedings were comprehensively reported; the 'CW' at the end of Mabbott's version probably stands, with initials reversed, for William Clark, the army stenographer who reported so vividly the Putney debates. Some of these transcriptions are fuller than others and differ in phraseology but not in substance: they have not been contested by royalists subsequently and indeed the official transcript was relied upon at the 1660 trials. The exchanges between Bradshawe, Cooke and the King given in this book come down to us virtually verbatim and the quotations – with grammatical and linguistic updating and editing – reflect these original texts. Uncertainties remain about the interjection by the masked 'malignant lady' rumoured to have been Lady Fairfax and as to whether Downes openly manifested his dissent as he later alleged, but they do not much matter: it is not disputed that there were two interjections from the gallery to which Axtell responded or that Downes and some judges were in favour of granting the King's request to address a joint sitting.

The most important legal proceedings in English legal history have rarely been analysed. The irresponsible decision to entrust editorship of the *Notable British Trials* volume published in 1928 to the fanatical royalist J. G. Muddiman ensured that this important publication was perverse in scholarship and barely readable. The first seventy pages comprise a diatribe against Cromwell, dotted with tributes to the 'saintly' King and accounts of his travails at the hands of ill-bred tormentors. Muddiman's account of the trial opens with an incredible story that a woman who shouted support for the King in Westminster Hall was 'branded with hot irons on her shoulders and her head so her flesh smoked and her hair set on fire' – under the gaze of thousands, none of whom ever mentioned this spectacular combustion. This incident, as Wedgwood shows in her *Trial of Charles I* (p. 236, note 27) was invented many years later by a woman prisoner in order to cadge money from a bishop. It is typical of the improbable allegations with which Muddiman litters his account. There was probably a political motive for his choice as editor: the Tory Lord Chancellor, Birkenhead, notes in his introduction that 'the present volume definitely supersedes the account of the trial in *State Trials* . . . a whig compilation'. In 1990 the American Notable Trials library republished Muddiman, with a confused foreword by Alan Dershowitz. The work at least contains in its appendices the official report (the so-called *Bradshawe's Journal*) and an accurate text of John Cooke's 'speech', although Muddiman accepts as factual Wharton's untrue libels on Cooke and makes the elementary mistake (on p. 66) of confusing him with another barrister of the same name, from Westminster not Leicester, who had been admitted to Gray's Inn in 1594 – fourteen years before Cooke was born!

In 1964, C. V. Wedgwood published *The Trial of Charles I* – a readable (if discursive) book that has become, for want of any rival, the classic account. It judiciously exposes some of Muddiman's partisan errors but makes some elementary mistakes: 'Cooke launched into the charge with evident enjoyment', writes Dame Veronica (p. 129) – an enjoyment evident to nobody at the time, since Cooke did not read the charge. She upbraids him for writing to his wife 'in this hortatory vein' (p. 221) a letter that was written to someone else. This fine historian of the period lacks the legal insight to understand John Cooke.

The regicide trial quotations are taken from *An Exact and Most Impartial Account of the Indictment Arraignment Trial and Judgement (According to Law) of Nine and Twenty Regicides, the Murtherers of His Late Sacred Majesty of Most Glorious Memory*. It appeared on 31 October 1660, just a fortnight after Cooke's execution: on 6 November Pepys 'found good satisfaction in reading thereof'. According to Anthony Wood it was edited by Bridgeman from Heneage Finch's notes, and this 'official' transcript was reproduced in *State Trials* and has never been questioned. However it is certainly not impartial and is demonstrably inexact. For example, in Cooke's case Bridgeman deals with arguments made by the defendant that do not appear in his transcribed speeches, which must therefore have been edited; there are statements attributed to Bridgeman which read fairly but seem to have been inserted for presentational reasons, since they are either out of context or are promises upon which the court never delivers. However, the evidence and the detailed arguments are substantially reproduced. Although the account was hastily produced for the propaganda purpose of satisfying people like Pepys of the rightness of the proceedings, the bias of the court comes through loud and clear.

The Speeches and Prayers of the Regicides together with several occasional speeches and passages on their imprisonment was acquired by Thomason on 1 December 1660 and to a large extent republished by the editors of *State Trials*. While some of the prison dialogue is questionable, most later historians of the period, including Christopher Hill and C. V. Wedgwood, have seen no reason to doubt the general authenticity of the work. The scaffold speeches were heard by numerous witnesses (many of them hostile) and would undoubtedly have been declared as forgeries at the trials of Brewster and other publishers, had that bloodhound censor L'Estrange found any evidence (in respect to Cooke's scaffold speech in particular) that they did not approximate to reality. Indeed, Justice Hyde's condemnation of Cooke assumed that his 'letter from the Tower' and his gallows address as published by Brewster in the seditious volume were authentic.

J. G. Muddiman, horrified that these 'horribly blasphemous lies' had been accepted by editors of the *State Trials* and by entries in the *Dictionary of National Biography*, devoted many articles in *Notes and Queries* (19 April 1913 onwards) under the pseudonym of 'J. B. Williams', to alleging that they were forgeries. He overlooks the trial of Brewster, and rests his case upon the fact that Henry Muddiman, reporting for *Mercurius Publicus*, described Cooke as 'penitent' on the scaffold. But Henry Muddiman was the government licensor who refused to allow any report of Cooke's speech to be published. His own brief news despatch contained only two details, namely that Cooke had 'heartily prayed' for Charles II and had asked that Peters might be reprieved for he was in no condition to die. Significantly, both details appear in Cooke's scaffold speech, as published in *The Speeches and Prayers*. The reflection on Peters's cowardice would certainly have been omitted if the publication were (as J. G. Muddiman contends) a forgery intended to whitewash all the regicides. Cooke's forgiving remarks about Charles II ('I say as to the King's majesty I have not heard any hard thoughts concerning him: my prayers shall be for him that his throne might be upheld for truth and mercy') were a prelude to his request that the King should spare the lives of Peters and the other regicides, and were not, in context, any sort of apology for his part in prosecuting Charles I. J. G. Muddiman argues that Cooke's letter from the Tower is a forgery, on the grounds that anyone who has read Cooke's 'scurrilous and semi-literate pamphlets' would realise that the letter was written by 'a more highly educated man than Cooke'. Here, royalist venom gets the better of reason: Cooke was one of the most highly educated men of his time and the 'letter to a friend' is written in exactly the same style as the *Vindication* and his other pamphlets. It is, in fact, vintage Cooke – if it were a forgery (and why bother?) it would have purported to come from Newgate (from which prison letters were readily smuggled) rather than from the Tower.

J. G. Muddiman is a strange obsessional figure whose undoubted familiarity with the newsbook literature of the period gives his writings a certain interest, but his ignorance of the law and his morose hatred of Cromwell and Cooke make his own commentaries upon them unreliable. His fixation with refurbishing the reputation of his ancestor, Henry Muddiman, verges on the comical: he seems to have used the pseudonym 'J. B. Williams' whenever promoting Henry's work, so that readers would not recognise his family connection. He makes a fetish of preferring accounts in news-sheets to trial transcripts, but this reliance on what Nalson called 'the paper bullets of the press, scandalous and calumniating' is the equivalent of writing the history of modern Britain using *The Sun* as the primary source. His attacks on John Cooke, in short articles in obscure historical magazines early in the twentieth century, are in their twisted way a tribute to the lawyer he sets out to diminish.

Westminster Hall, by Hollar. The head of John Cooke was placed on a pole above the door, (left): Pepys saw it from the opposite side of the courtyard

Notes

Chapter 1: A Man of the Middling Sort

1. Isaac and Elizabeth Cooke lived at Sketchley, a hamlet of Burbage, where the minister, Anthony Grey, was an aristocratic Anglican. See Nichols, John, *The History and Antiquities of the County of Leicestershire* (Wakefield, 1970), Vol IV, p468.
2. J Craigie (ed), *The Basilikon Doron of King James VI*, (Edinburgh, 1944), I p81.
3. Speech to judges in Star Chamber, (1616) C.H. McIlwain (ed) *Political Works of James I*, (Cambridge, 1918) p327.
4. *The True Law of Free Monarchies*, written by James in 1598 when he was King of Scotland.
5. Especially as he tells it: see Coke, *Reports*, 1600–1659, 12.41. The most commonly quoted version of the encounter is given in John, Lord Campbell, *Lives of the Chief Justices* 2nd Ed, (Oxford 1858), p272.
6. See Austin Woolrych, *Britain in Revolution, 1625–1660*, (Oxford, 2002), p20. In *Calvin's case* (1608) all the judges – including Coke and Bacon – accepted that the King's authority came from God.
7. Coke 'gave Englishmen an historical myth of the English constitution, parallel to Foxe's myth of the English religion . . .' He did not reinvent Magna Carta, but 'made it the possession of every propertied Englishman': Christopher Hill, *Intellectual Origins of the English Revolution Revisited*, (Oxford, revised 1997), p228–30. Note that Coke's advice 'to the grave and learned writers of histories is that they meddle not . . . with the laws of this realm, before they confer with some learned in that profession.' (p201)
8. Nichols, above note 1, p486, gives the pedigree of Cooke of Sketchley, from the 'Visitation' – a census taken by the King's officials – in 1619. Unfathomably, John Cooke is given an alias – 'Brodfield' – which originates with Abraham's father and attaches to the first-born son thereafter – Abraham, Isaac and John.

379

9. See David Underdown, *Rebel Riot and Rebellion: Popular Politics and Culture in England, 1603–1660*, (Oxford, 1985), p10.

10. C. S. L Davies and Jane Garnett, *Wadham College* (Oxford, 1994) p20.

11. Walter Ralegh, *History of the World*, 1736 ed, Preface XV.

12. John Cooke, *Unum necessarium* or *The Poor Man's Case, an expedient to make provision for all poor people in the Kingdom* (London, 1648), p44.

13. See Glen Burgess, *Absolute Monarchy and the Stuart Constitution* (Yale, 1996), p5

14. John Cooke, *The Vindication of the Professors and Profession of the Law* (London, 1646) p94.

15. *ibid*, p56.

16. *ibid*, p13.

17. Sibbes, *The Sword of the Wicked*, cited (note 68) by Mark E. Dever, 'Moderation and Deprivation: A Reappraisal of Richard Sibbes', *Journal of Ecclesiastical History*, Vol. 43 No3 July 1992.

18. Noel Henning Mayfield, *Puritans and Regicides*, (London, 1988), p57.

19. *The Five Knights Case* is reported at (1627) 3 State Trials, 1.

20. The controversy continues in academic circles. Compare J.A. Guy, 'The Origins of the Petition of Right Reconsidered', in 25 *Historical Journal* 2, (1982), p289, with Mark Kishlansky, 'Tyrrany Denied: Charles I, Attorney General Heath, and the Five Knights' Case 42 *Historical Journal* 1 (1999), p53. The judges' excuse to parliament was disingenuous: their ruling upheld the King's absolute right to detain 'by special command' for any reason, and for a period which might not have been indefinite but which they had declined to limit. See James Hart, *The Rule of Law 1603–60*, (Harlow, 2003), p126.

21. Conrad Russell, *Parliaments and English Politics 1621–29*, (Oxford, 1979), p352.

22. Wilfrid R. Prest, *The Rise of the Barristers* (Oxford, 1986) p270.

23. Simon Schama, *The British Wars, 1603–1776: A History of Britain*, Vol II, (London, 2001), p76.

24. *The King's Declaration Showing the Causes of the Late Dissolution*, 10th March, 1629, S. R. Gardiner, *Constitutional Documents of the Puritan Revolution*, (1625–1660), (Oxford) 3rd Edition, p83.

25. *Eliot's Case* is reported at (1630) 3 State Trials 293.

26. Chief Baron John Walter, who was suspended and threatened with dismissal: Edward Foss, *Judges of England*, Vol VI, p372 (London, 1848–64). The threats to Walter were recalled in 1689 during the drafting of the Bill of Rights, which provided that judges cannot be removed except by a two-thirds majority in both Houses of Parliament (a provision which has yet to be invoked).

27. G. M. Trevelyan, *England Under the Stuarts*, (1904) (Folio Society ed, London, 1996). p124.

28. *Clarendon's History of the Rebellion and Civil Wars in England*, (Oxford, 1888, repr 2001), Vol. I, p5.

Chapter 2: Strafford, Ship Money and a Search for Self

1. Lacey Baldwin Smith, *Elizabeth Tudor: Portrait of a Queen* (Boston, 1975), p105–6.
2. John Winthrop, *A Modell of Christian Charity Written on Board the Arbella on the Atlantic Ocean*, Winthrop Papers II, p282. As Frank Lambert puts it, 'The Puritans viewed themselves as a chosen people, an American Israel, who had entered into a covenant with God to plant a Holy Commonwealth in the New England wilderness': *The Founding Fathers and the Place of Religion in America,* (Princeton, 2003), p74.
3. David Hackett Fischer, *Albion's Seed*, (Oxford, 1989), p17. The hardships of the first few years made Winthrop think that God had 'stripped us of our vain confidence'. He gritted his teeth, and told his wife 'It is enough that we shall have heaven, though we should pass through hell to it.' See Francis J. Bremer, John Winthrop, *America's Forgotten Founding Father*, (Oxford, 2003), p194. For Peters' role at Harvard, see Samuel Eliot Morison, *The Founding of Harvard College* (Cambridge, 1935), p303–4.
4. Fischer, *ibid*, p112.
5. *Vindication*, p18.
6. John Adair, *A Life of John Hampden*, (London, 2003), p92.
7. George Wharton, *Mercurius Elencticus*, (No. 56), 6 February, 1649. Wharton was an astrologer and cavalier propagandist: his claim that by 1634 Cooke was an experienced litigator and crooked marriage-broker, who decamped to Ireland with a client's money, is demonstrably false.
8. Irish judges routinely accepted lavish gifts from great landowners like the Earl of Cork. Judge Sarsfield, who had convicted an innocent man of murder in order to seize his land after his execution, was sent to the Star Chamber for punishment. See R. L. Rington-Ball, *The Judges in Ireland* (Dublin, 1993) p248.
9. See CV Wedgwood, *Thomas Wentworth First Earl of Strafford, A Re-evaluation* (London, 1961), p172–3.
10. Hugh F Kearney, *Strafford in Ireland,* (Manchester, 1959), pxii
11. Wedgwood, above note 9, p160.
12. *The Poor Man's Case*, p21.
13. Wharton, *Mercurius Elencticus* 56, above note 7. This libel is false on two scores: the statutes were printed in 1635 while Cooke was in Strafford's service, and the young lawyer was back in England in 1641, offering to help Strafford's defence.
14. Cooke's Letter to Strafford, in *Papers Relating to Thomas Wentworth, First Earl of*

Strafford, ed. C. H. Firth, Camden Miscellany, ix, Camden Soc, NS/iii (1895), p19.

15. *Vindication*, p57.

16. *ibid*, p93.

17. Edward Chaney, *The Grand Tour and the Great Rebellion*, (Geneva, 1985), p276.

18. Paul Johnson, *The Offshore Islanders* (Penguin, 1972), p272.

19. Cooke's two travelling companions were well-connected: Nicholas Weston (son of the Earl of Portland) and Edward Ironside, probably the son of the future Bishop of Bristol – Chaney; note 17 above), p276–7.

20. Wharton, *Mercurius Elencticus 56*, 6 February 1649.

21. *A Union of Hearts*, (London, 1647), p50–51.

22. Edmond Ludlow: *A Voyce From the Watch Tower*, part 5 (1660–62), edited by A. B. Worden (Camden Fourth Series, Volume 21), p229. The *Memoirs of Edmond Ludlow*, first published in 1702, state that Cooke 'at Rome had spoken with such liberty and ability against the corruptions of that court and church, that great endeavours were used there to bring him into that interest. But he, being resolved not to yield to their solicitations, thought it no longer safe to continue among them; and therefore departed to Geneva where he resided some months in the house of Signor John Diodati, Minister of the Italian church in that city' (Vol. III, *Sands Edition*, Edinburgh, 1751, p57). Blair Worden argues persuasively (see his '*Roundhead Reputations*', London, 2001) that Ludlow's authentic 'Voyce' and its earlier lost parts were heavily edited by John Toland in the interests of the Whig revival. (This passage is part of his evidence, on the basis that Toland added biographical detail about Diodati which he knew from researching his 'Life of Milton').

23. *ibid*. The fact that Cooke conducted himself as a pious Calvinist is omitted by Toland from Ludlow's 'Memoirs'.

24. John Milton, *Second Defence of the English People*, see Milton, Works (Oxford 1991), p322. Milton's close friend from his Cambridge days, Charles Deodati, was the theologian's nephew.

25. *Vindication*, p89.

26. See J Cooke, *King Charles: His Case*, in J. G. Muddiman, *The Trial of Charles I* (Notable British Trials, London 1928), p251–2.

27. See Cooke's letter to Strafford, note 14 above.

28. Obvious, after watching 'Celebrity Big Brother'. The original Latin is: '*Qui nimis notus omnibus ignotus deoritur sibi*'. This fear of popularity seems to have obsessed the youthful Wentworth: he scribbled it on the flyleaf of a devotional book, changing 'deoritur' to 'moritur' ('he who is too well known to everyone, dies without knowing himself.'), C. V. Wedgwood (above note 9), p25.

29. Act of the Privy Council on the Position of the Communion Table at St Gregory's.

S. R. Gardiner, *Constitutional Documents* (Oxford, 3rd edition, 1906), p103.

30. Wedgwood, *Thomas Wentworth*, above, note 10, p236.

31. But see D. L. Keir, *The Case of Ship Money* (1936) 52 *LQR* 546, who argues that Hampden's legal tactic of 'demurring' to the writ meant that the King's claim that the realm was in danger had to be taken at face value. But the face of the writ did not at first make such a claim, and a national emergency could not rationally be deduced from the occasional depredations of pirates. That the King's factual claim was so obviously bogus was grist to those (like Cooke) who interpreted the majority judgements as a blank cheque for the King to override the law whenever he might whimsically think it 'necessary'.

32. R v Hampden is reported at (1637) 3 State Trials 825–1316.

33. Wilfrid Prest, *The Rise of the Barristers*, (Oxford 1986), p229, citing Augustine Baker's *Memorials*.

34. Cooke writes in *What the Independents Would Have* (1647), p1 that at this time he 'read with a single eye' (i.e. critically) the writings of dissenters like Ainsworth, Jacob, Robinson and Johnson – separatists who had set up their church for Anglican exiles in Holland early in the century. The pilgrim fathers on *The May Flower* had been separatists, not mainstream puritans of the kind who followed Winthrop to Massachusetts.

35. *Vindication*, p49.

36. Margaret Pelling, *Medical Conflicts in Early Modern London: Patronage, Physicians and Irregular Practitioners* (Oxford, 2003) p150.

37. *The Poor Man's Case*, p62.

38. Harold J Cook, *The Decline of the Old Medical Regime in Stuart London.* (Cornell, 1986), p130.

39. Adair, above note 6, p124.

40. Prest, *Barristers*, (above note 33), p253.

41. Petition of Twelve Peers for summoning a New Parliament: S. R. Gardiner, *Constitutional Documents*, (above, note 29), p134.

42. Sir Philip Warwick, *Memoirs*, quoted in Pauline Gregg, *Freeborn John: The Biography of John Lilburne* (London, 1961, repr Phoenix), p34.

43. Cooke's letter is found in *Papers relating to Thomas Wentworth, first Earl of Strafford*, ed. C H Firth, Camden Miscellany IX, Camden Soc, N S Liii (1895). It was transcribed by William Knowler – the original has disappeared.

44. It demonstrates the falsity of Wharton's allegation (See note 13 above) that Cooke had absconded with money given him by Strafford and only dared to return to England after the Earl's execution. On the contrary, Cooke was back in England well before that event, daring to help his old employer in his hour of need.

45. *Tryal of Thomas Earl of Strafford*, Complete State Trials, (London, 1719), Vol. I, p361.

46. *ibid*, p372.

47. The Solicitor General, Oliver St John, frankly accepted that legislation – the Act of Attainder – was necessary for declaring doubtful cases of treason. Recent academic studies argue that the Act extended the definition of treason to make it a crime against the <u>government</u> of the realm rather than specifically against the King: see Roberts, C., *The Growth of Responsible Government in Stuart England* (Cambridge, 1966); W R Stacey, 'Matter of Fact, Matter of Law and the Attainder of the Earl of Strafford' (1995) 29 *American Journal of Legal History* 323, at 325, 328; Conrad Russell, 'The Theory of Treason in the Trial of Strafford' (1965) 80 *English Historical Review* 30, 31, 45–7; Allan Orr, *Treason and the State* (Cambridge, 2002), p61 et seq. But it was still the King's realm: in 1641, the notion of Strafford's attainder as a jurisprudential bridge between treason against the King and treason *by* the King would have been a bridge too far.

48. One of them, Richard Starkey, claimed that Cooke was actually 'accused for debt' at this time. Although this was prejudicial evidence given at Cooke's trial in 1660, Cooke did not dispute that he scraped a living in this period by giving tutorials.

49. As Ludlow remarked, 'This choice man, when propounded to the Parliament for employment, was represented a light person, and incapable thereof.' *Voyce*, above note 22, p239.

Chapter 3: A King in Check

1. The most recent estimate suggests that about 800,000 died in the British Isles as a result of the civil wars. The heaviest casualties were in Ireland. See Diane Purkiss, *The English Civil Wars: A Peoples History* (HarperPress, London, 2006).

2 Act for the Abolition of the Court of Star Chamber, S. R. Gardiner, *Constitutional Documents*, (Oxford, 3rd Edition, 1906), p179. Act Declaring the Illegality of Ship Money, *ibid*, p191. For the continuing potency of the abolition of Star Chamber, see the House of Lords decision in <u>A v Home Secretary</u> (2006) 1 All ER 575, which refused to countenance the admission in UK tribunals of evidence obtained by torture.

3. Nicholas Canny, *Making Ireland British 1580–1620* (2001) p469–492.

4. S. R. Gardiner, *History of England from the Accession of James I to the Outbreak of the Civil War*, 10 Volumes (Oxford, 1883/4), Vol. X, p140.

5. Marten said in a House of Commons debate that 'it was better that one family should be destroyed than many' and was sent to the Tower when he admitted he was speaking of the royal family. He was soon released, but expelled from the House and not allowed back until 1647. Mark Noble, *The English Regicides* (London, 1798) Vol. II, p41.

6. Cromwell penned this telling metaphor in a private letter consoling his brother-

in-law for the loss of his son: Abbott, *Letters and Speeches* (1904) letter 21, 5 July 1644.

7. This was true of other Presbyterians, but not of Manchester, who had fought bravely at Marston Moor but suffered shell-shock from the carnage. He soon retired from public life, re-emerging in 1660 to welcome Charles II and, as Lord Chamberlain, to organize his coronation.

8. Where the King's gay cavaliers were not as gentlemanly as legend would have it. Anthony Wood provides a less romantic snapshot of their occupation of Oxford: 'though they were neat and gay in their apparel, yet they were very nasty and beastly, leaving at their departures their excrements in every corner, in chimneys, studies, coal-houses and cellars. Rude, rough, whoremongers; vain, empty, careless.' Paul Johnson, *The Offshore Islanders*, (Harmondsworth, 1975), p296.

9. But the religious fanaticism of their forces took iconoclastic toll of churches left with stain glass shattered and baptismal fonts full of urine. Their worst atrocity was committed on the night that Naseby was won, when a party of roundheads massacred a group of Welsh prostitutes found with the royalist baggage train. The true shame of this episode is not so much that it occurred (the women had attacked them with kitchen knives) but that it was never investigated, leaving the suspicion that they were executed as whores rather than suppressed as rioters.

10. *Vindication*, p75.

11. See Francis J. Bremer, *John Winthrop – America's Forgotten Founding Father*, (New York, 2003), pp335–6.

12. *A Union of Hearts*, p17.

13. State Trials, Vol. 5, p1074.

14. See John Lilburne, *The Legal Fundamental Liberties of the People of England* (1649), Thomason E560, p62.

15. *Vindication*, p26. This case may have been the basis of Wharton's false allegation in *Mercurius Elencticus No 56* that in 1633 Cooke was a marriage broker who pocketed £1,500 from a client then decamped to join Strafford.

Chapter 4: The Breath of an Unfee'd Lawyer

1. Cooke, *Letter to the Lord Deputy*, August 1655, printed in E Maclysart, *Irish Life in the Seventeenth Century*, (Cork, 1950), p442.

2. Ludlow, *Memoirs*, (Sands Edition, Edinburgh, 1751), Volume I, p246.

3. Wilfrid R Prest, *The Rise of the Barristers*, (Oxford, 1986), p2.

4. Donald Veall, *The Popular Movement for Law Reform, 1640–60*, (Oxford, 1970), p73.

5. St Luke, chapter 11, verses 46, 52.

6. C W Brooks, *Pettyfoggers and Vipers of the Commonwealth*, (Cambridge, 1986), p112–3.

7. Sergeants-at-law read for a special degree at the Inns and served (like modern recorders) as part-time judges of assize: see John H. Baker, *An Introduction to English Legal History* (4th edition. London, 2002), p157–8 and 21.

8. This benefit was intended for the gentry and clergy but was not, in practice, their preserve. Criminals able to read (or at least to memorise) the 'neck verse' might also be freed.

9. As in the case of the Gunpowder plotters. Common lawyers were reluctant to admit that torture could be justified in English law – as Fortesque said, it was something done by the French. Sir John Fortescue, *On the Laws and Governance of England* (Cambridge 1997, written in the mid-fifteenth century) Chapter 22, p31–4. Under civil law, torture of suspects was regularly ordered by continental magistrates.

10. Aubrey says of Bacon 'He was a homosexual. His ganymedes and favourites took bribes, but his lordship always gave judgement according to justice and honesty'. Aubrey, *Brief Lives* (London, Folio Society, 1988), p38.

11. Gerald E. Aylmer, *King's Servants*, p89, 93–94.

12. Prest, *Barristers*, (note 3 above), p311.

13. *Vindication*, p80 (although this reference may refer to Fairfax's father).

14. *Letter to the Lord Deputy*, in Maclysart, above note 1, p445.

15. *A Union of Hearts*, p24.

16. See Prest, *Barristers*, (above, note 3), p123–4.

17. *Letter to the Lord Deputy*, in Maclysart, above note 1, 1655, p438–440.

18. Entitled *Some Advertisements for the New Election of Burgesses for the House of Commons*, this pamphlet was published in connection with the election of 'recruiter' MPs who replaced those who had defected to the King at Oxford. It was republished a few months later under the more sensational title.

19. Shakespeare, *Henry IV*, part 2, Act IV, Scene 2.

20. *Vindication*, p35.

21. *Vindication*, Epistle Dedicatory.

22. *Vindication*, p58.

23. *ibid*, p3.

24. *ibid*, p57.

25. Prest, *Barristers*, (note 3 above) p292.

26. *Vindication*, p13.

27. *ibid*, p19.

28. *ibid*, p23.

29. *ibid*, p22.

30. *ibid*, p25.

31. *ibid*, p33–4.
32. Prest, *Barristers* (note 3 above), p27.
33. *Vindication*, p40.
34. *ibid*, p58–9.
35. *ibid*, p26.
36. *Vindication*, p66 and see Veall (above, note 4), p220–1.
37. *ibid*, p76, 96.
38. Veall, *Law Reform* (above, note 4), p73.
39. Benjamin Woolley, *The Herbalist* (London, 2004), p240.
40. Pauline Gregg, *Freeborn John*, (London, 1961), p102.
41. Margaret Pelling, *Medical Conflicts in Early Modern London*, (Oxford, 2003), p148.
42. Royal College of Physicians, B Hamey to Isaac Dorislaus, 20 August 1646 (copy supplied to author by Dr Prest).

Chapter 5: What the Independents Would Have

1. 'The English Revolutionaries, because of the conservative nature of the English character and because of the pervasive influence of their legal education, had to find a precedent even for an innovation.' Stuart E. Prall, *The Agitation for Law Reform During the Puritan Revolution, 1640–60*, (The Hague, 1966), p6.
2. Henry Parker, *Observations Upon Some of His Majesty's Late Answers and Expressions* (1642), Thomason E 153 (62).
3. A. K. Kiralfy, *Potter's Introduction to English Law and its Institutions*, (1958) 43; cited by Prest, *Barristers*, p235.
4. *A Union of Hearts*, p12.
5. *ibid*, p8.
6. Woolrych, *Britain in Revolution*, (Oxford, 2002), p335–6.
7. Cited in Tristram Hunt, *The English Civil War at First Hand*, (London, 2002), p151.
8. S. R. Gardiner, *Constitutional Documents of the Puritan Revolution*, 3rd Ed, (Oxford, 1903), p315.
9. John Cooke: *What the Independents would have, or a character declaring some of their tenets, and their desires to disabuse those who speak ill of that they know not* (London, 1647).
10. *ibid*, p3.
11. *Union of Hearts*, p37.
12. *ibid*, p68–9.
13. *ibid*, p8.
14. *ibid*, p10.
15. *ibid*, p14.

16. Gardiner, *Constitutional Documents* (above Note 8), p335.

17. The debate over the King went on for several days, and became so heated that William Clarke, the army stenographer, was ordered to stop recording it. The exchange between Harrison and Cromwell appears in his notes for November 11. See John Morrill, 'Oliver Cromwell', *Oxford Dictionary of National Biography* (Oxford 2004).

18. Tristram Hunt, *The English Civil War*, above note 7, p163–4.

19. S. R. Gardiner, *History of the Great Civil War*, (London, 1987), Vol. IV, p5.

20. *ibid*, p30. Stories about Cromwell and Ireton disguising themselves as tipplers at the Blue Boar Inn at Holborn, waiting to intercept riders with the King's letters sewn into their saddlebags, have the flavour of invention – correspondence from Carisbrooke to the Queen in Paris was not likely to have been routed via London.

21. Gardiner, *Constitutional Documents* (above note 8), p335.

Chapter 6: The Poor Man's Case

1. *Cooke's Poor Man's Case*, The Retrospective Review (November, 1853), p21.

2. John Cooke, *Unum necessarium; or The Poor Man's Case, an expedient to make provision for all poor people in the Kingdom* (London, 1648).

3. *The Poor Man's Case*, p42.

4. *ibid*, p43.

5. *ibid*, p44 & 65.

6. *ibid*, p68.

7. *ibid*, p64, 65.

8. *ibid*, p66.

9. *ibid*, p68: Cooke refers to his 'dear father's' objections to the profession.

10. Hugh Peters, *A Word for the Army*, 11th October, 1647.

Chapter 7: Malignant Blood

1. *A Declaration of the Commons of England in Parliament assembled expressing their reasons and grounds for passing the late resolutions touching no further addresses or Application to be made to the King* dated 11 February, printed 15 February, 1648 under the hand of Henry Elsing, clerk to Parliament. This very important document does not appear in Gardiner or Kenyon's collections of constitutional papers of the period.

2. S. R. Gardiner, *History of the Great Civil War*, (London, 1987), Vol IV, p119 – citing Allen's Narrative, in *The Somers' Collection of Tracts*, ed. Walter Scott (London, 1811). vi, 500.

3. Gardiner, *ibid*, p191.

Notes

4. Gardiner, *ibid*, p217.
5. In a petition to Parliament on 18 October. See *Perfect Occurances*, 13–20 October, 1648.
6. *The Remonstrance* was published in *Perfect Occurances* for 17–24 November. It was signed by John Rushworth as secretary of the Army Council and dated 18 November. It too is unaccountably omitted from Gardiner (*Documents*) and Kenyon, *The Stuart Constitution 1603–1688* (Cambridge, 1966).
7. *Perfect Occurrances*, 17–24 November, entry for 20 November.
8. *Perfect Occurances*, 29 September – 6 October, entry for 2 October (Thomason E 5 26).
9. *Monthly Mercury*, 8 November 1648.
10. See Gardiner, *History* (above, note 2), p249–53.
11. The situation in the first week of December was confused: Ireton and his Army colleagues and their Leveller allies, true to the principles of the *Remonstrance*, wanted the Long Parliament dissolved. But the Independent MPs with whom they met over the next few days urged a purge of Parliament, not a dissolution.
12. *Perfect Diurnall*, 4–11 December. It notes that Major Rolph had written from Carisbrooke to inform Parliament of Fairfax's order to take the King to Hurst: some officers had demurred, but most felt the General's command had to be obeyed.
13. Ludlow, *Memoirs*, (Edinburgh, Sands 1751), 1, p211–12.
14. *The Perfect Diurnall* 4–11 December (entry for 6th December).

Chapter 8: To Clutch the Swimming Hare

1. Acquittals were rare, but not unknown: if they occurred, the jurors would be summoned by the Star Chamber to explain themselves. See John Bellamy, *The Tudor Law of Treason*, (London, 1979), p171.
2. John Cooke, *Monarchy No Creature of God's Making* (Waterford, 1651), p115.
3. Recent unpersuasive attempts have been made to attribute a 'neo-Romanist' republicanism to some of the early parliamentarian leaders, based on their familiarity with Cicero and the Roman historians. They rely too much upon 'neo-classical' concepts in Harrington's *Oceana*, but that was not published until 1656 and had no influence on men like Cooke or Peters or other leading Independents. The basic influences on the regicides were the common law, Magna Carta and the bible. 'Neo-romanism' as a factor in the English revolution is being given far too much credence (notwithstanding the presence of Roman law expert Isaac Dorislaus on the prosecution team at the trial) e.g. by Quentin Skinner, *Classical Liberty, Renaissance Translation and the English Civil War*, in *Visions of Politics, Volume II: Renaissance Virtues* (Cambridge University Press, 2002); Adam

389

Tomkins *Our Republican Constitution* (Hart, Oxford, 2005), p52–56; Jonathan Scott, 'What were the Commonwealth Principles?' *Historical Journal*, Vol. 47, No 3 (Cambridge, 2004).

4. Hosea, 8:4; 13, 9–10.

5. *Monarchy*, above note 2, Preface. Although written two years later, *Monarchy* is an elaboration of the beliefs that Cooke, Peters and others held at the time of the trial.

6. *ibid*, p20.

7. *ibid*, p29.

8. *Ibid*, p93.

9. *Ibid*, p103.

10. *Ibid*, p50.

11. Drunken cavaliers were quarrelling in the Strand and threatening each other with pistols: see *Perfect Occurrences* 17–24 November, entry for 23 November.

12. *A Vindication of the Ministers of the Gospel*, 27th January 1649, cited by Elliot Vernon, *The Quarrel of the Covenant: The London Presbyterians and Regicides*, in Jason Peacey (ed.) *The Regicides and the Execution of Charles I* (Basingstoke, 2001), p202.

13. See Margo Todd, 'Isaac Dorislaus', *Oxford Dictionary of National Biography* (Oxford, 2004).

14. See Ruth Spalding (ed.), *The Diary of Bulstrode Whitelocke 1605–1675* (Oxford, 1990), entry for 19 December 1648.

15. Cooke had been retained in a legal capacity by the Army. In *Monarchy no Creature* (above note 2) at p60 he refers to 'the army whereby I was sometimes advocate, and count it honourable to be a member of an army fighting for Christ . . .'

16. *A Perfect Diurnall*, 28 August – 4th September (E526) report for 31 August. Sir Thomas Herbert records their presence at Newport in his memoirs, reproduced in Roger Lockyer (ed.), *The Trial of Charles I*, (London, 1971), p42.

17. Quoted in Robert Partridge, 'O Horrable Murder', *The Trial, Execution and Burial of Charles I*, (London, 1998), p49.

18. See Lockyer, note 17 above, p61.

19. Most commentators fail to notice that the meeting was at the Duke's request. (See *Perfect Occurrances* 8–15 December – 'Upon a letter from Duke Hamilton, Lieutenant General Cromwell is gone to Windsor and intends suddenly to return to Westminster.' Cromwell's main interest in meeting the Duke would have been to find out whether any Presbyterian MPs were complicit in 'the engagement' or supportive of the Scott's invasion, although he might have suggested that the Duke pass on the offer of a 'plea bargain' – abdication in return for exile – to the King, who would shortly join the Duke at Windsor.

20. *Perfect Diurnall* 11–18 December, entry for 16 December. Interestingly, the Rump,

for all its closeness to the Army, seems to have had no inkling of the decision to bring the King to London. On 15th December it ordered that 3 falcons and loads of shot be sent to Hurst (obviously for Charles' sport) together with large quantities of gin and a Union Jack to fly from the battlements to signify a King in residence – for what they must have supposed would be some time.

21. *ibid*, 18–25 December, entry for 18 December.

22. See G. Robertson and A. Nicol, *Media Law* (London, 2002), p401.

23. John Bellamy, *The Tudor Law of Treason* (London, 1979), p234.

24. M. H. Keen, *The Laws of War in the Late Middle Ages*, (London, 1965 repr 1993), p53.

25. A common saying that reflected the law of war: see Pierino Belli, *de rei militari et bello tractatus* (1563), or *A Treatise on Military Matters and Warfare* (Vol. 2, Oxford 1936, translation by H. C. Nutting) Chapter II. 16 ('Whether a captured general of the enemy should be spared'). Gentili, always more humane than other jurists of the time, reluctantly agreed that captured enemy leaders and even Kings could be killed if their survival would imperil the peace or if they were treacherous: 'even Caesar thought it folly to spare men who had more than once figured as his opponents.' *De Jure Belli Libri Tres* (1612 Hanau; Oxford 1933) translated by J C Rolfe, p385; 477–481; 525.

26. Spalding, *Diary*, above note 14, at p226–7. Whitelocke, who could never bear to be away from the centre of power, returned to undertake judicial functions in early January.

27. Bishop Burnet's *History of His Own Time*, (Thomas Ward, 1724), p46.

Chapter 9: The Hare, Clutched: Cooke's Charge

1. *Journal of the House of Lords*, X641, See S. R. Gardiner, *The Great Civil War*, (London, 1987 ed), p288.

2. *Perfect Diurnall* of some passages in Parliament, 18–25 December, entry for 23 December.

3. *Perfect Diurnall*, 25 December – 1 January, entry for 27 December.

4. Rushworth, in Lockyer, *The Trial of Charles I* (London, Folio Society), p71.

5. Bishop Burnet's *Life and Death of Sir Matthew Hale* (1682), p13 erroneously claims that Hale 'was not suffered to appear'. The King made no application to be represented by Hale, who advised him in private.

6. S. R. Gardiner, *History* (note 1 above), p288–9.

7. *Journal of the High Court of Justice*, as attested by Phelps, published by J. Nalson on January 4th, 1683. See Muddiman, *The Trial of Charles I*, Appendix A, p193.

8. Rushworth, in Lockyer, *Trial*, (note 4 above), p76–7.

9. C. V. Wedgwood, *The Trial of Charles I*, (London, 1964), p102.

10. Lucy Hutchinson, *Memoirs of the Life of Colonel Hutchinson*, (Phoenix, 1995), p235. She points out that the King's trial was urged in petitions presented by the regiments of the very men – especially Fairfax and Ingoldsby – who come the Restoration were to pretend most strenuously that they had opposed the trial.

11. *Perfect Occurrances*, 22–30 December, report 27 December.

12. According to a report in *Perfect Occurrances* for 3rd January, possible prosecuting counsel were discussed as early as that date.

13. Lucy Hutchison, above note 10, p234.

14. John Cooke, *King Charles: His Case*, published in Muddiman, *Notable British Trials, Trial of Charles I* (London, 1928), p258.

15. *ibid*, p257.

16. Historians assume too readily that the lawyers rather than the politicians were responsible for the length of the first draft charge. Cooke asserted at his own trial that 'it will appear, I hope, that some would have had a very voluminous and long charge, but I was utterly against it'. (*An Exact and Most Impartial Accompt*, p119.) Had his prosecutors found any evidence to the contrary (and they had witnesses – e.g. Nutley – to the painted chamber proceedings) they would have called them to testify against Cooke. Nutley instead pointed the finger at Harrison as the source of the pre-war allegations ('let us blacken him what we can'). Cooke made clear that this additional material – about Charles conniving at parricide, the Irish atrocities, Eliot's death, the loss of La Rochelle, etc – was irrelevant to his charge of treason and tyranny. See the preface to *King Charles: His Case*. Sean Kelsey's valuable demonstration that the outcome of the trial was not pre-ordained does not gain from his strange notion that the MPs took over Cooke's charge and watered it down so the King would have a better chance of acquittal. (See below, note 28 to Chapter 10) On the contrary, the final narrow charge was much more devastating for the defendant than the original blunderbuss indictment.

17. R v Charles I, 4 State Trials, p1070–1072. The procedural decisions related on p142–4 are found in the short minutes taken by Phelps at all meetings of the Court.

Chapter 10: The King's Trial

1. This story has been routinely accepted by historians to embroider their accounts of the trial, although it is derived from a highly dubious source – a very partisan prosecution witness at the regicide trials eleven years later. It was told then to implicate Marten by the spy Purback Temple, who claimed to have bribed the custodians of the Painted Chamber to let him hide in the recess behind the tapestry. From which hiding place, of course, he could not have seen the ruddy-complexioned Cromwell blanch. And the answer attributed as a stroke of genius

to Marten was very similar to the formula that the court had already agreed the previous day (as Phelps' minutes confirm), namely that Cooke would present the charge 'in the name and on the behalf of the people of England'.

2. They resolved that if the King 'in language or carriage towards the court be insolent, outrageous or contemptuous' the Lord President should decide whether to ignore or admonish him, or order him to be taken away or else adjourn the court.

3. Richard II, Act 4, Scene 1. See Charles Carlton, *Charles I – The Personal Monarch*, (London, 1995), p336.

4. 4 State Trials, p1078–9.

5. *ibid*, p995.

6. *The Moderate. No 28*, 16–23 January 1649 (p228), Sir Thomas Herbert, in his self-serving (and hence Charles-serving) memoirs claims that he scrabbled around for the silver tip, but he was on the other side of the King and could not reach it. (Herbert, *Memoirs* (3rd edition, 1815), p165.

7. 4 State Trials, p995 and see p1073.

8. *Ibid*, p995–7 and p1073–6.

9. *Ibid*, p1074.

10. *Ibid*, p1075.

11. *Ibid*, p1076.

12. See Testimony of Thomas Richardson, R v Peters in 1660, ('*An Exact Account* . . .'), (London, 1660), p162.

13. Sir Philip Warwick, *Memoirs of the Reign of King Charles I* (London, 1701), p380. The ubiquitous Peters seems to have had the run of St James's Palace while the King was there.

14. J. G. Muddiman, (ed.) *Notable British Trials, Trial of Charles I* (London, 1928), p98.

15. Testimony of James Nutley, R v Cooke (1660), *An Exact and Most Impartial Accompt* . . . , p107.

16. *ibid, Regicide Trial*, R v Peters, Testimony of Mr Chase, p167–8.

17. 4 State Trials, p1079–80.

18. *Perfect Occurrances*, 5–12 January, entry for 10 January. Prynne had been committed to prison for contempt of Parliament. Whitelocke was back on the Bench, which granted the *habeus corpus* after he had conferred with the Commons. See Spalding, *Diary* (above), p228.

19. Thus Fairfax was urged by Colonel White, one of his senior officers, to court-martial the King rather than to put him on trial: See S R Gardiner, *History of the Great Civil War*, (London, Windrush, 1987), Vol. IV, p302.

20. *Regicide Trial*, p111, evidence of Joseph Herne.

21. 4 State Trials, p1081–2.

22. *Ibid*, p1082–3.

23. *Ibid*, p1084.

24. *Regicides' Trial*, Herne, p112.

25. John Cooke, *King Charles, His Case* in Muddiman, p235.

26. *Ibid*, p250.

27. *State Trials*, p1096.

28. *Ibid*, p1093.

29. *Ibid*, p1098.

30. *Ibid*, p1098–9.

31. See Muddiman, *Trial*, p211. Muddiman erroneously labels these minutes, taken by Phelps, as 'Bradshawe's Journal'.

32. Sean Kelsey, for example, thinks that 'somebody was playing for time' because 'the colourful wartime recollections of a handful of non-entities . . . constituted extremely weak evidence indeed.' On the contrary, the evidence of common soldiers, from both sides, proved beyond doubt that the King bore command responsibility for the sufferings of ordinary people in the wars. The incriminating documents Cooke tendered for examination – the King's intercepted messages – provided the best evidence of his guilt. Kelsey's notion that 'Parliamentary commanders and leading civilian politicians could have easily provided far better evidence' is also mistaken: what better cue for royalists to cry 'victor's justice' had the likes of Cromwell or Haselrig testified against Charles? See Kelsey, 'Politics and Procedure in the Trial of Charles I', *Law and History Review*, Spring 2004, Vol. 22 No.1, p19–21.

33. 4 State Trials, p1099–1113. The public turned up as usual at Westminster Hall, so Dendy and the usher were sent to tell them to depart – the Court was sitting in private in the painted chamber: *Perfect Occurrances*, 18–25 January, entry for 24 January.

34. Muddiman, *Trial*, p214. Holder's successful plea against self-incrimination was on Thursday, 25 January.

35. *ibid*, p1108, Testimony of John Vinson.

36. *ibid*, Testimony of Will Cuthbert.

37. *ibid*, Samuel Lawson, p1105–6.

38. *ibid*, Humphrey Browne, p1107.

39. *Ibid*, Richard Price (the scrivenor who engrossed Cooke's charge, and who had met the King in 1643 as an emissary on behalf of the Independents).

40. *ibid*, Henry Gooch, p1111.

41. *Ibid*, p1113.

42. Regicides' Trial, Starkey Testimony, p116–7. Starkey at first put this evening meeting after the second or third trial session but then thought it rather 'in the interim of time before the sentence, for there was an adjournment for a day or two'. This would sensibly date it (if it took place at all, which Cooke denied) on either the Thursday or the Friday night.

Notes

Chapter 11: Farewell Sovereignty

1. Whitelocke, *Memorials of the English Affairs from the Beginning of the Reign of Charles I to the Happy Restoration of Charles II*, (London, 1682), Vol. II, p507.

2. 4 State Trials, p1115–6.

3. The following exchanges are from 4 State Trials, p1122–4.

4. See *Regicide Trial*, ('*An Exact and Most Impartial Accompt . . .*'), London, 1660, Axtell's trial, p189–92. Royalist legend attributes both interjections to Lady Fairfax, although if she was involved it is likely only to have been on the first day, when her husband's name was called.

5. Under the agreed court rules, Downes was entitled to secure an adjournment, without self-indulgent flourishes, simply by asking for one. Had he done so publicly there was no reason why the reports would not have indicated the fact. The only report which records his interjection is that of Nalson, a royalist whose version was not published until 1684. (See 4 State Trials, p1125).

6. Whitelocke, *Memorials of English Affairs*, above note 1, p509.

7. *A true and humble representation of John Downes Esquire touching the death of the late King, so far as he may be concerned therein*, 1660. Downes was a businessman-MP who played very little part in the Long Parliament, but made a fortune by buying and reselling royalist estates. His 'peevishness' had been displayed earlier in the month when he had accused another member of the court, the theologian John Fry (forebear of author/actor Stephen Fry), of blasphemy, forcing Fry's withdrawal from the trial and his suspension from Parliament until he cleared his name.

8. Downes said at his trial that he raised a further point, encouraged to do so by Peters and by 'private whispers' from another he declined to name but gave sufficient clues to identify as Cooke. Downes described this person as 'one of them that is gone and hath received his sentence and doom'. Downes was tried on 16 October 1660, the day that Cooke was executed. See Regicide Trial, p261–2.

9. Regicide Trial, p244.

10. *ibid*, p269.

11. Lucy Hutchinson, *Memoirs of the Life of Colonel Hutchinson* (Phoenix, 1995), p234.

12. Muddiman, ed., *Notable British Trials* (London, 1928), p235.

13. Richard II, Act III, Scene III, Lines 87–89. The Bishop of Carlisle, later in the play, predicts that 'children yet unborn shall feel the day as sharp to them as thorn', Act IV, Scene I, Lines 322–3.

14. 4 State Trials, p1008–16.

15. See Genesis 9, Verse 35.

16. 4 State Trials, p1017 and 1128.

17. *ibid*, p1128.

18. 'Bradshawe's refusal to allow the King to speak after his conviction was the final suggestion of a show trial' say Kishlansky and Morrill in their entry for Charles I in the Dictionary of National Biography (Oxford, 2004). On the contrary, it was customary criminal procedure at the time.

19. Amongst the commissioners recorded at this meeting was John Downes – which casts doubt on his post-restoration claim that he spent this time weeping in the speaker's office. Downes signed the death warrant on the following Monday.

20. See *King Charles: His Case*, in Muddiman, *Notable British Trials* (London, 1928), p235.

21. Rushworth in Roger Lockyer (ed.), *The Trial of Charles I* (London, Folio Society, 1974), p133–4.

22. See Muddiman, above note 12, or 4 State Trials, p1018–22.

23. State Trials, p1025.

24. *Ibid*, p1032.

25. See Theodore Meron, *War Crimes Law Comes of Age*, (Oxford, 1998), p8–9.

26. A Gentili, *De Jure Belli Libri Tres* (1612) Carnegie edition translated, J C Rolfe, 1933, p74. See Meron (above), p128.

27. See Cooke, *King Charles: His Case*, in Muddiman, p248.

28. The argument is developed by D. Allan Orr, *Treason and the State*, (Cambridge, 2002), p52.

29. A Gentili, *De Jure Belli Libri Tres* (1612), Carnegie edition translated, J. C. Rolfe, 1933, p122.

30. *The Trial of Charles I*, ed Lockyer (above note 21), p122.

31. She was the wife of Sir William Wheeler. See Lockyer, *op cit*.

32. *Regicide Trial*, evidence of Ewer (p247).

33. C. V. Wedgwood, *Trial*, p195.

34. The axe-man was probably Richard Brandon, the common hangman who had disposed of Strafford and Laud and could be expected – it was his professional duty – to perform the execution without a hitch. There is no doubt that he was brought with his instruments to Whitehall that morning by a troop of soldiers despatched by Axtell, and the sheer professionalism of his performance – the executioner knew to tuck the hair inside the victim's cap and to bend for forgiveness – indicated a man born to this grisly trade, which Brandon had inherited from his father. Although his published 'confessions' are inauthentic, there is some evidence that he accepted £30 in half-crowns for the job and that the King gave him an orange laced with cloves that he sold in Rosemary Lane, where he lived, for 10 shillings. See Thomason Tracts (British Library) E561 (12 + 14). It is very likely that his disguised assistant was a soldier, trusted by the army to take Brandon's place if the hangman quailed at the last moment. William Hulet, from

Colonel Hewson's regiment, is the likeliest candidate: he was convicted at the regicides' trial of beheading the King, but subsequently pardoned: see Chapter 19.

35. The description of the King's last moments is taken from the account by John Rushworth in Lockyer (above note 21).

36. The 'universal groan' was an early essential of royalist mythmaking, although it begins as a metaphorical lament at the funeral not the execution. Thus in March 1649, the Bishop of Chichester published 'A *Deep Groan Fetch'd at the Funeral of that Incomparable and Glorious Monarch Charles I.*'

Chapter 12: 'Stone Dead Hath No Fellow'

1. J G Muddiman, *The Trial of Charles I*, Notable British Trials, (London 1928), p167.

2. *Mercurius Elencticus* 7 February 1649. Given Wharton's capacity for invention, the quote is probably apocryphal.

3. Purbeck Temple had the facility of being everywhere the prosecution in October 1660 needed him to be in January 1649 – it was he who claimed to have hidden behind the tapestry in the Painted Chamber and later to have heard the interjections of Lady Fairfax. Royalists bridle (still) at the suggestion that Jane was the King's mistress: they claim that their intimate embraces at Carisbrooke were to disguise the smuggling of letters.

4. Lockyer (ed.), *Trial of Charles I*, (Folio Society, London, 1974), p142–3. For the same reason, the ashes of the Nazi leaders were, after Nuremberg, strewn over a fast-flowing river so that no shrine would be available for future mourners.

5. Whitelocke, *Memorials*, p540.

6. Sir Charles Lucas, A *Penitential Ode for the Death of King Charles*, see Andrew Lacey, *Elegies and Verse in Honour of Charles the Martyr*, Jason Peacey, (ed.) *The Regicides and the Execution of Charles I* (Basingstoke, 2001), p235.

7. Whitelocke, *Memorials*, p517.

8. Hugh Ross Williamson, *The Day They Killed the King*, (New York, 1957), p154.

9. See S R Gardiner, *Constitutional Documents*, p381 & 384.

10. *ibid*, p385–6.

11. *The Tenure of Kings and Magistrates* in Orgel and Goldberg (eds.) *John Milton* (Oxford, 1991), p276.

12. The need to make good this comparison explains the false accusations at the regicide trials about how soldiers reviled the King and spat on him in the passageways, and note evidence of Tomlinson, *Regicide Trial*, p219, that the 'incivilities' amounted to smoking and keeping hats on in his presence.

13. 'The Englishman's proverbial 'love of lord', his admiring interest in 'the squire

and his relations' . . . the Englishman was, at bottom, something of a snob but very little of a courtier.' G. M. Trevelyan, *English Social History*, (Pelican, 1967), p267.

14. Ludlow, *Memoirs*, (Sands ed, Edinburgh, 1751) Vol 1, p251.

15. See Wedgwood, *Trial*, p215, Note 70. John Aske, Cooke's junior (i.e. assistant) counsel, was appointed to the Upper Bench on June 1st, 1649.

16. *The Weeping Onion, A Salt Tear at the Lamentable Funeral of Dr Dorislaus*, 16th June, 1649.

17. Muddiman, above note 1, p259.

18. 'None shall kill an enemy who yields and throws down his arms, upon pain of death' was a rule of a) the King's army in 1640, b) the Earl of Essex's army in 1642 and c) the Army of the Kingdom of Scotland in 1643. See a) F. Grosse, *Military Antiquities* (London, 1788), p118; b) Charles M. Clode *The Military Forces of the Crown* (London, 1869), Vol. I, p422–5; c) Grosse (above) p136.

19. Pauline Gregg, *Freeborn John*, (London, 1961), p64.

20. Which remained difficult: three centuries later William Joyce (the pro-Nazi broadcaster 'Lord Haw-Haw') claimed that as an American he could not be tried for treason to the British crown: <u>Joyce v Director of Public Prosecutions</u> [1946] AC 347.

21. *A Compleat Collection of State Tryals*, (London, 1719), p567.

22. See the author's judgement in *Prosecutor v Kondewa*, SCSL, 04–14–T-128–7363, Decision on amnesty provided by Lomé Accord. 25 May 2004.

23. *State Trials*, Volume IV, p1190.

24. See the Privy Council decision in <u>A G of Trinidad v Phillip</u>, [1995] 1 AC 396.

25. Bulstrode Whitelocke, *Memorials of the English Affairs*, Vol 2, p548.

26. See G. B. Nourse, *Law Reform under the Commonwealth*, (1959), 75LQR 512, p515. Debtors could obtain release by swearing that they did not possess more than £5.00, over and above 'bare necessities'.

27. John Lilburne, *The Hunting of the Foxes*, (21st March, 1649).

28. The Levellers at Burford were broken and repentant, as they watched their three convicted comrades face the firing squad (made up of men they had fought with at Preston and Naseby) without protest. They were locked in the church ('Anthony Sedley, prisoner 1649', can still be seen carved on the font) and later released – without charge, and without further rebellion. See Trevor Royle, *Civil War* (London, 2004), p513.

29. The seriousness with which the prosecution of the Leveller leaders was mounted, may be seen from the fact that no less than 6 counsel were appointed to prosecute – two sergeants and Steel, as well as Cooke.

30. The Trial of John Lilburne, *A Complete Collection of State Tryals from the reign of Henry IV to the end of the reign of Queen Anne* (London, 1719), Vol 1, p584.

31. *ibid*, p593, 603.
32. *ibid*, p626.
33. Gregg, above note 19, p308.
34. John Lisle surrendered the mastership to Cooke: Commons Journal, VI, 246 (30 June 1649).
35. Peter Hopewell, *St Cross — England's Oldest Almshouse* (Chichester, 1995). Cooke followed John Lisle (the MP for Winchester who had assisted Bradshawe at the King's trial) but Hopewell dates this to 1657 – an error which is widely repeated, notwithstanding the record of Cooke's appointment as Master on 30 June 1649 and his signature as Master on leases of St Cross property in September 1649 and May 1651. (Hampshire Record Office, document 111M94W/Q2/68/1 and p441–6). Cooke was succeeded by Richard Shute in 1655. Dr Lewis, who had been appointed by Charles I in 1627, was restored as Master in 1660.
36. *The Hospital of St Cross* (Guide, 1993).
37. Hopewell, above note 35, p80.
38. *The Moderate* No 49, June 12–19 1649: Cooke is made a trustee under the 'Act for the Maintenance of Preachers'.
39. Council of State, Proceedings for May 8, 1649. CPSD 1649–50, p130.
40. Council of State, Proceedings for May 23, 1649: Cooke's fellow Commissioners include John Wildman, presumably the Leveller lawyer. CPSD 1649–50, 154.
41. *The Moderate Intelligencer*, Jun 9–16, announces Aske's elevation. It reports (p84–5) a dinner at Sergeant's Inn over which St John presides and Whitelocke condescendingly tells the lawyers how helpful they have all been to the Commonwealth.
42. Cooke, Letter to Fleetwood (August 6, 1655). Republished in MacLysaght, *Irish Life in the Seventeenth Century* (Cork, 1950), p444.

Chapter 13: Impressions on White Paper

1. Speech to General Council, 23 March, 1649, W. C. Abbott, *The Writings and Speeches of Oliver Cromwell* (London, 1937–47), Vol. II, p36–39.
2. Letter from Hugh Peters, 16 August 1649, printed in the *The Perfect Diurnall*, 23 August 1649.
3. Shortly before the army arrived in mid-August, Michael Jones won a significant victory over Ormonde at Rathmines and was able to welcome Cromwell to a 'pale' – the protestant area of influence around Dublin – which had largely recovered its proportions.
4. The most recent treatment is by Tom Reilly, *Cromwell – An Honourable Enemy* (Phoenix, 1999). He argues that Drogheda was very different to the way modern Irish republican historians (and Simon Schama) have sought to portray it, as a

war crime. It was a victory for English Republicans over English-led Royalists, fought according to the contemporary laws of war.

5. Aston's last letter to Ormond, on 10 September, was prophetically signed 'Living I am, and dying I will end, my Lord.' This stout royalist, who had governed Oxford for the King, obeyed Ormond's orders against his better judgement. He died defiant, cut down by soldiers who sawed through his wooden leg which was rumoured to be packed with gold.

6. Cromwell to William Lenthall, speaker of Parliament, 17th September, cited Reilly (above note 4), p274. Such letters were invariably published.

7. The following account is taken from *A True Relation of Mr Justice Cooke's Passage by Sea* – published in 1650 with *Mrs Cooke's Meditations*.

8. *The Hector* survived to sail in Blake's republican fleet: it was sunk under Montague in 1665.

9. Abbott, above note 1, Vol. II, p186–7.

10. *The Memoirs of Edmund Ludlow*, Vol I, p246.

11. The houses – one with a slate roof, the other straw – were in Bariston Street and St John's Street, the former presumably occupied as his home. His farm at Kilbarry was listed in *The Civil Survey A.D. 1654–6, County of Waterford* Vol. VI (Robert C Simington (Gov. Pub. Office, Dublin, 1642)), p190–1. 'There a good house, ye ruines of a castle, a garden and an orchard hereupon.' Barnehay Castle, although ruined, features in *The Castles of County Cork* by James N. Healy (Cork and Dublin, 1988). These lands were settled by Act of 26 September 1653 'upon the said John Cooke and his heirs forever, for his good and faithful services in Ireland and in lieu of all arrears of pension due him for the same.'

12. This is necessarily speculative, given the absence of birth and burial records, but John refers in his letter to Freelove to re-uniting in heaven with her brother, 'dear D.' There is a hint that Frances may have been pregnant at the time of the storm. The evidence that Freelove was Mary's child, and a baby at the time of Cooke's death, is by no means conclusive: his 'letter to Freelove' appears to be addressed to a child rather than an infant.

13. Nicholas Canny, *Making Ireland British, 1580–1650*, (Oxford, 2001), p467–8. For contemporary descriptions of the atrocities, see 476–7; 484–5; 510–15; 535; 542; 546–8.

14. Colm Toibin, 'The Cause that called You', *New York Review of Books*, 19 Dec 2002, p53.

15. These statistics were from *Mercurius Politicus* No.136, Dec 30 1952 – Jan 6, 1953, reporting sittings in Kilkenny, Clonwell and Cork. Cooke was certainly a member of the bench in Kilkenny (*Politicus* No.125) and probably in Cork. These 3 – judge tribunals were usually chaired by the Irish-born member (Donnellan or

Lowther) but in the absence of records it is impossible to assess their work. Muddiman (as 'J.B. Williams') makes a typical generalized attack without even noticing the acquittal rate: *The Regicides in Ireland II*, Irish Ecclesiastical Record (5th series) 3, 1914, p180–194. In contrast Hickson, who studied and transcribed Judge Lowther's notes of the trials of O'Neil, Muskerry and others, salutes their fairness and mercy: M. A. Hickson, *Ireland in the Seventeenth Century*, (London, 1884), Vol. II, p174–7.

16. Hickson, above, p204. Judge Lowther presided, but the court's somewhat gratuitous reference to the Sicilian Vespers suggests that Cooke was a member. Compare *King Charles: His Case* in Muddiman, *Trial*, p234.

17. R Dunlop, *Ireland under the Commonwealth*, Historical series XVII, University of Manchester, 1915, p335 (Document 369, 15 April 1653).

18. e.g. the use of the 'common purpose' doctrine by the Apartheid courts in South Africa to convict the 'Sharpeville 6' and 'Upington 14' in the 1980s. See Geoffrey Robertson, *The Justice Game*, (London, 1998), p211.

19. Cooke, *Monarchy No Creature of God's Making* (Waterford, 1651), Preface, p28–30.

20. See T C Barnard, *Cromwellian Ireland*, (Oxford, 2000). p273.

21. *Monarchy* Preface, p44.

22. Dunlop (above) Vol 1, p142, Document 149. (28 Feb; 1652). Edward Wale refused the call.

23. Preface to *Monarchy No Creature . . .* , p44–6.

24. John Percivale to Thomas Pigott (his cousin), 25 September 1652: HMC, Egmont Mss I 514.

25. See Preface to *Monarchy* etc, p34.

26. The Petition is published as the Preface to *Monarchy* etc, see p14. It was referred to the Committee for Irish Affairs by the Council of State on 24 December 1650: P.R.O. SP25/15 f. 44.

27. Cooke's resignation letter, 6 August 1655, reproduced in MacLysaght, *Irish Life in the Seventeenth Century*, (Cork, 1950), p422.

28. *ibid*, p425.

29. *ibid*, p436.

30. *ibid*, p445, 435.

31. *ibid*, p433.

Chapter 14: The Protectorate

1. See Antonia Fraser, *Cromwell, Our Chief of Men*, (London, 1970), p383.

2. See Mary Cottrell, 'Interregnum Law Reform: the Hale Commission of 1652' (1968): 83 *English Historical Review*, p689. Whitelocke received the report on behalf of Parliament and was instrumental in blocking its proposals, even for the

registration of land (Cooke's proposal for this, in the *Vindication*, had received wide support).

3. S. R. Gardiner, *Constitutional Documents*, (Oxford, 1903, 3rd ed.), p400.

4. 'The Examination of the Jury that try'd John Lilburne at the sessions House, Old Bailey, 20 August 1653': *A Compleat Collection of State Tryals* (London, 1719) Vol 1, p638.

5. Gardiner, *Documents* (note 3 above), p405.

6. Henry Cromwell to Thurloe, 14 November, 1655. Thurloe State Papers IV, 198

7. MacLysaght, *Ireland in the Seventeenth Century* (Cork, 1950), p430.

8. *ibid*, p441.

9. *ibid*, p445.

10. Parliament's land confiscation program in Ireland had begun in 1642: almost 20% of arable land had been seized to satisfy the 'adventurers' who financed the army in the four provinces (Munster, Connaught, Leinster, Ulster). The Act for the Settling of Ireland provided for the forfeiture of the property of those who had fought for Ormonde (although the families might be given land of half its value) and Catholics were to be 'transplanted' to Connaught, where they would be granted two thirds of the value of the confiscated land. They would not suffer forfeiture at all if they had manifested 'constant good affection' to Parliament.

11. See Dunlop, Vol. I above, No 791, p569.

12. See J. P. Prendegast, *The Cromwellian Settlement of Ireland*, (London, 1870; 1996), p231–6. Lady Thurles was not forced to remove to Connaught, although as 'a popish recusant and transplantable' she lost her lands. She was still alive to welcome her son, who returned laden with power and honours at the Restoration. Prendegast, p125.

13. Thurloe State Papers V, p353–4, 28th August 1656.

14. And Christopher Love, tried by a third High Court of Justice in 1651. See *A Complete Collection of State Tryals* (London, 1719), Vol 1, p640.

15. See Todd M Edelman, *The Jews of Britain 1656–2000* (University of California Press, 2004).

16. See Woolrych, *Britain in Revolution* (Oxford 2002), p647.

17. Andrew Marvel, *The First Anniversary of the Government under His Highness the Lord Protector*.

18. *Monarchy – No Creature of God's Making*, p93.

19. *ibid*, p99.

20. *ibid*, p119.

21. Woolrych, above note 16, p617.

22. There is no record of Frances' death. On the strength of some evidence of his marriage to Mary Chawner, Frances must have died from consumption at this time, shortly after John revealed this usually fatal illness to Henry Cromwell.

23. It was soon dissolved, after a republican resurgence fanned by Arthur Haselrig, who was summoned to attend the Upper House but insisted on taking his seat in the Commons because 'this looks like a House of Lords. I tremble to think of wardships and slavery.' Barry Denton, *Only in Heaven: The Life and Campaigns of Sir Arthur Hesilrige, 1601–1661* (Sheffield, 1997), p205.

24. *The Tryal of John Mordaunt*, in *A Compleat Collection* (above note 14) at p813.

25. Andrew Marvel, *A Poem Upon the Death of His Late Highness the Lord Protector.*

Chapter 15: Tumbledown Dick

1. Thurloe to Henry Cromwell, 18 January 1659. Thurloe State Papers VII, p594

2. This is the assumption made both by T. C. Barnard, *Cromwellian Ireland* (Oxford, 2000), p275 – and by Prest in the *Oxford Dictionary of National Biography* entry for Cooke.

3. Cooke to Henry Cromwell, 1st February 1659, Thurloe State Papers, p605.

4. Henry (Lord Deputy) to Lord Protector (Richard), 4 January 1659. Dunlop, p979.

5. Cooke to Henry, 8th February, 1659, Thurloe State Papers, p610.

6. Absence of records makes it necessary to assume that Frances died in 1659 and John remarried. There is no burial record for Frances, although she is obviously very ill in early 1659 (Cooke's letter to Henry). The remarriage to Mary Chawner is based on a statement by Nicols in *Antiquities of Leicestershire* Vol. IV and upon parish records that show Mary as 'Mary Cook' at the time of her own remarriage in 1667. There is no baptism record for Freelove, who must have been born (if Mary's daughter) in 1660.

7. Noble, *Lives of The Regicides*, Vol. II, p62–3. The report is from Whitelocke: 'Bradshawe declared, a little before he left the world, that if the King should be tried and condemned again, he would be the first man to do it.'

8. Austin Woolrych, *England Without a King*, (London, 1983), p39.

9. *Memoirs of Edmund Ludlow* (1702), Vol II, p125–7.

10. Thomason purchased his copy on 7 December 1659. Cooke may have returned to London for Bradshawe's funeral and written it then. Proof positive of his authorship is lacking and Prest's attribution in the Dictionary of National Biography is tentative.

11. Aidan Clarke, *Prelude to Restoration in Ireland*, (Cambridge, 1999), p130. This supports the thesis that Monck and Coote were in cahoots before Monck's march into England, the timing of which may have been triggered by the coup in Dublin.

12. William Bray (ed.), *Memoirs of John Evelyn*, comprising his *Diary from 1641 to 1705–6* (London, Warne & Co, 1818), p263.

13. Samuel Pepys, *Diary*, ed. R. C. Latham and W. Matthews (London, 1970), p44.

14. 'These four lines were in almost everyone's mouths': *Diurnal of Thomas Rugg*, (ed

William Sachse for Camden third series, Vol XC1, London, 1961), p30.

15. Pepys, *Diary*, p21.

16. Formed and guided by James Harrington, author of *Oceana* – the republican's handbook, published in 1656.

17. Pepys, *Diary*, p52.

18. *ibid*, p61.

19. So-called because the writs for the April elections were not issued in the King's name.

20. Pepys, *Diary* (note 113 above), p77 and 79.

21. Rugg, *Diurnal* (note 114 above), p56–8.

22. Pepys, *Diary*, p87.

23. *ibid*, p87 and p125.

24. *Memoirs of Ludlow*, Volume II, p251.

25. Haselrig was to end his days in the Tower, where he died of a fever in January 1661.

26. Edmund Ludlow, *Voyce From the Watch Tower*, ed A. B. Worden, Camden Fourth Series, Vol 21 (London, 1978), p126.

27. Rugg, *Diurnal*, p71–2.

28. Lambert died in 1684 on a prison island off Plymouth. Standing orders were to shoot him in cold blood if hostile troops were ever sighted. D. N. Farr, 'Lambert, John 1619–84' *Oxford Dictionary of National Biography*, 2004.

Chapter 16: Endgame

1. Dunlop, Vol. II, p716–7, entry 7071, 30 November 1659.

2. *A Sober Vindication of Lieutenant General Ludlow and Others* (1660) p3. Aiden Clark, *Prelude to Restoration in Ireland* (Cambridge, 1999) cites *A Sober Vindication* without attributing authorship. But it is the only extant pamphlet answering Ludlow's description of the *Vindication* that he says (and he should know) was written by Cooke. See *Voyce*, p87. It bears Cooke's style, and was published by Giles Calvert, who had printed other Cooke pamphlets.

3. F.J. Routledge (ed.), *Calendar of the Clarendon State Papers in the Bodleian Library* (Oxford, 1932) IV, p628–9; (30 March); p639 (6 April).

4. They feared that Coote's intention in seizing Cooke was to sacrifice him prematurely. As Ludlow put it, 'that he (Coote) might have this lamb to offer up to the fury of his sacred majesty', *Voyce*, p87.

5. John William Willis-Bund, *State Trials* (Cambridge, 1879–82) Vol. II, Part I, p5.

6. *ibid*, p10.

7. Pepys, *Diary*, ed Latham & Matthews (London, 1970), p118.

8. S. R. Gardiner, *Constitutional Documents*, p465.

9. Pepys, *Diary*, p122.

10. Ludlow, *A Voyce from the Watch Tower*, ed. A. B. Worden, C. F. S. 2i (London, 1978), p153.

11. *Act of Indemnity and Oblivion*, Article XXXVI. As it happened, this provision was to secure their lives, but not their liberty. Most were imprisoned for life.

12. Evelyn's *Diary*, ed. Bray (London, 1818), p265.

13. Pepys, *Diary*, ed Latham & Matthews (London, 1970), p159, entry for 26 May 1660.

14. St John narrowly avoided a bill of attainder, but was excluded for life from holding public office. He published a groveling self-defence – *The Case of Oliver St John Esq., concerning his actions during the late troubles* – in which he distanced himself from Cromwell (his close relative) and Thurloe (who had been his personal assistant) and claimed to have heard, seen and spoken no evil throughout the 'troubles'. Deprived of all power and in fear of reprisals, he left for European exile in 1662.

15. Pepys, *Diary*, p181, entry for 22 June, 1660.

16. *Bishop Burnet's History of His Own Time*, Vol. I (Thomas Ward, 1724), p98.

17. Ludlow, *Voyce*, p126.

18. Rugg, *Diurnall*, p81.

19. In September, Coote would be made Earl of Montrath and Broghill became Earl of Orrery.

20. John Bysse had, ironically, taken many of the witness depositions for the High Courts of Justice on which Cooke served. He had been a legal assistant in the Upper Bench, but transferred his allegiance quickly enough to be appointed a judge in Ireland after the Restoration: Barnard, *Cromwellian Ireland*, p288.

21. 'An Exact and Most Impartial Accompt . . .' No 97, p960 (entry for Wednesday 6 June 1660).

22. *Speeches and Prayers* . . . (1660) p47. ('Mr Cooke's letter to a friend'). The sequestration order is reported in *Mercurius Publicus* for No 23, entry for May 24.

23. *Speeches and Prayers*, ibid, p42.

24. *ibid*, p25.

25. Ludlow, *Voyce*, p230

26. See Rugg, *Diurnal*, p104, 107.

27. Letter, Michael Boyle to Sir John Percivale, from Cork, May 29, 1660. Dunlop Vol II, p611. Boyle had criticised Cooke for delivering judgments against the Earl's interests.

28. Boyle was rewarded, however, by being made a Bishop – Rugg, *Diurnall*, p117.

29. 'An Exact and Most Impartial Accompt . . .' No 97 (Thomason, E186). Entry for Thursday 7 June. The House resolved that Cooke should be excepted, apparently without discussion. Its next resolution was that 'This House does accept his Majesty's gracious offer of pardon and indemnity to themselves and the Commons of England.'

30. See *The Parliamentary History of England from the Earliest History to the Year 1803*, (London 1808), Vol. V, p76–9.

31. Leopold von Ranke, *The History of England*, (London, 1860). p322–328. Sir Heneage Finch reported Clarendon as explaining that the King regarded the nation as guiltless of his father's murder: this was the work of 'a small band of wicked and misguided men'.

32. Evelyn, Diary, p267.

33. Rugg, *Diurnal*, p114, p126.

34. Evelyn, *Diary*, p266.

35. The gold coin was hung around the enlarged glands of the scrofulatic neck; see Benjamin Woolley, *The Herbalist: Nicholas Culpepper and The Fight for Medical Freedom* (London, 2004) p106–7. Culpepper in 1650 recommended pilewort to cure the King's Evil 'if I may lawfully call it the King's Evil now there is no King.' (p264).

36. These quotations are taken from Cooke's 'Letter to a friend' reproduced in *Speeches and Prayers*, p38–50.

37. It was this passage that Sir Robert Hyde was to declare 'horrid blasphemy' when it was read out at the Old Bailey. 'The Tryal of Thomas Brewster' in *Compleat State Trials* (London, 1719), p981.

38. *Speeches and Prayers*, p49.

Chapter 17: 'They All Seem Dismayed . . .'

1. William Holdsworth, *History of English law*, Vol. 6. (2nd ed) (London Methuen, 1937), p605. Bridgeman drew the deed that led to the establishment in the *Duke of Norfolk's* case of the rule against perpetuities.

2. Edmund Ludlow, *Memoirs*, (Sands, Edinburgh, 1751), Vol. 2, p303.

3. Cony's case is discussed in State Trials, p936–8 (*Administration of Justice During the Occupation of the Government*). Ludlow and other barristers condemned the two counsel for 'choosing rather to sacrifice the cause of their client, wherein that of their country was also eminently concerned, than to endure a little restraint, with the loss of their fees, for a few days.'

4. Ludlow, *Voyce*, ed Worden CFS21 (London, 1978), p198. The new sheriffs, Bolton and Beak, were sworn in on October 1st.

5. Sadakat Kadri, *The Trial: A History from Socrates to O. J. Simpson* (London, 2005), p91.

6. Kelyling reports that the meeting of judges and prosecutors resolved to charge 'compassing and imagining' because 'then, we might lay as many overt acts as we would, to prove the compassing of his death'. Kelyling's report makes clear that the judges were determined to frame a charge upon which the 'traitors' could

most easily be convicted Kelyng 7, 8; 84 English Reports 1056, 1057.

7. Statute 7 William III.

8. They even directed that the three prosecution lawyers should meet members of the grand jury in a private session in order to 'manage the evidence for finding the bill' – another unfair departure from custom, which was for a judge rather than a prosecutor to preside over the grand jury deliberations, to ensure some impartiality in its decisions to send defendants for trial.

9. The judges agreed, with some irritation, that until the law was changed the writs to the Lieutenant of the Tower, directing him to deliver the prisoners, would have to be in English, not Latin.

10. *Speeches and Prayers*, p50–56 ('A Letter written by Justice Cooke to his wife').

11. *Voyce*, p179.

12. Geoffrey Robertson, *Obscenity*, (London, Wiedenfeld, 1979), p21.

13. The grand jury and trial transcripts of proceedings against the Regicides were published by the Government at the end of October 1660, as *An Exact and Most Impartial Accompt of the Indictment Arraignment, Trial and Judgement (according to law) of nine and twenty Regicides, the murtherers of His late sacred Majesty (etc)*. The grand jury proceeding, with Bridgeman's speech, is at p7–16.

14. Bridgeman misunderstands Coke and willfully distorts the common law theory that the King has 'two bodies' – a political body that could never do wrong other than through ministers (who alone could be prosecuted) and a natural body capable of committing crime – although it was debatable whether a common law court had jurisdiction to try him. Bridgeman conflates these two separate concepts to produce a doctrine of absolute royal impunity.

15. See Coke, 3rd Institute (1648) (ed.) para 14.

16. Pepys, *Diary*, ed Latham & Matthews (London, 1970), p263.

17. On all but Hulet, a soldier rumoured to be the masked executioner. The prosecutors were unsure of his guilt, and the jury deliberated for two further days before indicting him.

18. Cooke was prisoner number 25. See *Mercurius Politicus* for that week.

19. Opening day of Regicide trial at Old Bailey: see '*An Exact and Most Impartial Accompt* . . .', p17–32 (10 October 1660).

20. Pepys, *Diary*, entry for 10 October (p263).

21. R v Thomas Harrison: '*An Exact and Most Impartial Accompt* . . .', p32–56.

22. '*An Exact and Most Impartial Accompt* . . .', Scroop's trial is at p57–72; Carew's trial p72–83; Scot p82–95; Jones p96–102. Gregory Clement pleaded guilty: p95–6.

23. Scot's speech in the commons was, in context, precisely the kind of occasion for which Parliamentary privilege can be justified. He was talking out a motion that aimed to encourage the lynching of Republicans by declaring the execution of Charles I 'horrid murder'.

Chapter 18: The Trial of John Cooke

1. The extracts are taken from 'An Exact and Most Impartial Accompt . . .' The official transcript of the Regicide Trial, as edited by Bridgeman. The case of R v Cooke is at p102–152, and it reproduced in Vol IV of The State Trials. 'An Exact and Most Impartial Accompt . . .' is not an exact account, as is proved by the omission of Cooke's opening remark that was reported in all the newsbook reports the next day: see Parliamentary Intelligencer No 14, p666, entry for October 13, and Mercurius Politicus for the same date.

2. This witness was probably George Starkey, of New Windsor, Berkshire, who had been admitted to Grays Inn in 1633 and called to the bar in 1641. He testified against Peters later in the day. There was another Starkey – Ralph (admitted 1632, called 1640) at Grays Inn. The list of prosecution witnesses, as presented to the Grand Jury, is at p16 of 'An Exact and Most Impartial Accompt . . .'

3. A reconstruction of scenes from the regicides' trial, shown on Channel 4 Television in February 2005, wrenched these words out of their context to give the false impression that Cooke had spoken them at the end of his trial, as a tribute to its fairness! In fact, at the end of his trial, after Bridgeman's summing up to the jury, Cooke said the very opposite: 'I confess I humbly make bold to say, I have not received satisfaction in my judgement' – see 'An Exact and Most Impartial Accompt . . .', p150.

4. Parliamentary Intelligencer No 14, for October 13, 1660, p667.

5. R v Thomas Paine, 22 State Trials, p357 (1792).

6. Brougham would, in company, mock his client. 'The Queen is pure in-no-sense.' See Flora Fraser, The Unruly Queen, (London, MacMillan, 1996).

7. John Lord Campbell, Lives of the Lord Chancellors, 4th ed 1857, Vol. IV, (London, John Murray), p75–6.

8. James Fitzjames Stephen, an ultra-monarchist judge and supporter of extensive treason and sedition laws, castigates Cooke for running this 'ignominious' and 'mean' defence, although he misdescribes it and mistakenly thinks it was Cooke's main defence. Stephen, A History of the Criminal Law of England, Vol. I, p371 (London, 1833). It was an arguable construction of the Act, but it did not reflect the intention of the majority of MPs in the Convention Parliament, which was to have Cooke condemned for his 'instrumental' part as trial prosecutor.

9. Mercurius Politicus, for 13 October, p667. Cooke had cited a biblical precedent – that of the lawyer Tertullus, whom St Paul forgave for pleading against the truth, because this was his calling.

10. 'An Exact and Most Impartial Accompt . . .', p120.

11. ibid, p118.

12. ibid, p147.

13. *ibid*, p150.
14. This was a formula in regular use by judges at the Old Bailey until 1979. At the much publicised trial in that year of *'Inside Linda Lovelace'* the elderly judge directed 'If this is not obscene, members of the jury, I don't know what is'. But the jury acquitted and the DPP announced that there would be no further prosecutions in Britain of the written word. See Robertson and Nicol, *Media Law*, (Harmondsworth, 2002), p155.
15. Whitchcott was admitted to the Inner Temple in 1638 and called in 1645.
16. <u>R v Peters</u>, see *'An Exact and Most Impartial Accompt . . .'*, p153 onwards.

Chapter 19: A Trembling Walk with God

1. R. C. Latham and W Matthews (eds.), *The Diary of Samuel Pepys* (London, 1970), p265.
2. Respectively, Dr Dolben and Dr John Barwick, whose encounter with Cooke in Newgate is reported by a relative of the latter. See 'Hugh Peters', *Notes and Queries*, Feb 15, 1913, p123.
3. *The Speeches and Prayers of Major General Harrison, Mr John Carew, Mr Justice Cooke . . .* (1660), p28–9. Statements attributed to Regicides in prison have a martyrological flavour but represent the kind of conversation with which they would have bouyed their spirits. The authenticity of this underground publication is discussed later in the text and in the Notes on Sources.
4. Robert Phayre, named with Hunkes on the execution warrant, had been brought from Ireland with Cooke, but was a last-minute omission from the regicide defendants, because of his marriage to the daughter of Sir Thomas Herbert, final companion of Charles I. Herbert was useful to the new regime as witness to the King's saintliness, and was rewarded by a baronetcy and by the pardoning of his son-in-law.
5. The witness Simpson admitted he did not know whether it was Lady Fairfax other than by rumour (p187); the gallery owner, Griffith Bordaroe, who would have sold the seat, does not identify her (p192–3) while Axtell, who would have recognised his General's wife and had no motive to lie on this point said 'who she was, I know no more than the least child here.' (p206). Sir Purbeck Temple, a royalist spy given to wild imagining (he compared the King's sufferings to those of Christ and claimed that he had seen the King's severed head smile at him) said that his sister, a Mrs Nelson, had accompanied Lady Fairfax and both were masked: he did not identify which of them had shouted. (p189–90) The prosecution went no further than to allege that the interjection 'Nol Cromwell is a traitor!' was from a 'noble person'. The identification of Lady Fairfax by Clarendon and Rushworth, in accounts written many years later, has been too readily accepted.

6. Regicide trial, p200–201.

7. *ibid*, p205.

8. *ibid*, p226. Bridgeman directed them that 'It is very plain he had a hand in this business. He was a principal agent in it, because he brought the King to the scaffold, he had the care of managing that business. He signed the warrant to the executioner. Either he is guilty of compassing the death of the King or no man can be said to be guilty.'

9. The trial of Hulet is in *Regicide Trial*, p227–240.

10. *Speeches and Prayers*, p28.

11. *ibid*, p30.

12. Descriptions by detractors, but credible at this point: see J. B. Williams (Muddiman), *Notes and Queries*, March 1913, p164–5.

13. Cooke's final speech and prayer is excerpted from *Speeches and Prayers*, p30–38

14. See *Mercurius Publicus*, 11–18 October 1660, when Muddiman concedes that Cooke 'carried himself at his execution much better than could be expected from one that acted such a part in that horrid arraignment of our late sovereign . . . taking notice of Hugh Peters (he) wished he might be reprieved because, at present, as he conceived, he was not prepared to die.'

15. *Philippians* 2, verses 17 & 18.

16. John Evelyn states that Cooke and others 'suffered for the reward of their iniquities at Charing Cross, in sight of the place where they put to death their natural Prince and in the presence of the King his sonn whom they also sought to kill.' *Diary*, ed Bray (London, 1818), p268. Evelyn muddles names and dates (e.g. this entry is for October 17, the day after Cooke's execution) but his closeness to the King and the court gives credence to his report of Charles II's attendance, at least for some of the week's executions.

17. This is Ludlow's version. Some royalist accounts have Peters dying 'sullenly and desperately'; others admit that he pulled himself together with a short prayer. See *Notes on Queries*, March 1913, p164–5. There can be no dispute that his death was greeted with loud shouts and acclamations.

18. R v Marten, Regicide Trial, p245–51.

19. Pepys, *Diary*, above note 1, p268.

20. Letter from William Smith to John Langley, 20th October, 1660. See the *Fifth Report of the Royal Commission on Historical Manuscripts* (London, 1876), p174.

21. Evelyn, *Diary*, p268.

22. Secretary of State Nicholas to Henry Bennet, October 18, 1660 'The heads of the traitors Harrison and Cooke are, by the King's orders, fastened onto two poles and pitched on the north end of Westminster Hall.'

23. Pepys, *Diary*, ed Latham & Matthews (London, 1970), p269.

24. *ibid*, p270.

Notes

Chapter 20: Long Live the King

1. See F. A. Inderwick QC, *The Regicides*, in *Sidelights on the Stuarts*, (London, 1888), p294.
2. Rugg, *Diurnall 1659–61*, ed Sachse (London, 1961), p128.
3. Pepys, *Diary*, ed Latham & Matthews (London, 1970) Vol. II (1661), p283.
4. *Mercurius Publicus*, 31ˢᵗ January, 1661. There is no reference to the body of Thomas Pride, of 'Prides Purge' which was to have suffered the same fate. Doubtless it was in too poor a condition to serve as a prop in the macabre pantomime.
5. Rugg, *Diurnal*, above note 2, p151.
6. *State Trials*, Vol. V, p1337.
7. Mark Noble, *Lives of the English Regicides*, (London, 1798), Vol 1, p155.
8. St Martin's church has an affecting tribute to Phelps, the court clerk, erected by descendants from Massachusetts. The remains of William Cawley, the Chichester MP and philanthropist who founded St Bartholomew's hospital, were later removed from St Martin's and brought to the family vault at Chichester cathedral.
9. *State Trials*, Vol. V, p1365 citing Hutchinson's *History of Massachusetts Bay*.
10. Nicholas Murray, *World Enough and Time: The Life of Andrew Marvell* (London, 1999). Marvell took up Milton's case, claiming that the £150 jail fees he was forced to pay were excessive, although given the alternative this financial penalty might be accounted poetic justice.
11. *Willis Bund's State Trials*, (Cambridge, 1879–82), Vol. II, Part I, p339.
12. See *Tongue's Case, ibid*, p381.
13. *Northern Rising Trial, ibid*, p383–6.
14. See Mark Noble, *The Lives of the English Regicides*, (London, 1798), Vol. I, p xliv-xlv.
15. Rasul v Bush, US Supreme Court (2004) 124 S.Ct. 2686, 159 L.Ed.2d 548. See judgement of Justice Stevens.
16. As early as 6 November, less than 3 weeks after the final trial, Pepys 'found good satisfaction' in reading this trial transcript: *Diary*, Vol I, 1660, p284.
17. Comparison between the official transcript and contemporaneous court reporting in *Mercurius Publicus* shows that Bridgeman cut out some of Cooke's best moments – including his opening sally – and his own summing up attributes arguments and authorities to Cooke which do not appear in '*An Exact Accompt . . .*' of Cooke's speech. It is this version, edited by Bridgeman, that appears in State Trials.
18. Many historians who should know better actually claim that the regicide trials were fair: see e.g. Howard Nenner – 'Bridgeman's rulings and conduct of the proceedings at all times were legally and judicially correct' (*ODNB* entry for Bridgeman, 2004) and Alfred Havinghurst: 'A careful reading leaves a conviction

that the accused had a normal hearing. Rules of procedure were carefully explained, the defendants were granted writing materials, and they were patiently heard in their own defence. Chief Baron Bridgeman took special pains to answer all questions'. *The Judiciary and Politics in the Reign of Charles II* – Law Quarterly Review, January 1950, p67. Even C. V. Wedgwood opines that 'The trials of the Regicides were not grossly unfair . . . it is surprising that standards of justice and decency were, on the whole, upheld.' *The Trial of Charles I*, (London, 1964), p219. These opinions are demonstrably wrong.

19. The trial of Twyn is reported in *A Compleat Collection of State Tryals* (London, 1719). He was convicted and executed for treason.

20. The trial of Thomas Brewster, reported in *A Compleat Collection of State Tryals* (London, 1719), p981.

21. Brewster the bookseller and Dover the printer both died in prison in April 1664, possibly from the plague. They stoutly refused to secure their freedom by naming others involved in the publication. Brewster was a republican and follower of Vane: over 3,000 people 'of the same stamp' attended his funeral: *The Newes*, 28 April 1664; *Notes and Queries*, September 13, 1913.

22. Charles II direction to trustees for Sir George Lane, 24 November 1660, Calendar of State Papers, Ireland, 1660–1662, p98. The King ordered that Lane was to have immediate possession: 14 March 1661 (CSP, 262).

23. There are records from Barwell Parish, near Burbage, which show that Mary Cooke, a widow, married John Shenton in 1669 and died in 1679. John Cooke's last letter to Freelove (extract p333) urged obedience to her mother and 'thy loving uncle and aunt Massey' (*Speeches and Prayers*, p75). In 1680 Elizabeth Massey of Northampton, by now a widow, made a will leaving a bequest to her niece Freelove, 'now the wife of John Gunthorpe of Antigua'. Gunthorpe was the island's provost-martial, later a major and a member of Antigua's parliament. In a land dispute in 1687 he was described in court papers as 'son-in-law to that egregious trayter John Cook, solicitor to the pretended High Court of Justice against King Charles the Martyr . . .' (see Vere L. Oliver, *History of Antigua*, Volume 3, p40). These traces give reason to believe that Freelove made a happy and fruitful life in the Caribbean: the Gunthorpes had a son (Robert) and other children. In the course of researching St Cross records I came across a curious postcard sent to the Master in 1913 by one Earnest Hampden-Cooke who presented him with a signed copy of the Regicide Trial and promised a portrait of Mr Justice Cooke. Mr Hampden-Cooke obviously aspired to be a descendant of John Cooke and probably of John Hampden as well. He is a curious figure – the author of a book explaining that the second coming of Christ has already been and gone. *The Christ has Come* (1891) is much discussed on American biblical websites run by preterists.

24. Anonymous, 1667, sometimes attributed to Edmund Waller; see *BBC History*, October 2001, p18.

25. Blair Worden, *Roundhead Reputations* (London, 2001), p130.

26. *Trial of Alice Lisle*, in *A Compleat Collection of State Trials* (London, 1719) Vol. III, p489. The fugitive was a preacher, and Lisle said she did not realise he had fought for Monmouth. Jeffreys sentenced her to hanging, drawing and quartering. James I, almost as cruel, resisted all requests to commute her sentence but allowed her the indulgence of beheading.

27. Worden, above note 25, p133.

Epilogue

1. Edmund Ludlow, *A Voyce from the Watchtower*, ed. Worden (London, 1978), p229.

2. G. M. Trevelyan, *England under the Stuarts*, 12th Edition (London, 1925), p516.

3. Clarendon, *History of the Rebellion*, Vol. VI, (Oxford, 1888), p475 (paragraph 220).

4. A pamphlet attacking Cooke's case against the King appeared in 1691, purporting to have been written by Samuel Butler, although it lacked the style and wit of the late author of *Hudibras*. Entitled *The Plagiary Exposed or An Old Answer to a newly-devised calumny*, it heavy-handedly rebuts some of the points in Cooke's closing speech and claims that the civil war was started neither by the King nor by Parliament, but by the Scots. It is represented in *The Somers Collection of Tracts* Vol. 5 ed Walter Scott (London, 1811). It appears to be a royalist response to a renewed interest in the good old cause ('There is risen amongst us a new race of the old Republican stamp who have revived the quarrel'). The pretence that Butler (who died in 1680) had written it in 1661 would help it sell.

5. See R. C. Richardson, *The Debate on the English Revolution*, Third Edition, (Manchester University Press, 1998), p88.

6. *ibid*, p59.

7. S. R. Gardiner, *History of the Great Civil War* (London, Windrush, 1987), p300.

8. Blair Worden, *Roundhead Reputations* (London, 2001), p244.

9. Keneth Rose, *King George V*, (London, 1983).

10. The standard site, 'national curriculum material – History at Key Stage 3, Unit 8 – The Civil Wars, Department for Education and Skills, website: http://www.standards.dfes.gov.uk/schemes/secondary. It is ironic that a nation with more history to be proud of than any other should undervalue its study. History is not compulsory for school study age 14 onwards, and parents are advised by the Department of Education that selecting it as a GCSE option will fit their children for a career as an 'archivist, museum attendant or researcher': *Which Way Now* (Dept Education and Skills, 2005) p10.

11. Donald Veall, *The Popular Movement for Law Reform* (Oxford, 1970).

12. Toby C. Barnard, *Cromwellian Ireland: English Government and Reform in Ireland 1649–1660* (London, 1975).

13. A. L. Rowse, *The Regicides and the Puritan Revolution*, (London, 1994), p97–100. 'Cooke removed superfluous offices and reduced fees, abolished judges' fees and put them on a straight salary, combined equity and common law practice, and held assize sessions in the country. He also bent over backwards on behalf of the poor. In England Cooke actually pleaded that lawyers and physicians should remit every tenth fee to the poor. He ridiculed the enthronement of precedent – 'this over-doting upon old forms' – and the obfuscation of laws by antiquated language and procedure. He favoured the use of English law in cases, in place of the Anglo-Norman gibberish which gave the profession a trade union monopoly.'

14. G. E. Aylmer, G. E., *The State and its Servants* (London, 1973), p276.

15. Antonia Fraser, *Cromwell Our Chief of Men*, (Phoenix, 2001), p283.

16. 'Charles I – Regicide and Republicanism', *History Today*, (1996), 46:1, p29–34. However, Dr Barber perceptively discusses some of Cooke's pamphlets in *Regicide and Republicanism*, (Edinburgh, 1998).

17. Derek Wilson, *The King and the Gentleman* (London, 1999), p416.

18. Christopher Hibbert, *Charles I* (London, 1968, repr 2001), p274.

19. Inderwick Q.C., *Sidelights on the Stuarts*, p290.

20. Mentorn Oxford Films, broadcast as part of Channel 4's 'Civil War Season', in February 2005.

21. Suzanne Trill, Kate Chedzoy and Melanie Osborne, eds., *Lay by your needles ladies, take the pen: writing women in England, 1500–1700* (London, 1997), p170. These authors offer no biographical details for Frances.

22. Mercurius Militarius, 17th – 24th April, 1649, p13, cited by Joad Raymond, *Pamphlets and Pamphleteering in Early Modern Britain*, (Cambridge, 2003), p305.

23. See Simon Schama, *Citizens – A Chronicle of the French Revolution*, (Harmondsworth, 1989), p659–661.

24. Versailles Treaty, Article 227. This recorded the allies' agreement in principle to establish a court of 5 international judges to try the Kaiser, but U.S. policy ensured that it remained a dead letter. He lived happily in exile in Holland until his death in 1941.

25. Report 1st June 1945, Jackson to Truman. Anne and John Tusa, *The Nuremberg Trial*, (London, 1983), p66.

26. Robert E. Conot, *Justice at Nuremberg*, (London, 1983), p68.

27. See generally Geoffrey Robertson QC, *Crimes against Humanity: The Struggle for Global Justice*, 2nd ed. (London, 2002).

Index

www.randomhouse.co.uk/vintage